2002

LLEWELLYN'S

SUN SIGN

BOOK

Forecasts by
Gloria Star

Book Editing and Design: K. M. Brielmaier
Cover Art: Giovannina Colalillo
Cover Design: Kevin R. Brown
Copyright 2001

Llewellyn Publications
A Division of Llewellyn Worldwide, Ltd.
P.O. Box 64383 Dept. 0-7387-0032-0 St. Paul, MN 55164-0383

2001

JANUARY
S	M	T	W	T	F	S
	1	2	3	4	5	6
7	8	9	10	11	12	13
14	15	16	17	18	19	20
21	22	23	24	25	26	27
28	29	30	31			

FEBRUARY
S	M	T	W	T	F	S
				1	2	3
4	5	6	7	8	9	10
11	12	13	14	15	16	17
18	19	20	21	22	23	24
25	26	27	28			

MARCH
S	M	T	W	T	F	S
				1	2	3
4	5	6	7	8	9	10
11	12	13	14	15	16	17
18	19	20	21	22	23	24
25	26	27	28	29	30	31

APRIL
S	M	T	W	T	F	S
1	2	3	4	5	6	7
8	9	10	11	12	13	14
15	16	17	18	19	20	21
22	23	24	25	26	27	28
29	30					

MAY
S	M	T	W	T	F	S
		1	2	3	4	5
6	7	8	9	10	11	12
13	14	15	16	17	18	19
20	21	22	23	24	25	26
27	28	29	30	31		

JUNE
S	M	T	W	T	F	S
					1	2
3	4	5	6	7	8	9
10	11	12	13	14	15	16
17	18	19	20	21	22	23
24	25	26	27	28	29	30

JULY
S	M	T	W	T	F	S
1	2	3	4	5	6	7
8	9	10	11	12	13	14
15	16	17	18	19	20	21
22	23	24	25	26	27	28
29	30	31				

AUGUST
S	M	T	W	T	F	S
			1	2	3	4
5	6	7	8	9	10	11
12	13	14	15	16	17	18
19	20	21	22	23	24	25
26	27	28	29	30	31	

SEPTEMBER
S	M	T	W	T	F	S
						1
2	3	4	5	6	7	8
9	10	11	12	13	14	15
16	17	18	19	20	21	22
23	24	25	26	27	28	29
30						

OCTOBER
S	M	T	W	T	F	S
	1	2	3	4	5	6
7	8	9	10	11	12	13
14	15	16	17	18	19	20
21	22	23	24	25	26	27
28	29	30	31			

NOVEMBER
S	M	T	W	T	F	S
				1	2	3
4	5	6	7	8	9	10
11	12	13	14	15	16	17
18	19	20	21	22	23	24
25	26	27	28	29	30	

DECEMBER
S	M	T	W	T	F	S
						1
2	3	4	5	6	7	8
9	10	11	12	13	14	15
16	17	18	19	20	21	22
23	24	25	26	27	28	29
30	31					

2002

JANUARY
S	M	T	W	T	F	S
		1	2	3	4	5
6	7	8	9	10	11	12
13	14	15	16	17	18	19
20	21	22	23	24	25	26
27	28	29	30	31		

FEBRUARY
S	M	T	W	T	F	S
					1	2
3	4	5	6	7	8	9
10	11	12	13	14	15	16
17	18	19	20	21	22	23
24	25	26	27	28		

MARCH
S	M	T	W	T	F	S
					1	2
3	4	5	6	7	8	9
10	11	12	13	14	15	16
17	18	19	20	21	22	23
24	25	26	27	28	29	30
31						

APRIL
S	M	T	W	T	F	S
	1	2	3	4	5	6
7	8	9	10	11	12	13
14	15	16	17	18	19	20
21	22	23	24	25	26	27
28	29	30				

MAY
S	M	T	W	T	F	S
			1	2	3	4
5	6	7	8	9	10	11
12	13	14	15	16	17	18
19	20	21	22	23	24	25
26	27	28	29	30	31	

JUNE
S	M	T	W	T	F	S
						1
2	3	4	5	6	7	8
9	10	11	12	13	14	15
16	17	18	19	20	21	22
23	24	25	26	27	28	29
30						

JULY
S	M	T	W	T	F	S
	1	2	3	4	5	6
7	8	9	10	11	12	13
14	15	16	17	18	19	20
21	22	23	24	25	26	27
28	29	30	31			

AUGUST
S	M	T	W	T	F	S
				1	2	3
4	5	6	7	8	9	10
11	12	13	14	15	16	17
18	19	20	21	22	23	24
25	26	27	28	29	30	31

SEPTEMBER
S	M	T	W	T	F	S
1	2	3	4	5	6	7
8	9	10	11	12	13	14
15	16	17	18	19	20	21
22	23	24	25	26	27	28
29	30					

OCTOBER
S	M	T	W	T	F	S
		1	2	3	4	5
6	7	8	9	10	11	12
13	14	15	16	17	18	19
20	21	22	23	24	25	26
27	28	29	30	31		

NOVEMBER
S	M	T	W	T	F	S
					1	2
3	4	5	6	7	8	9
10	11	12	13	14	15	16
17	18	19	20	21	22	23
24	25	26	27	28	29	30

DECEMBER
S	M	T	W	T	F	S
1	2	3	4	5	6	7
8	9	10	11	12	13	14
15	16	17	18	19	20	21
22	23	24	25	26	27	28
29	30	31				

2003

JANUARY
S	M	T	W	T	F	S
			1	2	3	4
5	6	7	8	9	10	11
12	13	14	15	16	17	18
19	20	21	22	23	24	25
26	27	28	29	30	31	

FEBRUARY
S	M	T	W	T	F	S
						1
2	3	4	5	6	7	8
9	10	11	12	13	14	15
16	17	18	19	20	21	22
23	24	25	26	27	28	

MARCH
S	M	T	W	T	F	S
						1
2	3	4	5	6	7	8
9	10	11	12	13	14	15
16	17	18	19	20	21	22
23	24	25	26	27	28	29
30	31					

APRIL
S	M	T	W	T	F	S
		1	2	3	4	5
6	7	8	9	10	11	12
13	14	15	16	17	18	19
20	21	22	23	24	25	26
27	28	29	30			

MAY
S	M	T	W	T	F	S
				1	2	3
4	5	6	7	8	9	10
11	12	13	14	15	16	17
18	19	20	21	22	23	24
25	26	27	28	29	30	31

JUNE
S	M	T	W	T	F	S
1	2	3	4	5	6	7
8	9	10	11	12	13	14
15	16	17	18	19	20	21
22	23	24	25	26	27	28
29	30					

JULY
S	M	T	W	T	F	S
		1	2	3	4	5
6	7	8	9	10	11	12
13	14	15	16	17	18	19
20	21	22	23	24	25	26
27	28	29	30	31		

AUGUST
S	M	T	W	T	F	S
					1	2
3	4	5	6	7	8	9
10	11	12	13	14	15	16
17	18	19	20	21	22	23
24	25	26	27	28	29	30
31						

SEPTEMBER
S	M	T	W	T	F	S
	1	2	3	4	5	6
7	8	9	10	11	12	13
14	15	16	17	18	19	20
21	22	23	24	25	26	27
28	29	30				

OCTOBER
S	M	T	W	T	F	S
			1	2	3	4
5	6	7	8	9	10	11
12	13	14	15	16	17	18
19	20	21	22	23	24	25
26	27	28	29	30	31	

NOVEMBER
S	M	T	W	T	F	S
						1
2	3	4	5	6	7	8
9	10	11	12	13	14	15
16	17	18	19	20	21	22
23	24	25	26	27	28	29
30						

DECEMBER
S	M	T	W	T	F	S
	1	2	3	4	5	6
7	8	9	10	11	12	13
14	15	16	17	18	19	20
21	22	23	24	25	26	27
28	29	30	31			

Table of Contents

Meet Gloria Star 5

New Concepts for Signs of the Zodiac 6

Understanding the Basics of Astrology 8

Signs of the Zodiac 9

The Planets 10

Using this Book 11

2002 at a Glance 12

Ascendant Table 14

Astrological Glossary 16

Meanings of the Planets 22

2002 Sun Sign Forecasts

Aries 28

Taurus 51

Gemini 74

Cancer 97

Leo 119

Virgo 142

Libra 165

Scorpio 188

Sagittarius 211

Capricorn 234

Aquarius 257

Pisces 280

2002 Sun Sign Articles

The Twelve Houses of the Zodiac...303

The Sun and the Outer Planets
  by David Pond...306

Sun Signs and Your Health
  by Jonathan Keyes...319

Earth Signs: The Role of the Earth in Your Birthchart
  by Kenneth Johnson...336

Astrology in the Workplace
  by Alice DeVille...344

Women and Astrology in the Twenty-First Century
  by Leeda Alleyn Pacotti..356

Keeping Your Sun Sign on Track
  by Phyllis Firak-Mitz..369

The Super Natural Planets
  by Marguerite Elsbeth...383

Sun Signs and Psychic Ability
  by Mitchell Gibson..395

Sun Signs and Your Business
  by Stephanie Clement...406

The Venus Factor
  by Dorothy Oja..421

It's a Trade-Off: World Predictions for 2002
  by Leeda Alleyn Pacotti..434

The Finer Points: Houses, Aspects, and Transits
  by Stephanie Clement...444

Activities Ruled by the Planets...475

Planetary Business Guide..476

Planetary Associations..477

About the Authors...478

Meet Gloria Star

All horoscopes and sign descriptions for this book were written by Gloria Star. An internationally renowned astrologer, author, and teacher, Gloria has been a professional astrologer for over two decades. She has written for the *Sun Sign Book* for Llewellyn since 1990, and has been a contributing author of the *Moon Sign Book* since 1995. Her most recent work, *Astrology & Your*

Child, was released by Llewellyn in December 2000, following her book *Astrology: Woman to Woman* (Llewellyn 1999). She also edited and coauthored the book *Astrology for Women: Roles and Relationships* (Llewellyn 1997). Her newest astrological computer software is an interpreter for children's charts. She also created the concept and text for *Woman to Woman*, a computer program released by Matrix Software in 1997. She writes a regular column for *The Mountain Astrologer* magazine.

Listed in *Who's Who of American Women*, and *Who's Who in the East*, Gloria is active within the astrological community, where she has been honored as a nominee for the prestigious Regulus Award. She has served on the faculty of the United Astrology Congress (UAC) since its inception in 1986, and has lectured for groups and conferences throughout the U.S. and abroad. A member of the Advisory Board for the National Council for Geocosmic Research (NCGR), she also served on the Steering Committee for the Association for Astrological Networking (AFAN), was editor of the *AFAN Newsletter* from 1992–1997, and is now on the AFAN Advisory Board. She currently resides in the shoreline township of Clinton, Connecticut.

New Concepts for Signs of the Zodiac

The signs of the zodiac represent characteristics and traits that indicate how energy operates within our lives. The signs tell the story of human evolution and development, and all are necessary to form the continuum of whole life experience. In fact, all twelve signs are represented within your astrological chart.

Although the traditional metaphors for the twelve signs (such as Aries, the Ram) are always functional, these alternative concepts for each of the twelve signs also describe the gradual unfolding of the human spirit.

Aries: The Initiator is the first sign of the zodiac and encompasses the primary concept of getting things started. This fiery ignition and bright beginning can prove to be the thrust necessary for new life, but the Initiator also can appear before a situation is ready for change and create disruption.

Taurus: The Maintainer sustains what Aries has begun and brings stability and focus into the picture, yet there also can be a tendency to try to maintain something in its current state without allowing for new growth.

Gemini: The Questioner seeks to determine whether alternatives are possible and offers diversity to the processes Taurus has brought into stability. Yet questioning can also lead to distraction, subsequently scattering energy and diffusing focus.

Cancer: The Nurturer provides the qualities necessary for growth and security, and encourages a deepening awareness of emotional needs. Yet this same nurturing can stifle individuation if it becomes too smothering.

Leo: The Loyalist directs and centralizes the experiences Cancer feeds. This quality is powerfully targeted toward self-awareness, but can be shortsighted. Hence, the Loyalist can hold steadfastly to viewpoints or feelings that inhibit new experiences.

Virgo: The Modifier analyzes the situations Leo brings to light and determines possibilities for change. Even though this change may be in the name of improvement, it can lead to dissatisfaction with the self if not directed in harmony with higher needs.

Libra: The Judge is constantly comparing everything to be sure that a certain level of rightness and perfection is presented. However, the Judge can also present possibilities that are harsh and seem to be cold or without feeling.

Scorpio: The Catalyst steps into the play of life to provide the quality of alchemical transformation. The Catalyst can stir the brew just enough to create a healing potion, or may get things going to such a powerful extent that they boil out of control.

Sagittarius: The Adventurer moves away from Scorpio's dimension to seek what lies beyond the horizon. The Adventurer continually looks for possibilities that answer the ultimate questions, but may forget the pathway back home.

Capricorn: The Pragmatist attempts to put everything into its rightful place and find ways to make life work out right. The Pragmatist can teach lessons of practicality and determination, but can become highly self-righteous when shortsighted.

Aquarius: The Reformer looks for ways to take what Capricorn has built and bring it up to date. Yet there is also a tendency to scrap the original in favor of a new plan that may not have the stable foundation necessary to operate effectively.

Pisces: The Visionary brings mysticism and imagination, and challenges the soul to move beyond the physical plane, into the realm of what might be. The Visionary can pierce the veil, returning enlightened to the physical world. The challenge is to avoid getting lost within the illusion of an alternate reality.

Understanding the Basics of Astrology

Astrology is an ancient and continually evolving system used to clarify your identity and your needs. An astrological chart—which is calculated using the date, time, and place of birth—contains many factors which symbolically represent the needs, expressions, and experiences that make up the whole person. A professional astrologer interprets this symbolic picture, offering you an accurate portrait of your personality.

The chart itself—the horoscope—is a portrait of an individual. Generally, a natal (or birth) horoscope is drawn on a circular wheel. The wheel is divided into twelve segments, called houses. Each of the twelve houses represents a different aspect of the individual, much like the facets of a brilliantly cut stone. The houses depict different environments, such as home, school, and work. The houses also represent roles and relationships: parents, friends, lovers, children, partners. In each environment, individuals show a different side of their personality. At home, you may represent yourself quite differently than you do on the job. Additionally, in each relationship you will project a different image of yourself. Your parents rarely see the side you show to intimate friends.

Symbols for the planets, the Sun, and the Moon are drawn inside the houses. Each planet represents a separate kind of energy. You experience and express that energy in specific ways. (For a complete list, refer to the table on the next page.) The way you use each of these energies is up to you. The planets in your chart do not make you do anything!

The twelve signs of the zodiac indicate characteristics and traits that further define your personality. Each sign can be expressed in positive and negative ways. (The basic meaning of each of the signs is explained in the corresponding sections ahead.) What's more, you have all twelve signs somewhere in your chart. Signs that are strongly emphasized by the planets have greater force. The Sun, Moon, and planets are placed on the chart according to their position at the time of birth. The qualities of a sign, combined with the

Signs of the Zodiac

Aries	♈	The Initiator
Taurus	♉	The Maintainer
Gemini	♊	The Questioner
Cancer	♋	The Nurturer
Leo	♌	The Loyalist
Virgo	♍	The Modifier
Libra	♎	The Judge
Scorpio	♏	The Catalyst
Sagittarius	♐	The Adventurer
Capricorn	♑	The Pragmatist
Aquarius	♒	The Reformer
Pisces	♓	The Visionary

energy of a planet, indicate how you might be most likely to use that energy and the best ways to develop that energy. The signs add color, emphasis, and dimension to the personality.

Signs are also placed at the cusps, or dividing lines, of each of the houses. The influence of the signs on the houses is much the same as their influence on the Sun, Moon, and planets. Each house is shaped by the sign on its cusp.

When you view a horoscope, you will notice that there appear to be four distinctive angles dividing the wheel of the chart. The line that divides the chart into a top and bottom half represents the horizon. In most cases, the left side of the horizon is called the Ascendant. The zodiac sign on the Ascendant is your rising sign. The Ascendant indicates the way others are likely to view you.

The Sun, Moon, or planet can be compared to an actor in a play. The sign shows how the energy works, like the role the actor plays in a drama. The house indicates where the energy operates, like the setting of a play. On a psychological level, the Sun represents who

The Planets

Sun	☉	The ego, self, willpower
Moon	☽	The subconscious self, habits
Mercury	☿	Communication, the intellect
Venus	♀	Emotional expression, love, appreciation, artistry
Mars	♂	Physical drive, assertiveness, anger
Jupiter	♃	Philosophy, ethics, generosity
Saturn	♄	Discipline, focus, responsibility
Uranus	♅	Individuality, rebelliousness
Neptune	♆	Imagination, sensitivity, compassion
Pluto	♇	Transformation, healing, regeneration

you think you are. The Ascendant describes who others think you are, and the Moon reflects your inner self.

Astrologers also study the geometric relationships between the Sun, Moon, and planets. These geometric angles are called aspects. Aspects further define the strengths, weaknesses, and challenges within your physical, mental, emotional, and spiritual self. Sometimes, patterns also appear in an astrological chart. These patterns have meaning.

To understand cycles for any given point in time, astrologers study several factors. Many use transits, which refer to the movement and positions of the planets. When astrologers compare those positions to the birth horoscope, the transits indicate activity in particular areas of the chart. The *Sun Sign Book* uses transits.

As you can see, your Sun sign is just one of many factors that describes who you are—but it is a powerful one! As the symbol of the ego, the Sun in your chart reflects your drive to be noticed. Most people can easily relate to the concepts associated with their Sun sign, since it is tied to their sense of personal identity.

Using this Book

A lthough we can examine a number of your needs and life situations from this information, working one-on-one with a professional astrologer would let you explore many other factors to help guide you. If you would like more information, you might appreciate the personalized information and insights you'll receive from a professional astrologer.

I've described the year's major challenges and opportunities for every Sun sign in the "Year Ahead" section. The first part of each section applies to all individuals born under the sign. I've also included information for specific birth dates that will help you understand the inner changes you'll experience during 2002. The section illustrates your fundamental themes for the year ahead. They will be the underlying principles present throughout the year. These cycles comprise your major challenges and opportunities relating to your personal identity. Blend these ideas with the information you find in the monthly forecast section for your Sun sign and Ascendant.

To best use the information in the monthly forecasts, you'll want to determine your Ascendant or rising sign. If you don't know your Ascendant, the tables following this description will help you determine your rising sign. They are most accurate for those born in the continental United States. They're only an approximation, but they can be used as a good rule of thumb. Your exact Ascendant may vary from the tables according to your time and place of birth. Once you've approximated your ascending sign using the tables or determined your Ascendant by having your chart calculated, you'll know two significant factors in your chart. Read the monthly forecast sections for both your Sun and Ascendant to gain the most useful information.

Your "Rewarding and Challenging Days" sections indicate times when you'll feel either more centered or more out of balance. The rewarding days are not the only times you can perform well, but the times you're likely to feel better integrated! During challenging days, take extra time to center yourself by meditating or using other techniques that help you feel more objective.

These guidelines, although highly useful, cannot incorporate all the factors influencing your current life situation. However, you can use this information for an objective awareness about the way the current cycles are affecting you. Realize that the power of astrology is even more useful when you have a complete chart and professional guidance.

2002 at a Glance

Evidence of our new millennium is now everywhere. Look around, and you cannot help but be amazed at the influx of change in our daily lives! The skyscape for the year draws our attention to the experience of globalization, and information technology and communication are the avenues we use to continue this experience. While the similarities we all share as human beings are now definitely easier to understand and appreciate, even more important is the treasure of diversity. This is part of the message illustrated by the collective energies of Uranus and Neptune continuing their cycles in the sign Aquarius. Our awakening and compassion are focused through the lens of universality.

The outstanding elements for the long-term cycles are the elements air and fire. This combination of qualities represents a period of inspired ideas and enthusiastic communication, or at least that's what we are hoping to find and create in our world now. Underneath it all, we may struggle to understand one another and to accept that we can have our differences and still get along.

This year, home and family take center stage due to Jupiter's cycle through the signs Cancer and Leo, and children's needs are more strongly focused. It's a good year to concentrate more energy on the home front, and to nurture a true sense of personal security within the concept of family. With Saturn in Gemini, education moves into the forefront, although this can indicate a restraint of fresh ideas. Pluto continues its cycle in Sagittarius, and even though some astronomers want to "downgrade" Pluto from its status as a planet, the influence of this energy is definitely something we can all feel. As Pluto makes its impact known in the middle degrees of Sagittarius, our laws are changing and our ideals and beliefs are being unmasked. We are not only exploring these ideals, but we're dealing firsthand with old prejudice that needs to be eliminated if we are to continue our evolution.

However, it is the crisis in consciousness represented by the eclipses that tells the real story: as a collective society, we need to approach learning from a broader level. It is time to create opportunities to instill a joy in learning and a desire to expand our understanding. This is true not only for our children, but for all of us. If anything, we now face the challenge of opening our minds to higher truth, and allowing that truth to guide our choices and actions.

This is the last *Sun Sign Book* I will be writing, and I want to take this opportunity to thank all of you who have shared this part of my journey. It has been my true honor to communicate with you through these annuals. I am still here, doing my lifework as an astrologer, and hold in my heart a continual flame of hope and love for all of you. Have an inspiring year!

Ascendant Table

Your Time of Birth

Your Sun Sign	6–8 am	8–10 am	10 am–Noon	Noon–2 pm	2–4 pm	4–6 pm
Aries	Taurus	Gemini	Cancer	Leo	Virgo	Libra
Taurus	Gemini	Cancer	Leo	Virgo	Libra	Scorpio
Gemini	Cancer	Leo	Virgo	Libra	Scorpio	Sagittarius
Cancer	Leo	Virgo	Libra	Scorpio	Sagittarius	Capricorn
Leo	Virgo	Libra	Scorpio	Sagittarius	Capricorn	Aquarius
Virgo	Libra	Scorpio	Sagittarius	Capricorn	Aquarius	Pisces
Libra	Scorpio	Sagittarius	Capricorn	Aquarius	Pisces	Aries
Scorpio	Sagittarius	Capricorn	Aquarius	Pisces	Aries	Taurus
Sagittarius	Capricorn	Aquarius	Pisces	Aries	Taurus	Gemini
Capricorn	Aquarius	Pisces	Aries	Taurus	Gemini	Cancer
Aquarius	Pisces	Aries	Taurus	Gemini	Cancer	Leo
Pisces	Aries	Taurus	Gemini	Cancer	Leo	Virgo

Your Time of Birth

Your Sun Sign	6–8 pm	8–10 pm	10 pm–Midnight	Midnight–2 am	2–4 am	4–6 am
Aries	Scorpio	Sagittarius	Capricorn	Aquarius	Pisces	Aries
Taurus	Sagittarius	Capricorn	Aquarius	Pisces	Aries	Taurus
Gemini	Capricorn	Aquarius	Pisces	Aries	Taurus	Gemini
Cancer	Aquarius	Pisces	Aries	Taurus	Gemini	Cancer
Leo	Pisces	Aries	Taurus	Gemini	Cancer	Leo
Virgo	Aries	Taurus	Gemini	Cancer	Leo	Virgo
Libra	Taurus	Gemini	Cancer	Leo	Virgo	Libra
Scorpio	Gemini	Cancer	Leo	Virgo	Libra	Scorpio
Sagittarius	Cancer	Leo	Virgo	Libra	Scorpio	Sagittarius
Capricorn	Leo	Virgo	Libra	Scorpio	Sagittarius	Capricorn
Aquarius	Virgo	Libra	Scorpio	Sagittarius	Capricorn	Aquarius
Pisces	Libra	Scorpio	Sagittarius	Capricorn	Aquarius	Pisces

How to use this table:
1. Find your Sun sign in the left column.
2. Find your approximate birth time in a vertical column.
3. Line up your Sun sign and birth time to find your Ascendant.

This table will give you an approximation of your Ascendant. If you feel that the sign listed as your Ascendant is incorrect, try the one either before or after the listed sign. It is difficult to determine your exact Ascendant without a complete natal chart.

Astrological Glossary

Air—One of the four basic elements. The air signs are Gemini, Libra, and Aquarius.

Angles—The four points of the chart that divide it into quadrants. The angles are sensitive areas that lend emphasis to planets located near them. These points are located on the cusps of the First, Fourth, Seventh, and Tenth Houses in a chart.

Ascendant—Rising sign. The degree of the zodiac on the eastern horizon at the time and place for which the horoscope is calculated. It can indicate the image or physical appearance you project to the world. The cusp of the First House.

Aspect—The angular relationship between planets, sensitive points, or house cusps in a horoscope. Lines drawn between the two points and the center of the chart, representing the Earth, form the angle of the aspect. Astrological aspects include conjunction (two points that are 0 degrees apart), opposition (two points, 180 degrees apart), square (two points, 90 degrees apart), sextile (two points, 60 degrees apart), and trine (two points, 120 degrees apart). Aspects can indicate harmony or challenge.

Cardinal Sign—One of the three qualities, or categories, that describe how a sign expresses itself. Aries, Cancer, Libra, and Capricorn are the cardinal signs, believed to initiate activity.

Chiron—Chiron is a comet traveling in orbit between Saturn and Uranus. Although research on its effect on natal charts is not yet complete, it is believed to represent a key or doorway, healing, ecology, and a bridge between traditional and modern methods.

Conjunction—An aspect or angle between two points in a chart where the two points are close enough so that the energies join. Can be considered either harmonious or challenging, depending on the planets involved and their placement.

Cusp—A dividing line between signs or houses in a chart.

Degree—Degree of arc. One of 360 divisions of a circle. The circle of the zodiac is divided into twelve astrological signs of 30 degrees each. Each degree is made up of 60 minutes, and each minute is made up of 60 seconds of zodiacal longitude.

Earth—One of the four basic elements. The earth signs are Taurus, Virgo, and Capricorn.

Eclipse—A solar eclipse is the full or partial covering of the Sun by the Moon (as viewed from Earth), and a lunar eclipse is the full or partial covering of the Moon by the Earth's own shadow.

Ecliptic—The Sun's apparent path around the Earth, which is actually the plane of the Earth's orbit extended out into space. The ecliptic forms the center of the zodiac.

Electional Astrology—A branch of astrology concerned with choosing the best time to initiate an activity.

Elements—The signs of the zodiac are divided into four groups of three zodiacal signs, each symbolized by one of the four elements of the ancients: fire, earth, air, and water. The element of a sign is said to express its essential nature.

Ephemeris—A listing of the Sun, Moon, and planets' positions and related information for astrological purposes.

Equinox—Equal night. The point in the Earth's orbit around the Sun at which the day and night are equal in length.

Feminine Signs—Each zodiac sign is either masculine or feminine. Earth signs (Taurus, Virgo, and Capricorn) and water signs (Cancer, Scorpio, and Pisces) are feminine.

Fire—One of the four basic elements. The fire signs are Aries, Leo, and Sagittarius.

Fixed Signs—Fixed is one of the three qualities, or categories, that describe how a sign expresses itself. The fixed signs are Taurus, Leo, Scorpio, and Aquarius. Fixed signs are said to be predisposed to existing patterns and somewhat resistant to change.

Hard Aspects—Hard aspects are those aspects in a chart that astrologers believe to represent difficulty or challenges. Among the hard aspects are the square, the opposition, and the conjunction (depending on which planets are conjunct).

Horizon—The word "horizon" is used in astrology in a manner similar to its common usage, except that only the eastern and western horizons are considered useful. The eastern horizon at the point of birth is the Ascendant, or First House cusp, of a natal chart, and the western horizon at the point of birth is the Descendant, or Seventh House cusp.

Houses—Division of the horoscope into twelve segments, beginning with the Ascendant. The dividing line between the houses are called house cusps. Each house corresponds to certain aspects of daily living, and is ruled by the astrological sign that governs the cusp, or dividing line between the house and the one previous.

Ingress—The point of entry of a planet into a sign.

Lagna—A term used in Hindu or Vedic astrology for Ascendant, the degree of the zodiac on the eastern horizon at the time of birth.

Masculine Signs—Each of the twelve signs of the zodiac is either "masculine" or "feminine." The fire signs (Aries, Leo, and Sagittarius) and the air signs (Gemini, Libra, and Aquarius) are masculine.

Midheaven—The highest point on the ecliptic, where it intersects the meridian that passes directly above the place for which the horoscope is cast; the southern point of the horoscope.

Midpoint—A point equally distant to two planets or house cusps. Midpoints are considered by some astrologers to be sensitive points in a person's chart.

Mundane Astrology—Mundane astrology is the branch of astrology generally concerned with political and economic events, and the nations involved in these events.

Mutable Signs—Mutable is one of the three qualities, or categories, that describe how a sign expresses itself. Mutable signs are Gemini, Virgo, Sagittarius, and Pisces. Mutable signs are said to be very adaptable and sometimes changeable.

Natal Chart—A person's birth chart. A natal chart is essentially a "snapshot" showing the placement of each of the planets at the exact time of a person's birth.

Node—The point where the planets cross the ecliptic, or the Earth's apparent path around the Sun. The North Node is the point where a planet moves northward, from the Earth's perspective, as it crosses the ecliptic; the South Node is where it moves south.

Opposition—Two points in a chart that are 180 degrees apart.

Orb—A small degree of margin used when calculating aspects in a chart. For example, although 180 degrees form an exact opposition, an astrologer might consider an aspect within 3 or 4 degrees on either side of 180 degrees to be an opposition, as the impact of the aspect can still be felt within this range. The less orb on an aspect, the stronger the aspect. Astrologers' opinions vary on how many degrees of orb to allow for each aspect.

Outer Planets—Uranus, Neptune, and Pluto are known as the outer planets. Because of their distance from the Sun, they take a long time to complete a single rotation. Everyone born within a few years on either side of a given date will have similar placements of these planets.

Planets—The planets used in astrology are Mercury, Venus, Mars, Jupiter, Saturn, Uranus, Neptune, and Pluto. For astrological purposes, the Sun and Moon are also considered planets. A natal or birth chart lists planetary placement at the moment of birth.

Planetary Rulership—The sign in which a planet is most harmoniously placed. Examples are the Sun in Leo, Jupiter in Sagittarius, and the Moon in Cancer.

Precession of Equinoxes—The gradual movement of the point of the Spring Equinox, located at 0 degrees Aries. This point marks the beginning of the tropical zodiac. The point moves slowly backward through the constellations of the zodiac, so that about every 2,000 years the equinox begins in an earlier constellation

Qualities—In addition to categorizing the signs by element, astrologers place the twelve signs of the zodiac into three additional categories, or qualities: cardinal, mutable, or fixed. Each sign is considered to be a combination of its element and quality. Where the element of a sign describes its basic nature, the quality describes its mode of expression.

Retrograde Motion—Apparent backward motion of a planet. This is an illusion caused by the relative motion of the Earth and other planets in their elliptical orbits.

Sextile—Two points in a chart that are 60 degrees apart.

Sidereal Zodiac—Used by Hindu or Vedic astrologers. The sidereal zodiac is located where the constellations are actually positioned in the sky.

Soft Aspects—Soft aspects indicate good fortune or an easy relationship in the chart. Among the soft aspects are the trine, the sextile, and the conjunction (depending on which planets are conjunct each other).

Square—Two points in a chart that are 90 degrees apart.

Sun Sign—The sign of the zodiac in which the Sun is located at any given time.

Synodic Cycle—The time between conjunctions of two planets.

Trine—Two points in a chart that are 120 degrees apart.

Tropical Zodiac—The tropical zodiac begins at 0 degrees Aries, where the Sun is located during the Spring Equinox. This system is used by most Western astrologers and throughout this book.

Void-of-Course—A planet is void-of-course after it has made its last aspect within a sign, but before it has entered a new sign.

Water—One of the four basic elements. Water signs are Cancer, Scorpio, and Pisces.

Meanings of the Planets

The Sun

The Sun indicates the psychological bias that will dominate your actions. What you see, and why, is told in the reading for your Sun. The Sun also shows the basic energy patterns of your body and psyche. In many ways, the Sun is the dominant force in your horoscope and your life. Other influences, especially that of the Moon, may modify the Sun's influence, but nothing will cause you to depart very far from the basic solar pattern. Always keep in mind the basic influence of the Sun and remember all other influences must be interpreted in terms of it, especially insofar as they play a visible role in your life. You may think, dream, imagine, and hope a thousand things, according to your Moon and your other planets, but the Sun is what you are. To be your best self in terms of your Sun is to cause your energies to work along the path in which they will have maximum help from planetary vibrations.

The Moon

The Moon tells the desire of your life. When you know what you mean but can't verbalize it, it is your Moon that knows it and your Sun that can't say it. The wordless ecstasy, the mute sorrow, the secret dream, the esoteric picture of yourself that you can't get across to the world, or that the world doesn't comprehend or value—these are the products of the Moon. When you are misunderstood, it is your Moon nature, expressed imperfectly through the Sun sign, that feels betrayed. Things you know without thought—intuitions, hunches, instincts—are the products of the Moon. Modes of expression that you feel truly reflect your deepest self belong to the Moon: art, letters, creative work of any kind; sometimes love; sometimes business. Whatever you feel to be most deeply yourself is the product of your Moon and of the sign your Moon occupies at birth.

Mercury

Mercury is the sensory antenna of your horoscope. Its position by sign indicates your reactions to sights, sounds, odors, tastes, and touch impressions, affording a key to the attitude you have toward the physical world around you. Mercury is the messenger through which your physical body and brain (ruled by the Sun) and your inner nature (ruled by the Moon) are kept in contact with the outer world, which will appear to you according to the index of Mercury's position by sign in the horoscope. Mercury rules your rational mind.

Venus

Venus is the emotional antenna of your horoscope. Through Venus, impressions come to you from the outer world, to which you react emotionally. The position of Venus by sign at the time of your birth determines your attitude toward these experiences. As Mercury is the messenger linking sense impressions (sight, smell, etc.) to the basic nature of your Sun and Moon, so Venus is the messenger linking emotional impressions. If Venus is found in the same sign as the Sun, emotions gain importance in your life, and have a direct bearing on your actions. If Venus is in the same sign as the Moon, emotions bear directly on your inner nature, add self-confidence, make you sensitive to emotional impressions, and frequently indicate that you have more love in your heart than you are able to express. If Venus is in the same sign as Mercury, emotional impressions and sense impressions work together; you tend to idealize the world of the senses and sensualize the world of the emotions to interpret emotionally what you see and hear.

Mars

Mars is the energy principle in the horoscope. Its position indicates the channels into which energy will most easily be directed. It is the planet through which the activities of the Sun and the desires of the Moon express themselves in action. In the same sign as the Sun, Mars gives abundant energy, sometimes misdirected in temper, temperament, and quarrels. In the same sign as the Moon, it gives a great capacity to make use of the innermost aims, and to make the inner desires articulate and practical. In the same sign as Venus, it quickens emotional reactions and causes you to act on them, makes for ardor and passion in love, and fosters an earthly awareness of emotional realities.

Jupiter

Jupiter is the feeler for opportunity that you have out in the world. It passes along chances of a lifetime for consideration according to the basic nature of your Sun and Moon. Jupiter's sign position indicates the places where you will look for opportunity, the uses to which you wish to put it, and the capacity you have to react and profit by it. Jupiter is ordinarily, and erroneously, called the planet of luck. It is "luck" insofar as it is the index of opportunity, but your luck depends less on what comes to you than on what you do with what comes to you. In the same sign as the Sun or Moon, Jupiter gives a direct, and generally effective, response to opportunity and is likely to show forth at its "luckiest." If Jupiter is in the same sign as Mercury, sense impressions are interpreted opportunistically. If Jupiter is in the same sign as Venus, you interpret emotions in such a way as to turn them to your advantage; your feelings work harmoniously with the chances for progress that the world has to offer. If Jupiter is in the same sign as Mars, you follow opportunity with energy, dash, enthusiasm, and courage, take long chances, and play your cards wide open.

Saturn

Saturn indicates the direction that will be taken in life by the self-preservative principle which, in its highest manifestation, ceases to be purely defensive and becomes ambitious and aspiring. Your defense or attack against the world is shown by the sign position of Saturn in the horoscope of birth. If Saturn is in the same sign as the Sun or Moon, defense predominates, and there is danger of introversion. The farther Saturn is from the Sun, Moon, and Ascendant, the better for objectivity and extroversion. If Saturn is in the same sign as Mercury, there is a profound and serious reaction to sense impressions; this position generally accompanies a deep and efficient mind. If Saturn is in the same sign as Venus, a defensive attitude toward emotional experience makes for apparent coolness in love and difficulty with the emotions and human relations. If Saturn is in the same sign as Mars, confusion between defensive and aggressive urges can make an indecisive person—or, if the Sun and Moon are strong and the total personality well developed, a balanced, peaceful, and calm individual of sober judgment and moderate actions may be indicated. If Saturn is in the same sign as Jupiter, the reaction to opportunity is sober and balanced.

Uranus

Uranus in a general way relates to creativity, originality, or individuality, and its position by sign in the horoscope tells the direction in which you will seek to express yourself. In the same sign as Mercury or the Moon, Uranus suggests acute awareness, a quick reaction to sense impressions and experiences, or a hair-trigger mind. In the same sign as the Sun, it points to great nervous activity, a high-strung nature, and an original, creative, or eccentric personality. In the same sign as Mars, Uranus indicates high-speed activity, love of swift motion, and perhaps love of danger. In the same sign as Venus, it suggests an unusual reaction to emotional experience, idealism, sensuality, and original ideas about love and human relations. In the same sign as Saturn, Uranus points to good sense; this can be a practical, creative position, but, more often than not, it sets up a destructive conflict between practicality and originality that can result in a stalemate. In the same sign as Jupiter, Uranus makes opportunity, creates wealth and the means of getting it, and is conducive to the inventive, executive, and daring.

Neptune

Neptune relates to the deepest wells of the subconscious, inherited mentality, and spirituality, indicating what you take for granted in life. Neptune in the same sign as the Sun or Moon indicates that intuitions and hunches—or delusions—dominate; there is a need for rigidly holding to reality. In the same sign as Mercury, Neptune indicates sharp sensory perceptions, a sensitive and perhaps creative mind, and a quivering intensity of reaction to sensory experience. In the same sign as Venus, it reveals idealistic and romantic (or sentimental) reaction to emotional experience, as well as the danger of sensationalism and a love of strange pleasures. In the same sign as Mars, Neptune indicates energy and intuition that work together to make mastery of life—one of the signs of having angels (or devils) on your side. In the same sign as Jupiter, Neptune describes intuitive response to opportunity generally along practical and money-making lines; one of the signs of security if not indeed of wealth. In the same sign as Saturn, Neptune indicates intuitive defense and attack on the world, generally successful unless Saturn is polarized on the negative side; then there is danger of unhappiness.

Pluto

Pluto is a planet of extremes—from the lowest criminal and violent level of our society to the heights people can attain when they realize their significance in the collectivity of humanity. Pluto also rules three important mysteries of life—sex, death, and rebirth—and links them to each other. One level of death symbolized by Pluto is the physical death of an individual, which occurs so that a person can be reborn into another body to further his or her spiritual development. On another level, individuals can experience a "death" of their old self when they realize the deeper significance of life; thus they become one of the "second born." In a natal horoscope, Pluto signifies our perspective on the world, our conscious and subconscious. Since so many of Pluto's qualities are centered on the deeper mysteries of life, the house position of Pluto, and aspects to it, can show you how to attain a deeper understanding of the importance of the spiritual in your life.

2002
Sun Sign Book
Forecasts

By Gloria Star

Aries . . . . Page 28

Taurus . . . . Page 51

Gemini . . . . Page 74

Cancer . . . . Page 97

Leo . . . . Page 119

Virgo . . . . Page 142

Libra . . . . Page 165

Scorpio . . . . Page 188

Sagittarius . . . . . Page 211

Capricorn . . . . . . Page 234

Aquarius . . . . Page 257

Pisces . . . . Page 280

ARIES

The Ram
March 20 to April 19

♈

Element:	Fire
Quality:	Cardinal
Polarity:	Yang/Masculine
Planetary Ruler:	Mars
Meditation:	With courage, I pursue my destiny.
Gemstone:	Diamond
Power Stones:	Bloodstone, carnelian, ruby
Key Phrase:	I am
Glyph:	Ram's head
Anatomy:	Head, face, throat
Color:	Red, white
Animal:	Ram
Myths/Legends:	Artemis, Jason and the Golden Fleece
House:	First
Opposite Sign:	Libra
Flower:	Geranium
Key Word:	Initiative

Positive Expression:	Misuse of Energy:
Valiant	Impatient
Innovative	Blunt
Assertive	Abrasive
Self-reliant	Rash
Energetic	Belligerent
Independent	Thoughtless

Aries

Your Ego's Strengths and Shortcomings

Following is simply not your style. You prefer a view of life from the head of the pack, forging ahead with enthusiasm, fueled by the courage of your convictions. Whether you're blazing trails or cutting through red tape, you're most comfortable in the fullness of the present moment. You, of all people, understand the power of "Be here now."

Your enterprising spirit stems from your need to fulfill your role as "The Initiator" of the zodiac. At those times when you feel you're in a world of observers waiting for someone else to get the job done, you're ready to move forward. The daring heat from the energy of Mars, your planetary ruler, fuels your courage and drive. However, since your natural impulse is to constantly move forward or to forge ahead, your actions can create an unsettling shock wave to others in your path. The easy fix to this oversight is to sharpen your awareness of the effects of your words and actions, instead of boldly cutting through, no matter what. This can be much easier than having to waste energy later in diffusing unnecessary hostility or conflict. Sure, you like a challenge, but you prefer the ones that take you to the heights!

Your zest and vitality have been present since your youth, and even during your older years you still feel the powerful urging of your inner and impatient child. It's this same quality that fuels your creative ingenuity and capacity for joy. Your strength and passion for life set the rhythm for progress, and your light can inspire others to have faith in possibility.

Shining Your Love Light

What's better than the rush of energy and desire that spark the games of love? While the idea of love can quicken your pulse, your spirit is fueled by the chase and the exhilaration of conquest. You can grow impatient if your intended is waiting around or hesitates too long, and will be happiest with a partner who can stand the heat of your desires. Over time, you may learn to appreciate the power of love, which holds a steady flame in the depths of your heart, but you can grow disenchanted with a relationship that seems to cool too quickly. A partner who nurtures your independence and knows how to tease your desires stands a much better chance of holding your own interest over time.

You're a fire sign, and may feel most at ease with the fiery temperaments of Leo, Sagittarius, and other Aries individuals—since you all share a love of adventure and independence. However, your attraction to your zodiac opposite—Libra—can be amazing. You'll adore his or her grace and style, but can feel pressured if he or she expects you to measure up to a set of standards that are uncomfortable for you.

The fires of love can burn bright with another Aries, but in competitive situations (including arguments) those flames can quickly burn out of control. Taurus prompts you to slow down and enjoy the sensual side of life, but you might get bored if the pace is too slow. With Gemini, a contest of ideas can fan your passion, and you can each enjoy exploring the trails of life together, and love sharing your stories from your separate ventures. Cancer can be comforting and you can feel at home—until you're scolded for missing a family dinner. Leo shines light into your heart and can ignite your greatest passions and desires, but your loyalty will be expected. You have positive connections with some Virgos, and the ingredients for lifelong support and friendship may exist. Scorpio can provoke unbridled intensity, but you're out the door if control games stifle your independence. It's the adventurous Sagittarius spirit that invigorates your interest, and you may feel you can pursue your dreams in this connection. Capricorn promises security, but if there are too many rules attached you may not be a willing player in the game. Aquarius can put you at ease—as though you've met a soulful friend—and that can be the perfect beginning for romance. Pisces can provoke your secret desires and you can feel mystically connected, even though you may never know exactly where you stand.

Making Your Place in the World
You can be highly ambitious, and once you determine a life path that helps you develop self-respect you can be unstoppable. A career that provides mental and physical challenges will be welcome, and you might enjoy working independently. Occupations in

politics, sales, tourism, and travel may be attractive. Your creative ideas can be exercised in careers in jewelry and fashion design, the beauty industry, auto design, and mechanics or metal working.

A job in medical fields, ranging from surgery to physical or occupational therapy, can be rewarding. But you might also relish the physically demanding work of coaching, dancing, police work, firefighting, or the military. You'll be most fulfilled when your work gives you room to exercise your leadership and provides a place to try out fresh ideas.

Power Plays

One thing is clear: you feel most powerful when you're certain you are in charge of your life. You love challenges, whether they arrive from a position of leadership or spring from an opportunity to engage in your favorite sports. Your confidence grows as you meet your goals, and others can be inspired by the light that shines from your spirit of celebration. However, your spirit can be weakened if you are filled with shame, mistrust, guilt, or anger, and if these feelings are not positively addressed you can turn your power against yourself. Your victory arises when you can identify your responsibility, and when you fully address those needs as part of your drive toward success.

Since you have chosen the spiritual path of self-knowledge, you can uncover a true sense of power when you use your independence and leadership in harmony with your spiritual essence. By joining forces with the light of truth, your courage and honesty will shine brightly, inviting others to follow your lead.

Famous Aries

Kofi Annan, Matthew Broderick, Jennifer Capriati, Roger Corman, Bob Costas, Gordie Howe, Eric Idle, Andrew Lloyd-Webber, Bob Mackie, Peter MacNicol, Elle McPherson, Rosie O'Donnell, Teddy Pendergrass, Martin Short, Scott Turow, Jacques Villeneuve

The Year Ahead For Aries

Your confidence and enthusiasm enrich the seeds of your success—and it all begins close to home. This is the year to expand the foundation that supports your dreams and to further develop your abilities and skills. With an eye on the future, you can reach into experiences you may never have dreamed possible, while you enjoy the fruits of your labors. The challenges? These reside in your ability to strike a pace that will yield longer term growth, since there's a temptation to exhaust your fortunes too quickly.

You began the expansion of your home base last year, and with Jupiter transiting in the sign of Cancer until August 2002 your security needs continue to demand extra attention. Family may be growing, too. While this can be a good time to move or remodel your home, it's also the perfect time to instill your family with a positive warmth that comes from mutual support and understanding of one another. The dilemma during this cycle is about knowing where to draw limits, since it's easy to go overboard or to spend too much. In August, Jupiter moves into Leo, marking a time of increased creative capacity. Since you're likely to feel like opening your heart more fully, this can be your year for true loving fulfillment. Watch those romantic urges, though, since by the late part of the year you may be fascinated by something (or someone) that's not quite what it appears to be.

Saturn continues its trek through the sign Gemini, and challenges you to focus on development of your skills and abilities. This may be a good year to enroll in continuing education classes, to begin training or classes in a new career field, or to get to work on those ideas that have been burning a hole in your soul for the last few years! However, dealing with your responsibilities may require a few adjustments on your part. Fortunately, you have a knack for enjoying yourself, even when you're hard at work. This cycle underscores that ability. But if you find yourself wondering when the fun is going to start, take a moment and look for what's holding you back. It may be as simple as clearing away unfinished business so you can finally get to that all-important countdown toward launch!

The slower-moving planets—Uranus, Neptune, and Pluto— continue to drive your impulse to try new things or to explore ideas that can have far-reaching impact. Changes in your relationships with friends can be especially significant, since you are testing these relationships for their ability to nourish your need to experience true unconditional love. Opportunities to learn can also be rather interesting, and whether you're in formal classes, sitting at the feet of a master, or reaching out to share your own knowledge and experience, you're feeling a powerful surge of spiritual fulfillment.

The eclipses of Sun and Moon underscore your growing need to nourish your mind and challenge your spirit. If you've been waiting for the right time to travel, study, write, or explore—your year has arrived! Plus, the interplay of Jupiter, Saturn, and Pluto emphasizes that such ventures can bring levels of self-realization which surpass your previous experiences. The key is to seek opportunities that are in harmony with your truest needs. In the process, you may also uncover a few mysteries, especially mysteries about yourself and your life purpose. In all truth, it's more like a treasure hunt. Now, how long has it been since you've done that?

If you were born from March 20 to 27, you may find that it's much easier to accomplish the goals you've set for yourself this year. Since Saturn and the outer planets have moved into supportive connections to your Sun, you may feel more in control of your destiny. There are no new blocks in your path, and you can enjoy particularly rewarding success if you are following a life path that's much like following your bliss. Your primary challenge arises from the transit of Chiron—an influence suggesting that you are seeking to fulfill your calling or vocation. If your career or work does not echo the song of your heart, the discontent you experience is likely to arise from this life challenge. From August through October, you can take advantage of Jupiter's trine to your Sun. This can be an excellent time to showcase your talents, launch a special project, or make a declaration of love.

If you were born from March 28 to April 3, you're feeling spiritually uplifted while Neptune transits in sextile to your Sun. This year, your ability to tap into the most productive source of your imagination can lead you to become more confident about expressing your creativity. This cycle can be spiritually uplifting, and marks a time when you can confirm your trust in your intuitive voice. You just have to take the time to listen! From January through April, Saturn's supportive influence helps you make choices that create a foundation from which to launch your dreams. This could also be an excellent period to combine practice and discipline with your creative impulse. However, since Uranus is transiting in a semi-square to your Sun, you may jump into situations before you're ready. For this reason, if you take full advantage of Saturn's support, you can set out plans or goals that add strength and structure. Then, you can feel more confident about some of the experiments stimulated by that Uranus transit! You may also feel that you want to do something to make the world a better place. After all, Neptune's influence brings a strong measure of compassion into your life, and that energy needs to be expressed somewhere. Outreach through charitable efforts, or working with others to make a difference where you feel it counts, can be especially rewarding.

If you were born from April 4 to 10, you may finally feel that you understand the true source of your power. Pluto's cycle brings a positive, life-changing revitalization that can be like dusting off hopes and desires that have been impatiently waiting their turn. This is also a time of physical and emotional healing. Now is the time to forgive yourself and others so you can move on with your life. Are there destructive habits you've needed to break? Take advantage of Pluto's power to transform your subconscious drives by taking conscious control of your habits! In addition, you can explore ideas and places that bring true enrichment into your life. Whether you choose school, travel, reading, or you're making full use of modern technological outreach, it's the perfect time to share your ideas while you open your mind to other concepts. Saturn's influence during the spring and summer months helps you define which responsibilities and opportunities can take you further toward success and personal fulfillment. Do you have a paper to write, a course to complete, or a favor that's been unreturned? These are the months to focus on such endeavors. In your personal life, you may finally be ready to reach toward a deeper quality of love. While the thrill of desire can still drive you, your need to feel spiritually connected is even stronger. For this reason, you may decide that your needs for a soulmate are more profound than ever before. This union can come through connecting with another person. A profound desire to join with your higher self can drive many of your choices this year.

If you were born from April 11 to 20, you're feeling a tremendous drive from Uranus to break free and turn your dreams into reality. You've felt it building for a while, and now, with most obstacles out of your path, you're ready to let the world see you on your own terms. Positive changes in your relationships help speed your progress, and your friendships may become your life's truest treasure this year. This can be a wonderful time to become involved in community projects or to immerse yourself in your special interests. Plus, Saturn's cycle creates a strong base, indicating that you'll go further as you build a strong network of support. This network can come from other people, but it also includes your own capacity to bring many of your talents into a central focus. Your natural leadership can be part of this process, and others may look to you for guidance and support, too. Since the impulse of Uranus is to break free, it's not likely that you'll crave a large following. However, you love the idea of opening the way so that others with less courage or fewer opportunities can follow in the wake of your own success.

Tools For Change

You could just coast through the cycles this year, enjoying the positive affirmations of yourself and your progress. Or, you could take advantage of this remarkable time, harness the energy available to you, and move ahead by light years, spiritually speaking. With the supportive stability of the cycles of the slower-moving planets, this can be the best time to work toward your most meaningful goals. The best tool for that? Set truly meaningful goals! Long-range and short-range goals which stem from your yet unfulfilled needs can be more easily realized. Creative visualization, affirmations, and action focused through clear intent can bring phenomenal results.

If you've hesitated about developing your leadership abilities to the fullest, consider the exploration of interests or causes that stir your soul. This is a good year to join with others who share your ideals, and to take the lead when the way opens to you. Affirm your natural assertive drives by directing them into activities that improve the quality of life. You might also feel driven to strengthen your communication skills. Whether you're learning in a classroom, sending heartfelt e-mail to a good friend, speaking in a Toastmasters group, or making a presentation at work, circumstances that provide a chance to build your confidence in self-expression can be highly valuable.

To strengthen your connection to your spirituality, blend physical activity with enhanced inner awareness. Martial arts emphasize this concept, but you can just as effectively translate this idea into your favorite sports or fitness routine. Bring greater mindfulness into your activities: feel and experience the link of mind, body, and spirit. To tap into the more subtle levels of energy awareness, schedule an appointment with an acupuncturist, Reiki therapist, or body energetics expert. At home, create a space for your practice of the sacred. A quiet spot in your bedroom or den, or a meditation garden could serve as your space for reflection.

You might also want to take things into a different level. That adventure vacation you've considered may be just a phone call away! After July, travel can also be a significant stimulant to your creativity. However, during any time of the year, inner travel is a great idea. Make time to reflect on the best ways to bring unconditional love and joy into your daily life. All that's required is an open mind and a loving heart—and maybe a bit of practice to alter your routine so that there's time in your busy day to share.

♈

Affirmation for the Year

My thoughts, words, and actions pour forth from a loving heart.

Aries/January

In the Spotlight
After a few fits and starts, you can see real progress in career and community matters. The challenge is to balance family demands with career aims. Friends and professional allies help fill in the gaps.

Wellness and Keeping Fit
Allow a little more time for rest and relaxation through January 18, and focus on your "inner" fitness. Explore underlying causes of fatigue. Mars is in your sign after January 18, when you'll feel renewed and energized as you gradually increase your activity levels.

Love and Life Connections
Your friends are a key link to your self-confidence, and strengthening your ties lifts your heart. You can be on the receiving end of a favor after January 19. It's also possible that romance can spark from an introduction through a friend. Your love life gains momentum after January 18, when an old love may re-enter the picture. Romance fares best during the Full Moon on January 28, although your fantasies may be pretty active all month!

Finance and Success
Satisfaction from your career grows, and by working closely with others in positions of influence you can advance your pet projects—and your reputation! However, Mercury does turn retrograde on January 18, when a few projects may have to move to a side burner. While communication can seem inconsistent and negotiations uncertain, steady progress builds toward success after the New Moon on January 13.

Cosmic Insider Tip
Special attention to the details of a creative project can save your hide and your money from January 23 to 31. Double-check all figures, and know where you've left your keys.

Rewarding Days 1, 2, 9, 10, 14, 19, 20, 24, 25, 28, 29

Challenging Days 5, 6, 11, 12, 13, 26, 27

Affirmation for the Month I am listening to my intuitive voice.

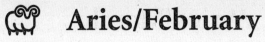 Aries/February

In the Spotlight

It's time to set out new goals that help you realize your dreams. After all, with Mars in your sign you have the energy and the drive. Now, all you have to do is direct it! You might be surprised how quickly you check off every item on your wish list!

Wellness and Keeping Fit

The supercharge you feel from Mars in Aries needs direction, and this is the time to concentrate on building strength and endurance.

Love and Life Connections

It's a meeting of the minds that sparks your interest in a love match from February 1 to 12. Yes, the physical attraction keeps the fires burning, too. Travel or a retreat from your ordinary routine can encourage you to expose your deepest feelings and share your hopes for the future. Are you playing a solo tune? A time-out from February 13 to 28 can inspire your creative passion. Give your imagination a place to roam free during the Full Moon on February 27.

Finance and Success

Reconsider a proposal while Mercury retrogrades through February 8. Your aims may be different from what they were when you first brought an idea forward. Plus, this is an excellent time to uncover previously hidden information or overlooked treasures. Surprising changes lead to profit and opportunity through the New Moon on February 12. While you can make progress by taking the lead, after February 13 you might move further ahead by allowing someone else to step into the spotlight (or take the heat!).

Cosmic Insider Tip

Saturn turns direct on February 7, and business enters a growth phase. You've been creating your strategy, and can take action that turns the tide from February 12 to 20.

Rewarding Days 5, 6, 7, 10, 15, 16, 17, 20, 25

Challenging Days 1, 2, 8, 9, 22, 23, 28

Affirmation for the Month My goals illuminate the best choices.

Aries/March

In the Spotlight
Softening your approach works like a charm. While you may have been driving pretty hard the last few months, now you're ready to enjoy the fruits of your labors. It's time to put your resources to work—but avoid the impulse to spend all your cash reserves.

Wellness and Keeping Fit
An overall health assessment from March 1 to 20 gives you a sense of control over your body. It's time for a physical tune-up, including a nutritional evaluation. Enhancing your flexibility puts the spring back in your step.

Love and Life Connections
Parties and social activities can feel like emotional spring-cleaning. New acquaintances spark unusual exploits after March 4. Plus, after March 8, when Venus moves into Aries, you're in the mood for love. If your aims seem unrealistic, take the time to explore possibilities. Be more attentive to resistance from others, since pushing too far can alienate affection. Then, take action during the Full Moon on March 28, when you're ready to stoke the fires of passion.

Finance and Success
Careful planning may not be your style, but you'll appreciate the effects of knowing where you stand. That makes it possible for you to take better advantage of fast-paced changes which open new doors from March 6 to 28. Enhance your portfolio by taking action after the New Moon on March 14. And if you've been waiting to showcase your talents, this is your month.

Cosmic Insider Tip
Everything seems to be moving forward, and with the momentum building, you're eager to satisfy your desires. Your reputation grows and your influence is stronger after March 20.

Rewarding Days 5, 6, 9, 10, 14, 15, 16, 20, 24, 25

Challenging Days 1, 7, 8, 12, 22, 23, 28, 29

Affirmation for the Month I am aware of the effect of my actions.

Aries/April

In the Spotlight
Network with others to expand opportunities for all concerned. It's one of those times when combined efforts raise greater rewards. Your ideas inspire progress through April 14.

Wellness and Keeping Fit
Extra caution can keep you out of danger, especially from April 1 to 12, and then after April 27. During these times you can be more accident prone, and it's also easier to fall victim to injury in high-risk situations.

Love and Life Connections
Expressing yourself with style and spontaneity can impress your sweetheart, but be careful with your promises, since it's easy to go overboard through April 5. After all, one element of communication is listening, and while you have fascinating things to share, your relationships may require that you yield to the needs of others some of the time. A getaway after April 14 can be just what you need to break the ice in a new love connection.

Finance and Success
Take another look at the numbers after April 4, since cost overruns can slow progress if you have failed to make room for them. Testing and experimentation help you create a wonderful finished product, and by the time the Aries New Moon occurs on April 12 you'll be ready to showcase your top-drawer project. After April 14 you may be ready to roll out a significant idea with the help of your friends.

Cosmic Insider Tip
Saturn and Neptune's harmony opens the way for greater satisfaction with your personal relationships from April 1 to 14. But you have to know what you want before you can have it!

Rewarding Days 1, 2, 6, 11, 12, 16, 20, 21, 28, 29

Challenging Days 3, 4, 5, 18, 19, 24, 25, 26

Affirmation for the Month I clearly define my aims and ideas.

Aries/May

In the Spotlight

Your fertile imagination and creative concepts can inspire a new life direction. One thing is certain: you're on the move, one way or another. This time is not about standing still.

Wellness and Keeping Fit

Outdoor activities keep your engine purring. Whether you're jogging in the park, hiking through the woods, or working in your garden—it's time to connect with nature while you get into shape. Get into a daily routine that allows ample time for fitness.

Love and Life Connections

Love blossoms in the light of shared interests and grows even stronger when you make time to celebrate your individual accomplishments. Show those you cherish how you feel from May 1 to 10, when there can be little doubt about your intentions or your desires. An old feud with a sibling can raise its head after May 8, and if you cannot reach an agreement, you may feel that it's time to put some distance between you for a while.

Finance and Success

Communicate. With Mercury, Venus, Mars, and Saturn emphasizing your mental abilities, it's the perfect time to travel, confer, write, speak, learn, or teach. Even after Mercury turns retrograde on May 15 you may feel inspired to keep your ideas flowing. Power plays can lead to a setback after May 5, but you can diffuse problems by working within established guidelines. Watch for legal traps, and avoid final agreements until you've completed thorough research.

Cosmic Insider Tip

Saturn opposes Pluto: what may have been a workable contract in the past can seem like a snare. If it's your battle to fight, move ahead with caution. If not, let somebody else take the potshots.

Rewarding Days 3, 4, 8, 9, 13, 14, 18, 26, 27

Challenging Days 1, 2, 15, 16, 22, 23, 28, 29

Affirmation for the Month The light of truth guides my steps.

Aries/June

In the Spotlight
Friction or turmoil at home may result from a benign situation, but it can still feel unsettling. The diversion of working toward your aims can keep you on a more even keel.

Wellness and Keeping Fit
Despite progress being made, burning the candle at both ends can be stressful. Since you're feeling some unfriendly fire from Mars, you'll need to be more diligent about your daily workouts. And remember to stretch, breathe, and honor your physical limitations!

Love and Life Connections
Are you making improvements at home, or moving? There's plenty going on that stems from good intentions, but you may feel that you're never able to satisfy everybody's demands. It's easy to get in over your head through June 8, but by the time the solar eclipse occurs on June 10 there's some relief. Venus waltzes into your love sector on June 15, and by opening your heart you can transform your life.

Finance and Success
Until Mercury ends its retrograde cycle on June 8 you may feel that you're a day late and a dollar short. Unanticipated chances can undermine your progress, and your competition seems to know when you're in trouble, too! By June 15 you may feel that you have a handle on the situation, although it can take a while for the dust to settle. Finances improve considerably by the Full Moon on June 24, but a conservative approach will serve your best interests.

Cosmic Insider Tip
The solar eclipse on June 10 emphasizes the importance of maintaining open communication, especially if there's a crisis brewing. Plus, it's a good time to finalize previously delayed plans.

Rewarding Days 4, 5, 9, 10, 14, 15, 22, 23, 27

Challenging Days 11, 12, 13, 18, 19, 20, 24, 25, 26

Affirmation for the Month I am attentive to my deepest needs.

Aries/July

In the Spotlight
Those projects that were simmering on the back burner may be boiling over, and keeping up with the demands of your busy schedule can leave you feeling harried. Your sense of humor saves the day. Besides, you appear to be making a tidy profit from it all.

Wellness and Keeping Fit
The primary downfall from July 1 to 13 is the temptation to push past your limits or take unnecessary risks. A little caution and common sense can save your neck, and you might still capture the record. Seek out fun-filled recreation to stay in shape after July 15.

Love and Life Connections
Home and family provide plenty of excitement, although you might have to be creative if you're going to squeeze in time for romance from July 1 to 12. After the New Moon on July 10 the tide begins to turn, although you may be face-to-face with the final end of an old relationship. Things are looking up though, since by the Full Moon on July 24 your love life may just move into blue-ribbon territory.

Finance and Success
Meetings and presentations open the way to success from July 1 to 9, although it's easy to overspend on "incidentals." Upgrades and improvements can be costly, so before you undertake that overhaul, do some comparative pricing. You may discover that last year's model will serve you quite nicely, as long as it works properly. Investments take a positive turn on July 22, although your best profits may come during the Full Moon on July 24.

Cosmic Insider Tip
Improvements at work streamline your efficiency and increase your enjoyment. However, disgruntled workers can undermine the situation after July 20. Address concerns when they arise.

Rewarding Days 1, 2, 3, 11, 12, 19, 20, 24, 29, 30

Challenging Days 9, 10, 15, 16, 17, 22, 23

Affirmation for the Month I look for joy each and every day!

Aries/August

In the Spotlight
Relationships take the lead, with enhanced potential to experience growing joy. Your creative impulses are supercharged, and can lead to tremendous innovation and financial reward.

Wellness and Keeping Fit
It's time to take a personal inventory and determine the best ways to further enhance your physical vitality. While you may be tempted just to coast for a while, overindulgence can be a problem, too. The impulse is to expand. Your choice is whether that expansion will be muscle or fat.

Love and Life Connections
Your light shines brilliantly and can be exceptionally attractive. But the most important stimulus from the planets is that it's easier to feel the pure love that flows from your heart. The New Moon on August 8 can bring you face-to-face with the answer to your dreams. Do something amazing, exciting, and memorable with the love of your life during the Full Moon on August 22. Celebrate!

Finance and Success
An inventive, unique, and valuable opportunity comes your way from August 1 to 5, and can be the key to establishing consistent financial rewards. From August 8 to 22 you can experience steady growth of your assets, but this is also an excellent time to develop and promote your talents and creative efforts. Concentrate on fine-tuning after August 24, when you'll appreciate a chance to catch your breath.

Cosmic Insider Tip
Jupiter moves into Leo for a yearlong trek, amplifying your creativity. But it's the high energy from Mars and Uranus that sets things in motion. It's up to you to run with it!

Rewarding Days 3, 4, 7, 8, 16, 17, 20, 21, 22, 25, 26, 30, 31

Challenging Days 5, 6, 12, 13, 18, 19

Affirmation for the Month I am grateful for abundance in my life.

♈ Aries/September ♈

In the Spotlight
Support from a partner or advice from a trusted mentor can raise questions, but may still be worth consideration. To continue your momentum, you may have to address the best ways to eliminate unnecessary situations or let go of things you no longer need.

Wellness and Keeping Fit
An old ailment or injury can slow you down. Instead of feeling trapped and stifled by fears, look further into root causes and adopt a holistic approach. Review your diet.

Love and Life Connections
After the New Moon on September 7, issues about trust and intimacy can lead to self-doubts. It's only your old fears knocking at the doors to your heart, and maybe you can finally let them out and bid them good-bye once and for all. If you're drawn to another person from September 14 to 25, take some time before you make a final decision. Venus and Neptune leave a heavy fog, so it's hard to see where the relationship might be headed.

Finance and Success
Legal matters and financial plans are best solidified early in the month, since Mercury turns retrograde on September 14. After that time your attention turns to troubleshooting and researching, and old business seems to come first on the agenda. Extra care with joint resources is necessary after September 7, and you might decide to pull out of a risky business venture near the Full Moon on September 21.

Cosmic Insider Tip
Power plays can undermine your success from September 8 to 20—but only if you're not paying attention. Keep your eyes open for signs of trouble, and address problems as soon as they arise.

Rewarding Days 4, 5, 12, 13, 17, 21, 22, 23

Challenging Days 1, 2, 8, 9, 10, 14, 15, 29, 30

Affirmation for the Month I show my appreciation for love.

Aries/October

In the Spotlight
Although it's tempting to burn the bridges you've crossed, it could be a waste of energy and might limit your future options! You're still eliminating unnecessary things from your life, but now you have to consider the effect your actions will have on the lives of others.

Wellness and Keeping Fit
Competitive sports or a healthy physical challenge can be the perfect answer to eliminating stress, but only if you are well prepared.

Love and Life Connections
Venus turns retrograde, and your feelings about a love relationship may also turn toward the past. Whether you're pining for a lost love, missing the sweetness of the early days of a relationship, or simply feeling remorse for what went wrong, it's time to look inside your own heart. Take a different approach to relationships during the New Moon on October 6. Then, by the time the Full Moon in Aries arrives on October 21, you'll be ready to move toward greater personal satisfaction.

Finance and Success
Review your finances during Mercury's retrograde through October 6, paying special attention to expenses that are wasting your resources. After that time, initiate a different plan of action that will allow you to recover losses and establish a sense of greater control. Aggressive growth from partnerships can lead to legal entanglements after October 16.

Cosmic Insider Tip
To move forward you may have to yield to old obligations first. This is not the time to run away from significant disagreements. However, adopting a posture that's too aggressive works against you.

Rewarding Days 1, 2, 9, 10, 14, 19, 20, 21, 24, 29

Challenging Days 5, 6, 7, 12, 13, 26, 27

Affirmation for the Month I am aware of my motivations.

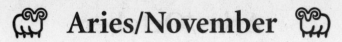 Aries/November

In the Spotlight

Competitive situations spark your vitality, although you might have trouble getting an accurate reading about your adversary. After November 19, better communications result, since you'll find it easier to locate your common values. That's called a friendly rivalry!

Wellness and Keeping Fit

Channel some of your competitive drives into your fitness routine, or get involved in sports that give you a chance to build upon your strengths and work on your weaknesses.

Love and Life Connections

The New Moon on November 4 stimulates your hidden desires, and if you bury them, resentment can result. Arguments over money are most likely power struggles—a question of who's in charge. Even though you might not like it at first, moving into the passenger seat can turn things around. After November 21 you may feel more at ease with talking about your hopes again.

Finance and Success

If your financial entanglements are working against your best interests, explore your options for discontinuing your association from November 1 to 18. If you try to pretend everything's okay, the underlying problems can blow your assets by the time the lunar eclipse occurs on November 19. However, you must also determine whether there are obligations you still need to fulfill, and if so, search for a workable solution.

Cosmic Insider Tip

The bottom line during the lunar eclipse on November 19 is about your personal values. Revamp your attitude to reflect your deepest truth, and the rest will fall into place.

Rewarding Days 6, 7, 10, 15, 16, 21, 25, 26

Challenging Days 2, 3, 8, 9, 18, 19, 22, 23, 29, 30

Affirmation for the Month I am willing to let go of the things I no longer need.

Aries/December

In the Spotlight

The Sun's eclipse stimulates a period of exposure. If you like solving mysteries, this can be pretty exciting. But if you feel vulnerable while dealing with underlying issues, then grab your jacket. Still, adventurous changes open the doors to new experiences.

Wellness and Keeping Fit

While you may think it's better not to know, you're always more adept at dealing with any situation when you can look it in the eye.

Love and Life Connections

Your partner may need more emotional support, or the opposite could be true: you might feel that your partner is not seeing who you are or what you need. Retreat from the everyday routine near the time of the solar eclipse on December 4, and give yourselves time to bond with one another. Reach toward the dream you share. Or, if you decide that there's nothing in common, seek a resolution to your relationship. On December 19, the Full Moon brings a time of enrichment, when you can uncover true love and more easily express what's in your heart. Honesty leads the way.

Finance and Success

Long-range financial planning can require that you take a more careful look at your debts. As you set up a plan to strengthen your assets, you may find that the challenge will require that you eliminate some spending habits that undermine your personal worth. A conservative attitude works best, but that doesn't mean you have to lose your pizzazz!

Cosmic Insider Tip

It's time to dig your way out of stubborn situations that inhibit your growth and progress. You don't have to go it alone. The universe provides help now, just when you need it most!

Rewarding Days 3, 4, 8, 9, 12, 13, 18, 22, 23, 31

Challenging Days 2, 5, 6, 20, 21, 26, 27, 28

Affirmation for the Month My stability comes from this moment!

ARIES ACTION TABLE

These dates reflect the best—but not the only—times for success and ease in these activities, according to your Sun sign.

	JAN	FEB	MAR	APR	MAY	JUN	JUL	AUG	SEPT	OCT	NOV	DEC
Move							7-21					
Start a class					1-14	9-17						4, 5
Join a club		11, 12										
Ask for a raise				12								
Look for work	1-3	4-12						6-25				9-31
Get pro advice	5, 6	1, 2, 28	1, 28, 29	24, 25	22, 23	18, 19	15, 16	11-13	8, 9	5, 6	2, 3, 29, 30	26, 27
Get a loan	7, 8	3, 4	2, 3, 30, 31	26, 27	24, 25	20, 21	17, 18	14, 15	10, 11	7, 8	4, 5	1, 2, 28-30
See a doctor			12-28					6-25				
Start a diet	3, 4, 30, 31	26, 27	26, 27	22, 23	20, 21	16, 17	13, 14	9, 10	6, 7	3, 4, 31	1, 27, 28	24, 25
End relationship			28, 29									
Buy clothes							22-31	1-5				
Get a makeover			8-31	12								
New romance						15-30	1-10	8, 9				
Vacation	9, 10	5-7	5, 6	1, 2, 28, 29	26, 27	22, 23	19-21	16, 17	12, 13	9, 10	6, 7	3, 4, 31

TAURUS

The Bull
April 19 to May 20

Element:	Earth
Quality:	Fixed
Polarity:	Yin/Feminine
Planetary Ruler:	Venus
Meditation:	I cherish and safeguard my environment.
Gemstone:	Emerald
Power Stones:	Diamond, blue lace agate, rose quartz
Key Phrase:	I have
Glyph:	Bull's head
Anatomy:	Throat, neck
Color:	Green
Animal:	Cattle
Myths/Legends:	Isis and Osiris, Cerridwen, Bull of Minos
House:	Second
Opposite Sign:	Scorpio
Flower:	Violet
Key Word:	Conservation

Positive Expression:	Misuse of Energy:
Prosperous	Avaricious
Loving	Covetous
Composed	Inflexible
Enduring	Uncompromising
Faithful	Lethargic
Stable	Resistant

Taurus

Your Ego's Strengths and Shortcomings

Sure and steady, you're driven by a need to create a secure and comfortable life. Your dependability is a trademark, since once you are committed, you're there for the duration. It's your ability to attract, evaluate, and accumulate the resources necessary for a happy life that help you play your role as "The Maintainer" of the zodiac.

Endurability is important to you, and that's one of the reasons you don't like to make changes—unless they're absolutely necessary. People and things that prove themselves worthy gain your life-long protection and appreciation. Through your natural connection to the energy of Venus, your planetary ruler, your loving energy embraces those who have your heart. They look to you for comfort and sustenance during life's ups and downs, and it warms your heart when you're brought closer together. Your Venusian qualities also attract and reflect artistry and beauty. As a result, your life is filled with beautiful people and valuable things.

Your consistent focus helps you develop your talents and artistic skills, and you may be a dedicated patron of the arts. However, you are also keenly aware of a need to preserve Earth's resources, and know that some things simply cannot be replaced or duplicated. It's the struggle to understand that you are more than what you have that may have lead to disappointment or frustration. But it is also letting go of what you no longer need that allows you to grow—spiritually and emotionally. After all, you have a connection to the continuous spiral of never-ending love from the Source—and it flows directly into your own heart.

Shining Your Love Light

You may attract more romantic relationships than you develop, since you are looking for the kind of love that will endure through time. For you, love is not a revolving door. Your tenderness, sensuality, and sweetness distinguish you as a first-class lover, but you look for commitment before you give your heart. If you feel a lack of support in a relationship or if your self-worth is threatened, you can be a victim of unwelcome jealousy. Losing someone you love can deal a crushing blow to your heart. Over time, though, you learn that love involves continual evolution and transformation. That's how it grows!

It's easiest for you to be comfortable with the other Earth signs—Taurus, Virgo, and Capricorn—since they share your need for practicality. However, your attraction to Scorpio, your zodiac opposite, can be especially intense and passionate. Unfortunately, you can both be highly possessive, so sustaining that relationship requires exceptional tolerance.

You're attracted to Aries, but can be disappointed if she or he wants to move on before you've settled in. With another Taurus you can feel completely at home, but you can also fall into a terrible rut unless you strive to keep your love alive. Gemini challenges you to develop greater flexibility, since he or she appreciates variety. An easy contentment with Cancer can lead to a secure home and family life. With Leo, ego conflicts can arise, although the passions you share can lead to forgiveness as long as you both have self-respect. You may feel that Virgo is your ultimate lover: hungry for the sensual experiences of love, but also sensible about priorities.

Libra's classy demeanor and grace can be enticing, although his or her indecisiveness can drive you nuts. You can savor the generosity and playfulness of Sagittarius, as long as you don't mind the periods of separation. Capricorn may be your perfect match, especially if your ideals and aims are mutually supportive. Aquarius may be interesting, but can fall short when it comes to providing sufficient attention to your needs. Pisces invites you to create a place to bring your dreams to life, and you can share wondrously romantic times together.

Making Your Place in the World

Building a lifelong career or body of work helps you focus your energy and creativity. Your natural business sense can be applied to the world of banking, finances, real estate, or investment. And you might also enjoy retail or restaurant trades. As a counselor, your patient understanding can help others develop to their fullest.

If you are drawn to an artistic career, you might excel in music or art, or might prefer to develop a lucrative gallery or world-class museum. You can filter your sense of structure into carpentry, wood working, building, or architecture. Gardening, farming, ranching, forestry, or the floral industry is also fulfilling. Environmental work can be satisfying, and you can also be a highly effective fund-raiser.

Power Plays

Your personal power emerges when you feel secure. In fact, your ability to maintain a focused course helps you develop the ample resources and loyal friends and family that serve as the anchor for your security. You'll show appreciation for those who have proven themselves, but can be a stubborn opponent to others who pretend to the throne or abuse their position or power.

When you feel most vulnerable, possessiveness or greed can overtake your better judgment as you strive to protect yourself. The desire "to have" versus the experience "to be" is part of your life lesson about attachments. After all, anything or anyone you perceive as yours will be difficult to release. But graciously closing a chapter or saying good-bye when the situation requires it will ultimately fortify your power. As you accept the value of others in your life and share your resources, the kinship that results can withstand all tests.

It's Mother Nature that teaches the most profound lessons of all—illustrating the natural cycles of rebirth and renewal. Incorporating this understanding into your life work, relationships, and sense of self ultimately provides a power that sustains your soul.

Famous Tauruses

Eddie Albert, Madeleine Albright, Tony Blair, T. Berry Brazleton, George Carlin, Joan Chen, Richard M. Daley, Tony Danza, Roma Downey, Dale Earnhardt, Lesley Gore, Jan Hooks, Casey Kasem, Jay Leno, Willie Mays, Al Pacino, Tim Russert, Renee Zellweger

The Year Ahead For Taurus

Your network of support grows, adding confidence in your ability to bring your dreams to life. It's by strengthening your skills and understanding that you further develop your life work, and shed light on the path for others to follow. There may be upsets in leadership that test your personal aims, but these can also lead to paths you might never have uncovered! The greatest challenge you face is that of building a more workable approach to managing your material resources, since waste is almost intolerable to you now.

The year 2002 is a time to express your ideas and enhance your ability to communicate them. Whatever your manner of communication, Jupiter's cycle from January through August helps you strengthen your confidence and skills. Travel can be uplifting and may also provide the keys to linking your ideas with others. Plus, connecting with others from different cultures can enhance your creativity. You may not have to go anywhere, either. After all, with tools like the Internet, you can travel the globe without leaving your house! During the last four months of the year, you're expanding your home base. Whether you redecorate, remodel, or move, you may feel a strong need to enhance the value of your home. Family can grow, too.

Saturn's influence in Gemini draws your attention to finances, and you may feel more inclined to learn about the best ways to manage your resources, too. It's a good year to utilize planning and organizational tools to give you a handle on your finances. While you may be more conservative with your spending, you may also discover that you're ready to put your money to work for you. The value of your time is also accentuated.

The slower-moving planets—Uranus, Neptune, and Pluto—continue their treks in the same signs as last year. The cycle of Uranus awakens you to the potential development of a different life path or career. You may feel an inclination to either strike out on a more independent path, or seek work that allows more opportunities to show your special genius. In addition, Neptune's cycle can provide some confusing stimulation, since you could lose your objectivity in a fog of illusion. It's important to explore opportunities for their realistic potential, since you can be more vulnerable to deception. However, you also may be drawn to focus your aims on charitable efforts or to follow pursuits that fulfill your spiritual inclinations. Pluto's cycle helps you uncover some of your hidden motivations, and stimulates a need to explore the deeper, hidden issues in your closest relationships.

The solar and lunar eclipses emphasize your self-worth and basic values. In addition, you're exploring the underlying value of those you hold dear, and may be questioning your emotional attachments and their merits (or lack of merit). Changes in your finances—even positive changes—can stimulate questions about the best ways to put all your resources to use.

If you were born from April 20 to 25, it's time to clear out a few closets. Pluto is transiting in sesquiquadrate to your Sun, indicating that you're ready to eliminate some of the things that no longer fit your life. There are subtle changes in your focus and self-expression—the kind of thing that you don't notice overnight, but becomes more apparent as time moves along. You may feel you're ready for a make-over—from the inside out! There's a potential problem with this cycle, though, since the discomfort you feel might be coming from a source that's difficult to pinpoint. Fortunately, your inborn patience can help, since careful adjustments will help you make determinations that promote personal growth. One of the key ingredients in your decisions can stem from changes in a close relationship. If you feel that your needs have changed, but the relationship has not grown to accommodate those needs, you may have serious thoughts about how to make alterations. It could come down to a careful assessment of your approach to intimacy and discarding those old fears about allowing someone to be that close to your heart and soul.

If you were born from April 25 to May 3, you're feeling an awakening of your talents and abilities, since Uranus is traveling in quintile aspect to your Sun. While this is a subtle cycle, if you have the inclination to develop your artistry or talents, this influence indicates that you can move into the creative flow with greater ease. Plus, you can feel an enhanced confidence about expressing your unique qualities in any situation. What you may not have considered a talent can also come to the forefront and advance your career or reputation.

If you were born from April 25 to May 5, you've reached a platform from which you can springboard onto another level. Saturn transits in semisquare to your Sun starting in May, and continuing until spring 2003. The hard work you put forth two years ago is now paying off, and you feel ready to move into a different life situation. Your career can advance, your relationships can deepen. However, you may have to leave a comfortable situation behind. It's like breaking in new jeans, when your well-worn pair is much easier to zip—except this is your life that's being tested! If you feel you need to develop your skills or understanding more fully, then Saturn's support can be helpful, aiding your ability to discipline your time and focus. But, you're just as likely to be given new responsibilities that require you to "learn as you go"—and that's the kind of exposure you can experience. Have you ever jumped on a trampoline or practiced diving from a springboard? The lift allows you to go higher into the air. In fact, you can even do more while you're up there! But the safety and security of standing on solid ground is missing for a few moments. This year, your life is like that trampoline. It's up to you to figure out how to handle being airborne—for a little while, at least. Visualize the way you want to land—it will provide security.

If you were born from April 28 to May 2, you're very sensitive while Neptune transits in square aspect to your Sun. There's a plus to this cycle: you can tap into your creativity more easily, and your imagination is enhanced. On top of that, your resistance to change dissolves, allowing you to step into the flow with greater ease. What's the down side? You could be so enthralled by the vision that you forget your life-vest. The problem with Neptune's influence is a potential lack of clarity, increasing a tendency to fall victim to illusion or deception (including self-deception). You're also uncovering some hidden talents and strengths while Pluto transits in biquintile to your Sun. This combination of influences suggests that as you reinforce this connection to your inner self, you will maintain a sense of harmony as you follow your dreams. To some extent, your life can be deeply transformed, since probing your inner self can be quite illuminating. The conflict could be that you have difficulty determining what is and is not important to your personal growth. To make the most of this period of extraordinary awareness, tap into your own truth. You can be unusually sensitive to the influence of others, and if you feel, deep within yourself, that some of these influences are misguiding, then take a time out to re-evaluate. Consulting with a trusted advisor on significant decisions can also serve as an anchor.

If you were born from May 4 to 10, you're making a series of adjustments this year while Pluto transits in quincunx aspect to your Sun. Think of this as a time to trim away excess and to fine-tune your life to fit the person you have become. In many ways, this can be a year of exceptional clarity—although you might not like everything you see! Situations beyond your control can present you with a series of upsets, and can undermine your self-confidence. To regain your momentum, trust your common sense. After all, you're a master at evaluating the strength of most situations. It's just that you can be thrown off-track, and that uncharacteristic wobbly feeling can be quite unsettling. You may just have to alter your priorities in order to maintain what's truly important. If health issues arise, consider this the perfect time to investigate until you get to the core of the problem. Ignoring physical symptoms can lead to a loss of control, but probing discomforts to discover their cause can put you right back in the driver's seat.

If you were born from May 6 to 20, it's time to take steps that bring your life to a higher level. Saturn is transiting in semisextile to your Sun. This particular cycle does not stimulate dramatic change, and usually gives you a better view of yourself and your needs. However, since you're stepping up, you may have to let go of a few things until you've established yourself on terra firma. Or, there can be a sense of delayed gratification—waiting until you've completed certain steps before you reach the rewards. Persistence, focus, and prioritizing are the keys to making the most of this cycle during 2002.

If you were born from May 16 to 20, the lunar eclipse on November 19 has special significance, since it is right on your Sun. While this is not the kind of influence that lasts for months, the changes you make during this time can have a lasting impact. Try to arrange a period of reflection or introspection near this time, since this can be a period of enhanced awareness.

Tools For Change

Your easygoing style can seem like a faded memory under some of the unsettling influences you're experiencing. To regain a sense of control and stability, develop your support network. You might also enjoy the expanded awareness derived from learning experiences—ranging from classes, to reading, to travel. It's easy to feel that you've lost your objectivity, and an increased database can certainly help in that department. Enhance your communication skills, or take advantage of technological tools that help you extend the range and effectiveness of what you need to say to the world.

Underneath it all, you may be taking a careful look at your deep-seated values. For this reason, it's a good idea to explore all the "stuff" you keep around the house or crammed into closets. As you begin to clear away clutter, you're likely to uncover a few poignant memories—and buried hurts, too. In the process, you have a chance to release your attachment to things, people, and emotions that create an unnecessary tie to your past. Of course, you don't have to give everybody their marching orders, but alterations in your priorities will certainly provide clues to those who need to understand your changes. This is your time to make way for an expression of personal values that will generate stability.

Then, there's the question of getting up to speed in this new century. While the high-tech tools like the Internet and broadband communications may have seemed futuristic a decade ago, now they're a part of your life. If you have not found a use for some of today's technical wizardry, this is the time to make friends with those wizards!

On a more personal level, you're also at a stage when your own resistance can work against you. Strive to develop a more flexible body and mind. Exercises that focus on stretching can have all sorts of wonderful effects on your overall health. And, as you stretch your body, you may discover that you're ready to stretch your consciousness, too. Visualize yourself as a limber, free, and powerful presence in the world. See yourself dancing to the most beautiful new music. Better yet . . . for just a moment, imagine that you are taking off and soaring above your daily existence. Look down to see a different perspective on your world. Bring the feeling of free flight and powerful vision with you as you land, back on Earth . . . and get to work making your dream a reality!

Affirmation for the Year

I use all my resources in a way that brings
more abundance into my life!

Taurus/January

In the Spotlight
High on creative inspiration, you're ready to make some dreams come true. Friends provide the cheering section, but you may also get a thrill from lending a helping hand to a deserving colleague.

Wellness and Keeping Fit
A vacation can give you that second wind you've been craving, but try to get back into your routine before January 15. Stress and strain at work can zap your energy, so some extra B-vitamins might help you maintain your mental clarity.

Love and Life Connections
Your pursuit of the sweetness of love yields delectable rewards from January 1 to 17. Watch your signals, though, since from January 7 to 12 misunderstandings can undo your best laid plans. The New Moon on January 13 opens the way for clarification. Family demands can squeeze your private time after January 20, although this is a good time to celebrate together.

Finance and Success
Conferences, presentations, and marketing schemes reap tremendous rewards from January 1 to 16. If you're targeting a different direction or meeting new people, the momentum is on your side after January 13. But watch out, since Mercury turns retrograde on January 18, and your careful planning can be undone by unexpected developments. The problem can be compounded by undermining from a competitor, so remain alert, particularly after January 24 and through the Full Moon on January 28.

Cosmic Insider Tip
Confusion can lead people to leap to the wrong conclusions from January 7 to 11, and again after January 27. In fact, it's the problems earlier in the month that are likely to crop up again!

Rewarding Days 3, 4, 12, 13, 16, 17, 21, 22, 23, 30

Challenging Days 1, 2, 7, 8, 9, 14, 15, 28, 29

Affirmation for the Month Truth and integrity light my way.

Taurus/February

In the Spotlight
While you're in a favorable position at work, you may also be drawing fire from competitors. A low profile helps, but it will be to your advantage to take the stage after February 18. Profits from your career improve, giving your confidence a hefty boost.

Wellness and Keeping Fit
That draggy feeling may be the result of too little sleep—or restless sleep. Mars stimulates your need to release energy and tension at a very basic level. Exercise helps immensely, but relaxation is crucial.

Love and Life Connections
You may have a different perspective about your parents, especially if there are significant family changes during the New Moon on February 12. After that time you're also establishing a more powerful link with a close friend. Take care, since a conflict or power struggle can drive a wedge between you and your partner after February 24. Disagreements about your shared resources can bring out the beast during the Full Moon on February 27.

Finance and Success
Since Mercury continues its retrograde through February 8 you may feel that you're repeating things you thought were already settled! Fortunately, there's room for negotiations from February 4 to 13, and these can resolve a number of issues. Careful budgetary planning midmonth can help you avoid unnecessary cost overruns. Hold your horses, though, since red tape or contract issues can slow or halt progress after February 25.

Cosmic Insider Tip
There's a shakeup in the works during the New Moon on February 12, although there's no reason to panic. Wait for the dust to settle, and finalize deals on February 13 and 14.

Rewarding Days 8, 9, 13, 14, 18, 19, 23, 26

Challenging Days 3, 4, 10, 11, 12, 24, 25

Affirmation for the Month My friends light up my life!

Taurus/March

In the Spotlight

Your drive and energy get a boost, since Mars cycles in your sign all month. With your eye on important goals, you're making steady progress and can strengthen your reputation in the process. Misdirected communication can create setbacks, however—so stay alert!

Wellness and Keeping Fit

To make the most of the high-powered fuel from Mars, concentrate on a fitness program that allows you to emphasize your physical strengths while paying attention to your weaknesses.

Love and Life Connections

Emboldened by the reassurance that your feelings are right on the mark, you're ready to share what's in your heart. Show your affections from March 1 to 8 to help erase doubts, since even small gestures can have a strong impact. You'll appreciate time to melt into romantic moments with your sweetheart, but can get lost in fantasy from March 12 to 16. Back on a heading toward a significant promise, it's time to make future plans from March 16 to 28.

Finance and Success

Combine your energy with colleagues whose talents and ideas measure up to your high standards. Brainstorms from March 1 to 7 advance your aims, and during the New Moon on March 14 you can take things to yet another level. Double-check plans, structures, and budget details from March 9 to 18—since a weak link can spell trouble. There's a buzz of excitement from March 12 to 29 that strengthens your attainment.

Cosmic Insider Tip

Give yourself a couple of days around the Full Moon on March 28 to withdraw from the action and regroup. Otherwise, your enjoyment of the success you're experiencing can be exhausting.

Rewarding Days 7, 8, 12, 13, 17, 18, 22, 23, 26, 27

Challenging Days 2, 3, 9, 10, 24, 25, 30, 31

Affirmation for the Month I deserve to have my dreams fulfilled!

Taurus/April

In the Spotlight

Your flair for artistry and sense of elegance sparkle under the heavenly influences this month. It's time to put your best foot forward, and let the world see what you have to offer.

Wellness and Keeping Fit

Graceful motion is much easier when you're in top shape. Since you might be tempted to spend more time lounging about after April 13, consider altering your routine to include slower, more deliberate exercises. Hatha yoga, Pilates, or similar practices can work nicely.

Love and Life Connections

The stimulus near the New Moon on April 12 will alter your old patterns in order to get things moving. In fact, you're likely to feel an attraction to someone that simply knocks you off your feet. To determine if it's infatuation or the real thing, you'll prefer a test run instead of just thinking about it. By the time the Full Moon arrives on April 27 you're reading signals that tell you whether or not you can delve further into the magic of love.

Finance and Success

Measured financial growth brings the kind of reassurance you appreciate. However, there are a few jolts from the powers that be that can rattle your nerves from April 4 to 11. An open mind can help you determine the best course of action. Review and revise your fiscal picture after April 20. If you're considering legal action, auspicious times are April 13 to 17, and then April 23 to 27.

Cosmic Insider Tip

You know in your heart whether you're in the right place. Alterations that improve your life and your relationships can make that place even sweeter from April 13 to 26.

Rewarding Days 3, 4, 5, 8, 13, 14, 15, 18, 19, 22, 23

Challenging Days 6, 7, 20, 21, 26, 27, 28

Affirmation for the Month Love lights my way.

Taurus/May

In the Spotlight

Money matters take top focus. This is the time to lay out plans and take actions that help to secure your long-term future. The first priority is to eliminate situations that are too costly or that place an unnecessary strain on your resources.

Wellness and Keeping Fit

Nervous tension can result from worry, and the resulting restlessness can destroy your concentration. To prevent stress from taking its toll, stay active, but also concentrate on your breathing. During meditation and exercise alike, focus on breathing is invigorating.

Love and Life Connections

Even if your work creates periods of separation from those you love, close communication helps maintain your ties. However, if you're not seeing eye-to-eye, the friction can lead to arguments. Before you jump to the conclusion that your relationship is doomed, explore the underlying issues. Try a different approach to exploring your feelings and needs during the Taurus New Moon on May 12.

Finance and Success

A careful and conservative examination of the costs involved in a project reassures your confidence in it. You're in no mood to skip over these fine points, and those who insist on speeding ahead may drive themselves right out of the picture. The momentum improves after May 12, but once Mercury enters its retrograde cycle on May 14 progress can be interrupted. Useful ideas emerge after May 22, when repairs get you up and running again.

Cosmic Insider Tip

Hidden problems come to the surface from May 8 to 16. It will cost more to ignore them than to deal with them—even if it's not much fun. The lunar eclipse on May 26 proves the point.

Rewarding Days 1, 2, 7, 10, 11, 12, 14, 20, 28, 29

Challenging Days 3, 4, 9, 17, 18, 24, 25, 30, 31

Affirmation for the Month I protect the things I value most.

Taurus/June

In the Spotlight

The solar eclipse brings attention to your need to establish a fresh direction for your material security. Correspondence with your network of talented and influential individuals helps you broadcast your successes and extend your own effectiveness.

Wellness and Keeping Fit

Getting outside to commune with Mother Nature helps you feel more alive. A vacation or weekend jaunt to your favorite beautiful spot inspires your creativity, and gives you a second wind, too. It's definitely time to smell the roses.

Love and Life Connections

Doubts may have cast a shadow on your intimate relationship, but you can recover trust by opening your heart. During the solar eclipse on June 10, reach into your soul to determine how you truly feel. Whether you are ready for a new love or working to strengthen an existing relationship, a generous heart attracts greater satisfaction. A romantic rendezvous turns the tide on June 24.

Finance and Success

Regroup during Mercury's retrograde through June 8, when another look at your portfolio can be an eye-opener. Profits from your ideas and efforts zoom along from June 9 to 22. However, it's important to leave room for unanticipated innovations after June 23. Meetings and presentations benefit your advancement from June 1 to 7, and again after June 22. Broadcast the outcome, since notice from an unusual source can be beneficial.

Cosmic Insider Tip

Practical ideas always carry weight with you. However, this month they may come from an unconventional source. Such developments keep life quite interesting!

Rewarding Days 2, 7, 8, 12, 16, 17, 24, 25, 29, 30

Challenging Days 10, 14, 15, 20, 21, 27, 28

Affirmation for the Month Change is safe.

Taurus/July

In the Spotlight
Close to home, your focus on family matters can cover a lot of territory. Changes, even those you welcome, can be unsettling and upset your normal routine. Call in reinforcements when you need them.

Wellness and Keeping Fit
Unless you enjoy your fitness regimen, you'll ignore it this month. Find something that feels more like fun, instead of a "work" out. After July 10 you'll also gain benefits from body therapies like massage or reflexology to help fine-tune your physical energy.

Love and Life Connections
Concise communication can heal old hurts, but leaping to a conclusion will widen the gap. Your intention during and after the New Moon on July 10 may be to enhance the beauty and comforts of home. However, others may protest unless they are happy about the arrangements. Fortunately, generosity wins out from July 8 to 20, and you can reach a lovely settlement. Affairs of the heart blossom after July 10, although there's a rough patch from July 21 to 25.

Finance and Success
A disturbance on the career front arises from July 1 to 6, when your values run headlong into differences with your superiors or other authorities. While you may want to dismiss these, due consideration can work to your benefit. Your talents give you the edge after July 9, and joining forces with others can enhance your recognition through July 20. Investments fare best from July 10 to 21. After that, reconsider options that seem to compromise your resources.

Cosmic Insider Tip
Connect. This is not a time to isolate yourself, since getting out there not only keeps you in the know, but the contact can inspire tremendous enthusiasm.

Rewarding Days 4, 5, 9, 10, 13, 14, 22, 23, 26, 31

Challenging Days 11, 12, 17, 18, 24, 25

Affirmation for the Month I welcome new ideas.

Taurus/August

In the Spotlight

Even if somebody's drawing a line in the sand, it may not be your battle. Before you get into the fray, weigh the potential costs against the outcome. Despite the turmoil, your creativity is on fire. Of course, it could be because of the turmoil!

Wellness and Keeping Fit

A healthy challenge can help you build muscle and tone your body. There's a tendency to hold too much tension, though, so add extra time for stretches before and after your workout. High-risk situations are treacherous after August 17, when a mistake can be costly.

Love and Life Connections

Mars burns its way through your home sector, unleashing plenty of friction. If you're moving or remodeling, then it's pretty clear what's up. Otherwise, you may need to pick a quiet corner and wait for the storm to blow over. Fortunately, your love life shows signs of improvement. It's just that family matters can disrupt the romance during the Full Moon on August 22.

Finance and Success

A competitive situation that's been brewing at work can explode in full force from August 1 to 5. Your allies and experience work to your benefit, though, and that challenge can give you a foothold for progress. Your strategies gain momentum after August 8. Financial profits from August 6 to 24 can provide a strong incentive to take on a new project next month.

Cosmic Insider Tip

Volatile situations beyond your control can be unsettling after August 18. Look for an opening that allows you to move into more creative territory.

Rewarding Days 1, 2, 5, 9, 10, 18, 19, 23, 28, 29

Challenging Days 7, 8, 14, 15, 20, 21, 22

Affirmation for the Month I know my strengths and limitations.

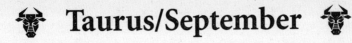

Taurus/September

In the Spotlight

This month, it's all about relationships of one kind or another. The day-to-day contacts at work can be unpredictable, but partnerships bask in Venus's agreeable glow. The biggest trap can come from family expectations, so keep track of your obligations!

Wellness and Keeping Fit

Lighthearted competition can spark your fun-loving nature. In fact, you'll enjoy a challenge from a good friend or family member—so issue an invitation for people to join you in fitness class or accompany you on your morning walks.

Love and Life Connections

With Venus and Mars warming up your passions, an intimate relationship intensifies. If you're in the market for love, put on your most fetching smile and start looking during the New Moon on September 7. Listen to your heart, since you can trip over your own inhibitions during the Full Moon on September 21. Perhaps it's time to abandon some of those fears—if you've established a trusting connection.

Finance and Success

Teamwork enhances your productivity through September 10, but after that you may be taking directions from somebody else. While this can throw your plans into a tizzy, you're not alone. Mercury turns retrograde on September 14, adding miscalculations, indecision, and poor communication to the mix. Dust off those unfinished projects if you want to make progress.

Cosmic Insider Tip

It might look like Mercury's retrograde is the culprit, but the ambush from Mars and Pluto is the real problem. For you, it's a question of creative control. If you made it, do you own it?

Rewarding Days 2, 6, 7, 14, 15, 19, 24, 25

Challenging Days 4, 5, 10, 11, 16, 17, 18

Affirmation for the Month I can accommodate changes.

Taurus/October

In the Spotlight

Take your time exploring your real feelings about your most intimate relationship. If your true needs are not reflected and fulfilled, discontent rises to the surface. However, it's also time to consider how to make the most of a wonderful connection.

Wellness and Keeping Fit

A consultation with a nutritionist and others on your holistic health team can aid you in maximizing your health. This is the perfect time to fine-tune your daily routine, diet, and fitness.

Love and Life Connections

Venus, the energy of love, glides around in your partnership sector—but she's in retrograde after October 10. That means you're rethinking your commitments and wondering what you're getting for your efforts. Love talk turns the tide after the New Moon on October 6, and a romantic getaway after October 11 can provide the perfect ambience. After October 24, deal with any misdirected signals immediately, or you'll have a big mess to unravel.

Finance and Success

Mercury's retrograde lasts until October 6, but you're uncovering some old trouble spots—so it can be to your advantage! Your creative ideas and sensible approach can place you in high demand through October 16. Strike agreements from October 7 to 10, and take another look at existing contracts after October 10. You may discover that your obligations have changed.

Cosmic Insider Tip

An old love can return to the scene after October 23—just in time to confuse your priorities. It could be a test; but it's also possible that you have unfinished business to address. You'll know.

Rewarding Days 3, 4, 11, 12, 16, 21, 22, 23, 26, 27, 31

Challenging Days 1, 2, 7, 8, 14, 15, 28, 29

Affirmation for the Month I am honest with myself about my feelings and needs.

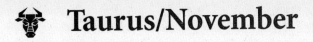 # Taurus/November

In the Spotlight
The loving attention you've given to a relationship pays off, although your decisions can ruffle a few feathers in the family. The lunar eclipse invites you to do some soul-searching.

Wellness and Keeping Fit
Tension on the job can drain your vitality. Even if you have to adjust your schedule, the time you spend working out can dissolve much of the stress of the daily grind. Emotionally charged situations can be especially tiring, so honor your need for rest, too.

Love and Life Connections
With Mercury and Venus highlighting partnership matters, it's time to communicate openly about your needs, hopes and dreams. No more clamming up—if it's important to you, confess. The Taurus lunar eclipse on November 19 can stimulate a period of vulnerability, but, more important, it's a powerful reality check. The truth is out, and a healthy relationship grows stronger, but you may need to leave a demoralizing connection behind.

Finance and Success
While Venus retrogrades through November 21, eliminate the products, projects, investments, and situations that show a history of lackluster results. This purging can free your time and resources for more viable opportunities. Misleading information can send you on a wild goose chase from November 3 to 7, when signing contracts is not a good idea, either. Extra care with investments is necessary throughout the month, and rash actions can be costly.

Cosmic Insider Tip
The essence of Venus retrograde is an examination of values, and it's significant for you. Venus is your planetary ruler, and this cycle prompts you to explore what's important and why.

Rewarding Days 8, 9, 13, 17, 18, 19, 27, 28

Challenging Days 4, 5, 10, 11, 20, 25, 26

Affirmation for the Month I treasure the power of nature.

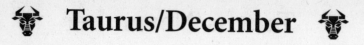

Taurus/December

In the Spotlight

Passionate moments make splendid memories, and you're in blue-ribbon territory. Whether you funnel your dedication into your love life, your work, or your family, your rewards depend upon the clarity of your intent. In other words, know what you want!

Wellness and Keeping Fit

A probe into the body-mind link of physical distress can be illuminating. The solar eclipse on December 4 emphasizes the need to explore repressed or unresolved emotional issues.

Love and Life Connections

Venus and Mars join together to bring a power punch to your relationship. If you've felt stalled or frustrated, it's time for that to end. Your partner may be the one who initiates the action, although a journey together can also unlock your romantic fervor. Are you available? After December 9, traveling single could lead to love. Infatuation can lift you right off your comfortable perch from December 8 to 17, although it could be true affection.

Finance and Success

Joining forces with a partner or others whose efforts complement your own can prove to be successful and profitable. Agreements forged now can carry weight for a long time, and you may derive significant benefits from mutual investments. Presentations, promotions, or teaching can advance your reputation quite effectively after December 8. Take a break from the action from December 9 to 16, but return to negotiations or planning after that time.

Cosmic Insider Tip

The healthy connection from generous Jupiter to powerful Pluto can propel you into the spotlight along with your talented cohorts. Just remember: credit where credit is due.

Rewarding Days 5, 6, 10, 11, 15, 16, 20, 24, 25

Challenging Days 1, 2, 7, 8, 9, 22, 23, 28, 29

Affirmation for the Month I am grateful for the love I receive.

TAURUS ACTION TABLE

These dates reflect the best—but not the only—times for success and ease in these activities, according to your Sun sign.

	JAN	FEB	MAR	APR	MAY	JUN	JUL	AUG	SEPT	OCT	NOV	DEC
Move							22-31	1-6				
Start a class	12, 13						7-20					
Join a club			13, 14									
Ask for a raise					12							
Look for work	3-31	1, 2, 13-28	1-11					27-31	1-30	1, 2, 11-31		
Get pro advice	7, 8	2, 3	2-4, 30-31	26, 27	24, 25	20, 21	17, 18	14, 15	10, 11	7, 8	4, 5	1, 2, 28-30
Get a loan	9, 10	5-7	5, 6	1, 2, 28, 29	26, 27	22, 23	19-21	15, 16	12, 13	9, 10	6, 7	3, 4
See a doctor			29-31	1-12				27-31	1-13	11-30		
Start a diet	4-6	1, 2, 28	1, 28, 29	24, 25	22, 23	18, 19	15, 16	11-13	8, 9	24, 25	2, 3, 29, 30	26, 27
End relationship				26, 27								
Buy clothes								6-25				
Get a makeover				1-25	12				6, 7			
New romance							11-31	1-5				
Vacation	11-13	8, 9	7, 8	3-5	1, 2, 28, 29	24-26	22, 23	18, 19	14, 15	11-13	8, 9	5, 6

GEMINI

The Twins
May 20 to June 21

Ⅱ

Element:	Air
Quality:	Mutable
Polarity:	Yang/Masculine
Planetary Ruler:	Mercury
Meditation:	My mind is linked to the source.
Gemstone:	Tourmaline
Power Stones:	Ametrine, citrine, emerald, spectrolite, agate
Key Phrase:	I think
Glyph:	Pillars of duality, The Twins
Anatomy:	Hands, arms, shoulders, lungs, nervous system
Color:	Bright colors, orange, yellow, magenta
Animal:	Monkeys, talking birds, flying insects
Myths/Legends:	Peter Pan, Castor and Pollux
House:	Third
Opposite Sign:	Sagittarius
Flower:	Lily of the valley
Key Word:	Versatility

Positive Expression:	**Misuse of Energy:**
Articulate	Gossipy
Perceptive	Distracted
Rational	Fickle
Quick-witted	Prankish
Resilient	Inconsistent
Curious	Duplicitous

Gemini

Your Ego's Strengths and Shortcomings

Always on "alert" status, you're fascinated with the endless diversity of life. Your focus is intellectual, and communication is soul food for you. You're an admirer of clear intelligence and may know people from a variety of backgrounds. As a result, you seem ever-youthful, playing your role as "The Questioner" of the zodiac in your life.

Known for your quick wit and intellectual sparring ability, you can also be a topnotch negotiator. When it's important to establish common ideals or elements that can lead to consensus, you have a knack for bringing people together. These diplomatic qualities can serve you well in your personal and professional life, although you may be accused of playing both sides against the middle if you're in a tight spot! Your love of travel and literature may prompt you to pursue academic goals, even in your later years. This is an outreach of your natural connection to the communicative energy of Mercury, your planetary ruler. The continual juggling act that results from your endless curiosity about all sorts of possibilities can frustrate those who prefer consistency and predictability.

Despite your inclination toward intuitive thinking, you're more comfortable with logical ideas. However, it is when you link logic and intuition that your genius emerges. After all, the natural duality of Gemini involves an ability to locate the nexus—that point which connects. Ultimately, your challenge is to reach into the space which connects your mind with the source of all knowledge. From there, you uncover the answers to your insatiable questions, and then shed light so that others can find their way.

Shining Your Love Light

Although the mysteries of love can be spellbinding, you'll be more at ease playing the field in relationships until you've sorted through your priorities. While one person may never be able to fulfill all your needs, finding that special someone to share and focus your life requires an intellectual affinity and mutual appreciation for personal freedom. Even though you can be a supportive partner, you may never be comfortable dealing with the complexities of deeper emotional issues. However, the right meeting of the minds can unlock the love in your heart, making it much easier to simply let go and enjoy the experience!

You are an air sign, and your desire to socialize and interrelate is most at ease with those born in Gemini, Libra, and Aquarius—all air signs. You may be most magnetically drawn to Sagittarius—your zodiac opposite—although you'll have to cope with Sagittarian wanderlust if the relationship is going to last.

Aries' freewheeling exuberance is simply captivating. Taurus brings out your sensual side, but you can become bored if he or she moves too slowly. Another Gemini can bring loads of fun into your life, but you can distract each other if your personal boundaries are too pliable. With Cancer's care and comfort you can let go and take it easy, but you may not agree on how to handle your shared resources. Leo's brilliant light stimulates the best of your own ideas, and you can develop a powerful bond of understanding.

You may feel at home with Virgo's thought-provoking and analytical mind, but you can go crazy if she or he goes too far with all those details. It's easy for you to love Libra, whose kindness inspires your creative artistry. You're engaged by Scorpio's intensity but can lose patience with his or her enigmatic nature. However, connecting to a Capricorn can be like working a perplexing puzzle, since just when you think you're getting close, the rules change. With Aquarius, you can develop a soulful connection, sharing your philosophies while you each reach for the utmost. Finally, although you might crave the joys of fantasy-filled nights with Pisces, during daylight hours you may be continually confused about what he or she really wants.

Making Your Place in the World

Blending intellectual challenges with creative imagination will provide a fulfilling career path. Your idealism can lead you to pursue a career in counseling, ministry, artistic expression, or public service, although you might prefer more mentally focused fields like writing, teaching, public speaking, politics, broadcasting, or advertising.

Pursuits which exercise your mind and use manual dexterity—drafting, design, music, or computers—can be rewarding. In fact, high-tech fields may be especially fascinating, and can provide the kind of diversity that will hold your interest. In sports, you may be an adept tennis player and might like instruction and commentating. In the performing arts, you're a natural mimic, and might also enjoy clowning, comedy, acting, and storytelling.

Power Plays

You're very familiar with the truth of the principle, "What you think, you become." For you, the power of the mind is illustrated every day. You may be a champion for improvements in education, and an advocate for youth, since you know that mental development is a key to personal power throughout life. For you, keeping an open mind is empowering, since the pursuit of fresh ideas and uncharted paths enlivens your spirit.

Part of your life work is building bridges—creating a path that links what has gone before with what is yet to come. By coupling your contagious enthusiasm with inspired ideas rooted in wisdom, you tap into your greatest power. Although you can be content with using your wit to get you out of a rough spot, your desire is to be known for much more. The most significant bridge you create is the one that connects your mind to higher consciousness. From there, your challenge is to share your understanding as a means of lifting the spirit of humanity to heights that empower us as a whole.

Famous Geminis

Drew Carey, Courteney Cox, Miles Davis, Christopher J. Dodd, Rudolph Giuliani, Anne Heche, Patrick Henry, Jewel, Anna Kournikova, Frank Oz, Jonathan Pryce, Joan Rivers, Richard Scarry, Maurice Sendak, Dr. Ruth Westheimer

The Year Ahead for Gemini

The focus you direct into your top priorities opens the way for you to test the importance of your most cherished dreams. This is your year to embrace your responsibilities and to make them work for you. Clarity emerges, and it's easier to identify your needs. You are shaping your identity based upon more realistic assumptions and possibilities, and can establish a significant foundation from which long-range growth emerges.

The most significant cycle you're experiencing this year is the continuation of Saturn's transit in Gemini. Since this cycle last occurred (1971–72), a lot has happened, and, after the middle of 2003, it will be another twenty-nine years before this happens again. As you can see, Saturn moves slowly, spending about two-and-a-half years in one sign. Saturn's influence is one of dedication, testing, discipline, and clarification. As a result, you can see the reflection of yourself and your life more clearly. The question is whether or not you like what you see! This is the time to bring situations to a close, particularly anything that is no longer relevant to your life experience. However, it is also a time to concentrate on building and strengthening circumstances that resonate with the essence of your true self. Your attitude toward your responsibilities is important, too. The obligations you need to complete to move forward can be demanding, but will bring rewards you can measure.

Jupiter's cycle emphasizes the significance of putting your resources to their best possible use. From January through the end of July, you may need to exercise some extra self-discipline when it comes to spending, since Jupiter's influence can stimulate a desire to spend more than you have. After July, Jupiter moves into the communication sector of your chart, providing an excellent period for developing a network of support. This will also be a wonderful period for travel, and is the perfect time to showcase your ideas.

The planets Uranus and Neptune are both transiting in the sign of Aquarius, highlighting your visionary capabilities and opening the way to expanded consciousness. Your spirituality can become a significant factor in your life, and your creativity can take flight. However, since these planets spend several years in one sign, the influence of their cycles takes a while to be fully realized. It is the year when these planets make an exact connection to your Sun that will bring the most significant opportunities for change. (See the sections that follow to determine if this is your year!) Pluto reaches the midpoint of its travel through the sign Sagittarius, stimulating an emergence of deep-seated issues. This is particularly true in the realm of relationships.

The solar and lunar eclipses have special significance for you during 2002. These cycles mark a time to become more clearly aware of what you need and want from your relationships, especially partnership and/or marriage. The cycles of Saturn and Pluto connect directly with the eclipse cycles for 2002, underlining their importance. Ties which need extra attention and care can demand more from you, but will grow stronger. Conversely, those situations which are not in your best interest may be more difficult to hold on to. Your deeper feelings seem to come to the surface, and if you've been postponing addressing issues, they can reach a crisis point during June and December, when the solar eclipses occur.

If you were born from May 20 to 28, you can breathe a bit easier this year. Saturn has moved along and, after a year of trial and testing, has left the conjunction to your Sun. Your confidence and enthusiasm gain momentum this year, particularly during the spring months, when you may feel that there are few barriers between you and the realization of your dreams. However, the Moon's North Node is transiting in a conjunction aspect to your Sun, marking a year when it's very important to explore your underlying motivations and deeper feelings. Since some of the external pressures in your life may be lifting, you can more easily afford to take the time to explore your inner self. Weaving a positive connection between your childhood and your current dreams and aspirations can give you a sense of continuity during this spiritually significant cycle.

If you were born from May 29 to June 3, you're experiencing a bit of magic in your life while Neptune transits in trine aspect to your Sun. Your imagination and artistic expression can be more easily developed now. You may also find that it seems more natural to reach out toward others in a more charitable manner, extending your time and resources to make a difference in the world. This cycle deepens your compassion, and you may find that it's also easier to forgive old hurts so you can move on. Plus, from January through April, Saturn will complete the cycle of a conjunction to your Sun (that cycle began in the summer of 2001). During these months, your commitment to values and experiences which help to anchor your hopes can give you just the right foundation for launching your dreams. Then, for the remainder of the year, your ability to trust the processes of life make it easier to "go with the flow." In December, the solar eclipse has special significance for you, since it opposes your Sun. This can be a critical time in a relationship, when you can reach a clear realization of the effects a special relationship has in your life. It's likely that the crisis will be a time of outreach and celebration, when you can finally let go of your fears and move into a deep commitment.

If you were born from June 4 to 10, your life is undergoing a powerful transformation this year while Pluto travels in opposition to your Sun. This is a cycle of regeneration and rebirth, when the things you no longer need drop away. Think of this time as a period of transformation, much like the metamorphosis experienced when a caterpillar is cocooned and changing into a butterfly. It's a vulnerable period, because your new self is not yet fully formed, but you can feel the power emerging. At the same time, you are experiencing endings, since you know you must bid good-bye to situations, people, and attitudes which no longer fit into your life. In addition, during the months from April through June, Saturn travels in conjunction to your Sun, adding intensity to the processes of completion. During these months, you may feel that your choices are limited, but perseverance and a positive attitude can see you through. Nobody has ever said that transformation is easy, but when you are given the opportunity to surrender to your highest needs, you finally express the essence of your true self. The most difficult elements of this cycle can involve your own resistance to change. In fact, you may discover a hidden stubborn quality that surprises you. But you should also expect that others may not be as cooperative as you'd like, and power issues can surface which expose the true nature of the situations you're in. Keep in mind that this is a cycle of healing, and that you are finally uncovering the jewels of your spirit. Little by little, the light glimmers, until ultimately your magnetism shines brightly.

If you were born from June 11 to 21, you're experiencing the sobering cycle of Saturn as it travels in conjunction to your Sun. Saturn's influence slows things down, and while you may have been Mr. or Ms. Speedy, now you're settling into a more careful pace. Think of this as a year of mellowing, while you grapple with the processes of becoming more patient. Since you tend to be filled with exceptional ideas and strong ideals, you're not always particularly patient. After all, once you've gotten something clearly in your mind, you're ready to go for it! This cycle lets you know exactly how much effort will be required, and over and over again you may feel that you're being tested. You are. Where you've previously been distracted, your responsibilities can require that you pay more attention. This is an excellent year to devote your time and energy to studying and building skills and understanding. Extra care with your health can also bring positive rewards, since establishing a regimen now that supports your needs can put you on a solid course. It is not the time to ignore physical problems, since they could become even more bothersome if you do. The same is true with emotional issues, because now is the time to address and explore what you do and do not need.

If you were born from June 14 to 20, this is your year to let your individuality shine through while Uranus transits in trine aspect to your Sun. This cycle adds a bit of fun and experimentation to your life experience. The freedom urge you feel can encourage you to express your talents with greater ease. Plus, since you're also experiencing the stability of Saturn's connection to your Sun, you may want to take some risks, but only if they seem worthwhile. Travel and cultural experiences can add a measure of depth and wisdom to your life. However, getting out of your old ruts can also bring you face-to-face with different relationship options. Whether you're finally willing to surrender to a new love that lets your spirit fly, or opening new doors in an existing relationship—you are not likely to settle into any defined patterns right away. This is your time to test possibilities in all areas of your life, including relationships. If you were a computer, you'd be getting an extensive upgrade!

Tools for Change

Even if you're comfortable taking a more conservative approach to life this year, Saturn's influence can have a dampening effect on your spirit. To lift some of the weightiness, be particularly attentive to the times when your thinking becomes too negative. Worry can be a drain on your vitality, and may simply represent the power of your fears. By becoming more mindful of the emotions that are blocking you, you can more easily let go and move onward. Affirmations can be an extremely beneficial tool this year, since now, more than ever, your mind is the key to your contentment.

While you're filling your mind with uplifting ideas, you might also decide that you need to affirm, develop, and trust your intuition. Seek out books, classes, or videos which help you understand the relationship between science and spirituality. A study of ancient techniques might be especially interesting. This is an excellent time to access the most mystical qualities of your life. You'll also benefit from the creation of a space in your home that's meant for contemplation or meditation. Whether you're building a zen garden, fashioning a comfortable corner of your bedroom, or creating another space—the feeling of a place that's meant to take you away from the everyday pressures will be reassuring.

Physically, concentrate on developing your flexibility while you build endurance. From simple stretches to hatha yoga or innovative techniques like Pilates—it's important to extend your outreach. Your nervous system may also need some extra nutritional support, and supplements of B-vitamins, omega-3 fatty acids, or mind strengtheners like ginkgo biloba can be beneficial. Polarity therapy can also be helpful to your overall sense of well-being.

Ⅱ

Affirmation for the Year

I make the best use of my energy and resources.

Gemini/January

In the Spotlight

Your drive to accomplish your ambition can definitely lead to success, but you may not be satisfied with the outcome if others are alienated in the process. Before you decide to buck the system, explore the rules. They may be more sensible than you first realized.

Wellness and Keeping Fit

Tension can drain your vitality through January 18, but staying on top of your fitness routine helps diffuse stress. To give your energy a boost, enroll in an innovative fitness class after January 20.

Love and Life Connections

A breach of trust can result from unrealistic expectations, although you can avoid this pitfall by clarifying your mutual hopes. The New Moon on January 13 stimulates intimacy issues, when you may run into inhibitions leftover from long-ago hurts. Family tensions can interfere with your personal time through January 20, but after that, a getaway can revitalize your love life. Be ready to open your heart during the Full Moon on January 28.

Finance and Success

A competitive situation in your career can be frustrating, but after January 18 you're past most of the battle zones and ready to enjoy the rewards for your hard work. Mercury will turn retrograde on January 18, when a review of existing contracts can help you define a future plan of action. Deal with details of financial arrangements from January 1 to 16, and then concentrate on gathering interested supporters who'll be part of promoting your new project.

Cosmic Insider Tip

Give in to your creative impulses during the Full Moon on January 28. It's time to open to inspiration and see where it leads.

Rewarding Days 5, 6, 14, 15, 19, 20, 24, 25, 28, 29

Challenging Days 3, 4, 9, 10, 16, 17, 18, 30, 31

Affirmation for the Month My intuitive impulses offer meaningful direction.

Gemini/February

In the Spotlight

Raring to go, you're eager to bring others into the action—where you can make a powerful difference within your community or even on a larger scene. Your ideas spark enthusiasm from others, and can even inspire new goals of your own.

Wellness and Keeping Fit

If you're into winter sports, then get your equipment ready and head out! Otherwise, some intense action at the gym is in order, since this is the time to build strength and increase your endurance. Watch sweet cravings after February 13; they can be your downfall.

Love and Life Connections

Your search for a love that keeps your heart singing and also nourishes your spirit may be over, since the New Moon on February 12 marks a time when you're awakening to fresh possibilities. An existing relationship can take a miraculous turn. If you're single, you may find a sweet smile during your travels or right there next to you at the library. Shared ideas and similar philosophies will bring you closer together.

Finance and Success

Use Mercury's retrograde cycle through February 8 as a time to reconnect with business associates or to follow through on current projects. Publishing, travel, and education fare nicely, although promotional efforts work best through February 13. The build-up of momentum after February 8 leads to a test of your plans during the Full Moon on February 27.

Cosmic Insider Tip

Business deals that have stalled gradually regain momentum after Saturn and Mercury turn direct on February 8. Progress starts like a locomotive, but will ultimately be more like a rocket.

Rewarding Days 1, 2, 10, 11, 15, 16, 20, 21, 25, 28

Challenging Days 5, 6, 7, 13, 14, 26, 27

Affirmation for the Month Truth is my strongest ally.

Gemini/March

In the Spotlight

While you're raking in awards and enjoying some acclaim, you may be craning your neck to try to peer around the next corner. Pulling back from the action can give you a better view of that future!

Wellness and Keeping Fit

While Mars treks through the sector of your chart that functions like your storage closet, you'll feel an impulse to clear out clutter from your past. This is a time for rejuvenation. Schedule time at the spa or with your massage therapist.

Love and Life Connections

Deal with family matters early in the month. Then, make time to celebrate with your friends, since you're ready to enjoy the easy flow of unconditional love. A special lunch or dinner can restore your connection, but a Full Moon party on March 28 might be a great way to enjoy those who share your ideals. Romance is favored most after March 21, since prior to that it's easy to get stuck in strange conversations that lead your affections astray.

Finance and Success

Time spent in association with your professional colleagues is truly worthwhile after March 8. The hierarchy at work can take a different direction after March 14, and knowing your allies can help you stay on a productive track. Watch for potential power struggles to emerge from March 16 to 25, when contracts and legal matters can hamstring progress. Your talent for negotiation comes in handy, but you have to know when to step out of the line of fire!

Cosmic Insider Tip

This is one of those times when you have to wait for everyone else to catch up with your far-reaching ideas. Try to bring your plans down to earth before the Full Moon on March 28.

Rewarding Days 1, 9, 10, 14, 15, 19, 20, 21, 24, 28, 29

Challenging Days 5, 6, 12, 13, 26, 27

Affirmation for the Month My goals reflect my true values.

Gemini/April

In the Spotlight

A slower pace gives you a chance to see which way the wind is blowing before you head out toward new horizons. This is a time to take careful steps and build structures that provide a reliable support. Rash actions can exhaust your energy and your resources.

Wellness and Keeping Fit

Failure to pay attention can result in accidents from April 1 to 15. When Mars enters Gemini on April 13 you'll be more energetic, and a reasonable pace will work to your advantage.

Love and Life Connections

An infatuation can have ridiculous consequences, and might be much more fun in your fantasies than it is in reality. Part of the problem in your close relationship can be getting your signals straight, although a friend can help you sort through your differences during the New Moon on April 12. Love fares better after Venus enters your sign on April 25, although you might prefer to take things slowly just to savor the experience.

Finance and Success

Introducing innovations into an unwelcome circumstance can be a real headache from April 1 to 14. You might even run into undermining from those who are threatened by change. To be more effective, invite questions and comments from others. Imaginative ideas move things forward, and everyone wants to share in the experience—as long as it's not too strange.

Cosmic Insider Tip

The Full Moon on April 27 can stimulate a desire to withdraw from the public eye for a while. With Venus and Mars dancing in your sign, you might want to make that a romantic experience!

Rewarding Days 6, 7, 11, 16, 17, 21, 24, 25

Challenging Days 1, 2, 8, 9, 10, 22, 23, 27

Affirmation for the Month I am healthy, happy, and strong!

Gemini/May

In the Spotlight

This is your time to shine. Showcase your top-drawer ideas, and take steps to assure your professional reputation. In the process, you may break ties with others who've been your anchor.

Wellness and Keeping Fit

To feel your best, concentrate on breath work. That's right: breathing. Of course, exercise increases your respiration, but boosting your breathing capacity can have amazing effects.

Love and Life Connections

It's not every day that Venus and Mars travel together in your sign, and that makes this a very special month for love to light up your life. Recently initiated situations move quickly, but even a long-standing relationship can reach new heights near the New Moon on May 12. Partnership issues are highlighted during the lunar eclipse on May 26, when renewing your commitment goes a long way toward healing old wounds.

Finance and Success

Even though you might not remember brewing up a magic potion, the positive turns your life takes can make it appear that you certainly have! With a serious focus on bringing your ideas to life, you can establish yourself as a viable resource, and others are likely to seek your input or guidance. However, contractual agreements will be more successful if you complete them before Mercury turns retrograde on May 15.

Cosmic Insider Tip

Some Mercury retrograde cycles work to your advantage. This is one of them. With Mercury in your sign for two months, you have more time to keep your ideas afloat.

Rewarding Days 3, 4, 8, 9, 13, 14, 18, 22, 23, 30, 31

Challenging Days 5, 6, 7, 20, 21, 26, 27

Affirmation for the Month I choose my words carefully to be certain that I say what I mean!

Gemini/June

In the Spotlight

It's a time for celebration, and sharing your joy with others inspires you to create new goals. However, in your exuberance you can go overboard with spending.

Wellness and Keeping Fit

Extend your fitness routine to make sure you have sufficient endurance. If you participate in marathons, this is an excellent time to do well. However, during the eclipse on June 10 you can run out of steam unless you're well trained and prepared.

Love and Life Connections

Mend fences in your relationships by extending an olive branch during the Gemini solar eclipse on June 10. Carrying a grudge can be entirely too weighty, and even if the other person does not want to let go of past hurts, you're ready to move on. Honor your obligations, though, since this is no time to skip out on your responsibilities. Instead, consider this a fresh start—when you're armed with knowledge and experience to assure a more successful venture of the heart.

Finance and Success

Reconsider a proposition or work toward solutions during Mercury's retrograde through June 8, but don't expect to get a new project going until June 10. Finances may improve dramatically after June 14, although travel or promotional activities can cost more than you anticipated. Be particularly careful with the fine points of a legal agreement from June 20 to 26. Extra caution saves money!

Cosmic Insider Tip

The Moon's eclipse on June 24 can carry an unseen threat to your stability, particularly if you're failing to safeguard your assets.

Rewarding Days 4, 5, 9, 10, 14, 18, 19, 27, 28

Challenging Days 2, 3, 16, 17, 22, 23, 24, 29, 30

Affirmation for the Month I am a caring guardian of all that is precious in my life.

Gemini/July

In the Spotlight

Grand plans can exact a dear price, but you may be willing (and able) to cough up the cash if it's important. Transportation has a strong impact, and that means you might be going somewhere or deciding to upgrade the way you get there.

Wellness and Keeping Fit

Emotional stress or worry can leave you feeling tired from July 1 to 10, but after that your vitality is on the increase. Even if you're still dealing with a stressful situation, your ability to cope improves. A daily walk or time in fitness class can help you turn the tide.

Love and Life Connections

A getaway with your honey adds spice to your love life from July 1 to 10, particularly if your day-to-day hassles don't go along on the trip. Extra attention to home life and family matters absorbs much of your creative time after July 11, although there is the potential for disagreements about preferences or priorities to spoil a celebration. It's during the Full Moon on July 24 that you have a chance to demonstrate the value of taking the high ground.

Finance and Success

Market your pet project from July 1 to 9, or at least send up a test balloon to determine whether or not it will fly. The resources and support you need to make things happen will gain a foothold after July 21, but you also can quietly build your connections until then. A partner may decide to take a different approach to handling things, and that can strain your budget.

Cosmic Insider Tip

Call on your experience to help you figure out a problematic situation, but try to avoid risky situations. The cosmos shows that you do not have much of a cushion if there's a hard landing.

Rewarding Days 2, 6, 7, 8, 11, 12, 15, 16, 24, 25, 29

Challenging Days 13, 14, 19, 20, 21, 26, 27, 28

Affirmation for the Month I honor traditions of the past.

Gemini/August

In the Spotlight
You've heard it said that the real gold mine is in your own backyard. Well, grab your tools, because the treasure you seek may be right in front of you. Putting your energy and enthusiasm behind your inspired ideas attracts support from others, too. Enjoy yourself!

Wellness and Keeping Fit
A consistent approach to fitness gives you more energy to relish the rewards your life brings during the New Moon on August 8. It's no time to be self-indulgent, although time out for a weekend's play or an adventurous vacation can give you another burst of vitality.

Love and Life Connections
Conversation with a sibling leads to new insights into your relationship, and may be the best way to handle family obligations. But after August 6, romance is a top priority, and you may be intrigued by a powerful and unexpected attraction during the New Moon on August 8. While this can lead to a passionate encounter, it's also an excellent time to break prohibitive inhibitions.

Finance and Success
Your success inspires others to follow your lead, and the more you advance, the more your opportunities increase. Call it a windfall— but your success will be measured by the way you handle the situation. It's quite possible that your fifteen minutes of fame will last longer, and during the time the spotlight shines, you also have a chance to give a friend a boost. It just doesn't get better than that!

Cosmic Insider Tip
The unexpected can turn the tide. Although you might be in the right place during the New Moon, it's the way you deal with the next wave on the Full Moon (August 22) that seals your fate.

Rewarding Days 3, 4, 7, 8, 11, 12, 20, 21, 22, 25, 26, 30, 31

Challenging Days 9, 10, 16, 17, 23, 24

Affirmation for the Month I spread the message of abundance.

Gemini/September

In the Spotlight

Put your talents to work for you and reap the rewards! But watch for turmoil on the home front, since your aims or aspirations can take your focus away from the demands others expect of you.

Wellness and Keeping Fit

Look for fun-filled options to stay on top of the fitness game. Repetitive routines can squash your enthusiasm, but a challenge that's more like play can help you overcome an old limitation.

Love and Life Connections

Pure excitement pours from your heart from September 1 to 7 and can open the way for greater contentment. The experiences you've hoped to share alter the depth of intimacy and trust with your lover. An old relationship can be reborn, but you have to decide if you want to pursue it further. If your needs are different, you may decide that it's not worthwhile to take that road. Watch for jealousy near September 21, since your imagination may be working overtime.

Finance and Success

Investments grow early in the month, but take a different turn when Mercury turns retrograde on September 14. To secure your assets, make alterations just after the New Moon on September 7, but avoid drastic measures. Contracts and legal matters can grow complex after September 15, and even though you're making headway during the Full Moon on September 21, you may not be out of the woods. Back away if you're in over your head.

Cosmic Insider Tip

Reconsider the roles you've taken on during Mercury's retrograde after September 14. You may be wearing too many hats, and that can give you a king-sized headache!

Rewarding Days 1, 2, 4, 5, 8, 9, 17, 18, 22, 26, 27, 28

Challenging Days 6, 7, 14, 15, 19, 20

Affirmation for the Month My words and actions follow careful consideration of potential outcome.

Gemini/October

In the Spotlight
Consider whether or not you're happy with your work situation. Alterations made now can help lighten your load, but may also result in closing out one circumstance so you can pursue another.

Wellness and Keeping Fit
Tension mounts, and unless you are making a conscious effort to address stress, your health can suffer. An old problem resurfaces, but a more holistic approach can change the way you handle it. Work with a personal trainer can be especially helpful.

Love and Life Connections
Arguments at home can raise buried resentment from October 1 to 15. However, your desire to create harmony and peace during the New Moon on October 6 can diffuse much of the tension. You may have simply fallen into a stale routine, and now that your needs are changing, it's time to alter the way you respond to love. Open your heart to the flow of love, and then by the Full Moon on October 21 you'll feel a surge of energy as love returns to you.

Finance and Success
Reconsider your investment strategy while Mercury retrogrades through October 6, but wait until October 15 to make alterations. Unexpected developments can change your timetable. Others are most receptive and supportive of your plans after October 17, although there's potential deception in the ranks after October 24. To safeguard your position, explore those rumblings and address the concerns of your coworkers or employees.

Cosmic Insider Tip
Venus retrogrades starting October 10, and for the next six weeks you may doubt your relationships. It's really a question of how comfortable you are when asking that your own needs be considered.

Rewarding Days 1, 2, 5, 6, 14, 15, 19, 24, 25, 29

Challenging Days 3, 4, 12, 16, 17, 18, 31

Affirmation for the Month I deserve to have the love I need.

Gemini/November

In the Spotlight
High levels of creative energy lift your spirits, but you might also make more work for yourself in the process. To enjoy the experience more, invite others whose talents complement your own.

Wellness and Keeping Fit
Recreational activities keep your enthusiasm alive. Laughter becomes your best medicine, since dealing with a pesky problem can get on your nerves if you let it. Healing touch can have a powerful effect on your vitality; schedule a massage for the lunar eclipse on November 19.

Love and Life Connections
Your assertiveness might be welcome, but you can run into problems if you and your partner are not on the same wavelength. Steer clear of issues that simply create friction, but make an effort to explore mistrust—especially mistrust of your own feelings. Failure to deal with your true feelings can lead to physical distress. A retreat or time for reflection can help you come to grips with what you need and want.

Finance and Success
Dust off that pile of unfinished business during the New Moon on November 4, and reprioritize. Maybe it's time to delegate a few tasks to others so that you can concentrate on projects that make better use of your talents and resources. If you continue to focus on activities that are not in your best interest, they can quickly drain your assets around the time of the Moon's eclipse on November 19.

Cosmic Insider Tip
Blending reliable traditions with innovative technology or fresh ideas stimulates growth and profit from November 16 to 27.

Rewarding Days 2, 3, 10, 11, 15, 16, 20, 21, 25, 29, 30

Challenging Days 1, 6, 7, 12, 13, 14, 27, 28

Affirmation for the Month I happily let go of the things I no longer need.

Gemini/December

In the Spotlight

The Sun's eclipse draws your attention to partnership, marriage, and contractual agreements. You're looking for improvements, but may not be willing to do all the work yourself. The question is whether you're working overtime to take up the slack.

Wellness and Keeping Fit

Irritation with the slow pace of change leads to unnecessary tension, and can interfere with your sleep and rest. Relaxing herbal teas, like skullcap and kava kava, can help—but you may need to vent your hostility. It's time to give your counselor a call.

Love and Life Connections

Communication with your partner may be improving, but you can also feel like you are on "information overload." Before you try to take on the burden of repairing your relationship all by yourself, step back to assess your motivations during the solar eclipse on December 4. Reflection may show you that your needs have changed, but that your partnership has not. Talk about your concerns during the Gemini Full Moon on December 19.

Finance and Success

Improvements at work enhance productivity, although there can be a breakdown in the system after December 5 if someone is not pulling his or her weight. The potential for deception exists, and if you're distracted by irrelevant circumstances, your assets can dissolve in a mist of confusion. Stabilize the situation before December 15 by joining forces with those who can see the situation clearly.

Cosmic Insider Tip

Venus and Mars are mystified by Neptune's foggy energy through December 14. Make the distinction between spirituality and illusion if you want to avoid a major loss.

Rewarding Days 8, 9, 12, 13, 17, 18, 19, 22, 26, 27

Challenging Days 3, 4, 5, 10, 11, 24, 25, 31

Affirmation for the Month I am willing to abandon false ideals.

GEMINI ACTION TABLE

These dates reflect the best—but not the only—times for success and ease in these activities, according to your Sun sign.

	JAN	FEB	MAR	APR	MAY	JUN	JUL	AUG	SEPT	OCT	NOV	DEC
Move								6-25				
Start a class		11, 12					22-31	1-5, 8				
Join a club				11, 12								
Ask for a raise						10, 11						
Look for work			12	1-28						31	1-18	
Get pro advice	9, 10	5-7	5, 6	1, 2, 28-30	26, 27	22, 23	19-21	16, 17	12, 13	9, 10	6, 7	3, 4, 31
Get a loan	11, 12	8, 9	7, 8	3-5	1, 2, 28, 29	24-26	22, 23	18, 19	14, 15	1, 12, 13	8, 9	5, 6
See a doctor				13-29							1-18	
Start a diet	7, 8	3, 4	2-4, 30, 31	26, 27	24, 25	20, 21	17, 18	14, 15	10, 11	7, 8	4, 5	1, 2, 28, 29
End relationship					26, 27							
Buy clothes								27-31	1-13	11-31		
Get a makeover				25-30	1-19	10, 11						
New romance				6, 7				7-31	1-7	6, 7		
Vacation	14, 15	10-12	9, 10	6, 7	3, 4, 30, 31	27, 28	24, 25	20-22	16, 17	14, 15	10, 11	7-9

CANCER

The Crab
June 21 to July 22

Element:	Water
Quality:	Cardinal
Polarity:	Yin/Feminine
Planetary Ruler:	The Moon
Meditation:	I am in touch with my inner feelings.
Gemstone:	Pearl
Power Stones:	Moonstone, chrysocolla
Key Phrase:	I feel
Glyph:	Crab's claws
Anatomy:	Stomach, breasts
Color:	Silver, pearl white
Animal:	Crustaceans, cows, chickens
Myths/Legends:	Hercules and the Crab, Asherah, Hecate
House:	Fourth
Opposite Sign:	Capricorn
Flower:	Larkspur
Key Word:	Receptivity

Positive Expression:	**Misuse of Energy:**
Nurturing	Smothering
Resourceful	Defensive
Intuitive	Insular
Sensitive	Evasive
Responsive	Distrustful
Discreet	Manipulative

Cancer

Your Ego's Strengths and Shortcomings

You're the one others turn to when they need support and care, since you have a talent for sensing how others feel and what they need. With an easy connection to the natural ebb and flow of the cycles of life, you have a knack for handling change and cultivating growth. It's as though you have a partnership with Mother Nature—an expression of your role as "The Nurturer" of the zodiac. Your innate sensibilities serve you well whether you're fostering the progress of your family and friends or a company.

Your drive to establish a nest can be quite powerful, and includes a special need for the security of home and a desire to create your own family. Male or female, you're the one who seems to easily provide nourishment to your friends and family—an outreach of your affinity with the comforting energy of the Moon, your astrological ruler. Part of being a Moon Child can be seen through your enjoyment of gardening, crafts, cooking, or other domestic delights. Your collection of artifacts from the past and love of heritage is a reflection of this quality. The other side of this expression is your powerful intuitive sensibility. Your emotions can also be especially sensitive, and once you take someone into your heart, it's tough for you to let go. Knowing when to pull back and allow your fledglings to fly from the nest can be hard. However, your loved ones will appreciate your tenderness more if you check your tendency to become too smothering with your concern.

Since you are emotionally perceptive, you can feel especially vulnerable. To protect yourself, you may go too far and create a barrier that keeps others away instead of inviting them to get closer. Fortunately, your intuition signals you when it's time to open your arms or to quietly back away to give someone space. Above all, invite your intuition to whisper when it's the right time for change. "For everything there is a season."

Shining Your Love Light

A significant part of your personal fulfillment includes your desire for a lasting love that will nourish your soul and extend to building a family. You need a relationship that brings comfort and gives you a chance to let your passions transform you. The challenge is to know when it's safe to open your heart, since once you're hurt you can create nearly impenetrable barriers. That is, your on-the-mark intuition helps you understand when the time is right to share the secrets of your heart.

The water signs—Scorpio, Pisces, and other Cancers—share your affinity for emotional depth and will understand you when words simply will not suffice. It's the intense attraction to your zodiac opposite, Capricorn, that can be most irresistible. If it's the right Capricorn, the two of you can establish a foundation for a strong family and a balanced relationship.

Aries is attractive, but you can feel irritated with her or his seeming selfishness or immaturity. Earthy Taurus whets your appetites for love while providing solid friendship. Gemini encourages you to open your mind and enjoy sharing your dreams, but your emotional intensity can push him or her away. With another Cancer you may be able to create an enduring partnership, but you can drown in emotions if you're both upset. Leo adores your careful attention, but you may wonder if you'll ever have your turn!

You can be cozy with Virgo and can build a powerful understanding and acceptance of one another. Your attraction to Libra can be exciting, but you may wonder if you're up to his or her exacting standards. Mutual sensuality and passion fuel a breathless relationship with Scorpio, and you could be eternal lovers. Aquarius may be your confidant, although you might always feel that you cannot let down your barriers completely. Pisces may seem to be your soulmate, since you can share your dreams and easily open your hearts to a future filled with hope.

Making Your Place in the World

A career that gives you plenty of room to grow will be most secure. Since you have an ability to hold onto assets and possessions, you can become quite influential and wealthy through your work. Politics, investments, and real estate can be rewarding. You might also be drawn to the food industry, or the hotel or antiques business.

Teaching, counseling, social work, midwifery, or medicine can be fields that fulfill your needs to promote growth. Or, your love of the past can be exercised through archaeology, history, and anthropology. Ranching, farming, gardening, and floral or landscape design can also be rewarding.

Power Plays

For you, power equals preservation. Sustaining valuable traditions from the past is part of your personal power. But to feel strong, you need a secure base. Certainly family and home are part of this picture, but when you can confidently protect those you love, you feel significant. You need to be needed! Through your link with your family, you experience the importance of connecting what has gone before with what is yet to come. You're able to identify situations and people that can strengthen such bonds.

By discovering the best way to modify traditions within the framework of current trends, you'll feel more hopeful about the future—for yourself, and for those who will follow in your footsteps. Through learning how to build a positive shelter from the storms of life you develop your ultimate strength and provide encouragement to others who look to you for guidance and support. The most empowering quality of all, however, is the shimmering thread that binds you to the source, reminding you that everyone and everything comes and goes through the currents of time and ever-changing seasons of life.

Famous Cancerians

Roone Arledge, George W. Bush, David Dinkins, David Alan Grier, Sean P. Hayes, King Henry VIII, Derek Jeter, Sydney Pollack, Fred Savage, Patricia Schroeder, Carly Simon, Ringo Starr, George Steinbrenner, Patrick Stewart, Dave Thomas, Jesse Ventura

The Year Ahead for Cancer

A s your confidence grows stronger, you experience true hope for the future. It's your turn to reap rewards for your persistent efforts, although you may still feel that you have a way to go before you're absolutely comfortable. For you, the reminder that you're on the right path adds tremendous reassurance.

There are reasons to celebrate, since Jupiter travels in your sign through the end of July. This cycle began last summer, and many of the opportunities that started then will ripen during the first half of 2002. This can be an exceptional period of personal growth, and certainly marks a time when your influence will extend further than you realize. The only downfall of this particular cycle is the tendency to take for granted the good things that are happening. Certainly it's important to enjoy the rewards you're experiencing, but knowing when you've reached your limits might be difficult to ascertain. Target healthy forms of expansion to avoid the less-desirable possibilities—like expanding your waistline! From August through December, Jupiter's influence moves into the financial sector of your chart. This is a time to make the most of your resources without overextending them.

Saturn continues its trek through the closets of your imagination and dreams, testing the validity of your hidden hopes. Sorting through your illusions can be pretty interesting, since you uncover the things from your past that make up the fabric of your soul. However, you're also bidding farewell to a lot of those past situations, especially the ones you no longer need. It can be uncomfortable to say good-bye, but there's also a freedom that emerges when you grow beyond your old limitations.

The slowest-moving planets—Uranus, Neptune, and Pluto—have very long-lasting influences. The changes indicated by these cycles take a while to manifest, although your awareness of the changes will be strongest when these planets are making an exact connection to your Sun or other planets in your chart. Uranus brings in the most intimate aspects of your life: a close sexual relationship, the things to which you have the strongest attachments, and your thoughts and feelings about death and healing. Neptune is also traveling through the same sector of your chart, and both of these influences together can enhance your intuitive and psychic sensibilities. Pluto's influence this year points to the ways you care for your physical needs. If you've been ignoring your health, this cycle can certainly bring your physical weaknesses to the surface!

The solar and lunar eclipses for 2002 emphasize your need to understand the nature of your past and how it influences your life today. Also, there's a stimulus to make adjustments that simplify and enhance your daily routine. Your dreams can be especially significant this year, and if you do find that you remember them, keeping a dream journal could be a fascinating and insightful exercise. Even if you do not recall the images in your dreams, your feelings about them can be illuminating.

If you were born from June 21 to 28, you're experiencing a year of self-discovery while Chiron travels in opposition to your Sun. This cycle can manifest in unusual ways, although your primary trouble spot may very well be your relationship and approach to dealing with the needs of others. If you've been going overboard taking care of your partner's or another's needs while ignoring your own, you may have to give up that caretaking role and focus on yourself for a change. Even if you're single, relationship issues can be trying, since either way, you're sorting through a pile of buried emotions about being a partner. As you open your heart to your real needs, it will be easier to make use of the heightened awareness you're experiencing from another cycle. Neptune is transiting in biquintile aspect to your Sun. This can bring a subtle, but positive, enhancement of your intuitive abilities. It's an excellent time to explore the meanings of symbols and to look beyond the surface for the deeper messages your inner self offers. Then, there's a special reward: during September and November, the universe opens the way for a deeper expression and understanding of love, since Venus will be transiting in a helpful trine aspect to your Sun during both months. Let your heart be your guide!

If you were born from June 28 to July 4, you may feel uneasy while Neptune transits in quincunx aspect to your Sun. While this can be a time of spiritual initiation when you're more powerfully aware of the subtle forces at work in your life, you can be thrown off balance by your new insights. Some of your defenses seem to drop away during this cycle, and the added vulnerability you feel can lead to unnecessary worry. As you carefully navigate your way through an unfamiliar course, your confidence builds, and you can make use of the sure-footed steps offered from January through April while Saturn transits in semisextile to your Sun. Setting priorities will help immensely, adding structure that will allow you to explore the mysteries that are opening before you. A careful course is best now, and if you're concerned about health issues, it's necessary to explore them instead of pretending they don't exist. Denial can get you into trouble! That's especially true since Uranus is transiting in sesqui-quadrate to your Sun—a period when an inaccurate assessment of a situation can be costly. In your personal relationships, you may discover hidden issues about intimacy that you've carefully tucked away. If you're truly interested in becoming whole and powerful, perhaps you should consider opening to the truth of your needs, fears, and hopes. You might actually like the end results, and it can do wonders for your soul.

If you were born from July 5 to 12, you're eliminating situations that can undermine your quality of life. Pluto is transiting in quincunx to your Sun, a cycle that lasts throughout 2002, but with an influence that can have long-range effects. This cycle can be like peeling an onion—just as you get through one layer, you find you've exposed another one! Health issues may be a primary concern, especially if you're dealing with a chronic condition or an old problem. Fortunately, the adjustments and treatments you apply now can be highly effective, since this is a time of healing and rejuvenation. Beyond physical concerns, the impact of the changes you make now can also have a powerful effect on your approach to life. You can pry your way out of stale routines or circumstances in which you feel stuck. Take a serious look at your job, since if it does not fit, this is an excellent time to make necessary alterations or to find a different line of work. You may not be able to walk away from circumstances that are your responsibility, though, since Saturn is also semisextile your Sun during the spring—from April through June. During these months, your careful concern with your obligations can help you complete the things that are holding you back. After that, you'll find it less complicated to make alterations.

If you were born from July 13 to 22, you're feeling the unsettling influence of Uranus traveling in quincunx aspect to your Sun. The ultimate effect of this cycle is an expression of your uniqueness and individuality, but there's some resistance to the process. Identify the source of the resistance first. If the source is you, then start by exploring your attitudes toward yourself, your needs, and your talents. However, if you discover that the resistance arises from your connection in a relationship, then it's time to make alterations in the relationship that will make allowances for the special needs of everyone concerned. It's also important to explore your attitudes toward finances, especially your long-range plans that stem from partnership, inheritance, or other similar issues. Most of the difficulties which arise from this cycle are due to unanticipated changes. (Consider it a test of your personal adaptability!) Fortunately for you, from July through December, Saturn transits in semisextile to your Sun, adding some stability to the changes that seem to come out of the blue. These two influences together mark a time to take well-considered steps in response to situations beyond your control. This can be a breakthrough year. As always, what you make of it is up to you!

Tools for Change

With so many cycles stimulating your questions about your priorities, this can be an excellent year to explore your psyche and soul. Whether you choose to work with a trusted therapist, astrologer, healing arts specialist, or all of the above, this is an excellent year to turn over a few rocks to see what's hidden beneath the surface. Extra attention to your health can make a huge difference, too—especially if you're feeling the effects of stress. Some cycles also create an effect of feeling scattered, which can interfere with your ability to focus or to be as effective as you like.

One key to re-integrating yourself is dream work. You can start by keeping a dream diary—writing notes to yourself about what you've experienced, felt, or seen during your dream time. You might want to explore the meaning of dream symbols, or take a class on lucid dreaming. Symbolic language can also be especially significant now, and work with oracles that use symbols—like runes, tarot, or I Ching—can be highly illuminating. The rich symbology of astrology might be of interest, so consider taking a class or reading some of the excellent material currently in print.

Go even deeper with your explorations by uncovering your past. Genealogy research might uncover fascinating information. To understand the history of your soul, consider work with regression hypnosis. Sometimes, combining these two explorations can be especially fascinating.

During your meditations, concentrate on opening your consciousness. Start by following your breathing, and with each breath let go of the pressures you feel. Once you're relaxed, continue to go deeper into the labyrinth of your psyche. Take time to fully explore the corridors of your mind until your mind disappears and you are simply one with the source. This sense of unity is what you seek now, and by carrying it with you into your daily life your self-confidence and awareness will continue to expand.

Affirmation for the Year

I am whole and strong.
My life is filled with true abundance in all things!

Cancer/January

In the Spotlight
Your energy and enthusiasm go a long way toward overcoming any obstacles in your path. Outstanding progress on the career front results from promotional efforts, cultural exchange, publishing, or academic pursuits.

Wellness and Keeping Fit
Step up your fitness program from January 1 to 18, when sports or training yield excellent results. After January 20 it's easy to misjudge situations or run into trouble if you've gone past your limits.

Love and Life Connections
High levels of attraction and pleasure enhance your love life, and even if you're in a partnership that needs some work, you can still enjoy yourself. Time away from your daily routine or a splendid vacation can inspire romance from January 1 to 17. Even a day or two can turn the tide if your intentions are pure. Contentious family issues create choppy emotional waters after January 19.

Finance and Success
Work out the details of an agreement or legal matter, and then take advantage of the growth-producing energy of the New Moon on January 13 to launch your plans. Progress continues up through January 17, and then you may need to sort through trouble spots during Mercury's retrograde from January 18 to 31. Evaluate budgets and tax matters with care after January 20, since an underestimation of liabilities can thwart progress later.

Cosmic Insider Tip
The Full Moon on January 28 clouds details involving mutual financial matters and partnerships. Tread carefully if you've ventured into unfamiliar territory.

Rewarding Days 3, 7, 8, 16, 17, 22, 26, 27, 30

Challenging Days 5, 6, 11, 12, 13, 19, 20

Affirmation for the Month I reach out to show my appreciation for others.

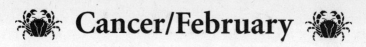 # Cancer/February

In the Spotlight
Underlying weaknesses in relationships only peek above the surface, but can still be difficult to repair. Competitive circumstances at work can take most of your time, and may be a source of the rift in your family.

Wellness and Keeping Fit
Emotionally charged circumstances can drain your vitality unless you're dealing with them. Staying active helps, but talking over your concerns with a counselor can alleviate some of your ills, too. A vacation eases tension and soothes your soul after February 19.

Love and Life Connections
An old relationship can emerge from the shadows from February 1 to 11. Even if you're not face-to-face with the person, the leftover issues can come to life. It's time to clear out your old attachments and feeling of guilt so you can move on. New love or a renewal of your close relationship results from exploring your shared ideals after February 12. By the time the Full Moon arrives on February 27 you may take the next steps toward true intimacy and trust.

Finance and Success
Problems with an agreement can be the central issue during the Mercury retrograde through February 8, and the bone of contention is control over finances. Plus, your drive to accomplish your aims is so strong that you might run roughshod over the wrong territory. After February 20, you can restore confidence and trust, although you may be looking for a way out of your current situation.

Cosmic Insider Tip
Prickly issues may be unavoidable, but it's difficult to ascertain how far to go. Consult a mentor or expert after February 12 if you need a helping hand.

Rewarding Days 3, 4, 13, 14, 18, 19, 22, 23, 27

Challenging Days 1, 2, 8, 9, 10, 15, 16, 17

Affirmation for the Month In all matters I seek the path of truth.

Cancer/March

In the Spotlight

You're building a firm platform from which to launch your most treasured hopes, and have the support of good friends and professional allies. Travel, academic, and political or public relations efforts go a long way toward advancing your career and reputation.

Wellness and Keeping Fit

To maintain your fitness routine, round up your best friend and head out to the gym, yoga class, or your daily walk. Besides that, sharing your goals with a buddy can be fun.

Love and Life Connections

Your most soulful yearnings are easier to express now, and disclosing your truest dreams to your sweetheart can reinforce intimacy during the New Moon on March 14. Love grows as you explore the recesses of your heart, and even if you're single your spiritual quest can fill you with joy. It's time to reach out and let your joy spill over into the lives of others.

Finance and Success

Business meetings and presentations are favored from March 1 to 8, but the momentum for progress really gets going from March 14 through the Full Moon on March 28. Forming a coalition with others who share your ideals works to the benefit of everyone after March 12, since prior to that time there are hidden factors that can undermine your progress. You may have to cut your ties to those who are not pulling their weight.

Cosmic Insider Tip

Jupiter's trek changes when it moves into direct motion on March 1, opening the way for stalled situations to get moving. You might also feel freshly inspired, so follow your hopes!

Rewarding Days 3, 4, 12, 13, 17, 22, 23, 26, 27

Challenging Days 1, 7, 8, 9, 14, 15, 16, 28, 29

Affirmation for the Month I confidently move toward the fulfillment of my dreams!

Cancer/April

In the Spotlight

With sweeter rewards for your efforts, you're flying high and sharing your success with your loyal supporters and friends. It's crucial to take careful steps after April 14, since you could alienate someone and not be aware of it at the time. Keep your radar on high alert!

Wellness and Keeping Fit

Tone your muscles and build endurance from April 1 to 15, then concentrate even more on enhancing your flexibility. You're entering a period of rest and rejuvenation after April 14, when scheduling time at the spa or a retreat can be just what the doctor ordered.

Love and Life Connections

A friendship can head toward unexplored territory, confusing the issue of personal boundaries from April 4 to 14. It's also possible that a partnership is changing, and you may have to determine whether or not you can trust the relationship. While your passions can be genuine, you may not be able to tell where they're actually taking you, so caution can be helpful. Despite this, love continues to grow, and it can blossom during the Full Moon on April 27.

Finance and Success

Community concerns or special interests provide an opportunity to exercise your leadership and form significant coalitions. A change of the guard puts everything on a fresh track from April 2 to 13, and a clear consensus can be difficult to establish immediately. Investment in your own talents or projects that have significance to you work much better than funding something you know little about.

Cosmic Insider Tip

The Scorpio Full Moon on April 27 emphasizes bounty and joy from your offspring. That can range from your children to your own creative efforts.

Rewarding Days 8, 9, 10, 13, 18, 19, 23, 26, 27

Challenging Days 3, 4, 5, 11, 12, 24, 25, 30

Affirmation for the Month I share my good fortune with others.

Cancer/May

In the Spotlight

Withdrawing from the action gives you a chance to regroup, and that can be pretty helpful if you're dealing with stalled negotiations or working out plans for a different strategy. Attacks within the ranks can be harmful—unless you're prepared for them.

Wellness and Keeping Fit

If you're in need of a tune-up—physically, mentally, or otherwise—this is the time to call in your reinforcements and revitalize. Extra rest helps, too, although stress can keep you in knots. Seek out relaxation helpers, like regular massage and herbal teas.

Love and Life Connections

Past mistakes can haunt your dreams, especially if you are burdened by guilt. It's time to purge unnecessarily gloomy emotions so that your current happiness is not polluted by negativity. If you're harboring secret fantasies or involved in a clandestine affair, explore your motivations. After much soul-searching, you'll be ready to enjoy the emergence of pure love when Venus enters Cancer on May 20. However, you may not bring your feelings into the open until after the lunar eclipse on May 26.

Finance and Success

Power struggles at work can frustrate your progress from May 1 to 11, but during the New Moon on May 12 you can identify allies who'll help you move your agenda forward. During Mercury's retrograde from May 15 through June 8 you'll have a chance to review problems and test different options.

Cosmic Insider Tip

Even before Mercury is retrograde on May 15 you'll see signs of failures in communication and equipment. Identify weaknesses where you can so that your efforts are not severely hindered.

Rewarding Days 6, 7, 15, 16, 21, 24, 25

Challenging Days 1, 2, 8, 9, 22, 23, 28, 29, 30

Affirmation for the Month I cherish my inner voice.

Cancer/June

In the Spotlight
Despite a few setbacks, this is an excellent time to take action that strengthens your professional reputation. But the real energy is happening in your personal life as love relationships blossom, adding sweetness to your life.

Wellness and Keeping Fit
Set a steady pace, since Mars travels in your sign all month, and you can be tempted to burn the candle at both ends. Increase muscle tone to keep your energy in top form, especially if you're preparing for competitive situations after June 23.

Love and Life Connections
No hinting around: if your heart is inspired with feelings of love, let love shine through! Mars and Venus travel in your sign, radiating passionate affection. You can attract amazing good fortune through love, and may have a second chance in a situation that's been in trouble. Romantic moments inspire a more profound commitment during the lunar eclipse on June 24, although this results from the dance of love that starts early in the month.

Finance and Success
Despite Mercury's continued retrograde through June 8, you're making professional strides. The key is to promise only what you can deliver, since if you go overboard, regrets follow right behind. Finances can improve dramatically during the solar eclipse on June 10, although a conservative approach to managing your good fortune will be more reassuring. Another opportunity emerges after June 24, when even your strongest competitors can be agreeable.

Cosmic Insider Tip
Celebrations are especially sweet this month, and can leave a lasting impression. It's wonderful when you're making good memories.

Rewarding Days 2, 3, 7, 8, 11, 12, 13, 16, 17, 20, 21, 29, 30

Challenging Days 4, 5, 18, 19, 24, 25, 26

Affirmation for the Month Love guides my words and actions.

Cancer/July

In the Spotlight

Your influence extends into far-reaching directions, and others follow your lead. With enthusiasm and confidence, you can take bold steps that become part of your legacy. However, problems can arise from distractions that can weaken your financial security.

Wellness and Keeping Fit

An adventurous or active vacation can be completely revitalizing, but even if your schedule is too demanding to get away, staying active makes a huge difference. An element of risk can be invigorating in sports, as long as you're prepared and in top shape.

Love and Life Connections

Your passions can be overwhelming—in a good way—from July 1 to 13. If you're looking for love, a powerful relationship can be ignited during the Cancer New Moon on July 10. While your vulnerability can keep you on edge, if you're clear about your feelings then there's little that can stop you. Intimacy deepens as you share your ideas and discover your common interests, or rediscover the passions that pulled you together in the first place.

Finance and Success

Watch your spending—although you may be at the top of your game, you can go overboard if you're spending on impulse. A careful assessment of your investments helps you determine whether or not it's time to alter your allocations, and it's safest to make changes from July 10 to 20.

Cosmic Insider Tip

With Mars and Jupiter conjunct in your sign, you may feel exceptionally confident. Use the momentum during the New Moon on July 10 to launch something personally important to you.

Rewarding Days 4, 5, 9, 10, 13, 14, 17, 18, 26, 27, 28

Challenging Days 1, 2, 15, 16, 22, 23, 29, 30

Affirmation for the Month I am grateful for the abundance that fills my life!

Cancer/August

In the Spotlight

Extra attention to the way you're handling your resources is crucial. Money is only part of the picture. Keep in mind the precious quality of time. Unanticipated disruptions can create setbacks near the time of the Full Moon on August 22.

Wellness and Keeping Fit

It's marathon time. However, the greatest test of your endurance may arise from your busy schedule. Know your limits—around mid-month it's easy to get in over your head.

Love and Life Connections

Reach out to your family, especially if fences need to be mended. Gatherings at home can be special, but even if you're not in the same place, making the connection is what's important. Communication is easiest after August 6, although evasiveness can lead to misunderstandings, leaving others to leap to conclusions that may be unfounded. If there's something you need to say, get it out there.

Finance and Success

To get your budget right, you may have to go back to the drawing board more than once. Costs for necessary innovations can escalate, although you may be able to restore or revitalize an existing situation and save yourself both time and money. Business meetings and presentations provide the framework for your future success after the New Moon on August 8. A trusted supporter may drop out of the picture unexpectedly after August 20, sending you scrambling.

Cosmic Insider Tip

Jupiter enters Leo, and for the next year you're attracting more resources—and spending more, too. With Mars fueling your desires, it's easy to go overboard. Debt is not your friend!

Rewarding Days 5, 6, 14, 15, 23, 24, 28

Challenging Days 7, 11, 12, 13, 18, 19, 25, 26, 27

Affirmation for the Month Before I act, I carefully consider the impact on my future.

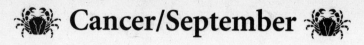

Cancer/September

In the Spotlight

With a crowded schedule, you may have to hustle to get everything done—but your creative ideas and the joy you find in the process make it all worthwhile.

Wellness and Keeping Fit

While you're on the go, you'll appreciate the extra vitality you gain by staying physically active. To fine-tune your body, get into a fitness class or work with a personal trainer. Launch your new program during the New Moon on September 7.

Love and Life Connections

Special touches at home enhance your comfort zone and invite you to enjoy your down time (when you have some). You're writing your own love story after September 9, when Venus waltzes into your romance sector. But uncertainty can creep into the picture from September 14 to 21 if you're separated from your sweetheart. To make amends, sneak away to your favorite haunt just before and during the Full Moon on September 21.

Finance and Success

Others are most receptive to your plans and ideas from September 1 to 15. Once Mercury enters its retrograde cycle on September 14 you may have to backtrack and bring the latecomers up to speed. There's a power play on the horizon from September 16 to 30, involving situations and people not producing what you expect. Rash actions to cut your losses can create unnecessary turmoil, although some divisions may be required.

Cosmic Insider Tip

Watch for smoke-and-mirror tactics from business partners (or potential business partners) from September 15 to 23.

Rewarding Days 2, 3, 6, 7, 10, 11, 19, 20, 25, 29, 30

Challenging Days 8, 9, 14, 15, 16, 21, 22

Affirmation for the Month I use my talents in harmony with my higher needs.

Cancer/October

In the Spotlight

Your heart is overflowing with love—whether you're directing your creative passions into your work or your family, the gratification you receive can be amazing. It's one of those times when you can see that the more you put into something, the more you'll gain from it.

Wellness and Keeping Fit

Recreation needs to be fun to hold your attention, so if you've become bored with your fitness routine, change it. Activities that add grace will also improve your self-confidence.

Love and Life Connections

Since Venus is living in your love zone for the remainder of the year, an intimate relationship can flourish. However, Venus does turn retrograde on October 10, and questions about your true feelings can emerge. Expectations can become problematic—especially those which are not fulfilled. To avoid being the victim or perpetrator of disappointment, maintain open and honest contact about what you can and cannot give or accept.

Finance and Success

During Mercury's last few days of retrograde through October 6, you may need to review plans and complete an ongoing project. Afterward, you'll want to be free to explore other options, since fresh ideas emerge and whet your appetite for different and new possibilities. Investments can grow beyond your expectations, and fall just as quickly.

Cosmic Insider Tip

The tides of business change: Venus and Saturn retrograde. Hedge your investments by focusing the bulk of your assets on proven commodities. Speculate only when you can afford a loss.

Rewarding Days 4, 7, 8, 16, 17, 22, 26, 27, 31

Challenging Days 5, 6, 11, 12, 13, 19, 20

Affirmation for the Month Love's rewards are worth the effort.

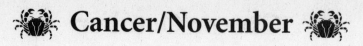 Cancer/November

In the Spotlight

An old love re-enters the picture—you may just be reminiscing when you hear that favorite song on the radio, or your paths can cross. Either way, it's time to address your true feelings.

Wellness and Keeping Fit

Agitation and worry can keep you in knots, making your workouts more important than ever. Increase your attentiveness when you're exercising (and driving), since distraction can lead to accidents.

Love and Life Connections

Your exploration of the truth of love continues, and the question this month is honesty versus fantasy. During the New Moon on November 4, explore the pure motivation in your heart, and search for the areas of intimacy you tend to avoid. In a trusting relationship there's room to investigate your fantasies, and playful romance help you let go of barriers. By the time the lunar eclipse arrives on November 19 you're ready to experience the complete flow of love—giving and receiving.

Finance and Success

A competitive situation arises in your career, and may come in the form of a sneak attack from November 1 to 10. Safeguard your resources, since you could lose something valuable if you're distracted. Your talents and expertise work to your benefit and are the likely source of your financial growth this month. Review productivity and losses now, since this is the perfect time to eliminate those situations that are simply draining your resources.

Cosmic Insider Tip

Venus is clouded by Neptune's foggy energy, and it can be difficult to assess the true value of things—or people. If you're uncertain about a situation, give yourself time before you act.

Rewarding Days 4, 5, 12, 13, 14, 22, 23, 24, 27

Challenging Days 2, 3, 8, 9, 15, 16, 17, 29, 30

Affirmation for the Month I seek honesty in all situations.

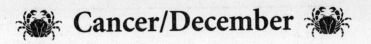 # Cancer/December

In the Spotlight
As the fog clears, you might be surprised about what's still intact. Lovers and children provide the most delightful diversions this month. However, on the practical level, it's sharing your talents and creativity that opens the way for others to give back to you.

Wellness and Keeping Fit
Your health takes a positive turn, and you may find yourself looking forward to your time at the gym or your daily walks. It's an excellent period to reclaim your energy and restore your vitality.

Love and Life Connections
With Venus and Mars joining the dance in your house of love, you have every reason to smile. The energy you put into your closest relationships is returning to you in amazing ways, so you can take action now that will have a powerful impact on the quality of your love life. Children bring special joy, and celebrating their accomplishments can bring you tremendous satisfaction. Your partner will appreciate knowing that you're tuned in to his or her needs.

Finance and Success
The solar eclipse on December 4 emphasizes your need to explore your satisfaction with your work. It's a great time to initiate new routines that will provide more enjoyment of your daily tasks, and to eliminate the things that are simply draining you. If you've been "sick of your job," you can easily see what it is that you don't like. After all, it's your life we're talking about! What can you change that will make you happy to go to work?

Cosmic Insider Tip
An infatuation can distract you from December 1 to 14—but oh, what a lovely distraction! Just keep your eye on your valuables.

Rewarding Days 1, 2, 10, 11, 15, 16, 20, 21, 24, 28, 29

Challenging Days 4, 5, 6, 12, 13, 26, 27

Affirmation for the Month I am the cocreator of my life.

CANCER ACTION TABLE

These dates reflect the best—but not the only—times for success and ease in these activities, according to your Sun sign.

	JAN	FEB	MAR	APR	MAY	JUN	JUL	AUG	SEPT	OCT	NOV	DEC
Move								27-31	1-13	11-31		
Start a class			2					6-25		7-12		
Join a club					12							
Ask for a raise							10					
Look for work			29-31	1-12							19-30	1-19
Get pro advice	11-13	8, 9	7, 8	3-5	1, 2, 28, 29	24-26	22, 23	18, 19	14, 15	11-13	8, 9	5, 6
Get a loan	14, 15	10-12	9-11	6, 7	3, 4, 30, 31	1, 27, 28	22, 23	18, 19	14, 15	11-13	8, 9	5, 6
See a doctor					1-31	1-30	1-7				19-30	1-8
Start a diet	9, 10	5-7	5, 6	1, 2, 28-30	26, 27	22, 23	19, 20	16, 17	12, 13	9, 10	6, 7	3, 4, 31
End relationship								23, 24				
Buy clothes											1-18	
Get a makeover				20-31		1-13	10					
New romance									8-30	1-9	4, 5, 22-30	1-31
Vacation	16, 17	13, 14	12, 13	8-10	5, 6	2, 3, 29, 30	26-28	23, 24	19, 20	16-18	12-14	10, 11

LEO

The Lion
July 23 to August 23

♌

Element:	Fire
Quality:	Fixed
Polarity:	Yang/Masculine
Planetary Ruler:	The Sun
Meditation:	My energy glows with light from the source.
Gemstone:	Ruby
Power Stones:	Topaz, sardonyx
Key Phrase:	I will
Glyph:	Lion's tail
Anatomy:	Heart, upper back
Color:	Gold, scarlet
Animal:	Lions, large cats
Myths/Legends:	Apollo, Isis, Helios
House:	Fifth
Opposite Sign:	Aquarius
Flower:	Marigold, sunflower
Key Word:	Magnetic

Positive Expression:	Misuse of Energy:
Self-confident	Self-absorbed
Loyal	Insolent
Vital	Domineering
Regal	Pompous
Bold	Dictatorial
Generous	Ostentatious

Leo

Your Ego's Strengths and Shortcomings

Your warm smile and magnanimous personality can light up a room. Whether you're in the spotlight or taking a supportive role, your vitality and flair for the dramatic can leave a memorable impression. You simply love life, and it's the power that emerges from your creativity that draws attention and builds your self-confidence. Your strong opinions are only one manifestation of your role as "The Loyalist" of the zodiac, since you are also the one who will stand by a friend no matter what.

In your heart of hearts, you believe that life is meant to be enjoyed, and your playful spirit endears you to others. Once your passion is ignited—for a person or an idea—you can let your talents shine forth and see no limitations. That's what keeps you in the forefront, and can also be your downfall if you go too far in pushing your own agenda. Like your ruler, the Sun, you shed light against the darkness, inspiring devotion and hope. For those who honor you with their praise, you can show enthusiastic appreciation. However, others need to understand that you take your promises seriously, since you may not easily forgive another who fails to honor agreements. By the same token, you may not recover from wounds to your pride, and you can be extremely demanding if you feel you're not receiving the attention you think you deserve.

Your courageous spirit inspires you to take a stand when it's most important. As you surrender your ego to the protection and guidance of your higher self, you become more aware of the true nature of devotion. From there, your life becomes a brilliant light shining with the power of eternal love.

Shining Your Love Light

Nothing matches the ardent passion you feel when you're in love, and your lavish affections can be unforgettable. It takes more than a few faltering steps on the path toward true love to discourage you. However, if you are hurt, you can close your heart or find it difficult to forgive. Fortunately, when you love, there's plenty of room to find healing.

As a fire sign, you truly enjoy the company of other fiery individuals—Aries, Leo, and Sagittarius—who share your appreciation for risk and flair for the dramatic. It's your attraction to your zodiac opposite, Aquarius, that can throw you off balance, since your needs for mutual autonomy can clash with your need for special attention. However, you can forge a powerful partnership once you create a bridge of understanding.

With Aries, you may have an instant attraction that ends as quickly as it begins. Taurus fascinates you, but you might dislike the possessiveness. Your imagination is stimulated by Gemini's wit, and you can become lifelong friends. Comfortable with Cancer, you can enjoy your retreats together but may not feel particularly passionate. Another Leo inspires powerful bursts of creativity, but ego conflicts will emerge unless you each have your turn in the spotlight.

Virgo's attention to perfection is appealing, although you may be better working partners than lovers. Libra's refined taste charms you, and you can feel that you're destined to share life's journey. Although Scorpio's sensuality can be breathtaking, the emotional intensity can choke your enthusiasm. Even though the flames of love are ignited by Sagittarius, you may be having so much fun that you fail to realize how deeply attached you have become; define your expectations to avoid heartbreak. Sustaining a relationship with Capricorn can seem more like work than fun. You're enchanted by Pisces, so much so that you can get in over your head before you know it.

Making Your Place in the World

A career with a secure future will garner more attention from you than "just a job." However, to be dedicated to your lifework you need to receive adequate recognition for your efforts. A position that commands authority or gives you a chance to exert leadership will be most rewarding. In the role of president, CEO, foreman, or admiral you can be a topnotch organizer and may influence lasting changes. As an attorney, teacher, or promoter, you're the one who can inspire a sense of self-importance in others.

Businesses that cater to recreation and entertainment—like nightclubs, theaters, casinos, or amusement centers—can be lucrative and enjoyable. You might also be drawn to the entertainment industry as a director, producer, actor, model, musician, or performer. In politics you can be an attention-getting candidate, but you could also be a dynamite campaign manager.

Power Plays

You know that power and influence are a sacred trust. Even as a child you may have had an attraction to power, and may still hold in your heart the inspiration you felt when your own personal power was kindled—by a teacher, parent, or mentor. Your desire for power may stem from a calling to champion the cause of human dignity. However, you might also be motivated to achieve a position of power for less lofty reasons. It's important to understand your motivations, since once you do have the ability to influence others, you can be especially good at it.

The distinction between becoming a benevolent ruler or dictatorial tyrant may depend upon your self-esteem. When you feel good about yourself, it's much easier to take charge with dignity. However, if you're reeling from hurt, you may use your influence to become unnecessarily self-indulgent. It's when you are working in harmony with others to reach a powerful goal that your efforts shine brightest. All in all, fleeting power can seem useless to you. You think in terms of permanence. For that reason, it's important to target hopeful goals that allow you to use your will in harmony with that of a higher power.

Famous Leos

Yasser Arafat, Amelia Earhart, Peggy Fleming, Peter Jennings, Don King, Lisa Kudrow, Gary Larson, Yves Saint Laurent, Matt LeBlanc, Karl Malone, Debra Messing, Jason Robards, Martin Sheen, Wesley Snipes, Danielle Steel, Helen Thomas

The Year Ahead for Leo

Revitalized by new goals, you're moving toward greater fulfillment during 2002. During part of the year you might prefer to keep a low profile, although that is likely to change when you advance into positions of prominence. The blend of responsible action and clear opportunity may be best expressed through your creativity or artistry—however you manifest your special talents.

From January through the end of July, the expansive quality of Jupiter stimulates your imagination. You may have grand dreams and can also feel an exceptional sense that you are protected. This connection to your spiritual nature can inspire you to focus more time and energy toward charitable efforts, and this can be an excellent time to work behind the scenes. Then, on August 1, Jupiter moves into Leo for its year-long trek in your sign. This is a signal that it's time to broaden your horizons. Since Jupiter transits in your sign only once every twelve years, this is, indeed, a special time to initiate changes that are truly important to you. It marks a period of open doors and clear paths, but can also be a time when you are tempted to overdo it. The results of excessive self-indulgence can slow your progress, so before you pull out your Platinum Card, consider the long-range effects.

Saturn's influence this year supports your ability to target goals that will help you accomplish the realization of your dreams. This year, exercises that provide a chance to work in concert with others who share your special interests can be especially productive. For that reason, work within your community can be meaningful. Plus, it's a time to solidify friendships or to get back in the groove with a friend from your past.

The slow-moving cycles of Uranus and Neptune bring challenges to your social relationships and can also alter the way you view partnership and marriage. Since these influences are a continuation of cycles that have been going on for the last few years, you may not notice a specific challenge. However, if this is the year Uranus or Neptune makes an exact opposition to your Sun, you'll definitely experience large-scale changes. Check in the sections that follow to see if this is your year to experience those cycles.

Pluto's influence emphasizes a rebirth of your creative talents. Love relationships may go through major alterations, and your family structure can change, too.

The solar and lunar eclipses draw your attention to the way you give and receive love. You'll feel the nagging deficiencies in your close relationships more intensely this year. Most important, if you've been blocking the power of love in your life this is an excellent year to explore why, and then release those blocks. What you may discover is an impasse in your ability to receive love and support from others. Whether this is due to a lack of trust, old hurt, or other fears, it's time to remind yourself that you deserve to receive the love you need!

If you were born from July 23 to 27, this year can be like unraveling a mystery. Pluto is transiting in sesquiquadrate to your Sun, marking a time when you may be asking questions about the reason you're here on Earth in the first place. This is your year to unmask your talents, develop your special abilities, and learn to trust your intuitive impulses when it comes to your self-expression. However, there can be traps and pitfalls, especially in situations that appeal to your desire to gain recognition. Consider this a test of your ego, and a chance to find out just how big it wants to be! If you're blinded by arrogance or self-centered motivations, you can run into trouble. That trouble could come in the form of someone else who takes unfair advantage of you or your resources. Just as important, though, is the possibility that you can trim away excess and move onto a more influential stage, ready to take on whatever comes your way.

If you were born from July 29 to August 8, you're being tested this year while Saturn travels in semisquare to your Sun. The primary lesson targets your ability to stick with your priorities. The goals you've established may need review or revision, and once you commit to those aims you can see significant progress. Pace yourself, since just when you think you've reached the plateau you may come to another hill! Because the climb can be steep, it's important to determine what to carry with you. That means you will have to let go of burdens that will not serve your best interests, including taking up the burdens of others (especially when they can carry things on their own). In many ways, this cycle serves as a springboard from your current situation to the next stage of your life. For that reason, the commitments you make need careful consideration, since you may have to live with them for a while. Hold the clear image of your hopes in your heart and continue onward, since the progress you make now can be marvelously self-confirming when you look back at it.

If you were born from July 31 to August 5, there's an element of confusion in your life this year. Neptune transits in opposition to your Sun, dissolving barriers and exposing a heightened awareness. In the beginning, this cycle can be troubling, since you can feel that you've lost your way. It's much like visiting a new place for the first time. The landmarks are unfamiliar, directions unclear, and even your destination can seem uncertain. Fortunately, the universe provides a nice foothold from January through April while Saturn completes its transit in a supportive sextile to your Sun. Establish your direction and priorities during this time. Then, as you carefully navigate, you will become more comfortable. The journey you're taking now is a journey inside yourself. This is a time of spiritual initiation, and from this time forward many of the things that have been part of your life may drop away. Transcendence is your goal: moving above the weightiness of earthly existence will bring you into a space of compassion, insight, and creativity. While some of the situations and people who are part of your life will continue onward with you, others will simply disappear—or at least that's how it will seem when you look back in a few years. You will also encounter situations that are not meant to last, but which simply serve as a means to help you move from this moment into your future. The primary pitfall can involve your health, since it's easy to ignore your physical needs or to abuse your body under this influence. The weak links in your body are exposed now, and you may be more sensitive to environment, food, or other elements of your life than you were in the past.

If you were born from August 7 to 12, you're moving into a position of increased power and influence while Pluto travels in trine aspect to your Sun. This exceptional cycle will not happen again in your lifetime. Whatever obstacles you encounter, it's easier to overcome them now. This time of healing has far-reaching effects, and the depth of insight that can occur during this phase takes you leaps and bounds ahead in your personal development. Also, during April and May, you get a little help from Saturn as it travels in a supportive sextile to your Sun. You are in a stable place and strongly energized, so you may feel much more confident about launching a major change in your life. Career moves can lead you onto a more fulfilling path, and alterations in your relationships can strengthen your sense of contentment. To top it off, you're blessed with a cycle from Jupiter. During the months of October through December, Jupiter conjuncts your Sun, opening the way for true abundance and prosperity. How you use these gifts is up to you. Just remember that gratitude and generosity will lift you even higher!

If you were born from August 13 to 22, this can be a time of clear direction. Saturn is transiting in sextile aspect to your Sun from June through December. Consider this a year when you can take stable, realistic steps toward manifesting your dreams. The effort you put forth now will definitely make a big difference, and others are likely to show their appreciation through their support. Career advancements will carry greater responsibilities, but you may be more than happy to shoulder them since they're getting you somewhere. If you have an opportunity to teach or learn, take it. The importance of long-range plans is easier to grasp, and while you may have an eye on the future, you're also firmly rooted in the present moment. From here, the promises you make can provide the basic structure of your life for years to come.

If you were born from August 16 to 23, expect a few surprises, since Uranus opposes your Sun for the entire year. Uranian cycles disrupt the status quo, and even though you have some stability from the Saturn cycle described above you may still feel eager to change yourself and/or your life direction—more than once. The big challenges come through your relationships, since what was once satisfying may now seem boring. Before you toss out everyone and everything, you're likely to reconsider (thanks to Saturn, and to your own sense of loyalty). However, you may still need to make sweeping changes. It's also conceivable that a few of those surprises will come from others. Your partner may change, and so your challenge can be to decide how those changes fit into your own life. Consider the things in your life that are blocking the expression of your individuality or the situations that stand in the way of your progress. These will be the most frustrating circumstances, and this cycle challenges you to find the best way to overcome obstacles, inhibitions, and limitations. The impulse may be to stage a rebellion. Before you torch the bridge, though, be sure you're not standing on it.

Tools for Change

Love guides your life this year, and the many expressions of loving energy can strengthen your sense of security and experience of joy. Your fulfillment stems from the love that flows in your heart through your creativity and personal relationships. Tools that will enhance your creativity can make a huge difference in your life. You might decide to make better use of technological advances, but you might also find that reaching back in time has its own rewards. A journey into sacred space through meditation can illuminate your path and choices, and altering the vibrations around you can be highly effective. Chimes, gongs, and chants can take you into a deeper consciousness and open your creative flow.

Music itself can be a valuable healing and balancing tool. The types of music you choose can completely change your focus. Set a creative mood for your work place, and, just as important, use music to create the perfect ambience enhancing your closest relationships. To deepen your connection to your partner, explore the teachings of Tantra. To heal your body, concentrate on vibrational medicine, energetic healing techniques like Reiki, or intensifying the flow of chi with techniques like acupuncture.

On a basic level, you are also creating a new mythology for yourself. Seeking inspiration from stories of those who've conquered their demons or influenced major change, you might inspired to study obscure myths. You may discover the symbology that helps you identify the essence of your own quest. A class in mythology can be an excellent beginning, as might a study of Jungian psychology. Work using symbols themselves can be especially significant, and for this reason astrology, runes, and tarot can be excellent tools.

ı̃ß

Affirmation for the Year

I welcome the changes that revitalize my life.

Leo/January

In the Spotlight
Competitive situations can seem more threatening, since your vulnerability is exposed. Fortunately, you're in a great position to call in reinforcements. Better yet, before the month ends you can scoot away from the turmoil to a much more enjoyable circumstance.

Wellness and Keeping Fit
The fine line between emotional tension and physical health gets blurred by excessive stress. The New Moon on January 13 ushers in a time to try out a different routine.

Love and Life Connections
Open lines of communication can help you avert problems with your partner. The trouble spot can be your own inhibitions, especially if you run into an old wound. If it's too painful to deal with right away, take the easy approach. Focus on your spiritual bond and your shared vision after January 20, when future plans can breathe new life into your relationship. Then, by the time the Leo Full Moon rises on January 28, you'll be ready to surrender to an uplifting commitment.

Finance and Success
Improvements in your work environment can increase productivity, but only if roles are understood. Otherwise, there can be too many cooks in the kitchen! Misleading information can delay progress, and after Mercury turns retrograde on January 18 things get even more confusing. Meetings and presentations benefit your reputation and can lead to a new source of revenue after January 18.

Cosmic Insider Tip
With a lot of ideas bantered about, things may appear one way even though you know something else is happening behind the scenes. Shine light on the real issues during the Leo Full Moon.

Rewarding Days 1, 2, 5, 6, 9, 10, 19, 20, 24, 28, 29

Challenging Days 7, 8, 14, 15, 16, 21, 22, 23

Affirmation for the Month I listen to the ideas of others.

Leo/February

In the Spotlight

A gracious action on your part can open the way for tremendous success. Not only can you return a favor, but you may be able to step into a situation that would not otherwise have been possible! Travel and promotional activities are prominently featured this month.

Wellness and Keeping Fit

Different scenery can inspire you to try a new health routine. An active vacation, with a balance of relaxation and fun, gives you a second wind. The change of pace makes a world of difference.

Love and Life Connections

With Mercury and Venus highlighting your need to reach agreeable solutions, this can be an excellent time to alter the course of your relationship. Expressing your needs and desires is easier, but you may also be more accommodating after the New Moon on February 12. Private time with your honey can be especially sweet after February 13, when your sensual nature can ignite a wave of passion. Be on the alert for sensitive issues after February 23, when you can run headlong into a power struggle before you know it!

Finance and Success

Your flair for the theatrical works to your advantage in promotional activities, when others are inspired by your leadership. Innovations and technological advances can help you streamline your efforts and move ahead of the pack from February 1 to 13. After Mercury leaves its retrograde cycle on February 8, you may need to fix a few leftover problems, though.

Cosmic Insider Tip

After Mercury and Saturn turn direct on February 8, business deals that were stalled can come back to the table. The question is: "Are you still interested?"

Rewarding Days 1, 2, 5, 6, 7, 15, 16, 20, 21, 25

Challenging Days 3, 4, 10, 11, 12, 18, 19

Affirmation for the Month I am eager to explore new horizons.

Leo/March

In the Spotlight
Driven to fulfill your ambitions, your courage shines forth. Competitive circumstances fuel your resolve, although you may have to modify an old partnership to keep a project moving forward.

Wellness and Keeping Fit
Are you feeling tired? It could be the weight of responsibility, but you might also be pushing beyond your limits. An evaluation of underlying causes of bothersome symptoms goes a long way toward restoring your vitality.

Love and Life Connections
Surprising news can alter your feelings about a relationship, although your imagination can get the better of you if you let it. Before you react to a situation, explore the truth. If you're available, travel or cultural pursuits can lead to a new love. With romance brimming, you may have little patience for family tension. However, it could be the contrast between your fanciful moments and the burdens of life that makes your love even more precious.

Finance and Success
Your enthusiasm for a new strategy adds to its momentum, but you can be distracted by power struggles with others who have an eye on your position. While your superiors may be impressed by your credentials, you still may have to prove your worth if you're going to advance. Showcase your talents or premiere a pet project between March 9 and the Full Moon on March 28. Meanwhile, keep a watch on the budget numbers, since cost overruns are a real probability.

Cosmic Insider Tip
Stubborn resistance from conservatives masquerading as do-gooders can create a setback. Play your cards close to your chest.

Rewarding Days 5, 6, 14, 15, 16, 20, 24, 25, 28, 29

Challenging Days 2, 3, 4, 9, 10, 11, 17, 18, 30, 31

Affirmation for the Month My dealings with others are forthright and fair-minded.

Leo/April

In the Spotlight

Your efforts bring you into the forefront, with a breakthrough in your career. While things may not go as you expect, the end result can be quite satisfying once the dust settles. Your influence can reach further than you think.

Wellness and Keeping Fit

Releasing tension is your top assignment from April 1 to 13, when dealing with all the changes can leave you feeling scattered and stressed. No more excuses! Enroll in a fitness class, join the office sports team, or hit the pavement on the New Moon on April 12.

Love and Life Connections

No matter what your age, you are likely to feel rebellion welling up in your heart from April 1 to 15. The old guard is dropping away, and it's time to strike out to fulfill your needs on your terms. If you've been focused on satisfying family or others instead of following your heart, it's likely that you'll push beyond those barriers and let your heart lead the way.

Finance and Success

To keep your wheels on the track to success may require that you steam through stormy opposition. Clarity emerges with the New Moon on April 12, when your goals are in sight and your spirit is refreshed. However, your promotional efforts continually build momentum throughout the month, and support from colleagues in your field can add to your advancement. Finances improve after April 25, when your income and outflow are more balanced.

Cosmic Insider Tip

With Saturn and Neptune in powerful harmony, you can make your dreams reality. To have what you want, you need to clearly determine your desires. Intention makes all the difference!

Rewarding Days 1, 2, 11, 12, 16, 20, 21, 25, 29

Challenging Days 6, 7, 13, 14, 26, 27

Affirmation for the Month Truth lights my way.

Leo/May

In the Spotlight
With all the excitement surrounding you, it can be difficult to keep your priorities in order. Your organizational skills will definitely come in handy.

Wellness and Keeping Fit
On the go, you might have trouble fitting your workouts into your schedule. With your vitality in overdrive, you can overdo it. However, this is the perfect time to step up your fitness routine.

Love and Life Connections
Love pours in from all directions, and that makes it easy to share the abundance of your life. With family, you're moving into a different role and can exercise positive influence. Children provide plenty of laughs, and your love life can improve by leaps and bounds. Make or renew vows before May 15, although you can thoroughly enjoy fun-filled travel through most of the month. The lunar eclipse on May 26 brings the potential to develop yet another dimension of love. It's all about surrendering to the music of your heart.

Finance and Success
Connections with your associates can provide the perfect opportunity to survey the breadth of talent that surrounds you. From there, you may be inspired to take on an exceptional task that could bring marvelous rewards. Delegate roles and tasks early, and then test drive your plans during Mercury's retrograde from May 15 to the end of the month. Work behind the scenes helps preserve your more sensitive plans after May 27.

Cosmic Insider Tip
Saturn opposes Pluto: structures are changing. The power base shifts. You can step into a position of strength, but only if you've done your homework.

Rewarding Days 8, 9, 13, 14, 17, 18, 19, 22, 23, 26, 27

Challenging Days 3, 4, 10, 11, 12, 24, 25, 30, 31

Affirmation for the Month *My goals reflect my passions.*

Leo/June

In the Spotlight
The solar eclipse on June 10 signals a time to reconsider your long-range plans. Directions you once pursued may have less value, and the path ahead can seem a bit hazy. Inner reflection adds confidence and clarity, and withdrawing from the action gives you a chance to regroup.

Wellness and Keeping Fit
The cosmos signals that this is your time to rejuvenate and revitalize. A vacation might be in order, or you just might prefer to take more time to yourself.

Love and Life Connections
Home and family can provide the haven you need most, and time nestled away in your favorite space brings reassurance. An old friend may reappear on the scene during the solar eclipse on June 10, taking you on a trip down memory lane. Then, on June 14, Venus enters your sign, marking a time when your affections deepen and others reach out to you. A fascination can take your breath away after June 21, when fantasies can come true.

Finance and Success
While Mercury retrogrades through June 8 you have a second chance with a situation that you may have thought to be lost. It's a good time to tie up loose ends. Then, quietly pull together your team of experts to design a new scheme for August. Finances are likely to improve, but you can lose track of details if you're not extra careful. At work, make improvements or try out a new approach to tasks during the lunar eclipse on June 24.

Cosmic Insider Tip
Take care of your health. If you're concerned, this is the time to see an expert. Start treatment before the Moon's eclipse on June 24.

Rewarding Days 4, 5, 9, 10, 14, 15, 18, 22, 23

Challenging Days 7, 8, 20, 21, 24, 27, 28

Affirmation for the Month My dreams are a source of healing.

Leo/July

In the Spotlight

A change of heart sparks alterations in your priorities. The super-charge you feel from Mars moving into Leo on July 13 can motivate you to drive more intensely toward your goals.

Wellness and Keeping Fit

To remain strong, a consistent pace is best. It's tempting to dive into a fitness routine or recreational activity without much preparation. However, what you can't see is likely to be more threatening than what you think is in front of you.

Love and Life Connections

Partnership can be topsy-turvy—whether you or your partner initiate changes, you can feel unsettled. You may be more enthralled with what you cannot have than with what is possible. What you have to determine is whether or not the desires that drive you will take you anywhere. Explore your motivations, and pull back if you sense trouble. Misreading signals can be especially likely during the Full Moon on July 24.

Finance and Success

Work in concert with your community or others whose concerns harmonize with yours, since together you can accomplish much more than you can do alone. Short-term agreements work nicely early in the month, and although you might be tempted to strike up a partnership after July 21, it may not be all it seems. Read the fine print, and consult an expert if you're still uncertain. The success you crave now might not come until next month.

Cosmic Insider Tip

Consider this to be an excellent time to research and explore possibilities. But consider your actions carefully, since Mars and Mercury are obscured by foggy Neptune after July 21.

Rewarding Days 2, 3, 7, 11, 12, 20, 21, 29, 30

Challenging Days 4, 5, 17, 18, 24, 25, 26, 31

Affirmation for the Month I am forgiving and compassionate.

Leo/August

In the Spotlight

Fasten your seat belt, and get ready for takeoff! With Mars and Jupiter in your sign, you're forging ahead with tremendous confidence. The momentum can carry you through for quite a while, and if you've been waiting for a time to move ahead, it has arrived!

Wellness and Keeping Fit

Now you can move out of your comfort zone and take a few reasonable risks. An innovative fitness routine or change of pace adds more energy, and strength-building makes a huge difference in your overall vitality. Avoid high risks after August 18, however.

Love and Life Connections

Your passion can certainly be attractive now, but you can also overwhelm those who are less sure of themselves. A journey can lead to serendipitous rewards, when you could meet the love of your life. Plus, during the Leo New Moon on August 8, your ability to make your desires known can lead to a powerful exchange. Even if you've been unsure of your commitment, it's important to review your needs and motivations.

Finance and Success

Your enthusiasm glows, and the impact of your words and actions can result in others joyfully following your lead from August 1 to 6. Trust your intuitive impulses, since all the facts may not arrive in time to make a significant decision. To complete or initiate a winning strategy, you're attracting a bevy of talent and can delegate the right tasks to the best people.

Cosmic Insider Tip

You may get the glory, but sharing the limelight with others gives you a very special joy. It's one of those picture-perfect times . . . the stuff that makes memories.

Rewarding Days 3, 4, 7, 8, 12, 16, 17, 25, 26, 30

Challenging Days 1, 2, 14, 15, 20, 21, 22, 28

Affirmation for the Month I am grateful for my life's abundance.

Leo/September

In the Spotlight

Razzle-dazzle works only so far, and while you have tremendous enthusiasm for your dreams and plans, support from others may seem to disappear. You're discovering who's talk, and who's action.

Wellness and Keeping Fit

Your energy reserves can be easily depleted, but that can prompt you to work more diligently toward building endurance. Setting limits can actually help—there's a tendency now to push beyond your capacities, or to overindulge in things that drain your vitality.

Love and Life Connections

Anticipation seems to lead into a black hole of disappointment. To avoid the crash from the cliffs of expectation, strive for clarity and well-defined communication. Partnerships are most vulnerable now, and you can end up feeling betrayed if you're not careful. The way you and your partner deal with money can be a source of friction during the Full Moon on September 21.

Finance and Success

Even in the best of times, spending beyond your limits is costly. The impulse from Mars tempts you to go out on a limb financially. With Jupiter's vision clouded by Neptune's illusions, you could end up buying something you do not need, or be hornswoggled by an unscrupulous character. Carefully consider your budget, and then look toward long-range possibilities. Since Mercury turns retrograde on September 14, you'll do yourself a favor if you wait to sign contracts until you've had more time to consider all the ramifications.

Cosmic Insider Tip

Ecstasy can take you to the heights, but unless your landing gear works, you're vulnerable. Use Neptune's dreamy phantasm to lift your creativity, but keep your credit cards in your pocket.

Rewarding Days 4, 5, 8, 12, 13, 21, 22, 23, 27

Challenging Days 7, 10, 11, 16, 17, 18, 24, 25

Affirmation for the Month Truth lights my way.

Leo/October

In the Spotlight

The comforts of home might be more of a hassle than anything else, even if your end goal is to make things better. There's also every possibility that you'll be on the move so frequently that you have little time to enjoy the comfort of your home as often as you like.

Wellness and Keeping Fit

All those calories add up—even when you aren't counting them! Trouble is, you may not have time to keep track of such details. Work out a tailor-made plan that will overhaul your daily routine. It will yield excellent results by the time the Full Moon rises on October 21.

Love and Life Connections

Emotionally charged issues at home can catch you off guard and add stress. Misunderstandings run rampant, although you can revisit the issues after October 17. To revive your sunny disposition, make an effort to clear the air, and bring problems into the open for discussion. You may simply have different viewpoints. Venus retrogrades for six weeks, starting October 10. This is the time to explore your true feelings and to work out your differences.

Finance and Success

Even after Mercury leaves its retrograde cycle on October 6, there's still fallout. Agreements can fall short, along with budgets, and the combination can leave you wondering how to make ends meet. Before you don your black armband, reconsider. This is the time to trim excess and eliminate nonproductive elements.

Cosmic Insider Tip

You're discovering just how resilient you are (or aren't). After putting on the brakes, take time to reconsider your options. Then, launch a different plan between October 15 to 20.

Rewarding Days 1, 2, 5, 6, 9, 10, 19, 20, 24, 29, 30

Challenging Days 7, 8, 14, 15, 16, 21, 22, 23

Affirmation for the Month I am secure in the midst of change.

Leo/November

In the Spotlight
Your focus turns to the home front, where close family gatherings and time spent cozying up to your sweetheart can warm your soul. Competitive situations at work calm, although you may still see signals that keep you on guard.

Wellness and Keeping Fit
Keep moving. To soothe stress, your daily workout can be your best tension-reliever. Work on flexibility, too, since those emotional knots you've felt lately may have buried themselves in your muscles.

Love and Life Connections
Mixed signals can lead you to believe what is not true. A new relationship is particularly vulnerable, since you're unfamiliar with one another or have not yet learned about your particular styles of doing things. However, mistrust is another thing, and if that's the case it's important to explore those feelings. While you may need to maintain some secrets, other secrets can undermine the honesty required for real intimacy. The lunar eclipse on November 19 draws your attention to family matters, when a crisis at home can lead to establishing different traditions.

Finance and Success
Confusion over finances can result from inattention to detail, although you're most at risk in situations which are not well-defined. If leadership is in question, and your budget and plans are not in sync with the "authorities," then you could be left in an unprotected position. Your professional allies can help you get out of a jam, and may be a resource if you're looking for new direction.

Cosmic Insider Tip
To avoid the trap of seeing only what you want to see from November 1 to 10, consult a trusted expert.

Rewarding Days 3, 6, 7, 15, 16, 20, 25, 26, 29, 30

Challenging Days 1, 4, 5, 10, 11, 12, 18, 19

Affirmation for the Month I am honest with myself.

Leo/December

In the Spotlight
The solar eclipse on December 4 leads to an illuminating creative experience. However, you may feel disappointed if you cannot do things on a grand scale. Concentrate on beautifying your home and putting more energy into family needs.

Wellness and Keeping Fit
An assessment of your physical needs can put you back on track. It's time to pull back and concentrate on boosting your nutritional support. Achieving a balance between work and rest is vital.

Love and Life Connections
Matters of the heart are emphasized during the Sun's eclipse on December 4, when love leads the way. You may have to surrender your control of a situation in favor of the needs of another, or otherwise suffer the consequences of somebody else having hurt feelings. To avoid resentment, keep channels of communication open, so you can sort through issues with siblings and family. Hiding your feelings might not be effective, and knowing when it's appropriate to speak can be most complicated from December 4 to 20.

Finance and Success
Hollow support will not suffice, and the surprise may be that your efforts and ideas are best received by an old ally from December 1 to 8. During this time, your competitors seem to have the edge, but what they offer may not have as much substance as they claim. Common sense saves the day, and unproven innovations may not fare as well as the "old standby."

Cosmic Insider Tip
Truth wins out, and the high moral ground is in the forefront during the solar eclipse on December 4. Empty propaganda will fall short, but it can have reached a pretty tall peak before it crashes.

Rewarding Days 3, 4, 12, 13, 14, 19, 22, 23, 27, 31

Challenging Days 1, 2, 7, 8, 9, 10, 15, 16, 29, 20

Affirmation for the Month I am strengthened by my heritage.

LEO ACTION TABLE

These dates reflect the best—but not the only—times for success and ease in these activities, according to your Sun sign.

	JAN	FEB	MAR	APR	MAY	JUN	JUL	AUG	SEPT	OCT	NOV	DEC
Move											1-18	
Start a class				12				27-31	1-13	6-31		
Join a club						10, 11						
Ask for a raise								8, 9				
Look for work	1, 2	8-12		13-29								9-31
Get pro advice	4, 5	10-12	9, 10	6, 7	3, 4, 30, 31	1, 27, 28	24, 25	20-22	16-18	14, 15	10, 11	7-9
Get a loan	16-18	13, 14	12, 13	8-10	5-7	2, 3, 29, 30	26, 27	23, 24	19, 20	16-18	12-14	10, 11
See a doctor	1-3	4-12					7-21					9-31
Start a diet	11-13	8, 9	7, 8	3-5	1, 2, 28, 29	24-26	22, 23	18, 19	14, 15	11-13	15, 16	12-14
End relationship								20-22				
Buy clothes						15-30	1-10				19-30	1-7
Get a makeover								8, 9				
New romance												4, 5
Vacation	19, 20	15-17	14, 15	11, 12	8, 9	4-6	1-3, 29, 30	25-27	21-23	19, 20	15, 16	12-14

VIRGO

The Virgin
August 22 to September 22

♍

Element:	Earth
Quality:	Mutable
Polarity:	Yin/Feminine
Planetary Ruler:	Mercury
Meditation:	I experience love through service.
Gemstone:	Sapphire
Power Stones:	Peridot, amazonite, rhodochrosite
Key Phrase:	I analyze
Glyph:	Greek symbol for containment
Anatomy:	Abdomen, intestines, gall bladder
Color:	Taupe, gray, navy blue
Animal:	Domesticated animals
Myths/Legends:	Demeter, Astraea, Hygeia
House:	Sixth
Opposite Sign:	Pisces
Flower:	Pansy
Key Word:	Discriminating

Positive Expression:	Misuse of Energy:
Analytical	Hypercritical
Practical	Tedious
Proficient	Petulant
Conscientious	Intolerant
Precise	Persnickety
Astute	Skeptical

Virgo

Your Ego's Strengths and Shortcomings

Your ever-busy mind helps you stay young, since you love to delve into an analysis of almost anything (or anyone!). Your quest for perfection fuels your ability to make improvements, and stems from your role as "The Modifier" of the zodiac—always looking for a better way. Your efficiency, skill, and attention to detail keep you in demand, and you feel most happy when you are assured that you've had a productive day.

A Virgo may have invented the word "tweak," since you understand that fine-tuning makes all the difference in quality. You can distill even the most complicated concepts into understandable language and procedure, and you're a natural teacher. Just as important, your own thirst for information stimulates lifelong learning. There's little that compares to an engrossing conversation with others you respect. All this mentality stems from your connection to the energy of Mercury, your planetary ruler, and because you are open to a wide range of ideas and curious about the way things work, you will always seem to be younger than your years.

Unfortunately, your attention to detail can lead to an excessively critical attitude, and even when you think you are offering objective advice others may interpret your intentions in the wrong way. Little do they realize that you continually keep that ultrasensitive microscope trained on yourself! It is your spiritual quest for excellence that drives you to purify your soul. However, you may never feel content until you learn to become more tolerant of your own humanity. Then, your efforts can shine brilliantly against a life path that reflects clear insight and compassionate understanding.

Shining Your Love Light

Your discriminating nature shows itself most in the way you approach relationships. There's a long list of qualifications that describe your soulmate, although you can be forgiving once you develop trust. Because you're seeking pure love, it may take a while before you let someone get close enough to discover your hidden sensuality. Love blossoms when you are with the right partner.

You are an earth sign, and Taurus, other Virgos, and Capricorn share your earthy element. That means you can enjoy the more measured pace and practical bent you all have in common. However, your resistance to intimacy can be quickly dissolved when you're with the right Pisces—your zodiac opposite. Together you can have an intensely emotional bond, although you may feel that you exist in different planes of reality!

Aries provokes a powerful passion, but can also be distracting when you're trying to focus. The stability and earthy creativity of Taurus is a real turn-on for you. It's the intellectual levity, quick wit, and continual curiosity that makes Gemini attractive to you, but you can be irritated by his or her scattered energy. With Cancer, friendship and open acceptance are easy, and you can become exceptional lovers if you decide to take your relationship in that direction. Leo's magnetic charm can knock you for a loop, but you may be reluctant to share all your secrets.

It's easy to be yourself with another Virgo, but don't make the mistake of thinking you're alike! You'll both need to be tolerant if your relationship is to last. You'll feel open and objective around Libra, but communication requires continual effort. Scorpio gets you going on all sorts of levels, and you can feel continual rapport with one another. You're right at home with Sagittarius, although you may not spend much time together. Aquarius stimulates fireworks and spiritual growth, but you may not feel that your personal needs get enough attention.

Making Your Place in the World

Even when you're not working, you're probably busy with a project. But in a career, you need a mental challenge and an opportunity to develop several skills. Whether you're in charge of your own business or working in concert with others, you need to feel there's room for growth. Watch your workaholic tendencies, since it's not usual for you to burn midnight oil. You may be a writer, editor, public speaker, or teacher. Or you might prefer to put your skills into office management, administrative services, systems analysis, desktop publishing, or scientific research.

Social service, counseling, or health professions can satisfy your desire to heal. You might also have a bent for careers requiring manual dexterity like drafting, crafts, design, graphic arts, or building. In performing arts, your attention to detail can be extended into fields like acting, directing, set design, editing, or musical performance.

Power Plays

The powers of change, growth, and evolution have a strong appeal for you, since you may feel that you're in the world to help make it a better place for everyone. However, the idea of power for its own sake can seem a waste. You're keenly aware of the power of the mind, and have a strong drive to be sure that others have an opportunity to learn and to make positive use of information. Your resourcefulness is the root of your personal power, and you can see learning and education as necessary tools. For this reason, you may determine that you need to take on the task of assuring that educational opportunities are there for others who need them, and that education itself is reformed to suit the needs of an evolving society.

Because you tend to think through things before you start to "work," you can accomplish many of your tasks with apparent ease. Only those who know you realize that you've been simmering the soup for a long time before it's ready to serve. As a result, your efforts may not be fully appreciated. It's also easy to fall into the trap of codependency, and knowing when to pull back and allow others to fail or succeed on their own is the ultimate test of honest power.

Famous Virgos

Terry Bradshaw, Jane Curtin, Queen Elizabeth I, Irving R. Levine, Branford Marsalis, Marlee Matlin, Christa McAuliffe, Reggie Miller, Jessye Norman, Jesse Owens, Itzhak Perlman, Jason Priestly, Leo Tolstoy, Conway Twitty

The Year Ahead for Virgo

Big goals call for increased efforts. Fortunately, your confidence is strong and your friends are there to lend a helping hand. Your greatest challenge this year comes from your need to maintain your focus on a significant project, or your work toward completion of a long-standing obligation. This is the year to take care of your responsibilities, while you work to eliminate unnecessary elements from your life that could hold you back in the future.

With Jupiter's optimistic energy highlighting your hopes, you're keeping your eye on the path ahead. Your objectives may be focused on making a difference in your community, or you may simply be more aware of the significance of setting your aims on what you truly need. It's time to hitch your wagon to a star and enjoy the good fortune and advancement you've worked hard to achieve. In August, Jupiter moves into Leo and nudges you to open to your spirituality. Your dreams can be truly visionary during the last five months of 2002, and some of the things you left behind in your past may also return to your life. Are there talents waiting to be used or further developed? If so, then this is a great year to shake off the dust and polish your abilities.

Saturn brings discipline and focus into your career. The hard work you've done to build your reputation can now elevate you to a position of greater responsibility, but you'll also feel that you are being tested in the process. If you're in a situation that no longer suits you, you may not be able to wiggle out of it—especially if your obligations dictate a need to stick with the program a while longer. However, you might be able to eliminate some unwanted elements in your career, or to focus your energy on delegating responsibilities so that you can be more attentive to the aspects of your work that call on your significant talent and skill.

The outer planets—Uranus, Neptune, and Pluto—each have long cycles in a sign. Their most significant impact occurs during the year when these planets make an exact contact to your Sun. Check the following sections for your birth date to determine if this is the year these planets will stimulate significant change. Uranus and Neptune continue to highlight your work environment.

Uranus's influence indicates a need to incorporate innovations, new technology, and experimental changes at work. Neptune's influence may prompt you to be even more involved in charitable efforts or to exhibit greater compassion through your work. Pluto's energy pulsates through your home environment and uncovers your deeper feelings about family. Maybe you need to use feng shui not only in the way you arrange your furnishings, but where you seat your family members during the holidays!

The solar and lunar eclipses for 2002 add further emphasis to the changes in your home and family circumstances. This may be a year when you experience a kind of "changing of the guard," with alterations in the overall structure of your family. The undercurrent of energy signified by the transiting cycle of the Moon's North Node draws your attention to your life work and true vocation. Your public profile may be very strong, but your desire to pull away from the limelight and deal with your personal needs also vies for attention. The trick is to keep a healthy balance, since too much energy taken from either can undermine your success.

If you were born from August 22 to September 6, you may feel like breathing a sign of relief, since Saturn is moving away from its tense aspect to your Sun. As a reward from the universe, you can even make progress in your creative self-expression. However, the first quarter of the year still shows that you need to stay on top of your obligations. Your talents and special gifts can shine through during the second half of this year, when Saturn moves into a supportive quintile to your Sun. The discipline and extra effort you put into your artistic talents can have a tremendous payoff. This aspect comes into effect in June, and lasts through the remainder of the year. You may also be involved in activities that support others in the development of their talents. In fact, if you teach or lend your energy as a mentor, it's quite likely that you'll meet others who have outstanding talents.

If you were born from August 23 to September 1, you may feel powerfully drawn to develop opportunities that will help you accomplish a greater sense of purpose. Just a "job" might not suffice, since you're digging deeper and are spurred by a need to experience more from life. Chiron transits in trine aspect to your Sun through-out the year, bringing the potential for deep healing into your life. It is through opening your heart to pure joy that you uncover drives that have been buried beneath the heavy weight of responsibility and obligation. Now, it's time for you to exercise those abilities and to feel the influx of energy that comes from blending your energy with your highest needs. This is also an excellent year to address physical complaints and to bring a healthier flow of physical vital-ity into your life. In other words, all the good things you do to take care of yourself will have a significant impact.

If you were born from August 31 to September 5, your spiri-tual yearnings need extra attention while Neptune travels in quin-cunx aspect to your Sun this year. Your need to retreat from the action can lead you to alter your schedule so that you have more time for reflection, meditation, or creative projects. While this is not necessarily a time of retirement, this cycle definitely has a mel-lowing effect. You may be more sensitive on every level, although it's your health that can seem most reactive. If you have allergies, they can be more intense. Or, your sensitivity to environmental pollutants can be more of a problem than in the past. The key to working with this cycle is to make adjustments to your lifestyle that will improve your vitality. In addition, from January through April, Saturn will complete its cycle in square to your Sun (this began last summer). The tension from this cycle can leave you feeling tired, particularly if you've been involved in a major undertaking of some sort. However, the recovery period that starts in April brings you to a realization of your real priorities.

If you were born from September 7 to 12, you may feel that your life is being completely transformed while Pluto transits in square aspect to your Sun. This year, you can eliminate situations and attitudes that stand in the way of your growth. You may experi-ence endings—ranging from the end of relationships to the end of an old way of life. Think of this time as a period of cocooning—when you are moving from one form of personal expression into another. The symbol of the butterfly is a good image to hold in your mind and heart, since you are now experiencing a metamorphosis that will renew your life and allow you to fly, beautifully and freely. Circumstances beyond your control can force a few issues, particularly in areas where you are resistant to change. This can feel like a profound test, especially if you've been ignoring important issues. At the least, this is a time when your awareness shifts dramatically and you have a rare chance to rebuild your life. The stress of this cycle will be strongest from April through June, as Saturn finally completes its cycle in a square aspect to your Sun. (The Saturn cycle was most intense from August through November of last year.) It's during these few months that you can run into resistance from others, especially in career matters. Power struggles can be an earmark of the Pluto cycle, and the areas in your life where you have control issues will be most emphasized. Even if you've always thought you were pretty tolerant, you'll definitely discover your limits. It's important to honor them, since restoration of yourself gives you an opportunity to create your life on your own terms, filling it with situations that reflect the best and most rewarding qualities.

If you were born from September 13 to 23, you're feeling the tension of Saturn transiting in square aspect to your Sun. You may sense that this energy is building up from January through May, and then, in June, the intensity peaks and continues to be powerful through the end of the year. It's much like piling on the weight of responsibility until you realize you've reached your limit. The trick is not to carry a load that's too heavy! For that reason, one of the most significant features of this year involves setting reasonable limitations and dealing with your responsibilities in a forthright manner. You may not be able to get rid of all your obligations. In fact, it's likely that you'll have to continue until you're certain that you've done what's required of you. It's like attending a course, and the pressure you feel when final exams roll around. If you've done your part, kept up with your studies, and learned what's necessary, the test can be stressful, but you'll perform well. However, if you've failed to live up to your obligations, the test can be much more grueling. In either case, setting priorities is necessary.

If you were born from September 14 to 21, it's time to make adjustments in your life which will free you from situations that are inhibiting your self-expression. Uranus is transiting in quincunx to your Sun. The impulse you feel from this cycle is a desire to get rid of everything and everyone you find irritating or intolerable. That's likely to be easier said than done! This is particularly complicated since you're also dealing with the Saturn cycle described above. But do you notice a complementary theme? Both of these cycles stimulate a desire to eliminate what you no longer need. The gift from Saturn is that you will be less tempted to burn the bridge while you're still on it!

Tools for Change

Health issues can be more prominent this year, since most of the high-impact cycles you are experiencing enhance awareness of your physical needs. While you may actually become stronger, old problems or injuries or the effects of aging are also likely to be more noticeable. Part of this is due to the fact that you can be a magnet for stress, and for that reason, you'll feel much more alive and in control of your life if you're continually aware of releasing tension. Daily relaxation and meditation can have an exceptional effect on your sense of well-being. A morning or evening walk can be just as effective, and combines physical activity with the act of letting go of tension. Nothing particularly complicated is required to release stress. In fact, the simpler, the better.

Of special benefit are exercise routines that emphasize stretching and flexibility. These can have a strong restorative effect. Healing therapies like acupuncture or therapeutic massage can keep your physical energy moving in its natural flow and rhythm. Vibrational therapies—ranging from music to pure sound to chimes and tuning forks—can be especially soothing.

At home, it's time to clear out clutter, create more open space, and eliminate things you no longer need or appreciate. To fine-tune the experience, consider incorporating principles of feng shui, which will help you bring a balance of all the elements of life into your personal space. Your relationships need some clearing, too. Establishing a better means of communication with those who share your life can be particularly important this year. Counseling can be an excellent tool, particularly if you're at an impasse. If changes in your family have had an unsettling effect (like empty-nest syndrome, or the loss of a family member), you may also be dealing with a surprising element of guilt. This is the time to forgive yourself for the things you cannot fix. It's also important to practice forgiveness of others, whenever and however you can.

During your meditations, focus on your heart. Tune in to its rhythm. Connect with the powerful flow of vitality that surges forth from the center of your being and throughout your body. Envision a pure and brilliant light, glowing within your heart. Feel it warming you, and then let that light shine forth into the world surrounding you. Then, during your days, remember this light and allow it to guide you, illuminating your path during times of joy and moments of despair.

♍

Affirmation for the Year

I am worthy of life's bounty
and my life is filled with abundance in all things.

Virgo/January

In the Spotlight
Progress on an important project inspires you to continue onward toward your goals. Your creative energy is amplified this month, and the work you do in association with others strengthens your reputation within the community.

Wellness and Keeping Fit
Your desire to enhance your vigor and vitality gets an extra push from Mars this month, and the more active you are, the more energy you'll have.

Love and Life Connections
Venus dances through the love sector of your chart, opening the way for romance, fun, and pleasure. A more fulfilling approach to love arrives with the New Moon on January 13, when even the most contentious situations in a relationship can lead to a joyful conclusion. Problems can arise with your partner through January 19, since power struggles over the best way to handle family situations can stimulate arguments and hurtful reactions.

Finance and Success
Your ability to emphasize practical elements of a project or plan works to your advantage through January 20. After Mercury enters its retrograde cycle on January 18, technical problems can be the fly in the ointment, stalling progress and frustrating your work environment. Keep track of important data, since losses near the time of the Full Moon on January 28 can cut more deeply than you realize at first.

Cosmic Insider Tip
Insightful ideas about the best way to handle a personnel problem or public relations issue can diffuse big troubles after January 20. Trust your intuition, but keep your documentation, too!

Rewarding Days 3, 4, 8, 12, 13, 21, 22, 23, 30, 31

Challenging Days 9, 10, 16, 17, 17, 24, 25

Affirmation for the Month My choices reflect my true needs.

Virgo/February

In the Spotlight
The planets test your ability to work well with others, particularly if someone else is not pulling his or her weight. It's time to cut your ties to situations that cost more than they are worth.

Wellness and Keeping Fit
Stripping away surface complaints and probing into root causes leads to faster healing. Holistic and alternative approaches can be especially effective. However, just as important will be your elimination of attitudes and habits that undermine your vitality.

Love and Life Connections
Renew friendships, and concentrate more on the unconditional aspects of your close love relationship. This is a time to blend your needs in a complementary harmony with your partner, and to renew your commitment to those who have your heart. The questions you have about your relationship, approach to intimacy, and issues of trust all surface. However, the New Moon inspires greater harmony with others.

Finance and Success
Questions of effectiveness and productivity arise while Mercury retrogrades through February 8. Test and experiment, and work toward final agreements, but keep a close watch on escalating production costs. You may be completing your obligations in a joint financial arrangement, and it's a good idea to give yourself some time before you take on another obligation. Clarify what you expect from partners to avoid losing valuable assets after February 14.

Cosmic Insider Tip
During the Virgo Full Moon on February 27 you may decide that it's time to finally let go of a long-standing association that no longer supports your growth or enhances your life.

Rewarding Days 4, 8, 9, 18, 19, 23, 26, 27

Challenging Days 5, 6, 7, 13, 14, 20, 21

Affirmation for the Month I acknowledge my true needs.

Virgo/March

In the Spotlight

Bold steps toward the fulfillment of a significant goal help you maintain your momentum. Travel, teaching, and publishing are prominently featured as means to achieving your aims. Those who were once your competitors may now want to play on your team.

Wellness and Keeping Fit

Even if you cannot take a full-fledged vacation, squeeze in time to pamper yourself. This is a period of renewal, and by allowing your body time to rejuvenate, you'll add a spring to your step and keep that ever-youthful glint in your eye.

Love and Life Connections

Improvements in an existing relationship arise from exploring your philosophical ideals. A retreat, vacation, or weekend getaway can provide the right setting to strengthen your spiritual bonds with your partner. Watch your expectations, since disappointments can result if you fail to clarify your needs, concerns, or commitments. To achieve the closeness you crave, abandon unrealistic expectations and strive for deeper understanding and trust.

Finance and Success

Contracts and legal maneuverings move along quite nicely until March 12, when mixed signals or hidden loopholes can undermine the entire process. Take things back to the drawing board during the New Moon on March 14, and target completing arrangements before the Full Moon on March 28. Conferences, business travel, and promotional efforts bring positive rewards.

Cosmic Insider Tip

It's time to blend practical ideas with visionary insight. You're the perfect person to spearhead efforts or coordinate activities that will bring people together to accomplish a common cause.

Rewarding Days 3, 7, 8, 17, 18, 22, 23, 26, 27, 30

Challenging Days 5, 6, 12, 13, 14, 19, 20, 21

Affirmation for the Month The principles of truth light my way.

Virgo/April

In the Spotlight

It's a time of celebration, accomplishment, and recognition for your efforts. Gracious actions on your part strengthen your position, but pridefulness can be damaging. The way you handle your success will determine whether or not spiteful challenges result.

Wellness and Keeping Fit

Although excessive risk-taking is not your style, you could be in a situation that spins out of control. Stay safe by watching out for the other guy. Ground your energy by connecting with the Earth.

Love and Life Connections

Your sensuality is awakened, and the right love connection can lead to a bountiful sharing of affection. Mend emotional hurts with your sweetheart, but set reasonable boundaries in situations where you feel a lack of trust. You're in no mood to repeat old mistakes. Clear communication about your needs and desires makes all the difference, and by the time the Full Moon rolls around on April 27, true romance permeates the spaces of your heart.

Finance and Success

Outline your preferences and requirements with those who seek your expertise, since you can sell yourself short if you're not careful from April 1 to 10. Budgets need extra attention during the New Moon on April 12, when it's time to whittle down your debt load and concentrate on profit margins. Professional meetings, conferences, and presentations give your career a boost after April 21, when your abilities are in demand.

Cosmic Insider Tip

Your influence can reach further, but it's knowing where to draw the line that's the tricky part after April 14. Think long-term before you agree to those offers that are rolling in.

Rewarding Days 3, 4, 5, 13, 14, 18, 19, 22, 23, 27

Challenging Days 1, 2, 8, 9, 10, 16, 17, 28, 29

Affirmation for the Month I know what I expect from myself.

Virgo/May

In the Spotlight

With the impact of so much energy filtered through Gemini, you may be wishing you were at least two people! You're probably wearing way too many hats, but after satisfying a long list of obligations, the hat that suits you best is comfortable by the end of the month.

Wellness and Keeping Fit

High levels of mental activity can get in the way of sleep. Decompress at the end of the day with a relaxing herbal tea or a warm bath.

Love and Life Connections

Are your arms getting tired while you try to juggle professional obligations and family needs? Take the weight off by maintaining open lines of communication and delegating responsibilities whenever possible. Your knack for keeping things organized helps you keep your sanity this month. Reinforcements arrive in the nick of time after May 20. They're called "friends." Denying their help could damage your friendship, so say "thanks," and then return the favor when you can.

Finance and Success

All forms of communication—writing, speaking, travel, publishing, etc.—are emphasized. Take advantage of technological assistance when possible in order to broadcast your ideas to the widest audience. Your high profile can make an impact, but careful choices of words is necessary after Mercury turns retrograde on May 15. It's one of those "foot-in-the-mouth" cycles, when your own words can be difficult to swallow.

Cosmic Insider Tip

The lunar eclipse on May 26 can add to the confusion resulting from a breakdown in lines of communication. Step out of the line of fire when you can.

Rewarding Days 1, 2, 10, 11, 12, 16, 20, 21, 25, 28, 29

Challenging Days 5, 6, 7, 13, 14, 26, 27

Affirmation for the Month I say what I mean.

Virgo/June

In the Spotlight
The eclipse of the Sun adds a powerful emphasis to your quest for a sense of fulfillment through your lifework. Communicating a sense of purpose through your career is important, and rewards for your efforts confirm whether or not you're on the right path.

Wellness and Keeping Fit
Increase your vitality by stepping up your fitness routine. Sports or a class at the gym can be fun to share with a good friend. Work with a personal trainer to fine-tune your routine.

Love and Life Connections
Family matters can reach a critical point during the solar eclipse on June 10 and are likely to involve changes beyond your control. In such situations, it's good to remember that the way you respond to these experiences is significant. Love flows into your life in wondrous ways from June 1 to 14. Whether it's a new relationship or a renewal of a long-standing commitment, it's time to let love lead the way. By the time of the lunar eclipse on June 24, romance begins to blossom.

Finance and Success
Your professional connections make all the difference, and relying on others to contribute their expertise pays off—but only if you've clarified expectations. Your efforts could be eclipsed by others who crave the spotlight at any cost, although those who appreciate your talents will know the truth. Consider it a test of your ability to stand up for yourself. Advancement is most promising after June 12.

Cosmic Insider Tip
While Mercury completes its retrograde through June 8, tie up loose ends and reconfirm significant agreements. Then, move forward with new plans after June 11.

Rewarding Days 7, 8, 12, 13, 16, 17, 21, 24, 25, 26

Challenging Days 2, 3, 4, 9, 10, 22, 23, 29, 30

Affirmation for the Month My talents shine brightly in all I do!

Virgo/July

In the Spotlight
Rewards for your efforts continue to bring you into the public eye, and this provides an opportunity to promote a special interest or concern that's important to you. Friends applaud your efforts, and you have a chance to help lift others to deserved prominence.

Wellness and Keeping Fit
Your physical vitality is strongest through July 14, but then your requirements for rest time increase. It's more important than ever to stick with your fitness routine, but complement your busy schedule with ample time out.

Love and Life Connections
Once Venus enters Virgo on July 10, expressions of love and appreciation are more abundant. However, you might discover that there are things about a relationship you simply cannot abide any longer, and could decide that it's time to close that chapter and move on. At the very least, your real needs and desires are clamoring for attention. Show yourself some appreciation.

Finance and Success
A few people failing to pull their weight can throw a monkey wrench in your careful plans from July 1 to 9, but help arrives with the New Moon on July 10. Fortunately for you, regrouping is something you do well. Community efforts can be especially successful from July 7 to 21, and by the time the Full Moon occurs on July 24 you're ready to let your hair down and celebrate your success. Give recognition where it's due, and enjoy that which comes your way.

Cosmic Insider Tip
Your reputation and past accomplishments lay the groundwork for your current success. New directions emerge midmonth, when you can see some of your dreams becoming a reality.

Rewarding Days 4, 5, 9, 10, 13, 14, 17, 18, 22, 23, 31

Challenging Days 6, 7, 8, 19, 20, 26, 27

Affirmation for the Month My hopes light the way toward success.

Virgo/August

In the Spotlight

They say the devil's in the details, and dealing with the fine points and sorting through facts and figures is your main focus this month. You're ready to slip behind the scenes for a well-deserved rest.

Wellness and Keeping Fit

Clear your mind of worry, and explore problems to determine what's really wrong. Regular periods of reflection, meditation, and relaxation are rejuvenating, but failure to listen to your inner voice can leave you exhausted.

Love and Life Connections

There's little doubt that the past can come back to haunt you, and unfinished emotional issues are right on your doorstep. Fortunately, you're ready to leave the past behind so you can regenerate your faith in love. The New Moon on August 8 stimulates your deeper needs and yearnings. This is a time of forgiveness, but it's also a time when you can draw boundaries when they need to be there. That makes you less vulnerable to the emotional "blackmail" that's hovering about midmonth.

Finance and Success

Extra attention to budget matters through August 7 helps you close the books on a project that's now complete. Fresh ideas arrive on August 6, although you might prefer to keep a low profile while you check out the possibilities. Innovations, equipment upgrades, or the help of talented people can enhance productivity through the Full Moon on August 22.

Cosmic Insider Tip

Changes in the hierarchy provide an opportunity for you to improve your work situation, but think twice before you take on new responsibilities.

Rewarding Days 1, 5, 6, 9, 10, 14, 15, 18, 19, 28, 29

Challenging Days 3, 4, 16, 17, 23, 24, 30, 31

Affirmation for the Month I make the most of all my resources.

Virgo/September

In the Spotlight
You're eager to move forward, and have the energy to put your best plans into action. Mars travels in your sign for the next six weeks, activating your courage, drive, and desires. Watch for competitors to challenge your position. Have they underestimated you?

Wellness and Keeping Fit
The great thing about Mars activating your sign is that you're quite driven. The difficult part is that you can be driven beyond your capacities. Set a pace you enjoy, since stress starts to build mid-month and can sap your vitality if you've been pushing too hard.

Love and Life Connections
Expressing your most tender affection strengthens your ties to those you love, but angry outbursts can undo your progress. Explore what's hidden in your heart during the Virgo New Moon on September 7, and search for any resentment or hurt buried there. Enhance a close relationship during a vacation or brief time away, when you can focus your time and energy on one another instead of work.

Finance and Success
Others follow your lead, although you might prefer to just be part of the team focused on getting a job done. Establish priorities that clearly define who's in control, since power struggles can emerge after September 6 and escalate through September 22. To avoid the threat of those who would undermine your position, align with trusted allies whose ideals echo your own.

Cosmic Insider Tip
Mercury turns retrograde for its three-week cycle on September 14—just in time for the chain of command to break down. Extra care is required to keep track of finances and valuable data.

Rewarding Days 2, 3, 6, 7, 10, 11, 14, 15, 25, 29, 30

Challenging Days 1, 12, 13, 19, 20, 21, 27, 28

Affirmation for the Month I follow the path of truth.

Virgo/October

In the Spotlight
Second chances do happen—and often at the best possible time.
You have to determine if you want to step back into an old situation, or if it's time to leave and say good-bye. Either way, reaching
closure in past situations can free you and open fresh pathways.

Wellness and Keeping Fit
Stress increases until October 12, and it's time to lighten your load.
For relief, concentrate on exercises that feature flexibility, but provide a good chance to burn off tension, too. Buried stress will
exhaust your energy reserves now.

Love and Life Connections
While Mars and Saturn square off you may feel that you simply cannot satisfy anybody—at least not without first twisting yourself into
a pretzel. Before you practice such contortions with your emotions,
explore the real issues. Shades of your childhood can echo loudly in
your current relationship. Venus turns around now, and during the
retrograde cycle that starts on October 10 you have a chance to
explore how you truly feel. Talk about your current needs and ability to flex with the challenges.

Finance and Success
Mercury completes its retrograde on October 6, and from October 6
to 11 you can take actions that stabilize your situation at work. Disputes over shared resources can become an issue after October 15,
when it's especially important to be alert to potential deception.
You're most vulnerable to the pitch that sounds too good to be true
after October 24, when good research is your best ally.

Cosmic Insider Tip
Dust off your talents that have been sitting on a shelf for far too
long. You may discover a gold mine!

Rewarding Days 3, 4, 8, 12, 13, 22, 26, 27, 31

Challenging Days 9, 10, 11, 16, 17, 18, 24, 25

Affirmation for the Month I am aware of the effect of my actions.

Virgo/November

In the Spotlight

An exchange of ideas and talents stimulates fresh directions in your lifework. However, your drive to get things done can lead to costly mistakes in the finance department. You're working hard and things are happening, but you may spend as quickly as you earn.

Wellness and Keeping Fit

Build endurance and muscle tone. Those targets for your fitness routine will extend the energy you have to accomplish all the tasks on your long list of things to do. The regenerative effect of bodywork (like massage therapy) is especially noteworthy during the New Moon on November 4.

Love and Life Connections

Romance fares best from November 4 through the lunar eclipse on November 19. A soulful connection inspires you to move toward a lasting commitment, or to renew your promise of love. However, since Venus remains in retrograde until November 21, you may still question whether or not this is what you really want. The real question could be, "What's stopping you?"

Finance and Success

Business meetings spur progress on the career front through November 19. Watch for misunderstandings through November 8, when your approach or methods could confuse those with less experience. Identifying your limits is the task on the financial front, although you still might let impulse get the better of you and spend beyond them. Consider long-term effects to avoid the trap of debt.

Cosmic Insider Tip

The lunar eclipse on November 19 emphasizes your need to reach into the spiritual dimensions of your life. It's time to rise above the ordinary and embrace what is rare.

Rewarding Days 1, 4, 5, 8, 9, 17, 18, 19, 23, 27, 28

Challenging Days 6, 7, 12, 13, 14, 20, 21

Affirmation for the Month I value the ideas of others.

Virgo/December

In the Spotlight

You may accomplish more this month than you've done in the last six months. Everything falls into place behind your careful organization. Or at least the things that count come along quite nicely. The friction comes from those who insist on sticking with tradition.

Wellness and Keeping Fit

Fill your mind with positive thoughts, and explore fun-filled options for fitness. You're ready for a change of pace, and will appreciate the benefits of special indulgences, like a day at the spa. Time away from your hectic tempo keeps your health in prime condition.

Love and Life Connections

Your heart's in great shape this month if you are surrounded by the people you adore. Your desire to show your love leads you to find delightful outlets to express your affection. However, disruptions at home can throw your schedule out of whack during the solar eclipse on December 4. Extra care is required from December 8 to 17, since you could send mixed signals, or might misread what someone else seems to be communicating.

Finance and Success

Whether you're in business meetings, sending out press releases, or online in a chat room, communication is the key to your success this month. Your ideas inspire others to join forces, if you need support. Or, you might be instrumental in bringing people together who can benefit from their mutual exchange of talents and ideas. Investments fare best near the Full Moon on December 19, although conservative actions produce better results.

Cosmic Insider Tip

Your ability to inspire others through your practical vision can open avenues you have not previously traveled. Call it progress!

Rewarding Days 2, 5, 6, 15, 16, 20, 24, 25, 29

Challenging Days 3, 4, 10, 11, 17, 18, 19, 31

Affirmation for the Month I am an excellent communicator.

VIRGO ACTION TABLE

These dates reflect the best—but not the only—times for success and ease in these activities, according to your Sun sign.

	JAN	FEB	MAR	APR	MAY	JUN	JUL	AUG	SEPT	OCT	NOV	DEC
Move											19-30	1-7
Start a class					10, 11					31	1-18	
Join a club							9, 10					
Ask for a raise									6, 7			
Look for work	4-18	14-28	1-11	30	1-14	9-30	1-6					
Get pro advice	16-18	13, 14	12, 13	8-10	5-7	2, 3, 29, 30	26-28	23, 24	19, 20	16-18	12-14	10, 11
Get a loan	19, 20	15-17	14-16	11, 12	8, 9	4-6	1-3, 29, 30	25-27	22, 23	19, 20	15, 16	12-14
See a doctor	4-31	1-3, 13-28	1-11				22-31	1-5				
Start a diet	14, 15	10-12	9, 10	6, 7	3, 4, 30, 31	1, 28, 29	24, 25	20-22	16-18	14, 15	10, 11	7-9
End relationship									20, 21			
Buy clothes	1-3	8-13										9-31
Get a makeover							11-31	1-6	6, 7			
New romance	1-18											
Vacation	21-23	18, 19	17, 18	13-15	10, 11	7, 8	4, 5, 31	1, 2, 28, 29	24, 25	21-23	17-19	15, 16

LIBRA

The Balance
September 22 to October 23

Element:	Air
Quality:	Cardinal
Polarity:	Yang/Masculine
Planetary Ruler:	Venus
Meditation:	I create beauty and symmetry.
Gemstone:	Opal
Power Stones:	Tourmaline, kunzite, blue lace agate
Key Phrase:	I balance
Glyph:	Scales of justice, setting sun
Anatomy:	Kidneys, lower back, appendix
Color:	Blue, pink
Animal:	Brightly plumed birds
Myths/Legends:	Venus, Cinderella, Hera
House:	Seventh
Opposite Sign:	Aries
Flower:	Rose
Key Word:	Harmony

Positive Expression:	Misuse of Energy:
Impartial	Conceited
Artistic	Distant
Gracious	Indecisive
Logical	Critical
Objective	Unreliable
Cultured	Argumentative

Libra

Your Ego's Strengths and Shortcomings

With an easy grace and fair-minded sensibilities, you're a natural diplomat. Others are drawn to your charm and elegance, and you invite dialogue in almost any situation. Your special knack for making others feel comfortable is valuable when you're called upon to be an impartial mediator. In your role as "The Judge" of the zodiac, you can apply your sense of logic and fair play—in your personal or professional life.

Your sense of refinement and love of beauty flow from your natural affinity with the energy of Venus, the planet of love. For you, everything stems from your sense of values, and while you know what you like, reaching the perfect decision can be torturous. Relationships are a high priority, although you may not feel secure about them until you have confidence in your own self-esteem. Measuring your value according to the wishes or desires of others can quickly lead to discontent. But when you apply your sense of relativity to the total picture, you can be more objective and keep everything (and everyone) in proper perspective.

In your attempt to balance the scales between the world surrounding you and your inner self, you can sometimes feel unsettled. Once you find a true sense of harmony with your inner self, that quality easily radiates into the world as a loving, peaceful energy that infuses everything and everyone you touch.

Shining Your Love Light

Although you might feel that life should be more like those steamy romance novels, the reality of your relationships can be more like a book of lessons. Fortunately, it takes more than a heartbreak to quell your desire to find the perfect partner, and once you find a harmonious connection you can develop a relationship based upon equality. The hard part is developing a tolerance for differences and patience with the evolutionary process of love itself. That perfection you seek can require time and patience while love refines and hones your relationship. In the long run, you may well discover that it's the process of loving that keeps your heart singing.

You're an air sign, and that means you crave communication and contact. The other air sign folks—Gemini, Libra, and Aquarius—will understand the importance that communication and social needs have in your life. However, the fireworks may blaze with Aries, your zodiac opposite, since your chemistry together can be phenomenal if you're on a similar wavelength.

With Taurus, you'll share a love for the aesthetic, although your tastes may have wide differences. Gemini's mental gymnastics keep you interested, and you'll enjoy travel and cultural pursuits together. Cancer's nurturing feels nice at first, but telling him or her to "back off" can be difficult if you're feeling overly protected. Leo can be your best friend and most unforgettable lover, since opening your hearts to one another is easy for both of you. Virgo's attention to quality and detail are right up your alley, and you can be everlasting friends whether or not you are passionate lovers.

Another Libra may equally treasure culture and beauty, and you may have a meeting of the minds despite a lack of stability in your relationship. Scorpio's tidal wave can engulf you and erase your personal boundaries; you have to decide if you can handle the intensity. With Sagittarius, the fun and adventure should be ceaseless and there will be plenty to write in your diary about this relationship. Your connection to Capricorn can be the stuff of legends, but control issues can dampen your enthusiasm. Love with Aquarius can encourage you to let go of your inhibitions and open to unbounded acceptance and mutual understanding. Pisces encourages your need to escape, but the emotionality can be overwhelming if you dive in too quickly.

Making Your Place in the World

A career path that allows you to develop your people skills and fine-tune your creativity can be especially fulfilling. You might prefer an artistic career as a designer, artist, costume designer, interior or set designer, decorator, or arts writer. You have a knack for seeing potential and can be successful in fields like counseling, personnel management, or image consulting.

Fields like public relations, politics, advertising, diplomatic service, or sales give you a chance to exercise your diplomacy. Through your social sensibilities and enjoyment of academics, you may go into teaching, the arts, or law. Or you may promote the arts by working in museums, galleries, and conservatories.

Power Plays

As you might suspect, there are at least two sides to the issue of power. On one hand, you realize that holding a position of influence gives you a chance to spark creative change. But on the other hand, you know that you cannot always please others when you assert your will against their own. For this reason, you're happiest in situations where you can work toward humanitarian ideals of justice for all concerned. Serving as witness to abuses of power can be unsettling, but with your balance of logic and diplomacy you can help spearhead revolutionary change. You'll enjoy the process more when you are working alongside others who share your ideals.

Emotionally driven prejudice can throw your balanced perspective right out the window. You can even lose track of your personal ideals if you're working too hard to placate someone else at the expense of your own self-esteem. Learning to be more realistic about your judgment of others and what makes them (or you) important arises as you establish stronger personal boundaries. You know what you like and what you value, and your relationships and work will prosper when you can blend your values with others you respect. The partnership you create with your source helps you build a life that illustrates the truth of love.

Famous Libras

Lorraine Bracco, William Faulkner, George Gershwin, Mark Hamill, Jesse Jackson, Madeline Kahn, Harvey Kurtzman, Rebecca Lobo, Anne Rice, Mickey Rooney, Will Smith, R. L. Stine, Gore Vidal, Christine T. Whitman, Serena Williams, Steve Young

The Year Ahead for Libra

Establishing a secure place within your community and professional sphere strengthens your ability to exert a positive influence. This is the year to refine your abilities, gather educational credits, publish your writing, teach, or join forces with others to make the world a better place. Your personal goals can be more easily answered, but your greatest joy may come from celebrating the successes of those you love. The year 2002 is about travel, learning, and intensified creativity, and marks a time when your heart is singing its most beautiful songs.

With optimistic Jupiter gliding through your career sector until the end of July, you're ready to expand your vocational options. This cycle marks a period of advancement and increased influence. However, it's also a time when your ability to work within reasonable limits will operate to your advantage. Think of it this way: you need to make the most of all your resources and the resources available to you through your work, but waste will expose your vulnerability. Meeting expectations works to strengthen your reputation, but falling short can just as quickly undermine your gains. Beginning in August, Jupiter's influence lifts your spirits and enlivens your goals. Not only can you make tremendous professional strides, but the associations and friendships you build can have a powerful impact in your life for years to come.

Saturn's disciplined energy emphasizes your need to develop your understanding of your philosophies and ideals. In addition, Saturn's cycle this year can aid your ability to concentrate, study, and work toward your aims. While this is a good time to test your belief systems, it's important to avoid dogmatic idealism, particularly if those ideals are uncomfortable or seem to ring as hollow truths.

The slow-moving cycles of Uranus, Neptune, and Pluto have their greatest impact when these planets make an exact connection to your Sun and the planets in your natal chart. The following sections will indicate whether or not these cycles are affecting you more directly. However, these influences can be charted against the backdrop of your life issues and experiences. Uranus and Neptune continue to influence your creative self-expression. Developing your artistry can lift your spirit in ways that move your life in a truly magnificent direction, and opening to true love breathes new life into your soul. Pluto's influence emphasizes your need to learn and to reach out to others with whom you can develop a real meeting of the minds.

The solar and lunar eclipses draw your attention to a need to share your ideas and ideals with others. This is definitely a year when you are reassured that "no man is an island," and when interaction with others can definitely be worth the effort! Along with the eclipses, astrologers study the motion of the nodes of the Moon, and this cycle adds strong emphasis to your need to establish a clear connection to higher truth. You may find that you're sorting through the differences between your beliefs, separating those based on emotional prejudice from those based on ideals that raise you to a higher level. This is the year to let go of convictions that you've adopted to satisfy someone else, in favor of following a path devoted to principles that have real meaning to you as an individual. Further information on the eclipses and their effect on your Sun sign is included in the monthly forecast sections.

If you were born from September 22 to 28, it's the perfect year to fine-tune your special talents and exercise your artistry. Uranus travels in biquintile aspect to your Sun, while Pluto transits in quintile aspect to your Sun. The combination of these two influences indicates a year of rare experiences. Consider this to be a time of serendipity—when your path leads you to situations that can be truly wonderful. If you decide to concentrate more time on artistic projects, you'll benefit from work with someone you consider to be a master teacher. It's also highly conceivable that your own talents will be sought by others, and an opportunity to mentor can be especially meaningful. As a result, you may meet more unique individuals and can establish communications in realms that might have been previously unavailable. Welcome to the true experience of a new millennium!

If you were born from September 29 to October 1, you're probing the question of your life purpose this year while Chiron travels in square aspect to your Sun. Chiron is the comet-like body in our solar system which astrologers study in relationship to multi-dimensional healing. We understand that healing is a multilevel experience, and during a cycle like this you can discover some of the deeper reasons your life may be lacking in certain things. That lack of content can spur you to move forward, but now, obstacles like self-doubt can block your path. The test rests in your need to uncover why you are heading in the direction you've been pursuing—in your work, your relationships, your spirituality, your creativity, and more. Your body can provide you with fascinating clues to your discontent. Physical pain may have physical causes, but probing further can help you discover the spiritual and emotional links which need to be addressed. In the process, you free your soul to take flight into expressions that add tremendous self-empowerment. Consider this a time to ask those ultimate questions, to find some fascinating answers, and to uncover even more questions.

If you were born from October 1 to 5, your imagination and creativity are boosted by Neptune's transit in trine aspect to your Sun. This fascinating cycle can aid you in your quest for inner peace, and helps you melt the barriers that have prevented you from expressing the love that burns in your heart. Whether you choose to express this loving energy through your creativity, within the context of your closest relationships, or in world service, it's an excellent time to exercise your talent to their fullest. Unfortunately, this cycle does not "feel" especially invigorating. In fact, the impulse is more like putting the oars in the boats and drifting. Although limited withdrawal can be beneficial now, disappearing from the scene could work to your detriment. Escapes that take you too far away can dissolve the foothold you've been working to accomplish. However, if you're ready to retire, take a sabbatical, or work in solitude, then this cycle certainly can aid you in such experiences. While Saturn completes its transit in trine aspect to your natal Sun from January through April, your ability to focus and prioritize is strongest. It's during these four months that you can design a plan to give you ample time to escape the everyday hassles, while still maintaining connections that are important to your continued success and security. Then, as the year continues to unfold, you can feel more confident about your temporary retreat from the limelight.

Such times can become the gestation of your most exceptional creative endeavors and spiritually illuminating experiences.

If you were born from October 1 to 7, you may feel that you're a bit out-of-step with the world. Uranus is transiting in a tricky sesquiquadrate to your Sun. The temptation during this cycle is to jump into situations for which you are unprepared. You might, by the grace of the heavens, emerge unscathed. However, you could also injure your reputation or other life elements you hold dear if you take actions without clear forethought. It's important to seek out expert advice in some situations, since your impression of a person or a circumstance may not be accurate.

If you were born from October 8 to 13, you're experiencing a year of regeneration while Pluto travels in sextile aspect to your Sun. This can be an invigorating year—physically, emotionally, and creatively. Travel can play a prominent role in your personal growth, but you can also alter your life by opening your mind to new ideas. Eliminating destructive habits is easier now, and you may also face less resistance from others if you need to make significant changes in your life. This is the perfect year to carve out priorities that give you a chance to take the lead in situations that are most important, or to join forces with others who are pursuing directions you truly appreciate.

If you were born from October 11 to 22, your self-discipline and practicality are awakened while Saturn transits in trine aspect to your Sun. Your attitude toward responsibilities is likely to improve, and you may feel more willing to take on obligations that add stability to your life. Educational pursuits fare especially well, although this can also be an excellent year to start a long-term project. Focus is the key element of this cycle, and the clarity emerging now can add tremendous confidence to your goals. Promotional activities, business travel, and publishing are also featured, and can provide the ingredients to take your reputation to a stellar level.

If you were born from October 16 to 21, your unique talents and abilities come to the forefront under the influence of Uranus transiting in trine aspect to your Sun. Developing your unique abilities is the hallmark of this cycle, since your individuality is what allows you to stand out above the crowd. Romantic relationships can be particularly intriguing this year, and you may feel much more experimental when it comes to love. Polish your artistry, too, since the more you immerse yourself into the creative experience, the more profound your awakening will become. It's your turn to be the trendsetter, and with your good taste and sense of style, you're likely to establish some fascinating and fabulous possibilities.

Tools for Change

With an explosion in consciousness and creativity, you may feel more enlivened this year, ready to take on the world! This is the year to secure the bridge between your mind and universal consciousness, and developing your spirituality may be a top priority. Expanding your grasp of knowledge can be personally gratifying and professionally rewarding, so whether you're enrolled as a student or teaching a class, you'll benefit from the learning that results. If you enjoy travel, an extended journey can become a rich resource, especially if you have an opportunity to immerse yourself in a different culture.

Deliberately seeking joy can be particularly beneficial, and will ultimately fuel your vitality, creativity, and ability to love more fully. For this reason, activities that make your heart sing can not only enhance your happiness, but will also add resilience to your spirit. Unlock your artistry, and if you feel blocked, consider exploring a supportive class or work with a mentor to help you uncover the depth of your creative expression. The path of the artist opens to you now, and if you are reluctant to follow it, the very inhibitions standing in your way are likely to hold the clues to physical disease and emotional discontent. Affirmations can be helpful tools, but you may need to go further. Work with a journal or diary to develop a connection to your inner voice. Alter your environment with music that soothes your soul, and enjoy the shimmering sounds of wind chimes in your personal space.

Simple play can be phenomenally beneficial to your life now, and for this reason spending time with children can awaken levels of laughter you've not felt for years. As you might guess, 2002 is a time to unlock your inner child. However, with your life experience and knowledge, you can serve as a protective guide to the parts of you that remain fresh and innocent. During your periods of contemplation, reach deep into your psyche and find your inner child. Give this part of your spirit space to grow and time to unfold. See yourself as eager, aware, and full of wonder. These are the qualities you're ready to weave into the tapestry of your life experience—with hues of bright, deep, and exceptional color.

Affirmation for the Year

My life is filled with the joy and wisdom of love.

Libra/January

In the Spotlight
As your reputation grows, your talents also blossom. Your resourcefulness makes all the difference, and your ability to keep the peace in awkward or tense situations places you in high demand.

Wellness and Keeping Fit
Consistency with your workout schedule may be difficult to accomplish, but staying active is crucial if you want to keep your energy up. You're in an accident-prone cycle after January 17—but that's no excuse for inactivity.

Love and Life Connections
Communicating what's in your heart is easy, although your forthright expressions can be startling to those who are less certain about their feelings or needs. Start at home during the New Moon on January 13, when quiet acceptance of your differences with others allows peace to settle into your home space. Romance is favored after January 20, and sharing passion with your sweetheart can take your breath away during the Full Moon on January 28.

Finance and Success
Improvements in your work environment enhance productivity from January 1 to 18, although you may have little patience for those who are not doing their part. Clearly defining expectations with your superiors and determining the rules of a situation are crucial elements in helping you maintain your good reputation. Once Mercury turns retrograde on January 18 you may have to retrace your steps in a situation under negotiation.

Cosmic Insider Tip
Imaginative escapes are extremely appealing from January 20 to 30. But if you're going to disappear from the action, take your cell phone along to be sure you're not completely out of touch.

Rewarding Days 1, 5, 6, 9, 10, 14, 15, 24, 25, 28, 29

Challenging Days 11, 12, 13, 19, 20, 26, 27

Affirmation for the Month I am honest about my feelings.

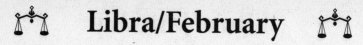 Libra/February

In the Spotlight

Filled with enthusiasm for life, you're attracting positive attention for your ideas and projects. However, this is also an excellent time to work in concert with others toward a successful enterprise.

Wellness and Keeping Fit

Competitive challenges, whether in sports or against a set of personal guidelines, help you maintain your fitness goals. Of course, you'll be more likely to stick with the program if you enjoy it. It's time to put more "play" into your "workout."

Love and Life Connections

The chemistry of love works like a magical elixir from February 1 through the New Moon on February 12, when breathing life into an existing relationship shows you how sweet love can be. However, tension can test your commitment, reminding you that the course of love rarely runs smoothly. A flirtation can be pure enchantment, but unless you're free to pursue it, you'll survive best by playing in the shallow end of the pool. Your ability (or lack of it) to reach into intimate levels of trust is exposed after February 14.

Finance and Success

A second (or third) look at your plans while Mercury completes its retrograde cycle through February 8 helps you uncover the cause of problems. Fortunately, your innovative ideas and ability to attract the right talent at the right time keep you ahead of the game. Pool your resources with others, but carefully define jobs and expectations if you want to maintain momentum through the Full Moon on February 27.

Cosmic Insider Tip

Mercury and Saturn both turn direct on February 8. That means business plans and communication are ready to move forward.

Rewarding Days 1, 2, 5, 6, 10, 11, 20, 21, 24, 25, 28

Challenging Days 8, 9, 15, 16, 17, 22, 23

Affirmation for the Month I attract the help I need.

Libra/March

In the Spotlight

Strife arises over joint finances or disputes involving inheritance or insurance. The nasty part is what you find when you turn over rocks during the necessary research. Don't be surprised if the other side does not play fair.

Wellness and Keeping Fit

An old physical problem can come to the surface, but this is an excellent time to deal with core issues and previously hidden weaknesses. The psychological dimensions of your physical health play a significant role in your healing this month.

Love and Life Connections

Some of the things you discover when you get close to someone are not especially pretty or nice. You have to decide how you're going to handle a situation that may not meet your standards. Open communication is easiest through March 10, but after then you may run into extrasensitive issues that neither of you wants to address. Slow and easy does it, but with the Libra Full Moon building tensions on March 28, you can be much more assertive about your real feelings.

Finance and Success

Legal battles and contract disputes can try your patience, and if somebody's hiding important information or assets then progress bogs down at the wrong time. Keep a careful watch on your spending, and talk over major purchases with your partner before you pull out your credit cards. The social elements of your business demand more time after March 9, but they are important.

Cosmic Insider Tip

Progress on the career front is happening, but there are so many distractions over the power plays that you might miss it. Delegate responsibilities when possible.

Rewarding Days 1, 5, 6, 9, 10, 11, 20, 21, 28, 29

Challenging Days 7, 8, 14, 15, 16, 22, 23

Affirmation for the Month I respect my power.

Libra/April

In the Spotlight

Resistance from others can throw a block in your path where money matters are concerned. The problem may be a difference of style or lack of agreement about priorities. Lower your expectations if you want to avoid frustration, since accordance could take a while.

Wellness and Keeping Fit

Worry is not your friend and can drain precious energy that you could use much more productively elsewhere. Old issues trigger buried anxiety, so this is the time to get to the core of problems.

Love and Life Connections

Your partnership can suffer from the slings and arrows of mistrust unless you deal with issues as they arise. Playing "nice"—pretending you're fine when you're not—can cause more problems than it solves. Open the way for mutual dialogue during the New Moon on April 12, and explore your concerns over serious issues. If you need to fix problems then time away from your regular routine after April 14 can provide a chance to locate the values that bind your hearts.

Finance and Success

Partnership agreements may require fine-tuning in order to accomplish the ultimate from your association. Probe into budgetary concerns from April 1 to 13, with an eye out for any situations that diminish returns on your investment. Schedule promotional efforts, conferences, and presentations after April 13, and invite others you respect to join your team. By April 26 you're attracting excellent support and garnering good reviews for your talents and endeavors.

Cosmic Insider Tip

If anybody can paint the best picture to illustrate the high points of a presentation, it's you. Target April 1 to 4, and then April 25 to 30, as excellent times to take center stage.

Rewarding Days 1, 5, 6, 9, 10, 20, 21, 24, 25, 28, 29

Challenging Days 7, 8, 14, 15, 16, 22, 23

Affirmation for the Month I value the ideas of others.

Libra/May

In the Spotlight

A rosy outlook for May arrives early in the month, raising your confidence and awakening all sorts of possibilities. Update your passport and pack your bags—it's time to travel, explore the world, and make an impact wherever you go!

Wellness and Keeping Fit

A spa retreat or vacation can do the trick, but if you cannot travel consider taking a day or two for special pampering. Holistic health applications can make a huge difference in your vitality.

Love and Life Connections

Nothing puts the zip back into your step like love, and with Venus and Mars doing a sexy rumba around the borders of your heart, you're inspired to dance along. If you're looking for someone new your paths are likely to cross during your travels, or you may meet in a classroom. An existing relationship moves into soulful territory, especially if you take time to talk about your hopes and desires. You may even run into an old lover after May 15. If so, sparks can fly. You have to decide if there's anything left to ignite.

Finance and Success

Despite Mercury's retrograde starting May 15, you're making tremendous headway in your career. Promotional activities and business travel raise your public profile. Legal matters fare best until May 21, but watch details in contracts. The lunar eclipse on May 26 brings an old association to a close so you can move toward different horizons.

Cosmic Insider Tip

A restructuring of the hierarchy occurs this month under Saturn's opposition to Pluto. As a result, you can step into an exceptional opportunity, but you have to be ready!

Rewarding Days 3, 4, 13, 14, 18, 22, 23, 26, 27, 30, 31

Challenging Days 1, 2, 8, 9, 10, 14, 15, 28, 29

Affirmation for the Month My actions are inspired by truth.

Libra/June

In the Spotlight

Work and career can absorb most of your time, with looming deadlines and ample opportunities to prove your merit. The solar eclipse on June 10 emphasizes your need to strengthen your unity with higher values stemming from your spirituality.

Wellness and Keeping Fit

Your health can suffer if you fail to set reasonable limits. Although you may be working late hours, balancing your schedule with adequate rest and exercise is still important if you're going to avoid burnout. Overindulgence takes its toll from June 1 to 14.

Love and Life Connections

Demands from family and parents can shrink your free time, and finding support when you need it most can be difficult. Friends prove to be a valuable resource after June 13, but your real strength comes from your devotion to your spiritual ideals. The key to maintaining emotional stability now rests in defining expectations. Leave room for the unexpected, since the lunar eclipse on June 24 tests your emotional resilience.

Finance and Success

Correspondence, conferences, publishing, teaching, and advertising—these forms of outreach can have a positive impact on your reputation. It's time to broaden your horizons, but without undermining your base. Review your plans while Mercury retrogrades through June 8, and line up your support. Then, during or after the Sun's eclipse on June 10, you'll be ready for launch!

Cosmic Insider Tip

The effects of reorganization and changes in the power base can be destabilizing, but between June 10 to 24 you can make alterations in your priorities that bring true prosperity into your life.

Rewarding Days 1, 9, 10, 15, 18, 19, 22, 23, 27, 28

Challenging Days 4, 5, 6, 11, 12, 13, 24, 25, 26

Affirmation for the Month I know and honor my limitations.

Libra/July

In the Spotlight
Competitive situations may be a challenge, but your talents and abilities shine through. Friends and professional associates provide valuable assistance or support, encouraging you to continue your pursuits. Your influence can also be helpful to someone else.

Wellness and Keeping Fit
To avoid accidents, you may need to be more attentive to what the other guy is doing. However, you can get into hot water on your own by going too fast or diving into a situation unprepared. Avoid high-risk activities, and take a guide along in unfamiliar territory.

Love and Life Connections
A difference of opinion within your family from July 1 to 13 can drive a wedge between you. It's up to you to determine how far you're willing to go to keep the peace. Pull back from the action to buy some time. Conversation on more neutral topics helps heal divisiveness after July 20. Your focus ultimately turns to affairs of the heart, and by the Full Moon on July 24 you're ready for a delightful romantic encounter.

Finance and Success
While you may have to go the extra mile to accomplish your goals from July 1 to 15, your efforts will be rewarded. An innovative plan or idea carries momentum through July 7, although you'll have to show proof of your claims if others are going to endorse your efforts. Conferences or community efforts give your reputation a boost after July 13. Investments show promise after July 24.

Cosmic Insider Tip
Your visionary sensibilities and creative talents are awakened during the Full Moon on July 24. It's a great time to be open to possibilities, but sweeping changes may not be comfortable.

Rewarding Days 6, 7, 8, 11, 12, 15, 16, 20, 24, 25

Challenging Days 1, 2, 9, 10, 22, 23, 29, 30, 31

Affirmation for the Month I am grateful for my life's abundance.

Libra/August

In the Spotlight

Rewards come your way—big time! Energetic Mars and optimistic Jupiter amplify your ability to make your dreams come true, but to get the most from these planetary helpers you have to put forth the effort. The hard part? You have to decide what you want.

Wellness and Keeping Fit

If you've put off getting into that fitness class or meeting with a personal trainer, you can get in step quickly this month and make progress in toning and strengthening your body. The New Moon on August 8 is a great time to get started on a fresh routine.

Love and Life Connections

Playful interaction with those you love can create marvelous memories. A getaway can spark a new love or improvements in an existing relationship from August 1 to 6. Once Venus enters your sign on August 7, romance can move into the top priority, with all those everyday necessities slipping behind. Celebrations with friends and family can be especially enjoyable after August 10, but the Full Moon on August 22 is meant for the sexy stuff.

Finance and Success

You're filled with enthusiasm and can experience advancements in your career that add even more confidence. While you may have to spend extra time at the drawing board from August 6 to 25, it will definitely be worthwhile. You can showcase your talents and still have something simmering on the back burner that takes your reputation further into the stratosphere.

Cosmic Insider Tip

Bring innovations into an existing situation if you want to see the most significant progress. If you do start something fresh, target the period from August 8 to 21.

Rewarding Days 3, 4, 8, 11, 12, 13, 16, 20, 21, 22, 30, 31

Challenging Days 5, 6, 18, 19, 25, 26, 27

Affirmation for the Month My friends are a marvelous treasure.

♎ Libra/September ♎

In the Spotlight

Extra time for reflection helps you deal with feelings of anxiety. You may feel that your past is coming back to haunt you, but there's also a greater potential that unfinished business will demand more of your time. Choose your words carefully.

Wellness and Keeping Fit

Uneasy sleep can result from worry, and a tendency to obsess over your concerns can make matters worse. Relaxation is a must, and releasing tension helps restore your vitality.

Love and Life Connections

Whether you're grappling with issues of trust with your current partner or still reeling from a disappointment that happened in the past, you can rob yourself of joy. It's time to forgive and move on—but this time with knowledge and understanding. After the Full Moon on September 21 you may feel that you've completed a deep emotional clearing.

Finance and Success

Fortunately, Mercury travels in your sign for the next two months. That means you'll be more comfortable with a forthright expression of your ideas. However, since Mercury retrogrades from September 14 to October 6, you may be more indecisive than usual. Concerns stemming from power struggles can escalate after September 18, and if you have a lack of communication in the process, problems can certainly be more daunting. Take time to regroup, rethink, and reconsider.

Cosmic Insider Tip

Watch your spending, since hidden costs can mess with your budget after September 12. Travel can be costly, too—particularly the way the other guy is driving!

Rewarding Days 4, 5, 8, 9, 12, 16, 17, 18, 27, 28

Challenging Days 2, 3, 14, 15, 21, 22, 29, 30

Affirmation for the Month I let go of what I no longer need.

Libra/October

In the Spotlight

Sorting through priorities helps you get back on track, and by mid-month you're sailing toward your goals. Diligent efforts, fine-tuned behind the scenes, work to your advantage until then. Safeguard secrets until you're sure it's safe to bring them into the open.

Wellness and Keeping Fit

An old injury or illness can create physical distress early in the month, but resolutions can come to light during the Libra New Moon on October 6. Focus your self-discipline on eliminating habits that undermine your health.

Love and Life Connections

Sometimes, the perfect moment simply does not present itself. Fortunately for you, once Mars enters Libra on October 15 you're not likely to let such trivial details stop you from going after what you want and need. A festive getaway can be an excellent opening for a change in the romantic atmosphere. During the weekend before the Full Moon on October 21, relationship issues reach their peak.

Finance and Success

It's back to the drawing board, and even though Mercury turns direct on October 6, you may not be satisfied with an idea or product until you can see it in action on October 16. Hidden problems continue to stand in the way of progress, especially if you're attempting to get ahead of the game. But bringing the bones of contention to the table helps you work through blocks and move forward from October 16 to 21.

Cosmic Insider Tip

With Venus in retrograde from October 10 to November 20, you may feel that no matter what you do, you seem to be financially behind the eight ball. It's a great time to re-use, recycle, and restore.

Rewarding Days 1, 2, 5, 6, 19, 10, 14, 15, 24, 25, 29

Challenging Days 11, 12, 13, 19, 20, 21, 26, 27

Affirmation for the Month I make the most of all my resources.

⚖ Libra/November ⚖

In the Spotlight

Finances take center stage, and the value of your time moves up the ladder of things you hold precious. Everything is about resources this month. You're ready to harness what you've got and take a ride along the road to success.

Wellness and Keeping Fit

Build strength and concentrate on toning your body while Mars travels in your sign this month. You can see results in your overall vitality, but also might like the way you look in your clothes. What good is that fabulous outfit if you can't wear it with pride?

Love and Life Connections

Your self-worth gets a workout. Once you get down to it, you may discover that you're looking for someone who really does like you for who you are, not what you own. Since Venus retrogrades until November 21, you'll be testing your relationships to determine if your values match up. The lunar eclipse on November 19 emphasizes intimacy—whether you've got it, or if it's only a myth.

Finance and Success

Coordinate your budget with long-range and short-term goals, and avoid impulse spending this month. Joint finances can be a source of contention until after the lunar eclipse on November 19. Your eagerness and self-confidence go a long way toward helping you accomplish your goals, and after November 19 your connections to experts and talented individuals speed your progress. Business meetings and presentations prove most successful after November 18.

Cosmic Insider Tip

Concentrate your attention on large-scale projects, and seek out opportunities to bring innovations into an existing situation from November 20 to 30.

Rewarding Days 2, 3, 6, 7, 10, 11, 20, 21, 25, 29, 30

Challenging Days 8, 9, 15, 16, 17, 22, 23, 24

Affirmation for the Month I am aware of my words and actions.

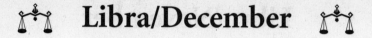 Libra/December

In the Spotlight

The Sun's eclipse lands in your communication sector, turning your attention to the need for clear understanding and agreeable expectations with others. Finances improve, but the temptation to spend beyond your means can drive you crazy.

Wellness and Keeping Fit

Building endurance may be your goal, but your motivation can sag from December 1 to 14. Part of the problem might be all those holiday goodies that seem to be everywhere you go. It's all a matter of portion control. Then you can have your cake and eat it, too!

Love and Life Connections

The warm feelings resulting from getting in touch with those you love can melt old tensions. Reach out from December 1 to 8, with a special effort to mend troubles during the Sun's eclipse on December 4. A pure heart helps, since your intentions shine through. Family matters take top priority after December 9, although you're likely to resist doing things just because someone expects it. However, you may have to compromise, especially where friends are concerned.

Finance and Success

Work out details of contracts and agreements from December 1 to 10, when business meetings also give your reputation a boost. In the spending department, your want list may be larger than your credit line, and investments drift into the uncertain category. If you stick with your budget, you should fare nicely, even though others may try to insist that you take on more than you can handle. Explore your motivations.

Cosmic Insider Tip

Innovative ideas open the way for advancement from December 1 to 6. After that, the tried and true takes the driver's seat.

Rewarding Days 3, 4, 7, 8, 17, 18, 23, 26, 27, 31

Challenging Days 5, 6, 12, 13, 14, 20, 21

Affirmation for the Month I am worthy of the love I need.

LIBRA ACTION TABLE

These dates reflect the best—but not the only—times for success and ease in these activities, according to your Sun sign.

	JAN	FEB	MAR	APR	MAY	JUN	JUL	AUG	SEPT	OCT	NOV	DEC
Move	1-3	8-12										9-31
Start a class							11				19-30	1-8
Join a club								8, 9				
Ask for a raise										6, 7		
Look for work			12-29				7-21					
Get pro advice	19, 20	15-17	14-16	11, 12	8, 9	4-6	1-3, 29, 30	25-27	21-23	19, 20	15, 16	12-14
Get a loan	21-23	18, 19	17, 18	13-15	10-12	7, 8	3, 4, 31	1, 2, 30, 31	24, 25	21-23	17-19	15, 16
See a doctor			12-28					6-25		2-10		
Start a diet	16, 17	13, 14	12, 13	8-10	5-7	2, 3, 29, 30	26-28	23, 24	19, 20	16-18	12-14	10, 11
End relationship										20, 21		
Buy clothes	3-16	13-28	1-11									
Get a makeover								7-31	1-6	6, 7		
New romance	19-31	1-12										
Vacation	24, 25	20, 21	19-21	16, 17	13, 14	9, 10	6-8	3, 4, 30, 31	1, 26-28	24, 25	20, 21	17-19

SCORPIO

The Scorpion
October 23 to November 22

♏

Element:	Water
Quality:	Fixed
Polarity:	Yin/Feminine
Planetary Ruler:	Pluto (Mars)
Meditation:	I achieve mastery through transformation.
Gemstone:	Topaz
Power Stones:	Obsidian, amber, citrine, garnet, pearl
Key Phrase:	I create
Glyph:	Scorpion's tail
Anatomy:	Reproductive system
Color:	Burgundy, black
Animal:	Reptiles, scorpions, birds of prey
Myths/Legends:	The Phoenix, Hades and Persephone, Shiva
House:	Eighth
Opposite Sign:	Taurus
Flower:	Chrysanthemum
Key Word:	Intensity

Positive Expression:	Misuse of Energy:
Healing	Destructive
Sensual	Obsessive
Passionate	Caustic
Rejuvenating	Extreme
Incisive	Jealous
Creative	Vengeful

Scorpio

Your Ego's Strengths and Shortcomings

Your traits of mystery and prolific creativity form an intriguing mix of attributes, endowing you with a tremendous charismatic quality. With a reservoir of curiosity and desire to explore the essential nature of life itself, your ability to uncover what others may only question is unmatched. You do not do anything halfway, and your intense focus helps you reach into the depths of yourself, too. As "The Catalyst" of the zodiac, you have the ability to stimulate healing change.

Confidentiality is important to you, and those who know your secrets are few and far between. Only rarely do you expose the details of your own life and feelings, and then only once you've established a bond of trust. In fact, the tests you devise for those who would share the circle of your life can be quite complex. Your motivation arises from your tremendous emotional sensitivity, and that may be one of your greatest secrets of all. Those who do not know you may feel that you operate with a hidden agenda, when, in fact, you are simply protecting yourself and those you love.

Your ability to be an agent for transformational change stems from your connection to the energy of Pluto. You understand that most situations involve a series of layers, and much of your inner strength comes from your penetrating insights. Your life path is that of the shaman: a journey of regeneration formed through an ability to tread between the worlds of joy and sorrow in search of truth. And the entrance to this path comes from forgiveness of yourself and others, so that you can experience the spiritual rebirth that drives you ever onward.

Shining Your Love Light

Getting close to someone emotionally takes time, since you are not likely to open your heart to just anyone. While your sex appeal and charm can be deliciously enticing, you are very protective of your gentle heart. To unlock the doors to your heart, you will test love long before you trust that it is real. If you are hurt by love, you may have so many layers that it will take a while for a potential partner to penetrate your inner sanctum. However, your ability to surrender to love and allow the pure transformation it can bring into your life inspires you to continue your search for the partner with whom you can build a life.

You are a water sign like Cancer, Pisces, and other Scorpios—and you can be more at ease knowing that you share a tendency to operate on an emotional level. You can feel either powerfully attracted or repelled by your opposite sign, Taurus. If you share a healthy balance of power, you experience steadfast devotion, but you can each be monumentally stubborn when you disagree. You have fun playing teasing games with Aries, but can be dissatisfied if you only scratch the surface. Gemini can be entertaining and witty, although you may distrust her or his inconsistency. Cancer's care inspires feelings of closeness and security, and you may become life-long companions. Leo's magnetism can feel awesome, but the relationship will not last if you feel he or she is too self-absorbed. With Virgo, you can develop an intense friendship that leads to abiding love and passion. You can be at ease with Libra, but may resent feeling that you have to make all the important decisions.

Another Scorpio can be just what you need, but your relationship can run the gamut from extreme passion to volatile power struggles. Sagittarius's self-reliance and fun-loving attitudes are appealing, but only if you do not feel left out. Capricorn can support your desire to achieve your aims and understands your security needs. You may feel strangely at home with Aquarius, but you won't reach the passion you desire if there's too much emotional distance. However, Pisces can be your ultimate lover, stimulating your creativity and desire for romance while providing a source of imaginative inspiration.

Making Your Place in the World

You are an excellent strategist, and will appreciate a career path that requires research, restoration, or creative thinking. You could be well suited to detective work, scientific or medical research, or a career in anthropology, archaeology, or history. You might also be drawn to the healing arts, where you could work in medical fields or as a counselor.

Public service fields such as politics, law, or social services can provide a chance to direct effective changes in society. Or, you might prefer to exercise your talents as a painter, producer, director, performer, or writer—where your artistic outreach can have a healing effect on others. Investment banking, career management, financial counseling, or the insurance industry could also be your cup of tea.

Power Plays

Scorpio and power are intrinsically linked. You can identify true power, but you may shun those who would steal power from others. The idea of the superhero, who could transform in a flash from ordinary person to extraordinary heroine or hero, was fascinating when you were young. As an adult, you know whether or not someone knows how to use her or his power, and hope that others will understand that you, too, have the ability to shape and create your own life. You also understand that some levels of power need to be contained until they are safe or ready for release. That's one reason why you have your secrets!

The ultimate powers of birth, life, sexuality, and death all represent the essence of transformation, and these experience may always intrigue you. Problems arise when you try to hold onto life's treasures, or when you become jealous of others who seem to have what you deeply desire. The essence of healing requires you to release what is no longer needed. From this knowledge you can restore your life when you've experienced loss or pain. Your warrior spirit continually guards you, but it is compassion that drives your ability to bring hope to a world filled with doubt.

Famous Scorpios

Daniel Boone, Barbara Boxer, John Cleese, Nadia Comaneci, Dale Evans, Paul Josef Goebbels, Ethan Hawke, Kevin Kline, Kweisi Mfume, Georgia O'Keefe, Ru Paul, Jane Pauley, Ann Reinking, Will Rogers, Meg Ryan, Rob Schneider

The Year Ahead for Scorpio

Your ideals and visions for the future open broader horizons during 2002, instilling hope during a time of change. While some circumstances beyond your control exert a destabilizing influence, your extraordinary insights allow you to make the most of things. You're leaving behind an old way of life and moving into a more gratifying expression of your true self. As a gift, by the time the year reaches its close, your creativity simply glows from a heart filled with pure love!

Optimistic Jupiter parades through the sector of your chart that's identified with cultural exchange, academic pursuits (like teaching or publishing), travel, and promotion through the end of July. It's time to get the word out and let the world know what you have to offer. In the process, you have an opportunity to learn and may be exposed to influences that add a fascinating dimension to your understanding of the world. You could benefit from a period of spiritual retreat, a sabbatical, or other circumstances that would provide a chance for you to expand your connection to higher mind. Then, in August, Jupiter enters the realm of your career and reputation, and you have an excellent chance to step into positions of influence or to advance a cause that's close to your heart.

The manner in which you handle the resources you share with others is under scrutiny this year, since Saturn continues its journey through this area of your chart. It's time to exercise greater self-discipline in matters of finance—especially the way you deal with indebtedness, taxes, or inheritance. You may find that others are less giving than in the past, especially if you do not see eye-to-eye on money matters, or if there is a power struggle in a close relationship. This test can be disturbing if you try too hard to maintain absolute control. The lesson could be that you have to allow someone else's needs to define priorities for a while.

The cycles of the very slow-moving energies—Uranus, Neptune, and Pluto—are most influential when they make a distinctive connection to your Sun. To determine if this is the year you will experience the impact of these influences, check the sections that follow (defined by your birth day). Uranus and Neptune exert a strong influence in your home and family life this year. Uranus's cycle stimulates disruptive change at home, and can signify a time when your family structure is changing dramatically. Neptune's influence stimulates a deep desire to reach into the space of your soul, and to create a personal environment that nourishes these soul-level needs. The influence of Pluto emphasizes your approach to handling your personal resources, indicating that this can be a significant time to revamp your finances and lifestyle.

The solar and lunar eclipses draw your attention to issues of intimacy. This involves more than sexuality, although sexuality can certainly be part of intimacy. What you are addressing is your approach to trust and close emotional and spiritual connections with others. You may experience a different insight into dealing with transformation, healing or death—when your outreach and support can be helpful to others experiencing transitional changes in their lives. It is the transit of the nodes of the Moon that indicates the soulful and emotional impressions most strongly emphasized, and this year you're uncovering and releasing old fears so you can move forward and heal your life.

If you were born from October 23 to 31, you're experiencing the stimulus of Chiron traveling in sextile aspect to your Sun. The alterations you can bring into your life this year start with a change in the way you think. You're also working toward healing old disappointments and hurts. First, you have to be honest with yourself so you can identify the source, then, with conscious effort, you can begin to chisel away at the restrictive or negative thinking that has resulted. You can see clear evidence of the profound impact the quality of your thoughts can have on the quality of your life.

If you were born from October 25 to November 6, the last six months of this year can be filled with time-consuming tests of your patience. Saturn travels in sesquiquadrate to your Sun beginning in June, when it's important to handle your obligations with great care. Although this cycle will have its full effect until midyear, you may see evidence of it earlier. Relationships can be a hot spot, and differences in the way you handle your resources can be a source of frustration. Or, people who owe you money (or other obligations) may not be repaying you. On a more fundamental level, the essence of this cycle is a test of your commitments. The deeper question can be what holds you to the situations that form the structure of your life. Are you there out of guilt? Or are you there because you want to be? Those situations that demand your time and attention and do not also have your real dedication can drag on for what seems an eternity. Consider it a time when you learn the significance of a promise—including the promise you did not know you had made!

If you were born from October 31 to November 5, you're feeling the illusory influence of Neptune traveling in square aspect to your Sun. Your sensitivity is marked on every level, but your desire to spend more time exploring the intangible experiences of life can be the most noticeable element of this cycle. While Neptune does enhance your imagination and artistry, you may find it difficult to bring your dreams into reality. Escape seems like a good idea, but once you're there, reconnecting to the day-to-day necessities can be difficult, if not impossible! Choose healthy escapes, since destructive choices like drugs or alcohol can easily become abuses or addictions during this time. The significance of this cycle is the invitation to experience a difference perception of yourself and of reality. Delve into your inner sanctum to experience the ecstasy of unity with your higher self, and let go of the restraints that have blocked your ability to surrender. The trouble can arise when you need to deal with everyday matters, or when you have to draw the boundary lines in a relationship. You may only see what you want to see, and fall into denial when it comes to dealing with the cold, harsh facts of a situation. To avoid falling victim to the negative elements of this cycle, devote time and energy each day to finding your center. Ground yourself and locate your focus. In other words, while you have your head in the clouds, remember to keep at least one toe on the ground!

If you were born from November 7 to 11, Pluto is transiting in semisextile aspect to your Sun this year. You are moving onto a different platform, taking steps to transform your sense of self, and eliminating a few negative habits in the process. Think of this cycle as helping to shed a layer of yourself—a kind of soulful "exfoliation" experience. This is the year to clear out your closets, rearrange your pantry, reorganize your files, and get rid of clutter. In some ways, you may feel that you're more vulnerable—and you are. However, that vulnerability arises from the fact that you are letting go of the inhibitions that block you from expressing the essence of yourself. Take small steps. This is not a marathon. It is, instead, a time to invite a healing process that unveils the radiance of your spirit.

If you were born from November 10 to 22, you are experiencing the cycle of Saturn transiting in quincunx aspect to your Sun. This cycle brings limitations, but they are more in the form of detours than an outright impasse in the path. You can feel as though you are moving one step forward, two steps back, and then . . . you have to hop on one leg for a while! This cycle reaches its full impact in June, and will remain in effect for almost twelve months more. However, your obligations will take a larger chunk of your time and energy as you move through the early months of 2002. Extra attention to health concerns is important, since bothersome symptoms can occur in time to alert you to a problem that could get much worse if you ignore it. For that reason, exploring ailments or injuries when they arise can put you in the driver's seat, instead of feeling that your body has taken control of your life. In other areas, explore your approach to work and relationships. You can fine-tune now, and the adjustments you make can bring the best elements of your life into focus.

If you were born from November 11 to 21, you're feeling the unsettling influence of Uranus transiting in a square aspect to your Sun. Unexpected changes are a hallmark of this cycle, particularly changes that happen beyond your control. However, you may also make alterations in your priorities or self-expression which are met with surprise from others. In some ways, this can be a period of rebellion, especially if you've felt inhibited by situations you want to leave behind. The changes you've needed to make, but have resisted, may happen anyway—especially if you've been hanging on for dear life because you are afraid. The answer to that dilemma is to address your fears. Look them squarely in the eye and figure out who's boss. It's time for you to break free, but it's not the best time to try to wipe the slate clean. There's an old saying: "Don't throw out the baby with the bath water." It definitely applies to your life this year. Granted, things are up and down, but you may discover that the roller coaster you're on has some elements of fun associated with it. Just be careful when you step off the ride.

If you were born from November 18 to 22, your special talents can emerge while Neptune transits in quintile aspect to your Sun. It's time to dust off your dreams and fine-tune your abilities. Or, if your inclination is to teach, acting as a mentor or teacher can bring you into connection with a gifted person who will blossom under your guidance.

Tools for Change

To keep a balance between body, mind, and spirit you may have to put forth extra effort this year. The cycles of the slower-moving planets indicate that your physical and emotional stress levels are likely to be more intense, but that you're also accomplishing a great deal. To maintain your focus and momentum, you may also have to do more work on the "inner" level, becoming more attentive to the quality of your thoughts and the nature of your deeper motivations. Meditation can be a powerful tool, but more intensive reflections can bring even greater insight and balance. A vision quest or lengthy spiritual retreat can help you let go of the trappings of the outside world so that you can clarify your spiritual focus. This can be especially helpful if your responsibilities seem to be crowding your creativity.

Take advantage of Jupiter's stimulus, and explore a broader life view by delving into spiritual teachings of the ages. By training your thoughts on wisdom, you can forge a more significant link to your true self. You might also enjoy work with a labyrinth as a means of uncovering the pathway through the transformations of life. Travel can fortify your spirit, too—especially if you have an opportunity to probe a place that holds real intrigue for you.

Since Uranus and Neptune can have a strong impact on your personal environment, you can also benefit from alterations in your personal space that allow your energy to flow more freely. A study of feng shui, or work with a feng shui master, can be the perfect complement to your intuitive insights about what you need to feel comfortable and to attract the greatest prosperity into your life. By bringing the elements of life into balance around you, you'll grow stronger in the face of change. On a physical level, you can alter your chi, or life force, by practicing techniques like qi gong, tai chi, hatha yoga, or the martial arts. Applying discipline to your physical efforts can be helpful, but you also may need to incorporate greater flexibility—mentally, emotionally, and physically.

♏

Affirmation for the Year

I joyfully release the things I no longer need.

Scorpio/January

In the Spotlight
Sparked by an infusion of creative vitality, you're able to dramatically express yourself. The question is whether or not the message is getting across, since illusions may seem to have a more profound effect than truth!

Wellness and Keeping Fit
A goal of increased endurance can be more easily reached through January 17. After January 19 you may be more accident prone, particularly if you're distracted at the wrong time. Focus.

Love and Life Connections
Passionate encounters refuel your faith in a relationship, and romance can be particularly enticing through January 20. Clarify your intentions during the New Moon on January 13, since assumptions can disrupt the smooth flow of communication with others. Your attempts to bring greater harmony into your home life can be met with resistance if someone else has a different idea. Try to keep an open mind and heart.

Finance and Success
Presentations or written communications fare best through January 16, since lost data or skewed information can throw a monkey wrench in the works once Mercury turns retrograde on January 18. Friction with coworkers or a disagreement over procedures can get out of control after January 21, when deception can also be a problem. Extra care with finances is necessary to avoid making a mistake in expenditures. Lost data can be a problem, too.

Cosmic Insider Tip
A tendency to rush can be a real problem from January 22 to 31, when Mars and Jupiter are squaring off and lighting a fire under your impatience.

Rewarding Days 3, 4, 7, 8, 12, 13, 17, 18, 26, 27, 31

Challenging Days 1, 2, 14, 15, 21, 22, 23, 28, 29

Affirmation for the Month I heed my limitations.

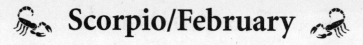

Scorpio/February

In the Spotlight
It's the little things that get on your nerves. If you let them, that is.
Your calm demeanor can automatically defuse some trouble spots,
but otherwise you may need to take breaks from the action.

Wellness and Keeping Fit
Worry can interfere with your rest and can also undermine your
effectiveness at work. Adequate relaxation can be especially helpful, and your nervous system may need extra nourishment, too.

Love and Life Connections
Unsettled situations at home can result from apparently "innocent"
circumstances that turn out to be a real pain. Escalation of tension
around the New Moon on February 12 can upset your need for
peace and solitude, although you can find novel ways to deal with
the problems. Part of the tension could be a need for more cuddling
and fun with your sweetheart, and that can improve dramatically
after February 12. Encounters with close friends can be especially
sweet during the Full Moon on February 27.

Finance and Success
Resolutions to old problems can arise in the easiest way during Mercury's retrograde through February 8. You may simply need to contact the right expert, and that probability looks good from February
4 to 13. Innovations prove their merit following the New Moon on
February 12, when your own ingenuity can also be sought after.
Investments fare best after February 20. However, you'll also gain by
showcasing your talents during the Full Moon on February 27.

Cosmic Insider Tip
Saturn and Mercury turn direct after February 7, when business
deals start to move and progress on agreements slowly emerges.
Concentrate on details that affect long-term goals.

Rewarding Days 3, 4, 8, 13, 14, 23, 27

Challenging Days 10, 11, 12, 18, 19, 25, 26

Affirmation for the Month I attract helpful relationships.

Scorpio/March

In the Spotlight
Relationships take center stage, with a special emphasis on partnerships. Competitive situations can become quite disagreeable if someone's bending the rules. Flexibility is one thing, but you're not likely to turn into a pretzel just because somebody has a power problem.

Wellness and Keeping Fit
A healthy physical challenge can take down that edgy feeling, but be sure you understand the conditions before you dive in. A lack of preparedness can be costly from March 7 to 20, when you'll also do yourself a favor by declining if you know you're not ready.

Love and Life Connections
Mars travels through your partnership zone, lighting fires of discontent and igniting anger. Even though you may have love on your mind from March 1 to 8, unless you're reading and sending the right signals you can end up getting into hot water before you know it. Try again during the New Moon on March 13, when sweet expressions of love help heal the hurt. The little things will definitely make a difference, and your persistence pays off if your heart is pure. It's the last part that's tricky. What do you really want, after all?

Finance and Success
Legal agreements can be more like arguments with nothing but conflict, particularly if the scale of power tips too far to one side. A reasonable contract is possible, especially if you agree on what you hold to be mutually valuable. Explore details after March 12, and try to initiate your project before the Full Moon on March 28.

Cosmic Insider Tip
Old issues are ghosts in the way of progress from March 13 to 17. If you think you've been in this place before, ask yourself if you want to be here again!

Rewarding Days 2, 3, 4, 7, 12, 13, 22, 23, 27, 30, 31

Challenging Days 9, 10, 11, 17, 18, 24, 25

Affirmation for the Month My actions positively influence others.

Scorpio/April

In the Spotlight

Soothing Venus moves in to soften the sharp edges in your relationships, and the benefits of your connections with others are easier to appreciate. Cooperative ventures offer rewards, although you may still be standing in the shadow of someone else for now.

Wellness and Keeping Fit

Extra care from April 1 to 14 can help you stay out of harm's way, especially when it comes to problems caused by the other guy. Later, the psychological dimension of a physical complaint becomes more apparent during the Scorpio Full Moon on April 27.

Love and Life Connections

Your priorities in a partnership can contrast with changing family demands or needs, and if you do not see eye to eye, a split could result during the first half of the month. Funnel your frustration into positive outlets to avoid turmoil, but seek the truth of your own heart first and foremost. Your sensitivity peaks during the Scorpio Full Moon on April 27, when you can finally surrender to the most pressing needs and move on.

Finance and Success

If a contract or partnership is not working out, this is the time to bring your concerns into the open and seek solutions or dissolutions. You may simply need to redefine your roles and expectations, or clarify the direction you now want to pursue. Deception is in the air, and mistrust can undermine the quality of what you're trying to accomplish. Even if faced with deceit, the choice reflecting integrity works to your advantage.

Cosmic Insider Tip

This is a time of renewal for you, when closing out the past is a part of opening the way for future change and opportunity.

Rewarding Days 3, 4, 8, 9, 18, 19, 23, 26, 27, 28

Challenging Days 6, 7, 13, 14, 15, 20, 21

Affirmation for the Month I am honest about what I truly need.

Scorpio/May

In the Spotlight

Research can expose a number of things previously unseen or misunderstood, and might even send you in a different direction. Travel light—you are likely to return with more than you anticipate.

Wellness and Keeping Fit

Surface solutions will not suffice, since you're eager to get to the core of physical distress and deal with it once and for all. Extract or eliminate problems, but watch a tendency to cut too deeply from May 7 to 14.

Love and Life Connections

Intimacy is the issue, as trust and vulnerability are especially complex this month. Your current situation may contrast sharply with a past circumstance that left you hurt, but the triggers still leave you feeling exposed during the New Moon on May 12. Explore your real feelings, and look carefully at the circumstance and needs you have now. Concentrate on the spiritual elements of your relationship after May 21.

Finance and Success

Shared resources can allow you a measure of security while you adapt to changes in a market or work situation. Clarify expectations before Mercury turns retrograde on May 15, since vague agreements will work against your best interests. Conferences or promotional events broaden your horizons after May 20, and open the way for another successful venture later this summer.

Cosmic Insider Tip

With Saturn and Pluto in opposition, it's crucial that you evaluate your resources in the current economic climate. Changes in the structure can lead to success, but you'll need to be flexible.

Rewarding Days 1, 6, 7, 15, 16, 20, 24, 25, 28, 29

Challenging Days 3, 4, 10, 11, 12, 18, 19, 30, 31

Affirmation for the Month I understand what others need from me and know what I can and cannot give to them.

Scorpio/June

In the Spotlight

Rewards for your efforts lift you onto a brighter horizon, and your confidence grows as a result. Promotional efforts bring fabulous results, but you may also see a spiraling success of your top-drawer project. It's time to enjoy the limelight.

Wellness and Keeping Fit

Staying active pays off, but you may not feel like pushing beyond your limits. That's okay—as long as you don't give in to overindulgence that can blow your diet or routine. Consider taking a vacation, or blend business and pleasure travel when possible.

Love and Life Connections

Your travels can open the doors of your heart, or you may still be riding high from an affair kindled late last month. Venus, Mars, and Jupiter join forces to help you trust the love you feel. Ask yourself: "If not now, when?" Action during the Sun's eclipse on June 10 can blast your inhibitions out of the water, but it's time spent basking in the perfect ambience of romance that brings a promise during the lunar eclipse on June 24.

Finance and Success

Renew negotiations or get back in touch with a business associate to reach closure while Mercury retrogrades until June 8. You may be able to put the finishing touches on an agreement or reassure others that you definitely mean business. Then, after June 10, you'll be ready to get started on a new project or take advantage of that extra publicity coming your way. Remember your friends while you're basking in the glow of success.

Cosmic Insider Tip

An offer made from June 20 to 23 may be less substantial than it appears. Let your intuition help you navigate uncertain pathways.

Rewarding Days 2, 3, 12, 13, 16, 20, 21, 25, 26, 29, 30

Challenging Days 1, 7, 8, 14, 15, 27, 28

Affirmation for the Month Truth lights my way.

Scorpio/July

In the Spotlight

Recognition in your career field continues to grow, and your influence increases. All means of broadcasting, travel, publishing, and teaching can work to your advantage. Take advantage of associations with professionals you respect.

Wellness and Keeping Fit

Stay strong by toning muscle and increasing endurance through July 13, when work with a trainer can also be especially effective. Then, concentrate on stress relief through activities like massage, meditation, and focused relaxation as a regular element of your day.

Love and Life Connections

Sometimes good things create conflict, especially if your heart pulls you in two directions. You might desire one person, but have a more meaningful connection to another. Explore the spiritual essence of your connection during the New Moon on July 10, when your higher needs help you clarify what's best. Then, when the Full Moon arrives on July 24, you may not be in such turmoil that you alienate the one you truly love.

Finance and Success

Your ideas or creative products garner an enthusiastic response and can place you and your talents in demand. Disruptive factors can be unsettling from July 1 to 10, but may simply be a result of bringing everything together. Launch a project or campaign, or allow yourself to be in the public eye more often after July 10. Then, after July 25, allow ample time to reflect on your success, study the reviews, and then withdraw to regroup for your next endeavor.

Cosmic Insider Tip

Your ability to show the best you have to offer is powerful from July 8 to 23. After that, competitors could shake your confidence.

Rewarding Days 9, 10, 13, 14, 17, 18, 22, 27, 28

Challenging Days 4, 5, 11, 12, 24, 25, 31

Affirmation for the Month I am confident in my abilities.

Scorpio/August

In the Spotlight
Define expectations, particularly in career matters. Contracts are a good way to accomplish this, but you have to know what you want before you agree. Assumptions and handshakes may not be the best indicator of commitment.

Wellness and Keeping Fit
Define your limitations, particularly in unfamiliar activities or situations that involve extra risk, if you want to avoid injury or setbacks. You're most vulnerable from August 1 to 6.

Love and Life Connections
Family tensions can be worrisome, although the biggest problem can be trying to satisfy the requests on the family front. Stormy circumstances call for an evenhanded response, since a knee-jerk reaction can stir up more trouble. Your vulnerability is most evident during the Full Moon on August 22 when arguments result if you're not playing the game. Maybe it's time to sit on the bench and watch the action—especially if it's not your fight anyway.

Finance and Success
Competitors rattle their sabers, but it might not be worthwhile to step into the arena. Define your goals and find out what your superiors or customers want from you before you change your strategy or alter your priorities. From August 6 to 14, consult with trusted experts about budget plans for your upcoming projects, and then look into costs of improvements before you move forward. Conservative attitudes prevail after August 18.

Cosmic Insider Tip
Information dredged up from the past makes headlines midmonth, but it may not have a significant impact on your reputation. Just think twice before you start slinging mud!

Rewarding Days 5, 6, 10, 14, 15, 18, 23, 24

Challenging Days 1, 2, 7, 8, 20, 21, 22, 28, 29

Affirmation for the Month My goals reflect my real needs.

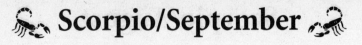 Scorpio/September

In the Spotlight
Fortune smiles your way, since Venus moves into a four-month trek in your sign. Your artistry is strengthened, and your marketability also improves, but you can lose momentum later in the month if you spread yourself too thin. Saying "no" can be the biggest test.

Wellness and Keeping Fit
Team sports or a fitness class can be just the right motivation to move you to a more efficient fitness level. You may push past your limits after September 20 if you become too caught up in the action and forget that your body can only do so much.

Love and Life Connections
Time spent with friends can be truly marvelous, and may lead to a deepening of love. Now you can transform your resistance and open to the music of your heart more easily. Tune in during the New Moon on September 7 to uncover your true feelings, and explore possibilities that were previously not available. Since Venus enters Scorpio on September 7, you'll be able to put your best face forward.

Finance and Success
Your professional associations add strength to your plans. Political activities step up a notch, and unfair or inaccurate information can surface after Mercury turns retrograde on September 14—so stay alert. Offer a more attractive alternative by focusing attention on the opportunities presented by following a different path or strategy. Your choice of the high road makes a huge difference in public opinion by the time the Full Moon arrives on September 21.

Cosmic Insider Tip
Excessively idealistic or unrealistic actions taken from September 15 to 25 can have troubling consequences. Careful research may be your only protection.

Rewarding Days 2, 3, 6, 7, 10, 11, 14, 15, 19, 20, 29, 30

Challenging Days 4, 5, 16, 17, 18, 24, 25, 26

Affirmation for the Month I know those I can trust.

Scorpio/October

In the Spotlight
Despite good times, caution with spending works to your advantage, since instability clouds the picture this month. The same is true about time obligations—anything you consider a resource may have to stretch further than you anticipated.

Wellness and Keeping Fit
Evaluate your health needs and set up a plan that will add endurance and elevate your mental focus. Nutritional support for your nervous system helps. Then, after October 16, incorporate more time for rejuvenation into your schedule for a few weeks.

Love and Life Connections
Restrictions or inhibitions in a close relationship test your feelings, and may lead you to change your focus. Once Venus turns retrograde on October 10, you may have more questions than answers about your love life. While the dream of escape can seem like a good idea, you'll benefit from exploring what's in your heart and taking steps to let go of what you no longer need. What are your concerns, and how is fear blocking you from knowing love?

Finance and Success
Those skid marks on the road toward your success can come from a withdrawal of support from a partner or investor. Reconsider your options while Mercury goes retrograde (through October 6), and then connect with proven allies to solicit their advice. Then, after October 24, you'll be ready to fine-tune and quietly build up another platform.

Cosmic Insider Tip
Saturn turns retrograde on October 10, and your economic picture can be altered as a result. Explore your obligations and trim where you can, since heavy debts now can inhibit your creativity.

Rewarding Days 3, 4, 7, 8, 12, 16, 17, 26, 27, 31

Challenging Days 1, 2, 14, 15, 21, 22, 23, 29, 30

Affirmation for the Month I joyfully let go of what I no longer need.

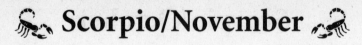 Scorpio/November

In the Spotlight
Things are looking up as Mercury and Venus in your sign support your ability to get your message across. This can be especially significant in your relationships, since making connections through a meeting of hearts and minds can be a wondrous thing, indeed.

Wellness and Keeping Fit
Your need for extra rest continues. You need to budget your time and energy so that you're not exhausting your reserves, and you will benefit from a vacation or change of pace.

Love and Life Connections
Mixed signals or misleading communication can be confounding from November 1 to 8. You may just need a little time apart, or more privacy in your daily routine. Clarify your needs on November 4 and 5, when honesty works much better than "protecting your feelings." What once worked may now be purely irritating, and you may have little patience for situations that have grown intolerable. The real test of a relationship comes during the lunar eclipse on November 19, when the balance of power becomes more apparent.

Finance and Success
Back at the drawing board, you're refining plans and exploring directions that are better kept secret until you can see how to market them. Put out feelers after November 4, but keep significant details to yourself until you're sure the coast is clear. Promises of support may be there, but situations that are not yet clear can still hamper progress. Besides that, once you've completed "tweaking" your project, you may have a different strategy altogether!

Cosmic Insider Tip
Since Venus continues its retrograde until November 20, you may be more conservative about long-term commitments.

Rewarding Days 1, 4, 5, 8, 9, 13, 14, 23, 24, 27, 28

Challenging Days 10, 11, 18, 19, 20, 25, 26

Affirmation for the Month I am mindful of my honest intentions.

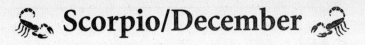 Scorpio/December

In the Spotlight
Your drive to accomplish your aims is fueled by the power of Mars and Venus. The joining of these forces in Scorpio marks an exceptional period of accomplishment created through the passion of your heart.

Wellness and Keeping Fit
You'll be glad you've taken a rest, since this month is about going and going. Fortunately, Venus helps calm the pace of Mars, and your drive can be softened by an intensified awareness of what makes you feel good. Do more of that.

Love and Life Connections
The lovers dance has you in the spotlight, and while Venus and Mars tango in Scorpio, your love life simply glows. If you want it to, that is. You might decide that you prefer to funnel this energy into your life work, your children, or your spiritual path—and even so, you can still enjoy the fruits of pure joy. If you've depleted that storehouse of joy, this is the time to replenish it, with ample amounts to share with those in the circle of your life. Celebrate!

Finance and Success
Your talents shine, and drawing others into projects that stem from your creative vitality leads to success. Finances improve, partly from the generosity of others, but mostly from the value of what you have to offer. Seek advancement, or petition the powers that be for a raise, after December 15. Meanwhile, invest your returns in your business to continue growth well into next year.

Cosmic Insider Tip
The solar eclipse on December 4 marks a time of insight about your personal values. Your self-esteem can improve, because you're willing to acknowledge just how special you are.

Rewarding Days 1, 2, 5, 6, 10, 11, 20, 21, 25, 29, 30

Challenging Days 7, 8, 9, 15, 16, 22, 23

Affirmation for the Month I am worthy of the love I need.

Scorpio Action Table

These dates reflect the best—but not the only—times for success and ease in these activities, according to your Sun sign.

	JAN	FEB	MAR	APR	MAY	JUN	JUL	AUG	SEPT	OCT	NOV	DEC
Move	4-17	13-28	1-11									
Start a class	1-4, 13	9-12					10, 11					9-31
Join a club									6, 7			
Ask for a raise											4, 5	
Look for work			29-31	1-12			22-31	1-5				
Get pro advice	21-23	18, 19	17, 18	13-15	10-12	7, 8	4, 5, 31	1, 2, 28, 29	24, 25	21-23	17-19	15, 16
Get a loan	24, 25	20, 21	19-21	16, 17	13, 14	9, 10	6-8	3, 4, 30, 31	1, 26-28	24, 25	20, 21	17, 18
See a doctor			29-31	1-12				27-31	1-30	1, 11-30		
Start a diet	19, 20	15-17	14-16	11, 12	8, 9	4-6	2, 3, 29, 30	25-27	21-23	19, 20	15, 16	12-14
End relationship											19, 20	
Buy clothes			12-28									
Get a makeover									8-30	1-5	4, 5, 21-30	1-31
New romance		12-28	1-7, 13, 14			11-13	9, 10					
Vacation	26, 27	22, 23	22, 23	18, 19	15, 16		5, 6		2, 3, 29, 30	26, 27	22-24	20, 21

SAGITTARIUS

The Archer
November 22 to December 21

Element:	Fire
Quality:	Mutable
Polarity:	Yang/Masculine
Planetary Ruler:	Jupiter
Meditation:	All things in harmony are possible.
Gemstone:	Turquoise
Power Stones:	Lapis lazuli, azurite, sodalite
Key Phrase:	I understand
Glyph:	Archer's arrow
Anatomy:	Hips, thighs, sciatic nerve
Color:	Royal blue, purple
Animal:	Fleet-footed animals
Myths/Legends:	Athena, Chiron
House:	Ninth
Opposite Sign:	Gemini
Flower:	Narcissus
Key Word:	Optimism

Positive Expression:	Misuse of Energy:
Philosophical	Condescending
Adventurous	Preposterous
Jovial	Opinionated
Broad-minded	Self-righteous
Exuberant	Extravagant
Wise	Irreverent

212 • Llewellyn's 2002 Sun Sign Book

Sagittarius

Your Ego's Strengths and Shortcomings

For you, life is all about the quest. Your plucky spirit shines brightly in your work, relationships, and optimistic attitude. While you may invite excitement in your role as "The Adventurer" of the zodiac, it's your desire to uncover truth that keeps your fiery enthusiasm alive. In your heart of hearts, you know that you can make your dreams come true. Your desire to do what's right invites support from others, although your candor can be disarming to those who prefer to maintain strict control.

Your fascination with the diversity of life can lead you to explore different cultures, languages, and philosophies. Asking questions is part of who you are—as anyone who's known you since childhood will confirm! Whether you learn through travel, study, reading, or interactive communication, you have a great appreciation for the many textures of humanity. While your soul and spirit reach out, you also discover plenty of joy. In fact, your jovial nature is an outpouring of the energy of Jupiter, your planetary ruler. Through your natural sense of expansion, your flights of hope reach the outer limits. This allows you to grow spiritually and encourages you to develop your connection to higher consciousness.

The problem is knowing when to stop. In fact, setting limits can be difficult—you tend to think in terms of possibilities instead of limitations. It's easy to promise, since you prefer to be as generous as possible with your time and resources. But it can be difficult to fulfill those promises if you're overcommitted. To strike a balance between your visionary ideals and the limits of reality requires a profound grace inspired by your connection to divine wisdom. After all, you—of all people—know that you are not alone.

Shining Your Love Light

True love: it may be the most intriguing of all your life quests. Although you adore feeling free and easy, the pleasures of sharing life with a companion whose ideals are as powerful as your own can be incomparable. The power of love gives you the courage to open your heart, even if you've been disappointed in your search for love.

As you explore, your sense of self matures, and you will find it easier to become a steadfast partner who understands that love provides a truly remarkable freedom of expression. From there, the rest is easy!

Since you're a fire sign, you might feel most inspired and at-ease around other fiery individuals—Aries, Leo, and Sagittarius. Your attraction to Gemini, your zodiac opposite, can be tremendously exciting, although establishing trust and understanding can require more patience than either of you are willing to give. With Aries, sharing the passions of your heart can lead to a deep and exceptional love. Taurus can provide healing comfort, but you may feel that your timing is off in your relationship. You can be intrigued by Cancer's safety net, but will resent feeling overprotected. With Leo, you can feel extremely alive and may share a blissful journey if your ideals are harmonious. Being around Virgo is fascinating until all the lists of proper procedures appear.

Libra can be your dear friend and a cherished lover. Be on the alert for Scorpio's allure, since you can be overcome and may feel trapped before you're ready to commit. Another Sagittarian who respects your ideals and shares your enthusiasm for life can be perfect—as long as you can both stay in step with one another! You'll find Capricorn's steadfast security inviting, but if you feel too controlled you may bolt and run at the first chance. Aquarius understands your need for freedom, and you admire his or her unmatched individuality. Pisces mystical manner definitely intrigues you, but you may tire of guessing games if there are too many mixed signals.

Making Your Place in the World

Just a "job" may never satisfy you. You need a career that fulfills a mission, and you measure success through your sense of enthusiasm and the feeling that you are developing yourself and your talents through work. Your ability to inspire and influence others through writing or speech can be used in fields like politics, law, the ministry, promotional activities, advertising, or diplomatic service. Intellectual challenges may be welcome, so a career in fields like journalism, writing, travel, broadcasting, or teaching can encourage you to continue to learn.

In business, you might find speculative investments, banking, real estate, or sales enjoyable and lucrative. The entertainment business may be right up your alley. Or, you might also excel in sports, and you can be an excellent promoter or agent.

Power Plays

You can get caught up in the active philosophical exercise of defining power, and know that power and liberty are inextricably linked. Such ideals inspire you to take risks that would send others running. The freedom to think and act in accordance with higher principles is part of your life quest, and human liberty is a precious commodity. Whether you dedicate your work to such ideals or simply live your life in accordance with meaningful principles, you're in it for enlightenment. Truth always shines the most brilliant light, even when it's hard to take. That can be especially notable when you're dealing with prejudicial ideas or beliefs—your own, or someone else's.

Your search for wisdom helps you keep an open mind. And it's the puzzle of the nature of abundance that can be most intriguing. Through sharing your bounty with others you uncover the essence of prosperity clothed in pure joy. Part of your continual study, writing, teaching, and travels is based on your desire to realize truth. As a result, you may discover that you have become an architect of a peaceful and prosperous future among all humankind.

Famous Sagittarians

Christina Applegate, Tyra Banks, Dave Brubeck, Thomas Daschle, Judi Dench, Brendan Fraser, Amy Grant, Bo Jackson, G. Gordon Liddy, Leonard Maltin, Donny Osmond, Cathy Rigby, Charles Schumer, Leslie Stahl, Jon Stewart, Lee Trevino

The Year Ahead for Sagittarius

Get ready for launch! Filled with fresh inspiration, you're eager to experiment with possibilities and explore different options. The universe does, of course, require that you file a flight plan before you head off into the wild blue yonder. Your focused effort can make all the difference, and by shouldering your responsibilities you'll move further, faster. From there, the journey has a lot to offer. This can be your year to set your dreams on cruise control and enjoy the ride.

The cycle of Jupiter, your planetary ruler, brings growth from your association with a partner from January through August. This is also an excellent time to explore some of the emotional issues left over from your past. As you open your soul and air your grievances, you may very well discover why you've run into problems with trust. One of the challenges of this cycle can be the manner in which you express your gratitude toward others, since taking unfair advantage of the good graces of others can be costly on several levels. From August through December, Jupiter travels in a more harmonious connection to your Sun, opening the way for rewarding educational opportunities, travel, cultural pursuits, and spiritual quests.

Saturn's travel continues its opposition to your sign—stressing the importance of mutual responsibility in your social and intimate relationships. Obligations you've undertaken in the past will demand more of your attention. This is definitely not the time to procrastinate, since you could delay progress unnecessarily. It's more a test of your ability to address the reality of your life situation and to accept the tasks in front of you. Obstacles in your path can be tests of your patience and ingenuity, but do not necessarily mean that your journey is over!

The slower-moving planets—Uranus, Neptune, and Pluto—continue along the same paths as last year. Uranus's awakening energy stimulates your mind and invites you to explore a different approach to the way you process information. Whether you're finally getting into the technology revolution or inventing new

216 • Llewellyn's 2002 Sun Sign Book

gadgets yourself, this is the time to give your ideas plenty of room to develop. Neptune's visionary qualities further emphasize a potential for enhanced awareness and imaginative communication. Pluto is now midway through its cycle in Sagittarius, offering opportunities for personal healing and self-empowerment.

The solar and lunar eclipses are also especially significant for you during 2002. The solar eclipses in the signs of Gemini (June 10) and Sagittarius (December 4) indicate a year filled with crucial developments. If you've been waiting for a breakthrough or an end to a drawn-out situation, then this is likely to be the year when the tides turn. Your challenge may be to strike a positive and healthy balance in your relationships, or to address your deepest feelings about your current relationship (or lack of one!). The transit of the Moon's nodes helps you reach into your deepest motivations so that you can feel more self-assured when you make life-altering choices this year.

If you were born from November 22 to 28, this is a year of soul-searching and a great time for personal reflection. Your questions reach a point of clarity during the lunar eclipse on May 26. However, the clarity does not come overnight during the eclipse! From January through May, you may feel that you're making a series of adjustments in the way you handle your resources, since Jupiter is traveling in quincunx to your Sun. This is the time to extend true gratitude to those who've made a difference in your life. On a personal level, consciously making the most of your time, money, and energy can have a huge impact. In fact, you may move from pinching pennies to counting your blessings this year! The reason? From August through October there's a change in the cosmic currents, with Jupiter transiting in trine to your Sun. To make the most of these cycles, give yourself ample time to seriously consider your true needs during May and June, when the influence of the Moon's eclipse is strongest.

If you were born from November 28 to December 4, you're experiencing a year of powerful creativity and imagination while Neptune transits in sextile to your Sun. It's time to let go of your resistance and allow your spirituality to light your way. In the process, you can take advantage of the stimulus to forgive, releasing the burdens of guilt or resentment so your spirit can fly free. This cycle lasts all year, and even extends into the year 2003 for a while. The greatest impact can be your rediscovery of your hope and faith. It's like finding the wind beneath your wings! Just in case you wonder if your tests are done, you are still dealing with the final challenges of Saturn's opposition to your Sun. However, this is most intense from January through April, when trial and testing are most noticeable. If you have not yet completed a significant project, then these four months are the time to buckle down and get it done. It's an excellent time to teach or learn, too, so academic pursuits can be very meaningful. The universe provides a special gift for you from October through December, when Jupiter transits in trine aspect to your Sun. Plus, the solar eclipse on December 4 falls right on your Sun, marking a time of rebirth and fresh directions. In a nutshell, if you're paying attention and putting forth an honest, dedicated effort, you can move from a period of restraint to a period of newfound freedom!

If you were born from December 2 to 8, it's time to dust off your talents and put them to good use. Uranus is traveling in quintile aspect to your Sun. Although this cycle can be subtle, if you're listening to your inner voice you will definitely know it's happening. Since you may have more self-discipline due to Saturn's opposition to your Sun, it can be the perfect time to fine-tune your skills. Or, you might find it an excellent year to work with a mentor to help you develop your abilities to their fullest. If you're at a stage in your life when your expertise is well established, discovering new techniques or utilizing innovative technologies can make a huge difference in your creativity. You may also be the one guiding someone else, and can attract truly gifted individuals.

If you were born from December 5 to 12, you're experiencing a once-in-a-lifetime cycle while Pluto transits in conjunction to your Sun. This is a very slow-moving cycle, and you've already felt some of the changes during the last year. That powerful stimulus to clear out all the clutter in the way of your progress is a very noticeable element of this cycle. Even more important, the influence of the transformations you're making this year can have a lifelong impact. One interesting element of this cycle is the kind of "stuff" that rises to the surface. All the things you've swept under the carpet are peeking through a well-worn hole. At the most profound level, this is a period of healing—when the circumstances in your life that drain your vitality need to be eliminated. From April through June, you're also feeling Saturn's drag on your energy while it transits in opposition to your Sun, and it is the combination of these two influences that can truly test your resolve. Physical challenges can be a test, but the underlying emotional and spiritual issues may be the most taxing—until you uncover them, that is. If you're stuck in a circumstance that is simply not good for you, it can become extremely difficult. But remember this: you do have choices about the way you handle the challenges of this time. Think of this as a period of spiritual, emotional, and physical purging. You're simply eliminating extra cargo so you can soar more freely and land with greater certainty!

If you were born from December 10 to 21, it's your year to break out of your inhibitions and let your individuality shine. Uranus is transiting in sextile aspect to your Sun, stimulating your need for independence. Your intuitive sensibilities can also be strengthened during this cycle, and trusting that special sense of things can make a huge difference in your life choices. But there's a monkey wrench in the works: from June through December, Saturn is also transiting in opposition to your Sun, testing your motivation and dishing out some extra responsibilities. For this reason, you'll do yourself a favor by not burning all your bridges while dancing to your freedom song during the first half of the year. Better yet, check to be sure you're not still standing on a bridge before you drop the torch! You may need to break away, but you're being tested to determine if you're balancing responsibility with liberty. It's a true Sagittarian test, since your natural motivation is to ride into the sunset without looking back. Just as important is an examination of your fears, since the other side of the challenge is to determine why you're holding back (if you are). Either way, your life direction may change. You have to determine how much to pack for the journey!

Tools for Change

There's a lot changing around you, but it's only a reflection of the tremendous shifts in your energy and focus. Physically, you may feel a bit tired this year, since Saturn's influence can bring an element of stress and tension. First things first: address your physical needs. Item One is to maintain your flexibility while you work toward extending your endurance. There's no way around it: exercise is crucial. It's a great year to work with a physical therapist, personal trainer, or instructor, and to consult with a nutritionist to help you tailor a program that suits your specific needs. To help you clear your energy, confer with an expert in body energetics. Techniques like acupuncture can help you get your energy flowing again, but you might also enjoy massage therapy as a means of releasing those tight muscles.

You're also ready to explore innovative or alternative approaches to enhancing your mental function. Add a nutritional boost to your mind by including plenty of foods high in B-vitamins and omega-3 fatty acids. Challenge your brain with mind-bending games. Reach into the recesses of your consciousness by exploring a labyrinth. Work with tuning forks to alter your physical, spiritual, and mental vibration. All these tools help you break out of the impact of everyday stimulus, and help you keep your energy open.

During your meditations, you'll benefit from going into the depths of your psyche. To get a sense of the experience, you might enjoy spelunking (exploring caves and caverns). Study the myth of Persephone—the maiden abducted into the underworld—and her personal transformation. You're experiencing something similar on a spiritual and psychological level. While you may want to soar above the clouds, you'll go further if you're discovered the treasures buried in the depths of your consciousness. This is no time to wade in the shallows!

Affirmation for the Year

I am filled with pure inspiration.
Each step I take is guided by the light of wisdom.

🏹 Sagittarius/January 🏹

In the Spotlight

Despite some friction at home, you're thinking about the future and moving ahead. Finances need extra attention, even though your resources are growing. The connections you make this month and planning you do now can set up a secure future.

Wellness and Keeping Fit

Keep your attention on what's in front of you, since accident-prone elements can be a problem from January 1 to 17. To boost your energy, get started on a new fitness schedule after January 21.

Love and Life Connections

Address long-standing issues, since this is the time to clear up misunderstandings or make necessary apologies. Your heart's on fire with passion after January 18, when a journey can lead to true love. An existing relationship can deepen, especially if you make time to break away from routine and focus on your shared interests. But if you're free to explore a new connection, the skyscape paints a rosy picture for meeting someone special after January 20.

Finance and Success

Put your head together with an expert in your field to break past barriers in a negotiation or presentation. Even if you're the one on the front lines, you'll go further armed with a solid network of talent and advice. Mercury turns retrograde on January 18, and after that you'll see the best success working on projects that are already underway. Watch budget details, since a miscalculation from January 21 to 26 can delay progress.

Cosmic Insider Tip

The Full Moon on January 28 reflects a powerful time for visionary ideas to grow. A phone call, letter, or e-mail can awaken powerful support from an old ally.

Rewarding Days 1, 5, 9, 10, 14, 15, 19, 20, 28, 29

Challenging Days 3, 4, 16, 17, 18, 22, 24, 25, 26, 30

Affirmation for the Month My actions come from the heart.

🏹 Sagittarius/February 🏹

In the Spotlight
Adventure, travel, and love highlight the month. But for Cupid's arrow to hit its mark, you may have to lay a little groundwork—or at least stay in one place long enough! Your creativity is at a peak, adding to your inspiration. In short, what's stopping you?

Wellness and Keeping Fit
Unless it's fun, you're not likely to show up at fitness class. But if you're enjoying yourself, you'll push harder and see more immediate results. You might decide to focus your fitness time on a sports activity, instead. Either way, it's the perfect time to build strength.

Love and Life Connections
With Mars blazing through the love sector of your chart, you're eager to stoke the fires of passion. Romantic travel can be the source of snapshots for your favorite memories from February 1 to 12, although after that you might prefer quiet time at home with your sweetheart. Family and home connections require attention after February 18, especially if your focus has taken you away for a while.

Finance and Success
Oops! A miscalculation can blow your budget while Mercury retrogrades from February 1 to 8, and you may not get things straightened out until the end of the month. Your reserves are strong, and there are plenty of people willing to lend a helping hand to bring your projects to a successful conclusion. A competitor can sneak below the radar screen during the Full Moon on February 27, so stay alert if you want to head off an unexpected challenge.

Cosmic Insider Tip
Although Mercury moves into direct motion on February 8, the fallout from the surprising changes and confusing messages takes a while to sort through. Concentrate on completing old enterprises.

Rewarding Days 2, 5, 6, 7, 10, 11, 12, 15, 16, 25

Challenging Days 4, 13, 14, 20, 21, 26, 27

Affirmation for the Month Right and truth prevail.

Sagittarius/March

In the Spotlight
A combination of inspiration and elbow grease opens the way for your continued success. You may not be in the headlines, but your priorities have a more personal tone this month.

Wellness and Keeping Fit
Fine-tune your health by altering your daily routine. Concentration on your flexibility helps keep your energy flowing. Attention to your immune system can keep you in shape while others are sniffling.

Love and Life Connections
Warm special touches add to the beauty and comforts of home, just in time to invite cherished friends or family to dinner. After March 8, you'll probably feel more inspired to visit your favorite haunts with your sweetie, or go on your own to enjoy a personal adventure. Inspired by true love, you're eager to let your heart lead the way after March 10, although you can get carried away from March 12 to 17. Make time for romance during the Full Moon on March 28.

Finance and Success
Arguments at work can result from equipment breakdowns or changes in procedure. Confer with experts from March 1 to 11 to keep momentum going on your top projects. Investments take off after March 9, but cautious spending works best until after the New Moon on March 14. Even then, careful evaluation of your options is necessary to avoid overextending your finances, since the Full Moon on March 28 indicates the possibility that costs will exceed your budget.

Cosmic Insider Tip
Jupiter turns direct on March 1, opening the way for an increase in abundance and stronger confidence in the future. This affects business and personal decisions.

Rewarding Days 5, 6, 9, 10, 14, 15, 24, 25, 28, 29

Challenging Days 12, 13, 19, 20, 21, 26, 27

Affirmation for the Month My creativity is inspired by my heart.

Sagittarius/April

In the Spotlight

Cooperative ventures with others provide benefits, but it can be a bumpy ride until you work out the power plays. To ease tension, focus on what you can control and let the rest fall into place.

Wellness and Keeping Fit

Competitive situations rev your engine, so whether you're involved in sports or working toward a personal physical challenge, you're eager to reach your goals. Problems arise if you push too far beyond your limits midmonth. Even though you don't like to admit them, they remind you they exist.

Love and Life Connections

Your fun-loving spirit is inviting to others who enjoy sharing your adventures, although you might not like it if they try to call all the shots. It's easier to work out your differences from April 1 to 13. Your heart opens to a more free experience of love during the New Moon on April 12, although your partner may seem resistant to your advances. You have to decide if the clash is worth the effort.

Finance and Success

By actively examining and fine-tuning your investment strategy, you'll be ready to move your funds into a more promising direction on April 12. Spend on necessary improvements, or purchase technology that will aid your productivity after April 10. Then, you'll be ready to hammer out an agreement with your cohorts at work. Put your plans into action before the Full Moon on April 27.

Cosmic Insider Tip

With Saturn and Neptune in happy agreement, you'll derive benefits from striking a bargain with a trusted partner. However, if you're in an unworkable situation, this may be the time to end it.

Rewarding Days 1, 2, 6, 7, 11, 12, 20, 21, 25, 28, 29, 30

Challenging Days 8, 9, 10, 15, 17, 22, 23, 24

Affirmation for the Month To work better with others, I honor the strengths we each bring into a situation.

Sagittarius/May

In the Spotlight

At least everything is out in the open. Or does it just appear that way? There's a lot rising to the surface when it comes to relationships. It's time to explore and discuss your feelings, and needs.

Wellness and Keeping Fit

If you've been fiddling around and ignoring your body's needs, you'll feel the effects now. With so much cosmic energy confronting your Sun, you need to vent. A holistic approach has never been more useful than it is right now.

Love and Life Connections

It's true confession time. The reality of your experience as a partner is staring back at you. The planets create a mirroring energy that allows you to see yourself and your partner in a very clear light. The good can shine brightly, and the parts of your relationship that are not working can seem to scowl. Even if you're single, you'll feel a need to explore what you want and need from others. By the time the Sagittarius lunar eclipse arrives on May 26 you're ready for answers. Chances are you'll be listening . . . and talking!

Finance and Success

Legal battles can be civil, but may have a devastating impact unless you're well prepared. This is a test of your ability to see beyond personal issues and into the long-range effects of actions and decisions. You can be quite convincing from May 1 to 13. Then, Mercury turns retrograde on May 15, and you may have to go over the same issues. Again. It's a test of patience and thoroughness.

Cosmic Insider Tip

The contests happening now can be really exciting and bring out your best talents. It's dealing with shortsightedness from others that's the true frustration!

Rewarding Days 3, 4, 8, 9, 18, 19, 22, 26, 27, 30

Challenging Days 1, 5, 6, 7, 13, 14, 15, 20, 21

Affirmation for the Month I take responsibility for my actions.

Sagittarius/June

In the Spotlight

Despite your desire to remain free, old emotional issues can still hold you back. This is a time to question why you're holding onto certain people, situations, and attitudes. The process involves cleanup and restoration. You may even uncover a few treasures!

Wellness and Keeping Fit

The link between body, mind, and soul proves to be especially significant. Some of your physical discomfort is likely to be resolved once you've gotten to the core of an old disappointment or hurt. Take time for a day at the spa, or, if you can, a vacation.

Love and Life Connections

Stimulus from Mars activates hidden issues, and arguments can work like a knife to cut to the core of your most sensitive emotions. You may crave true intimacy, but if there are power and control issues involved the comfort you seek can be difficult to find. By midmonth you may discover that your spiritual link helps alleviate the pain you feel.

Finance and Success

Mercury continues its retrograde through June 8. It's a good time to research and review, but you may not see significant progress. Fortunately, the rhetoric tones down after the solar eclipse on June 10, and by June 15 your confidence in a project is restored. Conferences and presentations are advantageous from June 17 to 30, but expect conservative attitudes to prevail during the lunar eclipse on June 24. Delay final decisions until you're comfortable with the costs.

Cosmic Insider Tip

The fallout from the solar eclipse on June 10 exposes trust issues. For this reason, you may not want to finalize lasting agreements until you're more sure of yourself—and the other guy.

Rewarding Days 4, 5, 14, 15, 18, 19, 22, 23, 27

Challenging Days 1, 2, 3, 9, 10, 16, 17, 29, 30

Affirmation for the Month I deserve to have my needs fulfilled.

Sagittarius/July

In the Spotlight
Promises made now have lasting value, and the changes resulting from your commitments can alter your life course. This does not mean the fun is squeezed out of your life! In fact, your joy can lead to an amazing revitalization.

Wellness and Keeping Fit
A fitness program that incorporates philosophical concepts inspires you to reach toward life-enhancing goals. You might even decide to teach others what you've learned.

Love and Life Connections
Renew or make vows to strengthen a partnership from July 1 to 7, especially if you've worked out your differences. It's time to make a promise to yourself that will help you reach an important milestone—whether you're single or connected. Pack your bags and get ready to explore exciting places after July 14. Keep your options open, since a journey during the Full Moon on July 24 leads to a profound exchange of ideas.

Finance and Success
Renew or restore items you've found during your recent cleanup, or put some effort into renovations at home. This is the time to make the most of your hidden assets, and inheritance and joint property can fortify your financial picture. Sorting details can get a bit dicey from July 21 to 27, though. Promotional efforts, publishing, and academic pursuits advance your career after July 14, and your influence can make a difference to someone else after July 22.

Cosmic Insider Tip
Imaginative and fantastic ideas and images carry extra weight during the Full Moon on July 24. You can make a deeper impression than you might realize.

Rewarding Days 2, 3, 11, 12, 19, 20, 21, 24, 25, 29, 30

Challenging Days 6, 7, 13, 14, 26, 27

Affirmation for the Month I am aware of the impact of my actions.

Sagittarius/August

In the Spotlight
Special interests and community activities add zest to your life, and travel can be a prominent feature. Most important are your long range plans, since this is the time to initiate changes.

Wellness and Keeping Fit
Your vitality is supercharged, and you're raring to go! A challenging hike, or weekends enjoying your favorite summer sports, can put an extra zip in your step. Take advantage of your love of the outdoors and indulge in an adventurous vacation with your favorite buddy.

Love and Life Connections
Sharing a journey can strengthen a partnership, taking your relationship to a deeper level during the New Moon on August 8. But if you're free to discover new love, then your travels can lead you into the arms of someone completely fascinating. Exhilarating romance can turn into a lifelong connection. While you're counting your blessings, your friendship with another who shares your spiritual yearnings will make your heart sing.

Finance and Success
Promotional activities advance your career and give you a chance to enjoy the spotlight. Launch an innovative campaign on or after August 8, but double-check requirements and rules to avoid a setback from August 17 to 26. Contractual and legal matters add potential profits and limit your potential liability. Jupiter's influence enhances your confidence for the next year, and this is the time to get started on projects that support your career aims.

Cosmic Insider Tip
Legal loopholes can frustrate your progress from August 10 to 16, but this is also a good time to test a product or an idea to determine any weak points.

Rewarding Days 7, 8, 12, 16, 17, 20, 21, 25, 26

Challenging Days 3, 4, 5, 9, 10, 23, 24, 30, 31

Affirmation for the Month My ideals have truth and integrity.

☌ Sagittarius/September ☌

In the Spotlight

Focused effort is required if you're going to accomplish your career aims this month, and even then there's plenty of competition. The challenge can spur your enthusiasm, and since your confidence is growing, even you might be surprised at your level of achievement!

Wellness and Keeping Fit

Limits? What are those? It's tempting to push yourself beyond your capacities. Adequate training and competent instruction can help you stay out of hot water, although situations beyond your control can test your capabilities after September 15.

Love and Life Connections

Love blossoms from September 1 to 9. After that, your passions can take an unusual turn, and you may find yourself fantasizing about an unreachable someone. By the Full Moon on September 21 there are contentious situations to deal with. The source of trouble can be a disagreement with your family, especially if there's some unfinished business that you've been trying to avoid. Just be aware that repairing a rift can have an overflow effect in your closest relationship.

Finance and Success

Momentum for your ongoing plans starts the month on a high note, and you're in line for advancement, too. Unexpected rewards from September 1 to 10 can be especially gratifying. Then, when Mercury turns retrograde on September 14, your most carefully designed plans may be up for revisions due to circumstances beyond your control. It's also easy to lose track of valuables or be seduced by unscrupulous individuals from September 14 to 21.

Cosmic Insider Tip

Safeguard important information and documents after September 13, since you could be a victim of theft and not even know it!

Rewarding Days 4, 5, 8, 12, 13, 17, 18, 22, 23

Challenging Days 1, 6, 7, 19, 20, 21, 26, 27, 28

Affirmation for the Month I am clear about my motivations.

⚹ Sagittarius/October ⚹

In the Spotlight

Resistance from others can stifle your enthusiasm. It's a test of knowing which battles are worth the effort and which will simply exhaust your resources. A careful evaluation of the rules and expectations helps you reprioritize so you can move forward.

Wellness and Keeping Fit

An old problem can become a real nuisance from October 1 to 15—especially if you've pushed your limits. With a little help and guidance from a talented professional, you can turn the tide and be well on your way to recovery before the Full Moon on October 21.

Love and Life Connections

A fundamental disagreement with your partner can create a wedge, blocking your ability to move beyond a difficult issue. A friend can offer objective support during the New Moon on October 6, but you may still have questions about your relationship. Venus retrogrades on October 10, beginning a six-week period of introspection about your needs. To heal the rift in your relationship, seek out your shared dreams and spend time away from everyday stress.

Finance and Success

Since Mercury is in retrograde through October 6, your career plans may be on hold—or in limbo. Plus, a change in the hierarchy can be unsettling for everyone. An open mind and positive attitude feed your tolerance, and by October 16 there's light at the end of the tunnel. Confer with your professional allies from October 12 to 23, since their support can help you through an uncertain period.

Cosmic Insider Tip

Saturn turns retrograde, too—and for you that means it's time to take yet another look at your relationship. If you're still not happy, the cosmos gives you another chance to work out solutions.

Rewarding Days 1, 2, 5, 6, 9, 10, 14, 19, 20, 29

Challenging Days 3, 4, 16, 17, 18, 24, 25, 31

Affirmation for the Month I accept the things I cannot change.

🏹 Sagittarius/November 🏹

In the Spotlight
To take the pressure down a few notches, let your allies take the lead for a while. Work behind the scenes can protect your ripening investments (or ideas) until you're ready to give the world a preview after November 20.

Wellness and Keeping Fit
Grab your best buddy and get serious about that fitness class you've been talking about. You're ready to get started—or to start over—with a program that suits your individual needs. Establish goals with your instructor during the New Moon on November 4.

Love and Life Connections
Withdrawing from the action gives you a chance to reconsider your needs and feelings through the lunar eclipse on November 19. Instead of escape, you can make this a time to uncover buried issues you've tried to outrun in the past. Then, after November 20, you'll feel more at ease moving forward without having to drag around those weighty issues. A romantic exchange or lighthearted getaway can enliven an old relationship after November 18.

Finance and Success
Career advances lift your confidence, but you may be worried about situations that are not clearly defined. Eliminate losses or nonproductive situations while Venus retrogrades through November 21. Hidden costs can undermine your budget, especially if you've lost track of your expenditures. Be prepared to take the lead after Mercury enters your sign on November 19.

Cosmic Insider Tip
The lunar eclipse on November 19 marks a time to retreat and honestly explore your inner motivations. Surrendering to your higher self helps answer your essential questions.

Rewarding Days 2, 6, 7, 10, 15, 16, 25, 26, 29, 30

Challenging Days 1, 4, 12, 13, 14, 20, 21, 27, 28

Affirmation for the Month My inner voice is my most trusted ally.

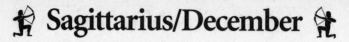 Sagittarius/December

In the Spotlight

The Sagittarius solar eclipse on December 4 sets the stage for significant new life directions. The dilemmas you've dealt with since May are finally reaching their conclusions, and it's time for you to take bold, but careful, steps to refocus your life path and priorities.

Wellness and Keeping Fit

Part of regaining your momentum involves striking a balance between your inner self and the outward focus of your life. Mars activates your unconscious drives, so it's a good time to explore the habits that are undermining your mental and physical well-being.

Love and Life Connections

Your secret desires may not be as secret as you imagine. But are you only infatuated? Give your dreams some time in the light of your inner self. Honest reflection helps prepare you for the challenges you're likely to encounter. You may break away from a relationship that no longer suits your needs, or you may be faced with changes beyond your control. Sort through your feelings during the Sun's eclipse on December 4, and explore your options before the Full Moon on December 19.

Finance and Success

Presentations and business meetings fare best from December 1 to 8. After that, you may have more questions than answers. It's easy to be hornswoggled from December 9 to 20, so watch out for the snake-oil salesman in the Armani suit. Practical matters are easier to understand after December 23, although you may have plans to get away from the action for a vacation.

Cosmic Insider Tip

After December 15, grand plans and schemes are very likely to have hidden costs, or can be more complicated than they appear to be.

Rewarding Days 3, 4, 7, 8, 9, 12, 13, 22, 23, 31

Challenging Days 1, 10, 11, 17, 18, 19, 24, 25

Affirmation for the Month I deserve to have my needs fulfilled!

SAGITTARIUS ACTION TABLE

These dates reflect the best—but not the only—times for success and ease in these activities, according to your Sun sign.

	JAN	FEB	MAR	APR	MAY	JUN	JUL	AUG	SEPT	OCT	NOV	DEC
Move			12-28									
Start a class	4-17	12-28	1-10					8,9				
Join a club										6,7		
Ask for a raise												4,5
Look for work				13-30				6-25		6-10		
Get pro advice	24,25	20,21	19-21	16,17	13,14	9,10	6-8	3,4,30,31	1,26-28	24,25	20-22	17-19
Get a loan	26,27	22,23	22,23	18,19	15,16	11-13	9,10	5,6	2,3,29,30	26,27	22-24	20,21
See a doctor				13-29							1-19	
Start a diet	21,22	18,19	17,18	13-15	10-12	7,8	3,5,31	1,2,28,29	24,25	21-23	17-19	15,16
End relationship												18,19
Buy clothes			29-31	1-12								
Get a makeover												3,4
New romance			8-31	12								
Vacation	28,29	24,25	24,25	20,21	17-19	14,15	11,12	7,8	4,5	1,2,28-30	25,26	22,23

CAPRICORN

The Goat
December 21 to January 20

♑

Element:	Earth
Quality:	Cardinal
Polarity:	Yin/Feminine
Planetary Ruler:	Saturn
Meditation:	I master the challenges of the physical plane.
Gemstone:	Garnet
Power Stones:	Peridot, diamond, quartz, black obsidian, onyx
Key Phrase:	I use
Glyph:	Head of goat
Anatomy:	Skeleton, knees, skin
Color:	Black, forest green
Animal:	Goats, thick-shelled animals
Myths/Legends:	Chronos, Vesta, Pan
House:	Tenth
Opposite Sign:	Cancer
Flower:	Carnation
Key Word:	Ambitious

Positive Expression:	Misuse of Energy:
Sensible	Apprehensive
Reliable	Miserly
Patient	Austere
Responsible	Rigid
Thrifty	Dictatorial
Disciplined	Machiavellian

Capricorn

Your Ego's Strengths and Shortcomings

Your determination and focus are tremendous assets as you drive toward accomplishing your ambitions. Few can push a project toward its success as effectively as you, since you're the ultimate efficiency expert. As "The Pragmatist" of the zodiac, you know how to make the most of the materials at hand and when to put your talents to work. Whether you're making your way up the ladder of success or striving to master what's personally important, you set priorities that help you get the job done.

Forward motion is definitely your preference, although if life deals you a setback, you're able to keep your eye on your goals and continue to make strides. While you may not always be patient, you do know how to get what you want from life. It's your affinity with Saturn's disciplined energy that helps you grasp the importance of building a solid foundation for your dreams. In fact, once you've set out on the path toward your goals, you are not likely to take "no" for answer. However, some of your hardest lessons can come from learning what it means to take responsibility and honor social limitations, and you may have learned early that bucking authority has its price. In personal and professional connections, your resistance can be infuriating to others, especially if you are struggling within yourself over issues about personal worth. On the other hand, you can just as easily be the one who offers a no-nonsense approach to tackling the tasks most would find impossible.

When you're in charge, you feel most confident, but you can also enjoy relinquishing control to a partner, friend, or student—giving you a chance to enjoy the ride. Just as when you reach your own goals, when those who share your life reach their own pinnacles you feel tremendous gratification. During the times you need to regroup, nothing tops getting back to basics to connect with the simple joys of life. That's how you keep that bright smile.

Shining Your Love Light

Because you express a reserved, matter-of-fact manner, others may mistakenly believe you are not romantic—but that's far from the truth! It's just that until you know it's safe to let someone see your tender side, you keep your guard up. Once you open your heart, you fully intend to nourish lasting love and affection. You seek a love that can stand the test of time, and intend to have a wonderful experience in the process.

In love relationships, you let your natural affinities emerge when you're with the other earth signs—Taurus, Virgo, and other Capricorns. Your mutual appreciation for practical concerns creates a comfortable understanding of your priorities with these signs. However, the sparks of attraction can fly with Cancer, your zodiac opposite. Together, you can create a strong foundation from which to build a sense of family.

Locking horns with Aries can stimulate your passions just as much as it frustrates your inability to keep him or her under control. With Taurus, your sensuality emerges and it's easy to let love flow freely. Gemini can get on your nerves, but your need to be in charge can be just as irritating to him or her. You may feel a powerful attraction to Leo, but mutual trust can take a long time to establish.

Virgo can be the perfect companion for your life journey, since you share mutual ideals and values. While you can have a legendary attraction to Libra, building emotional closeness can take on the vestiges of an epic quest. Magical alchemy and passionate devotion can grow with Scorpio, who may be your lifelong friend. Sagittarius inspires you to uncover your dreams, but you may not like it when you have to make room for her or his independence. It can be easy to get close to another Capricorn, but if you fall into stale routine the light of your love will dim. Aquarius can be your cherished friend, but your values often differ. A connection with Pisces can seem completely magical, inviting you to express and fulfill your heart's desire.

Making Your Place in the World

A highly respected position means a lot to you, and you'll feel most content when your lifework promotes your self-esteem. You're well suited for positions of authority, and might relish the world of business—particularly if you can exercise your administrative or executive abilities. However, you might also be a gifted teacher, especially in fields like geology, life sciences, or life skills.

Building things feels wonderful, and work as a designer, contractor, manufacturer, or craftsperson can be rewarding. Your need to stay in touch with nature can turn into the business of farming, ranching, forestry, or zoo-keeping. Metaphysical studies feel natural, and work in the healing arts as a therapist, herbalist, chiropractor, naturopath or holistic physician can provide practical applications of your understanding of energy and healing.

Power Plays

Even as a child, you've always known that if you did not use your power, someone else would. When you are in charge of anything, you feel much more content. Learning the rules makes a lot of sense, too, because you can exercise more control when you know how to play the game. Ultimately, you make your own rules. Power itself arises from the arduous task of learning what it means to be in control, and knowing when you have to let go and give in to situations beyond your control.

As you temper your personal power through the gentility of a loving heart, others will begin to see you as an icon. In all truth, you may not be interested in lording power over others, but instead you simply want to assure that progress is respected and meaningful traditions are honored. For you, responsibility is power, and whether you're practicing that truth or teaching it, others look to your example to see how well it works.

Famous Capricorns

Victor Borge, Cate Blanchett, Jim Carrey, Mary Higgins Clark, Katie Couric, Umberto Eco, Nancy Lopez, Ricky Martin, Charlie Rose, Vidal Sassoon, Diane Sawyer, Michael Schumacher, Bart Starr, Grant Tinker

The Year Ahead for Capricorn

As you devise more inventive ways to use your talents and resources, you're moving into different circles of influence. The support you receive from others opens pathways that allow you to grow and prosper, although you may still prefer to take an independent route whenever possible. The year 2002 can involve dedicated effort and hard work, but your rewards make it all worthwhile.

Expansive Jupiter travels in opposition to your sign through the end of July, challenging you to set goals that will push you to express and use your talents to their fullest. Yet this is also a time to give others a chance to shine, and to show your appreciation for their support. This cycle can push you out of your comfort zone, since you feel a need to offer extra assistance in return for the efforts of others, or to follow the lead of a partner or associate. Cooperative ventures can fare especially well, as long as your expectations are carefully defined. This becomes even more necessary after August, when Jupiter enters the sector of your chart that helps you uncover the truth of your relationships. It's time to come clean with yourself about your motivations, but it's also a period when you are learning lessons of trust. On a practical level, watch out for the temptation of excessive debt, since the resulting discomfort can undermine your creativity and sense of personal control. Keep a careful watch on your budget and follow your usual frugal approach to situations if you are the least bit unsure of their outcome.

Saturn, your planetary ruler, taps into the health sector of your chart for the entire year. That means you'll need to pay more attention to your body's needs, but you can also do something about any problems. This is the perfect time to get into a routine that helps you feel more in touch with your physical and emotional needs.

The slower moving planets—Uranus, Neptune, and Pluto—are still traveling in the same areas of your chart as last year. The times these planetary cycles have their greatest impact is when they make an exact connection to your Sun or one of the planets in your chart. However, their influence can be long-lasting. Uranus and Neptune both stimulate a need to explore the way you're handling your resources—time, money, and energy. Your values are also changing, and what was once important may not hold your interest now. Pluto's impact during 2002 helps you uncover your hidden motives, and also stimulates a more profound understanding of your dreams. The comet-planetoid Chiron travels in Capricorn during this year, marking a significant time of spiritual and psychological growth. This influence also indicates that you can hurt yourself by failing to honor what you know is right for you. It's the "shoot yourself in the foot" syndrome in operation.

The solar and lunar eclipses emphasize the balance between your psychological and physical health. This is the perfect year to learn about nutrition, and a great time to evaluate your personal needs. Your deeper feelings about yourself can be exposed, and you may gain an understanding of some of those destructive habits you need to break. The specific impact of each eclipse will be defined in the months they occur in the sections that follow.

If you were born from December 21 to 25, you're experiencing Pluto's energy in a semisquare aspect to your Sun. This cycle can leave you feeling uncomfortable with the status quo, especially if your current situation is not fulfilling your needs. Your unconscious motivations can lead you to make decisions that seem to fall apart. You may want or need one thing, but you do another. These actions can be clues that show you where to start when it comes to uncovering your real needs. It is not a time to pretend, or to repress your actual feelings, but it is an excellent time to take an honest look at yourself and the dreams you have not yet fulfilled. At the core of this cycle is your desire to feel fully empowered to be all that you can be. Ultimately, you are likely to look back on this time as a breakaway period in your life . . . the year when you decided to take the path that made all the difference.

If you were born from December 21 to 28, you're feeling the impact of Chiron transiting in an exact conjunction to your Sun. This rare cycle can bring significant changes in your attitudes toward what's most important in your life. Exploring your life purpose can be part of this cycle, and as a result you may alter your career. However, life purpose extends into your relationships, too. If you find yourself asking, "What am I doing in this situation?" you are seeing evidence of this cycle at work. From there, it's up to you to determine whether or not a circumstance needs to be changed. Or, your attitude may be in need of repair! What you can see is how you might be damaging yourself or your life through your actions and choices, and where you need to experience healing.

If you were born from December 28 to January 2, you are opening your awareness to another level while Neptune cycles in semisextile aspect to your Sun. The impulse from Neptune is to help you move beyond the ordinary and into the transcendent. You can do that by developing your creativity, being more charitable and compassionate, and listening more carefully to your inner voice. There is a subtle, muted quality to this cycle—an urging that encourages you to move out of your ruts and up to a different level. Physically, you can be more sensitive than you have been, so you may need to make adjustments to accommodate these changes. Pump up your immune system, too, since you can be more susceptible to colds or other ailments. In addition to Neptune's cycle, from January through March Saturn will complete the cycle that began last year—a quincunx aspect to your Sun. For this reason, you'll be more likely to experience the health-related elements of this cycle during the first quarter of 2002. After making reasonable adjustments, you'll feel that you are more in charge of your health.

If you were born from December 30 to January 5, it's time to break some useless habits while Uranus transits in semisquare aspect to your Sun. This can be an excellent period to experiment with changes you've wanted to make, without leaving everything behind in the process. In some ways, this cycle can be like a springboard, giving you a boost in your confidence when it comes to trusting your individuality. Flashes of insight are a common occurrence, and during these times you can peek above the day-to-day crush and see where your path leads. While you may not make sweeping changes this year, you can definitely eliminate unnecessary burdens and move into a life experience that brings renewal and a sense of personal freedom.

If you were born from January 4 to 10, there are deep changes occurring while Pluto transits in semisextile to your Sun this year. This is an important time to eliminate clutter, to let go of your past, and to move forward with a sense of personal conviction that you're doing the right thing. Since the primary influence of Pluto's cycle can be felt at a psychological level, you may feel most inclined to eliminate self-defeating attitudes—or to at least acknowledge that they exist! Think of this as a year to dig into that nagging feeling of discontent and to discover why it's there. Work with a counselor could be helpful, but you'll also benefit from incorporating time for reflection and contemplation. Alterations in your physical routine can make a difference, too, since this is a time to fine-tune your body and get in shape. Extra care may be necessary during April and May, as Saturn travels in quincunx aspect to your Sun. During these months you may be more inclined to deal with health issues. Then, for the remainder of the year, you can get on with the business of continuing your self-improvement.

If you were born from January 11 to 20, it's time to make adjustments in your priorities. Saturn is traveling in quincunx aspect to your Sun. This cycle does not get into full swing until June, but you will feel the build-up earlier. Changes can occur as an indirect result of situations that are coming to a close. However, you may also find it more difficult to end things, especially if you have doubts or fears about the outcome. Think of this as a time that's like pruning a tree or shrub. You may need to cut away some dead wood, or clip off branches in order to create the shape you desire. Problems can arise if you cut too deeply, but with care and forethought your efforts will meet with success. The most significant impact of this cycle can occur with your physical health. Destructive habits can have consequences that undermine your vitality, or you may be more prone to illness. A holistic approach to your health will work best, since the only way you may feel that your vitality is secure is to address the needs of your mind, body, and spirit. The good thing is that you can become stronger as a result of your actions.

If you were born from January 14 to 18, expect the unexpected. Uranus is traveling in quincunx aspect to your Sun, adding a very unsettled quality to your life this year. Since you are also experiencing the Saturn cycle described above, you can feel that your life is in a bit of a pickle. After all, you need to deal with your responsibilities (Saturn), but want to break free (Uranus). To deal with this cosmic juggling act, you'll benefit from making a conscious effort to maintain your sense of feeling grounded. Even if you are experiencing changes beyond your control, by maintaining a focus on your top priorities you'll be able to benefit from those changes. In addition, you probably have a few things you want to eliminate. Your relationships may need an overhaul, but since your values are changing, your finances can use work, too. It's all a part of creating a life that reflects and supports the essence of your most unique qualities.

Tools for Change

Many of the longer-lasting cycles you're feeling this year can have a significant impact on your health. However, the effects are more likely to be an enhanced awareness of what you need to either stay healthy or become stronger. The hard part is doing the work required! In fact, some of these same cycles can have a dampening effect on your vitality, so finding motivation will be more challenging.

First, develop your mindfulness. Mindful living encompasses focused attention on your thoughts and actions. Instead of allowing yourself to be driven entirely by impulse or habit, you can gain greater control over your time and energy by simply becoming more aware. You might make faster progress using a meditation machine that works to synchronize patterns of sound and lights to help you focus your mind. However, you can accomplish the same effect through regular meditation, or, if you need a focusing tool, using meditative music. You are more sensitive to the effects of vibration this year, and the quality of music and sound in your environment can make a significant difference in the way you feel. Subtle sounds can be especially influential.

Pay special attention to your dream time this year. Relaxation may come more easily if you stay active and keep your body supple.

However, if you need a little help to relax or sleep more peacefully, consider exploring techniques that help you get into deeper sleep. In addition, you might appreciate the insights you gain by becoming more aware of your dream images and feelings. Work with a dream journal can be especially helpful as you uncover your hidden motivations and release elements from your past.

Physically, strengthen your immune system by stepping up your aerobic activity. Then, consider adding techniques like gua sha, a traditional Chinese method designed to clear the lymphatic system. This is a time when you're experiencing the miracle of your body's self-healing ability, but you may have to help it along.

Vß

Affirmation for the Year

I am motivated by a desire to purify my life.

Capricorn/January

In the Spotlight

The year begins on a high note for you, with a special emphasis on communication and travel this month. Finances can provide confusion, especially if you lose track of significant information. Maybe it's time to try out that accounting software!

Wellness and Keeping Fit

There's plenty of vitality to meet your daily obligations, and more to spare for pure enjoyment from January 1 to 15. To start the year off right, get into a different and more challenging routine during the Capricorn New Moon on January 13.

Love and Life Connections

The urge to get away to your favorite place can be the perfect opening to initiate a love connection from January 1 to 18. Whether you're altering the course of an existing partnership or heading down the path of new love, it's easier to express what's in your heart during the New Moon on January 13. Friction at home demands your attention after January 20, although the turmoil could be the result of home improvements, a move, or changes in the family.

Finance and Success

Meetings and presentations move along quite nicely from January 1 to 16, when introducing your ideas can be met with strong support. However, dealing with budgetary concerns can be a real headache once Mercury turns retrograde on January 18. It's one of those times when you can misplace things easily, and lose information. Back up computer files to avoid slowing your progress.

Cosmic Insider Tip

A series of confusing elements comes into play during the Full Moon on January 28, when you and others could be misled by unscrupulous individuals.

Rewarding Days 3, 4, 7, 8, 11, 12, 13, 16, 17, 22, 31

Challenging Days 5, 6, 18, 19, 20, 26, 27, 28

Affirmation for the Month I make the best use of my resources.

ᛉ Capricorn/February ᛉ

In the Spotlight

Pressing toward your goals, you can run roughshod over sensitive toes. Fortunately, open communication goes a long way toward mending problems. Finances take a top priority, and innovations or new tools pave the way for speedy returns on investments.

Wellness and Keeping Fit

Integrative approaches to fitness, like martial arts, hold your interest. A visit to your acupuncturist or shiatsu expert during the New Moon on February 12 will help restore the flow of chi.

Love and Life Connections

Tension or turmoil results from Mars blazing through the home and family sector of your chart. It's a good time to repair rifts, but conflicts can get out of hand unless you make time to deal with them. Take a break in the action after February 14 and head out to explore a place of interest with your kids or your sweetheart, but keep plans simple to avoid extra strain. To rejuvenate a tired relationship, reach toward your common spiritual aims during the Full Moon on February 27.

Finance and Success

Mercury retrogrades until February 8, although it is an excellent time to sort through problems or get to the core of situations that are not working. From February 4 to 14 you're in a great position to bring practical ideas to the forefront. Working out details of a budget agreement can stall progress from February 16 to 21, but once you've worked out the bugs, there's little to stop you.

Cosmic Insider Tip

Some of the ideas you wanted to introduce or develop at the first of January get a second chance to shine from February 1 to 14. Mercury's retrograde works to your advantage—this time!

Rewarding Days 3, 4, 8, 9, 13, 18, 19, 26, 27

Challenging Days 1, 2, 5, 15, 16, 17, 22, 23, 28

Affirmation for the Month My life is filled with people I value.

⚹ Capricorn/March ⚹

In the Spotlight

Creative projects and experiences that flow from the heart revitalize your life. You can grow physically stronger, but, more important, you can strengthen your ties to those whose ideals and talents are mutually supportive. It's time to bring your aspirations to life.

Wellness and Keeping Fit

Uplifted by the consistency of Mars traveling in friendly Taurus, you're ready to take on the challenge of reshaping your body. Laughter is also great medicine, so seek out activities you enjoy.

Love and Life Connections

No waiting around—it's time to put actions behind your desires and let someone know how much you care. If you're uncertain, explore possibilities through conversation to give you a chance to gauge signals. Then, get things moving after the New Moon on March 14 when a romantic rendezvous can set the stage for memorable moments. Home fires need extra attention during the Full Moon on March 28, so be sure to leave time in your busy schedule.

Finance and Success

Business expenses can pile up from March 1 to 10, and even though you may be able to justify them, you will not be comfortable if you go over your budget. To assure that you have ample resources, re-evaluate your plans, and then reconsider your timetable. A more careful approach will feel best until after March 17, when those uncertain elements are finally out in the open. Meetings and presentations fare best from March 13 to 28.

Cosmic Insider Tip

Although fresh ideas are intriguing from March 1 to 10, you may not see much value in them until you've had a chance to put them to the test.

Rewarding Days 3, 7, 8, 12, 13, 17, 18, 26, 27, 30, 31

Challenging Days 1, 14, 15, 16, 22, 23, 28, 29

Affirmation for the Month I use my energy to do the most good.

Capricorn/April

In the Spotlight

Despite your preference for the practical, a bit of whimsy can overtake your life in the name of creative expression. This is the perfect time to exercise your talents, but it's also an exceptional period to surrender to love.

Wellness and Keeping Fit

If you've been waiting for the right time to get into a more challenging fitness routine, evaluate your needs with an expert, and then initiate your program after the New Moon on April 12.

Love and Life Connections

Venus and Mars are doing the dance of love, just in time for you to enjoy the essence of springtime with someone special. Indulge your sensual side from April 1 to 13, sharing the pleasures that come from opening your heart. Then, after April 14, look for unique ways to communicate your feelings. Friends play a more significant role during the Full Moon April 27, when a quiet gathering can solidify your connections.

Finance and Success

Invest in improvements to your property or assets that will strengthen their long-range value, but watch for costly disruptions from April 4 to 12. At work, there's a call for greater efficiency, and productivity is on the increase after April 13. Showcase your talents from April 2 to 24, when you'll have a more appreciative audience. But look for opportunities to tie your efforts to others in your field if you're seeking to make a greater impact.

Cosmic Insider Tip

Your base of operations is likely to change or undergo improvements. That will make things easier in the long run, but can try your patience near the time of the New Moon on April 12.

Rewarding Days 3, 4, 8, 9, 13, 14, 22, 23, 27

Challenging Days 11, 12, 18, 19, 20, 24, 25

Affirmation for the Month Love leads the way in all my actions.

Capricorn/May

In the Spotlight

Cooperative ventures with others can be especially rewarding, but will try your patience. Your timetable and the pace of everyone else may not match. It's one of those times when you may have to consider the value of adjusting to circumstances you cannot control.

Wellness and Keeping Fit

Knowing your limits and paying attention to them can be two different things—a lesson you may discover this month. However, after May 12 you're ready to try a more prudent approach to taking care of yourself. It's important to be watchful to avoid accidents.

Love and Life Connections

It's important to squeeze in some special time with your partner. A getaway during the New Moon on May 12 can revitalize your love. If you're running out of ideas to keep love alive, take your lead from your sweetheart. The easiest thing to do is to show more appreciation for others. In fact, such simple actions can have spectacular results after May 24.

Finance and Success

Incorporate new procedures or adjust job descriptions at work from May 1 to 14, when you're looking for increased efficiency. However, drastic actions can injure progress and may send a message that leads to a lack of trust. Once Mercury goes retrograde on May 15 you may feel that you're spending more time reviewing problems than moving forward. Those reviews can be exceptionally revealing, though, and are worth your time and attention.

Cosmic Insider Tip

Changes in the overall power base can be unsettling, but may happen even if you do not want them to occur. The lunar eclipse on May 26 indicates a major shift in your daily routine.

Rewarding Days 1, 2, 6, 10, 11, 12, 20, 21, 24, 28, 29

Challenging Days 8, 9, 14, 15, 17, 22, 23

Affirmation for the Month I know when to surrender control.

Capricorn/June

In the Spotlight

Clarity about your work emerges with the solar eclipse on June 10, when it's time to determine why you've made certain life choices. The viability of a working partnership intensifies, and that offers more options. This is no time to settle for what you do not need.

Wellness and Keeping Fit

Direct your competitive drive into healthy contests to diffuse tension. Your mind-body awareness intensifies as the Sun's eclipse nears, and after June 10 a new routine provides a chance to let off steam. Counseling can be beneficial if you want to uncover issues.

Love and Life Connections

Conflicts with your partner escalate, but may also be a source of healing. After all, there's nothing like bringing problems into the open—where you can address them directly. Love also grows, and from June 1 to 15 showing your appreciation for others goes a long way toward deepening your affections. The balance of power in your relationships becomes clear during the Capricorn lunar eclipse on June 24. It's time to find out who needs what, and from whom.

Finance and Success

The weak links at work create havoc during Mercury's retrograde through June 8. Whether people or machines are the problem is not the point. How you handle the disruption is the issue. Support from others can be exceptionally beneficial, and a working partnership can help you expand your financial base. To avoid disappointments, define expectations and make alterations when circumstances dictate.

Cosmic Insider Tip

If you're feeling a bit grumpy, you'll do yourself and everyone else a favor if you can pinpoint the cause. Your preference now is to celebrate and enjoy yourself.

Rewarding Days 2, 7, 8, 16, 17, 21, 24, 25, 29

Challenging Days 4, 5, 11, 12, 13, 18, 19, 23

Affirmation for the Month I am blessed with love and support.

Capricorn/July

In the Spotlight

Imagine a spiral of energy that carries you upward toward your ultimate dreams . . . that's the power you're experiencing from the cosmos. It's time to expand your horizons and trust the visions you hold for your future. Call it the birth of fresh ambitions!

Wellness and Keeping Fit

An instructor or trainer can help you get on the right track with your fitness routine from July 7 to 21. However, after July 14 you're most focused on delving into the root causes of any physical distress. A holistic approach works best, since there are more things than "symptoms" to address.

Love and Life Connections

No hemming and hawing: if you're serious, take the steps to solidify your commitment. You can be just as determined if you've decided to end a relationship, but only if you can reach some kind of closure. Issues about intimacy emerge after July 14, and whether you're exploring your own uncertainty or lack of trust from your partner, this is the time to reach into the depths.

Finance and Success

Contracts and agreements require special attention, but open the way for speedy progress on the career front. Just as important are the social elements involved in your rise up the ladder of success. Business travel and conferences give you a chance to shine after July 10. You may also uncover significant financial opportunities while you're there.

Cosmic Insider Tip

Even if you are not in total agreement with the way others are handling a particular project, you may still be able to participate and prosper from your association.

Rewarding Days 4, 5, 13, 14, 17, 18, 22, 23, 27, 31

Challenging Days 1, 2, 3, 9, 10, 15, 16, 29, 30

Affirmation for the Month My values light the path to my success.

✳ Capricorn/August ✳

In the Spotlight
Promotional activities enhance your career, but cultural and academic pursuits also offer promise. Friction comes from the financial front, with joint property, taxes, or inheritance serving as targets (or triggers) for most of the turmoil.

Wellness and Keeping Fit
Emotionally charged situations can drain your vitality, especially if stress is mounting. Tap into your network of health resources to get to the core of problems.

Love and Life Connections
Power issues rise to the surface in your relationship, and can escalate out of control by the time the Full Moon arrives on August 22. You do have options. First, talk about expectations, since the blame game will only create more trouble. Then, look for workable solutions to money matters. An attraction can stir flames of passion at the New Moon on August 8, but you may lose interest if you're tempted by another possibility during the Full Moon on August 22.

Finance and Success
Legal matters can resolve and clarify business deals, although court situations may lead to disappointments from August 12 to 17 when an old agreement creates problems. Strengthen your professional reputation by focusing on solutions, and invite experts to join your team to fill in weak links. The politics of your job can provide a chance for you to take the lead after August 18.

Cosmic Insider Tip
Innovations that link existing or established procedures and technology have an excellent chance for success. Breakthroughs move you beyond an impasse after August 17.

Rewarding Days 1, 2, 9, 10, 14, 18, 19, 23, 28, 29

Challenging Days 5, 6, 7, 11, 12, 13, 25, 26

Affirmation for the Month My future depends on resolving issues from the past.

⚳ Capricorn/September ⚳

In the Spotlight

Fresh pathways unfold to help you move further toward the success you crave. Whether your aims are personal or professional, tapping into workable visions increases your confidence. Misinterpretations of your words and actions can create setbacks, so strive for clarity.

Wellness and Keeping Fit

If it's been too long since you've hiked through the woods or climbed your favorite mountain trail, then this is the time to go. Communing with nature invigorates your spirit.

Love and Life Connections

Exploration of your spiritual path not only helps to reassure your confidence in your choices, but may also lend strength to a love relationship. You may discover a different level of love during the New Moon on September 7, when a meeting of the minds can lead you to open your heart. Love can become more complicated after September 21, when your differences are emphasized.

Finance and Success

Your professional reputation gains momentum. Your influence and expertise are more valuable, and others may seek your guidance or assistance. Depending upon your priorities, you may make time for them—but only if there's reciprocity. Once Mercury begins its retrograde cycle on September 14, regulations or red tape can slow your progress. Tap into your network of resources during the Full Moon to keep the momentum going.

Cosmic Insider Tip

Unrealistic Neptune spurs excessive Jupiter, and your list of wants is growing. You could be tempted to pay more than necessary if your impatience wins out. Research has tremendous merit.

Rewarding Days 6, 7, 11, 14, 15, 19, 24, 25

Challenging Days 2, 3, 4, 8, 9, 21, 22, 29, 30

Affirmation for the Month Divine wisdom shines its light on the best path, and I follow with confidence.

⚕ Capricorn/October ⚕

In the Spotlight
Despite a few setbacks at work, you're closer to realizing important goals. Consider this an excellent time to repair problems, heal hurts, and review your future plans.

Wellness and Keeping Fit
Maintaining consistent energy can be a challenge, since your daily routine may not leave much "free" time to exercise. Make your health a priority, with a special focus on increasing your flexibility. Special care dealing with tension is necessary midmonth.

Love and Life Connections
The value of friendship is emphasized, and an old friend returns to the scene. Renewing your connection can bring you closer, but situations evolving after October 20 can also show where you've grown apart. Philosophical differences can add stress to your personal relationships, although you may decide to keep your opinions to yourself in order to keep the peace. This is the time to evaluate your relationships to determine how they fit your current needs.

Finance and Success
Until Mercury completes its retrograde cycle on October 6 you may be stuck in a tense situation at work due to a change of the guard or problems involved with complicated rules and procedures. Conservative mistrust of unproven innovations can overwhelm experimental possibilities, although there's room for new plans to emerge after October 24. Your vulnerabilities are most apparent during the Full Moon on October 21.

Cosmic Insider Tip
You know about Mercury retrograde and problems with contracts, but Venus enters a six-week retrograde cycle on October 10. That marks a time to eliminate situations draining your resources.

Rewarding Days 3, 4, 7, 8, 11, 12, 13, 16, 21, 22, 23, 31

Challenging Days 5, 6, 19, 20, 26, 26

Affirmation for the Month I am clear about my intentions.

⚚ Capricorn/November ⚚

In the Spotlight
Combined efforts involving a community or special interest boost your reputation and inspire fresh ideas. Your drive to accomplish your aims can overpower your personal time, although inviting your friends and family to join in the effort might be a good approach.

Wellness and Keeping Fit
When it comes to fitness, the buddy system keeps you motivated—especially if you're trying something different. Consider accepting a friend's invitation to join a fitness class or start a team sport. After November 20, inner fitness is emphasized.

Love and Life Connections
During the times you're openly expressing your fondest dreams and hopes, the light of your spirit shines brightest. It's easiest to reach out with a trusting heart and share your innermost thoughts with a like-minded soul during the New Moon on November 4. It could spur a romantic interest or strengthen an existing bond. Then, by the time the lunar eclipse occurs on November 19, you may be ready to celebrate the culmination of an amazing connection.

Finance and Success
Careful attention to your budget helps prevent unnecessary strain from November 1 to 16, when an unforeseen expense can take the wind out of your sails. You might just as easily overlook an important meeting, so double-check your calendar. Otherwise, all systems are "go" for an amazing period of advancement and success. Your individual efforts shine.

Cosmic Insider Tip
The lunar eclipse on November 19 emphasizes your artistry, and is an excellent indicator that applied effort (in other words—hard work), combined with talents, can take you to the top this month.

Rewarding Days 4, 5, 8, 9, 12, 13, 18, 19, 27, 28

Challenging Days 2, 3, 15, 16, 22, 23, 24, 29, 30

Affirmation for the Month My future is bright!

℣ Capricorn/December ℣

In the Spotlight
Momentum toward progress continues, and your influence expands. While enlisting the support and talents of others in your field, your leadership abilities also take hold. Your vision and focus provide the direction for tremendous rewards, personally and professionally.

Wellness and Keeping Fit
While you're busy setting goals, include something on the list about health and fitness. Your vitality is strengthened under helpful planetary drives. Plus, letting go of a destructive habit can bring renewal during the Sun's eclipse on December 4.

Love and Life Connections
Friendship can turn to passion if the situation is right. But if you're attempting to cross impossible boundaries, you can quickly run into trouble and confuse everyone—including yourself. It's easier to work through differences or explore your desires in a more practical manner once Mercury moves into Capricorn on December 8, but mixed signals can still leave you scratching your head is disbelief until after December 20.

Finance and Success
Careful attention to detail from December 1 to 7 prepares you for a successful launch of your pet project. However, you may not be satisfied with budget numbers and might delay final countdown until December 15. Investments fare best after the Full Moon on December 19, when it's easier to determine the direction a plan is likely to take. Before then there are too many issues clouding the picture.

Cosmic Insider Tip
The solar eclipse on December 4 emphasizes your need to tie up the loose ends from the past. Those old ghosts can cast a shadow on what might otherwise be a time of prosperity.

Rewarding Days 1, 2, 5, 6, 10, 15, 16, 24, 25, 29

Challenging Days 3, 4, 12, 13, 14, 20, 21, 22, 26, 27

Affirmation for the Month My intuition is my ally.

CAPRICORN ACTION TABLE

These dates reflect the best—but not the only—times for success and ease in these activities, according to your Sun sign.

	JAN	FEB	MAR	APR	MAY	JUN	JUL	AUG	SEPT	OCT	NOV	DEC
Move			29-31	1-12								
Start a class			12-28						7, 8			
Join a club											4, 5	
Ask for a raise	13											
Look for work				30	1-31	1-30	1-6	27-31	1-13	12-31		
Get pro advice	26, 27	22, 23	22, 23	18, 19	15, 16	11-13	9, 10	5, 6	2, 3, 29, 30	25, 26	22-24	20, 21
Get a loan	28, 29	24, 25	24, 25	20, 21	17-19	14, 15	11, 12	7, 8	4, 5	1, 2, 28-30	25, 26	22, 23
See a doctor					1-14	9-30	1-6					
Start a diet	24, 25	20, 21	19, 20	16, 17	13, 14	9, 10	6-8	3, 4, 30, 31	26, 27	24, 25	20, 21	17, 18
End relationship		26, 27										
Buy clothes				13-29								
Get a makeover	1-18			1-25								
New romance					12							
Vacation	3, 4, 30, 31	26, 27	26, 27	22, 23	20, 21	16, 17	13, 14	9, 10	6, 7	3, 4, 31	1, 27, 28	24, 25

AQUARIUS
The Water Bearer
January 20 to February 19

≈

Element:	Air
Quality:	Fixed
Polarity:	Yang/Masculine
Planetary Ruler:	Uranus
Meditation:	My creativity is a quality of mindfulness.
Gemstone:	Amethyst
Power Stones:	Aquamarine, black pearl, chrysocolla
Key Phrase:	I know
Glyph:	Currents of energy
Anatomy:	Circulatory system, ankles
Color:	Iridescent blues, violet
Animal:	Exotic birds
Myths/Legends:	Ninhursag, John the Baptist, Deucalion
House:	Eleventh
Opposite Sign:	Leo
Flower:	Orchid
Key Word:	Unconventional

Positive Expression:	Misuse of Energy:
Progressive	Fanatical
Friendly	Careless
Kindhearted	Detached
Autonomous	Undirected
Innovative	Aloof
Altruistic	Anarchistic

Aquarius

Your Ego's Strengths and Shortcomings

You embrace the extraordinary and go out of your way to connect with unusual people and situations. Uniqueness is your trademark, since you are the consummate individualist, shining light on the untrodden path. You think globally, and as "The Reformer" of the zodiac, you seek to overturn that which blocks the way of progress. It is the clear, quiet whisper of your intuitive voice that guides your journey, and the pure quality of unconditional love that animates the song of your heart.

Your friends are the treasure of your life, and you enjoy the company of people whose ideals inspire change. Your stubborn individualism sometimes gets in the way of your acceptance by those who seek conformity, but following the herd is simply not your way. In fact, your revolutionary attitudes can stir others to take actions they might ordinarily fear. Freedom is not just an idea for you, it's a way of life! You may not learn the lessons (and value) of responsible action until you are beyond your years of youthful rebellion. It is your connection to the unpredictable energy of Uranus, your planetary ruler, that stimulates your unique perspective on life and encourages you to be part of establishing a new order. However, you can also feel isolated and unsupported in the world if you go too far beyond the fine line between future possibility and the acceptable bounds of reality.

Sometimes you can appear more aloof to others than you intend to be. It's just that you can travel light years within your thoughts, and when you're "out there," you're more difficult to reach. Your true friends understand that your quest can take you away from them from time to time. But it is your connection to the universal mind that shapes your originality, and from there, your ideas and creativity illuminate the wisdom of unconditional love.

Shining Your Love Light

A relationship that supports the individuality of both partners is your goal. You seek a commitment based on mutual respect and dual autonomy. You might even decide that you prefer to create your own "rules" of commitment instead of following more traditional definitions of relationship. You need a partner who can be your most profound friend and a passionate lover, and will appreciate someone who knows when to leave you to your own pursuits. It is through a meeting of the minds that you learn to trust love, although your desire to be logical can get in the way of letting love lead your heart. You know when you're looking into the eyes of love. The question is whether you're ready to make the commitment that will allow love to blossom.

A communion of ideas is most attractive and comfortable for you, because you are an air sign. With the air signs—Gemini, Libra, and Aquarius—you are in common mental territory and feel most at home. However, your zodiac opposite, Leo, stirs your passions like nobody else and the magnetic attraction can be mutually intense. The problems arise if he or she requires too much attention without returning the same to you.

Aries keeps you on the move and invites you to communicate everything that's on your mind. Taurus holds onto everything, including you, and that will feel good only if you can let go and allow it. Gemini's mental gymnastics can engage your heart and mind and may be a delightful lover. Cancer's need for contact can seem too much like work for you to enjoy the relationship. Intimacy with Virgo can be uneasy, although he or she stimulates your need to probe the depths of your soul and unlock your heart. With Libra, you feel a connection of spirit and the two of you can relish exploring the multiple dimensions of life's beauty together. Scorpio's passions can leave you feeling awash in a sea of complex implications. Sagittarius can be a lifelong friend, pure fun and an excellent companion for your journey. Capricorn may ultimately become a friend, but control issues makes this relationship uncomfortable. Another Aquarian can short-circuit your emotions, since you may be wired differently and blow your fuses too often. With Pisces, you understand compassionate ideals and concerns, but personal intimacy may seem impossible.

Making Your Place in the World
A job might seem okay for a while, but your have your heart and soul on a life path that will allow you make a difference in the

world. Work that gives you ample room to express your originality will be most fulfilling and draw your greater talents. Scientific fields—like computers, aviation, electronics, the space industry, meteorology, or theoretical mathematics—can be a wonderful challenge for your mind. Or, you might excel in fields like advertising, public relations writing, broadcasting, or anything in the communication industry.

You can be a natural in fields like psychology and astrology that require you to blend intuitive and rational thoughts. Marketing your uncommon creations or owning a unique business can be lucrative options. You might enjoy a career in fine arts, ranging from original music to visionary art. Or, theatrical fields may be your bent. Political service can be a positive endeavor, and doing charitable work provides an opportunity for humanitarian outreach.

Power Plays

Status quo can seem like a power bandit to you. While you appreciate timeworn tradition, which still provides a positive platform for growth, you are likely to confront situations that inhibit healthy change or steal the passion from the human spirit. You may not seek power for its own sake, but are likely to stand shoulder-to-shoulder with others whose influence can bring healing into the world. Your piercing visionary sensibilities allow you to see the life circumstances in which power is wasted or abused, and to feel united with your life purpose you may make it your quest to eliminate as many of those abuses as possible. It is important, however, that you watch out for your ego, since your inner shadow, driven by selfish motives, can steal the light you long to show to the world.

Famous Aquarians

Corazon Aquino, Mikhail Baryshnikov, Jeb Bush, Richard Cheney, Gregory Hines, James Joyce, Douglas MacArthur, Leontyne Price, Vanessa Redgrave, Mary Lou Retton, Chita Rivera, Tom Selleck, Eddie Van Halen, Chuck Yeager

The Year Ahead for Aquarius

Bringing your dreams to life invigorates and inspires you, so that even more creative energy emerges. This can be your year to rise onto a different social platform, and from this space you can develop new friends, strengthen your working partnerships, and invite participation from others whose talents garner your respect and admiration. The year 2002 is the time to make your presence known in the best possible manner, since the impression you leave now can remain for years to come.

Your work load can grow from January through July while Jupiter stimulates your job sector. The good news is that this same cycle can bring support from others who are willing to help, and whose efforts enhance your productivity. Nonetheless, it's still tempting to take on more than you can carry, or to make promises without carefully considering their full ramifications. The most difficult element of this cycle is in determining which opportunities will be most advantageous. In other words, you may have to say "no" some of the time! In August, Jupiter moves into Leo, drawing your attention to your expectations about partnerships. It's time to consider what you truly want from a partnership, and to think carefully about the kind of partner you want to become. While it's tempting to make this about the other person (or lack thereof!), the real growth comes from your own increased confidence and optimism about your ability to have the kind of relationship you truly need.

Saturn's influence brings support to your creative endeavors this year. The place to focus your discipline and extra effort is in the development of your talents and self-expression. If you have children or if you're involved in guiding the lives of children in some way, you may also be instrumental in helping a child establish his or her creative potential.

The slowest-moving planets—Uranus, Neptune, and Pluto— have cycles that last a long time. You'll feel the influence of these planetary cycles most during the one- to two-year period when they make an exact connection to the Sun or other energies in your chart. To determine if this is your year to experience these cycles, check the paragraphs that follow. Uranus and Neptune continue their transits through Aquarius, stimulating your desire to express your uniqueness and develop your spirituality more fully. Pluto's travel in your chart emphasizes a deepening of your friendships over the next few years.

The solar and lunar eclipses draw your attention to the way you express your individuality through love and relationships. Friendships are emphasized by the eclipses, however all relationships that tug at your heart strings need some extra energy from you during 2002. A bit of introspection can be quite helpful, since the deepest emotional stimulus comes from how much you truly love yourself. This is the time to allow the flame of love in your heart to burn brightly, radiating a true light that allows you to experience the magic of devotion. Anyone you take for granted will appreciate your outreach, and the strength this brings into your life will also return the flow of love to you.

If you were born from January 20 to 26, you are feeling friction from Pluto's transit in semisquare to your Sun. This influence stimulates your need to explore the hidden motivations behind your personal and professional goals. If you've not made a serious attempt to review your goals in a long while, then now is the time to examine them. And if you are not the person who has set goals in the past, you'll benefit from asking "why?" Your politics may also change under this influence, since the ideals and the people with whom you associate have more meaning now. On another level, you can also clear away the obstacles that have prevented you from getting what you want from your career. While you're looking underneath those rocks, you might also discover a few abandoned hopes and dreams. It's up to you determine whether or not you want to dust them off and turn them into something!

If you were born from January 26 to February 4, you might trip over a few impediments during the second half of the year. From June through December, Saturn will transit in sesquiquadrate to your Sun. Consider this a time to test your priorities and to examine your responsibilities. Are you carrying unnecessary burdens? If so, you'll find that your life becomes much more productive once you lighten your load. You're also exploring the question of whose approval validates you and your life choices. If you're struggling to satisfy your parents, a boss, a partner, or someone else in sacrifice to your true self, then the tension can block your progress. After all, doing something just so somebody else will be happy is not enough. On the other side of that coin is the question of which obligations you need to satisfy that you have ignored or not yet fulfilled. There may be only one course between you and that cherished degree. Or you might have one last chapter to write in your novel. What's stopping you?

If you were born from January 28 to February 1, this is a year filled with magic, imagination, and spirituality. Neptune's travel joins your Sun in a conjunction aspect—a once-in-a-lifetime experience of enhanced sensitivity and heightened intuition. It's easy to let go, forgive, and open to peace and tranquility. However, this cycle does not motivate action, since the impulse is to escape or turn inside and explore your inner self. It's a good year for a pilgrimage. Or, you might prefer to focus more on your creative artistry—since your muse is dancing up a storm! As a bonus, during the months of January through March you're feeling the support of Saturn transiting in trine aspect to your Sun. This is the time when adding some structure and discipline to your day can make a huge difference in your ability to complete projects or produce results. Charitable and humanitarian efforts can provide the perfect opportunity to bring your visions to life throughout the year. The only thing you'll need to watch is your tendency to give too many people the benefit of the doubt. Prudent choices require extra effort, and to avoid the vulnerability presented by this cycle you'll do well to consult a trusted advisor before investing your resources.

If you were born from February 3 to 8, you're empowered by the cycle of Pluto transiting in sextile to your Sun. The more energy and effort you put behind your hopes and aims, the more influential you can become. Opportunities to advance your reputation and to focus your involvement in projects that become your trademark can be especially significant. Situations can improve dramatically through a little extra effort during the months of April and May, when Saturn also trines your Sun. These are also the months when you are most likely to achieve professional advancement, or when your influence has the most profound impact. On a physical level, you can also reach into the core of any physical distress or health concerns so that true healing follows. Not only will surface answers seem inadequate, but your desire to uncover hidden elements of problems can help you uncover strength that you may have failed to recognize before. This is the time to heal yourself and your life.

If you were born from February 8 to 18, you're experiencing enhanced focus and clarity this year while Saturn transits in trine aspect to your Sun. This cycle is more powerful after June of this year. However, it's never too early to start getting organized! If you've been waiting for the right time to put extra effort behind the development of your special gifts, you'll make more progress now than you may have dreamt possible. The right teachers emerge, or your own inner teacher becomes more accessible. Your ability to guide others is also enhanced, and for that reason, you may decide that it's time to take someone under your wing. A mentor program can be particularly rewarding now. On a professional level, this cycle indicates an excellent time to make your talents more "real." Turn your writing into a published work, record your music, show your paintings . . . let your talents been seen!

If you were born from February 11 to 19, this is your time to feel the lightning bolts of Uranus transiting in exact connection to your Sun. Unless you live another eighty-seven years, you will not have another chance to experience this cycle. You may find yourself thinking, "I now can see some of the reasons why I was born." This is a time of awakening, and a period of profound self-expression. Any hesitation you may have experienced in the past seems to dissolve under the impulse that whispers, "Do it now!" Some of those impulses might be good, others might just be impulses that get you into big trouble. Much depends upon how well prepared you are before you take action. While your intuition is likely to be clear as a bell now, your patience may have evaporated. Yes, this is a great year to experiment with possibility, and it is also an excellent time to start being yourself. However, you may not be able to create a perfectly clean slate, since other elements active in your chart right now might indicate that you have certain responsibilities that also need your time and attention. The marvelous thing is that you can now meet those responsibilities on your own terms. This is your time to become completely yourself!

If you were born from February 16 to 19, you can feel the emergence of some of your hidden talents while Pluto travels in quintile aspect to your Sun. This is a subtle cycle, but because you are also feeling the impulse from the Uranus conjunction to your Sun (see above), it has more profound meaning. Pluto's influence encourages you to strip away excess so that you can bring the finest you have to offer into manifestation. Consider this a special gift from the universe. What you do with it is up to you.

Tools for Change

Since you are likely to burn excessive mental and nervous energy under the current planetary cycles, extra attention to this physical need will add vitality. Of course, a balance of work, exercise, and rest will help immensely, but you may also need to be more attentive to your dietary requirements. Foods containing ample B-vitamins, or a supplement of B-vitamins, can help reduce the stress you feel. An emphasis on minerals like calcium and magnesium can also help, especially when it's time to rest. A diet filled with fresh fruits and vegetables may seem more appropriate, too.

To rejuvenate your body, mind, and spirit, concentrate on opening your energy (or chi) and keeping that natural flow. Techniques like acupuncture, shiatsu, or bioenergetics can be especially beneficial. Vibrational medicine and incorporation of magnetic devices might be effective, too. In the evenings, take time to relax before you go to sleep, and make a conscious effort to bring quiet to your mind and spirit. Herbal teas and aromatherapy using pure essential oils can be helpful tools.

Another tool is more abstract, but just as effective. Your creative expression can have a profound healing effect in your life, and may also be the key to what you desire to accomplish in the world. Find ways to surrender to your creative impulses. Make time in your schedule to write, paint, play music, design, draw—whatever it is you're inspired to do. The more you allow these impulses to open, the more powerful your energy will become.

Last, but not least—look for joy. Fill the coffers of your heart with joy and laughter. Share your stores of happiness with others. Engage in frivolity just because it makes your heart sing. Locate the parts of your life that make you smile, and spend more time there. Your joy will heal your own life, but, even more important, it will spill over into the lives of others.

≈

Affirmation for the Year

I am a radiant being, with a heart that sings for joy!

Aquarius/January

In the Spotlight

Places to go and people to see . . . there's plenty of connecting going on, and it's time to get your message out there. Watch where your money's going, though, since costs can get out of control.

Wellness and Keeping Fit

Fight off sluggish energy by gradually toning and strengthening your muscles. A change of scenery or alterations in your daily routine can give your fitness a boost. Down time during the Full Moon on January 28 will help to recharge your batteries.

Love and Life Connections

Unfulfilled passions surface in your dreams, although taking them literally could lead you to believe something that is not yet true or real. Your inner whispers, and early in the month your meditation time, provide objectivity about your needs. It's after January 19, when Venus enters your sign, that love is ready to blossom. A romantic encounter during and after the Full Moon on January 28 helps to clarify whether or not your amour shares your feelings.

Finance and Success

Money seems to go out as fast as it comes in, and your reserves can dwindle. Fortunately, capital seems to be on the increase after the New Moon on January 13. You're also attracting support from others who enthusiastically endorse you or your plans. Make an extra effort to communicate or meet. Despite a few setbacks during Mercury's retrograde that begins on January 18, you can still make progress toward a successful conclusion.

Cosmic Insider Tip

Far-reaching plans and visionary pursuits lift you and your reputation into the stratosphere after January 20. It's your time to enjoy the fruits of your labors.

Rewarding Days 5, 6, 10, 14, 15, 19, 20, 24, 25

Challenging Days 1, 2, 7, 8, 21, 22, 23, 28, 29

Affirmation for the Month I make use of all my resources.

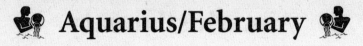 Aquarius/February

In the Spotlight
Travel and communication move you further toward realizing your aims. It's time to let people know what you have to offer, and to test your ideas against a backdrop of reality.

Wellness and Keeping Fit
Time in the open air can be especially invigorating, so take advantage of your favorite winter sports and get out there! Start a different fitness routine or initiate a daily regimen that better suits your needs during the Aquarius New Moon on February 12.

Love and Life Connections
The powers of attraction work in your favor through February 12, and a fascinating connection can be a sweet diversion from February 3 to 9. It's a great time to bring the fire back into an existing relationship, or to put out feelers if you're in the market for soulful contact with someone new. Value differences or concerns over money can taint the waters of love after February 17, especially if one or the other is stubbornly resistant. Dig deeper to locate the real source of the problem.

Finance and Success
Put a different spin on the situation at work to draw attention to the positive attributes of your plans or products from February 1 to 10. While Mercury retrogrades through February 8 you have a chance to uncover problems you may have overlooked. The New Moon on February 12 brings a fresh light on the path toward success, and those who've been slow to come around may finally lend you their support.

Cosmic Insider Tip
Some of the ideas that have been on hold finally come to life after Mercury and Saturn both move into direct motion on February 8. Dust off your dreams and bring them center stage!

Rewarding Days 1, 2, 6, 10, 11, 12, 16, 20, 21

Challenging Days 3, 4, 18, 19, 24, 25, 26

Affirmation for the Month I maintain communication.

Aquarius/March

In the Spotlight

Competitive situations add stress that can undermine your enthusiasm and vitality. The key to maintaining may be as simple as setting a more leisurely pace.

Wellness and Keeping Fit

You may need extra motivation to stick with your fitness routine. Concentrate on enhancing flexibility. Extra nutritional support helps keep your mental function in tiptop shape.

Love and Life Connections

Sibling relationships could use extra attention, particularly if family matters are stressful. Seek out your common ideals instead of concentrating on your differences. At home, watch for friction resulting from changes in family structure or in your home (like a move or renovation). To breathe life back into a love relationship, plan a getaway after March 20. At the least, retreat to your favorite romantic spot during the Full Moon on March 28.

Finance and Success

Market your ideas, attend meetings, or fine-tune your skills to keep you at the top of your professional game. While competitors can seem intimidating, once you discover what they have to offer you may feel much more confident. Misleading actions or information can throw you off track midmonth, but after March 19 you're back in the groove. Revise your budget from March 12 to 28, and make alterations that leave room for the cost of innovations.

Cosmic Insider Tip

Deception comes in an unexpected form, and may not be intentional. Still, the effects can create a setback from March 12 to 23. Alertness on your part makes all the difference!

Rewarding Days 1, 5, 9, 10, 11, 15, 20, 21, 28, 29

Challenging Days 2, 3, 17, 18, 24, 25, 30, 31

Affirmation for the Month My words and actions reflect a heart filled with kindness.

Aquarius/April

In the Spotlight

Your creative and artistic endeavors prove their merit and open the way for splendid success. Cooperative ventures are less stressful—as long as you can allow your individuality to shine through!

Wellness and Keeping Fit

Accidents are most likely if you're distracted from April 1 to 12, when even "safe at home" may not be too safe. Strive to maintain your center, and keep your focus directed at what you're doing at the present moment.

Love and Life Connections

Arguments at home can result from situations where you feel you've lost control, and are most likely through April 15 when you're feeling most uneasy. Romance quickens after April 14, when Mars stimulates your desire to be more expressive. But expect family to demand extra time near and during the Full Moon on April 27, even if you do prefer to stay more or less out of the picture. Obligations are obligations!

Finance and Success

Conferences and meetings clarify the direction requiring your focus, and the priorities you set during the New Moon on April 12 have a good chance of succeeding. Resistance to progress comes from those who do not understand the implications, and an explanation of your plans can diffuse that resistance. Try a "hands-on" approach, since not everyone has a grasp of abstractions. Speculative ventures are especially promising after April 25.

Cosmic Insider Tip

Practical idealism is the watchword of the Saturn trine Neptune cycle currently in effect. Use this concept to nudge others who have been reluctant to follow your lead.

Rewarding Days 1, 2, 6, 7, 11, 16, 17, 24, 25, 29

Challenging Days 13, 14, 15, 20, 21, 22, 26, 27, 28

Affirmation for the Month I am focused on this moment.

Aquarius/May

In the Spotlight
Your unique abilities are impossible to overlook, since your special talents are energized and their value is in demand. The only downside to this picture is deciding which offers to accept, which to put on hold, and which to reject.

Wellness and Keeping Fit
Recreational activities and sports may be the best way to stay fit, but you'll also enjoy exercise that incorporates an artistic element, like dance. One thing is certain: having fun is a key ingredient.

Love and Life Connections
To win the heart of your love, listen to your muse and take a truly inventive approach. After all, it's not like you to do anything in the "ordinary" way, so why approach love any differently? With Mercury, Venus, Mars, and Saturn all energizing your love sector, you certainly know how you feel, and the inspiration that comes from listening to your heart can be all that's required to get things moving. Make love a priority during the lunar eclipse on May 26.

Finance and Success
Bring together the best talent you can find to assure the success of a project. You can be part of a precedent-setting experience that challenges an outworn tradition. But don't expect the conservative elements to give up easily. There's a challenge, and you already know what you'll have to prove in order to gain the acceptance you require. Use Mercury's retrograde cycle after May 15 for follow-up meetings, further testing, and continual stages of development.

Cosmic Insider Tip
If you have children or if you're involved with kids in any way, you can find tremendous joy in their presence now. In fact, they may be the inspiration for your most amazing project yet!

Rewarding Days 3, 4, 8, 9, 13, 14, 22, 23, 26, 30, 31

Challenging Days 10, 11, 12, 17, 18, 19, 24, 25

Affirmation for the Month Love lights my way.

Aquarius/June

In the Spotlight

Now that you have the attention of others, all you have left to do is the work. The friends who gather to help you come from far and wide, and you can feel the momentum building during the Sun's eclipse on June 10.

Wellness and Keeping Fit

Your health can suffer if you push beyond your physical capacities. At the least, muscle strain is a possibility. Concentrate on extending your flexibility, and take a personal break during the lunar eclipse on June 24 that's health-focused.

Love and Life Connections

Work through your discontent with the actions of a friend by keeping an open mind and communicating honestly. This is no time to pretend you're happy if you're not, since the paradox can leave you feeling out of sorts. Look for the things you truly appreciate about others after June 14, and remind yourself that gracious acceptance of compliments sends a positive signal. Create a space for romantic fantasy from June 18 to 28.

Finance and Success

Adjustments at work fine-tune productivity, even though breakdowns or communication failures can be a hassle until Mercury leaves its retrograde cycle on June 8. Contract negotiations are intriguing from June 16 to 24, but hidden loopholes can be a much larger problem than you realize. Consult an expert, and if you're still not satisfied, postpone final agreements until next month.

Cosmic Insider Tip

Your insights about the weak links at work are right on the mark, and careful one-to-one communication can help diffuse major problems near the time of the solar eclipse on June 10.

Rewarding Days 1, 5, 9, 10, 18, 19, 22, 23, 27, 28

Challenging Days 7, 8, 14, 15, 16, 20, 21, 24

Affirmation for the Month I am sensitive to the needs of others.

Aquarius/July

In the Spotlight

Contentious situations spark a fresh creative direction, which might lead to even more competition. This can be dangerous at work if others are jealous. Know who your friends are.

Wellness and Keeping Fit

Emotionally charged situations can send your blood pressure through the ceiling, especially if you've been overdoing it. Plan some down time, and seek out the support of a personal trainer to help you get on track with a program that's tailor-made for you.

Love and Life Connections

A change of heart can have a profound effect on your partnership from July 1 to 9, especially if your relationship has run its course. You have to determine if you can still be friends, or if you want to create a new vision to share together. Once Mars moves into Leo on July 13, you may be more uneasy and less tolerant. Honest confrontations can heal, but deceit simply deepens a wound. Evaluate how you truly feel during the Aquarius Full Moon on July 24; it's time to forgive what you can, and let go of what you cannot change.

Finance and Success

Lay out plans and reasonable expectations on the job, but realize that situations beyond your control can throw a kink in the works near the time of the New Moon on July 10. Indirect criticisms can leave you wondering whether or not your priorities fit with your work situation. Finances can be a bone of contention from July 21 to 31, when your priorities seem out of alignment with your partner's.

Cosmic Insider Tip

Things are not what they appear to be. Patience and introspection are valuable tools, especially during the Aquarius Full Moon on July 24.

Rewarding Days 2, 3, 7, 8, 15, 16, 20, 24, 25, 29

Challenging Days 4, 5, 10, 11, 12, 17, 18, 19, 31

Affirmation for the Month I evaluate challenges carefully and completely before I act.

Aquarius/August

In the Spotlight

Good things are happening, especially in the realm of reputation and career advancement. There's one hitch: your competitors are definitely making their presence known, and the biggest one may be part of your inner circle. Call it a test of partnership!

Wellness and Keeping Fit

Your desire to increase your strength and agility can help you stay more active. You're a bit more accident-prone after August 18, when extra caution in unfamiliar situations can save your hide.

Love and Life Connections

Yes, you're right . . . there is another Aquarius Full Moon this month. That's two in a row. This exciting situation means that you're more aware of your needs. Partnership issues can be pretty dicey during the New Moon on August 8, but it's a good time to set up a different way of relating to one another that leaves out the guesswork and goes for direct communication. Then, by the time that Aquarius Full Moon rolls around on August 22, you'll be more likely to let your passions lead the way.

Finance and Success

Look at the bottom line, and do what you can to shrink your financial obligations. Then, focus your energy and time on promoting what you have to offer. Advertising, travel, publishing, or broadcasting can be especially successful after August 6. Old allies come to your aid, too, and may offer resources that speed your progress.

Cosmic Insider Tip

Your unique approach to problem-solving and innovative ideas go a long way toward advancing your reputation from August 16 to 22. But you could also feel a lot like the Pied Piper!

Rewarding Days 3, 4, 11, 12, 13, 16, 17, 20, 21, 22, 30, 31

Challenging Days 1, 2, 7, 8, 9, 14, 15, 28, 29

Affirmation for the Month I associate with those whose values complement my own.

🐾 Aquarius/September 🐾

In the Spotlight

The benefits of your partnership are emphasized, although you can see the weak points, too. While you're making your list of "likes and dislikes," take a careful look at what you've been avoiding. Honesty with yourself helps you make healthy choices.

Wellness and Keeping Fit

Explore root causes of physical complaints, since scratching the surface will only leave you unsettled. An old injury or illness can spell trouble during the New Moon on September 6. A holistic approach leads to significant progress.

Love and Life Connections

Intimacy is more than sexuality, although the physical elements of your close relationship can be a clue to underlying emotional distance. Trust can be a key ingredient to hidden issues, and if financial disagreements seem to be cropping up, then power is also a potential trouble. You may just be dealing with some old hurts that have nothing to do with your current situation. Either way, stay in the moment, talk about your needs, and listen to your partner.

Finance and Success

Legal matters move along best from September 1 to 8, although details of contracts can still be negotiated once Mercury enters its retrograde on September 14. Consider what you actually want and need, and reflect on your options after September 14. Look at the question of who's in control, since anything thwarting your independence now will seem intolerable.

Cosmic Insider Tip

The Full Moon on September 21 draws your attention to your spending patterns. Is there a link between emotional disappointment and spending? If so, do you want to change it?

Rewarding Days 1, 8, 9, 1,2 13, 17, 18, 22, 27, 28

Challenging Days 4, 5, 6, 10, 11, 21, 24, 25, 26

Affirmation for the Month I am aware of my real motivations.

Aquarius/October

In the Spotlight

Reconsideration of a proposal or an idea can result from information that's recently come to light. Changes in the hierarchy can also leave an opening for you to advance. Staying in the loop is important if you are to take full advantage of situations when they arise.

Wellness and Keeping Fit

Make an effort from October 1 to 14 to eliminate habits that drain your vitality. It's time to cut out the attitudes and offending elements that you no longer need, and to do more things that give you energy! Adventurous travel can be invigorating after October 19.

Love and Life Connections

Although you may not think you're one to hold a grudge, there may be something buried in your heart that stands in the way of forgiveness. Unburden guilt and let go of resentment from October 1 to 16, when you're ready to put things in their proper perspective. The spiritual quality of a close relationship helps you trust your feelings. A getaway helps immensely after October 12, or if you're seeking new love, you may very well find it along your journey.

Finance and Success

The details of an agreement may need to be revised, so take another look at them while Mercury is in retrograde through October 6. Then, sign final documents after October 12, but before the Full Moon on October 21. A change in the financial climate can leave you with uncertain choices after October 24, when a conservative approach to spending is the only option that makes sense.

Cosmic Insider Tip

Venus retrogrades for six weeks beginning October 10, prompting you to consider what you want to gain from your work in the world.

Rewarding Days 5, 6, 10, 14, 15, 19, 24, 25

Challenging Days 1, 2, 7, 8, 21, 22, 23, 28, 29, 30

Affirmation for the Month I clearly define the expectations I have in my relationships.

🌊 Aquarius/November 🌊

In the Spotlight

Emotionally charged communication may fly in the face of logic, although you can steer ideas into a more objective frame of reference. Despite this, you appreciate the thinking that conflict inspires.

Wellness and Keeping Fit

Nature beckons, and the more often you can enjoy the great outdoors, the more energized you'll become. Graceful, fluid movements help you get more in touch with your body.

Love and Life Connections

Family concerns leave you feeling spent, but you can balance the drain on your energy by incorporating ample time for daily reflection and a spiritual recharge. Memories stir a kind of yearning for simpler times, but when you honestly think back, you may realize that is partly illusion. It's time to allow the reality of this moment to dissolve illusions. The lunar eclipse on November 19 raises the question, "Are you tending to your soul?"

Finance and Success

Since the imagination of the public seems to be caught up in plenty of propaganda, your challenge is to extract the truth where you can and use it to illustrate different options. Use rich imagery and artistic elements strengthen presentations from November 1 to 20. Then, after November 21, concentrate on inspirational ideals to help influence your career course. Travel, publishing, teaching, or broadcasting can play significant roles in your work this month.

Cosmic Insider Tip

Look to the leadership of those you deeply respect for insights into the best way to strengthen your career following the New Moon on November 4.

Rewarding Days 2, 3, 6, 7, 10, 11, 15, 16, 20, 21, 29, 30

Challenging Days 4, 5, 17, 18, 19, 25, 26

Affirmation for the Month I am tolerant of the differences between myself and others.

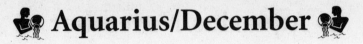 Aquarius/December

In the Spotlight
Your drive to accomplish your ambitions can be quite powerful, and it's easy to run roughshod over others in your climb up the ladder of success. Your friends may offer excellent advice, but it's only worthwhile if you use it!

Wellness and Keeping Fit
Buried stress can lead to tense muscles, requiring you to be more diligent about your fitness routine. Real time for rejuvenation makes a big difference, although you may be tempted to burn the candle at both ends.

Love and Life Connections
You may feel pulled in several directions, since the Sun's eclipse on December 4 emphasizes your need to spend time with close friends and special loves. However, Venus and Mars pull you toward family obligations, and there can be some confusion about whose needs are most important. Mixed signals abound from December 8 to 18, when you'll have to go out of your way to clarify what you mean. Fun and games return for the Full Moon on December 19.

Finance and Success
Professional alliances and good friends at work are most influential through December 8. Despite your attempts to treat everyone fairly, you may still run into trouble midmonth, especially if you've fallen short of somebody's expectations. Finances are most likely to become an issue after December 15, when impulse spending can lead to unforeseen difficulties.

Cosmic Insider Tip
The solar eclipse on December 4 can bring a few folks out of the woodwork, especially some friends you've not seen for quite a while. Consider it a gift for the holidays!

Rewarding Days 3, 4, 8, 9, 17, 18, 19, 27, 31

Challenging Days 1, 2, 15, 16, 22, 23, 29, 30

Affirmation for the Month I use my influence in the best way.

AQUARIUS ACTION TABLE

These dates reflect the best—but not the only—times for success and ease in these activities, according to your Sun sign.

	JAN	FEB	MAR	APR	MAY	JUN	JUL	AUG	SEPT	OCT	NOV	DEC
Move				13-29								
Start a class			29-31	1-12						6, 7		
Join a club												4, 5
Ask for a raise		11, 12										
Look for work							7-21			31	1-18	
Get pro advice	28, 29	24, 25	24, 25	20, 21	17-19	14, 15	11, 12	7, 8	4, 5	1, 2, 28-29	25, 26	22, 23
Get a loan	3, 4, 30, 31	26, 27	26, 27	22, 23	20, 21	16, 17	13, 14	9, 10	6, 7	3, 4, 31	1, 27, 28	24, 25
See a doctor	1-3	4-12					7-20					9-31
Start a diet	26, 27	22-24	22, 23	18, 19	14, 15	11-13	9, 10	5, 6	2, 3, 29, 30	25, 26	22, 23	20, 21
End relationship	28, 29											
Buy clothes					1-15	9-30	1-6					
Get a makeover	19-31	1-12										
New romance				26-30	1-18							
Vacation	5, 6	1, 2, 28	1, 28, 29	24, 25	22, 23	18, 19	15, 16	11-13	8, 9	5, 6	2-4, 29, 30	26, 27

PISCES

The Fish
February 19 to March 20

♓

Element:	Water
Quality:	Mutable
Polarity:	Yin/Feminine
Planetary Ruler:	Neptune
Meditation:	I surrender to the heart of divine compassion.
Gemstone:	Aquamarine
Power Stones:	Amethyst, bloodstone, tourmaline
Key Phrase:	I believe
Glyph:	Two fish, swimming in opposite directions
Anatomy:	Feet, lymphatic system
Color:	Sea green, violet
Animal:	Fish, sea mammals
Myths/Legends:	Aphrodite, Buddha, Jesus of Nazareth
House:	Twelfth
Opposite Sign:	Virgo
Flower:	Water lily
Key Word:	Transcendence

Positive Expression:	Misuse of Energy:
Idealistic	Gullible
Soothing	Confused
Imaginative	Codependent
Forgiving	Oblivious
Resilient	Victimized
Spiritual	Escapist

Pisces

Your Ego's Strengths and Shortcomings

With a special sensitivity to the many facets of life, your perceptions and insights fuel your compassionate soul. For you, life is meant to be an experience of magic and artistry, and the ideals of peace and spiritual enlightenment are among your personal goals. You play the role of "The Illusionist" of the zodiac, and whether you're involved in world service or enjoying a moment of whimsy, your actions can open others to possibilities they cannot envision as easily as you do. You know that it is necessary to be tolerant and flexible if you are to bring your dreams to life. But it's your belief in those dreams that keeps you going.

Even as an imaginative child you may have been perplexing to the more "down-to-earth" types, since the fine line between imagination and reality is your favorite perch from which to view life. Your sensitivity invites others to seek your insightful support, although it can be a challenge to draw the boundary lines between their needs and your feelings. It is your connection to the energy of Neptune, your planetary ruler, that helps you step into the spiritual realm, where you can let go of yourself and rise above the weighty issues of the day. This same flow of energy allows you to forgive, let go, and move on beyond the small stuff. Unfortunately, you can easily fall victim to corrupt individuals who would take unfair advantage of your kindness. By creating time and room to rejuvenate, and assuring that your actions are grounded by your highest needs, you can avoid many pitfalls. However, you can be tempted to go too far with your need to escape, and abusive or addictive escapes can exact a very dear price. Fortunately, you can surrender to the power of your spirituality to shed light on the best path. After all, it is from this source that you express the true magic of changing the world.

Shining Your Love Light

Your sensitivity and love of romance put you in the lead for "soulmate search," and love may be your ultimate quest in life. It will take more than a few disappointments in the romance department to convince you that your dreams of love do not have meaning. It is that deep yearning that fuels much of your creative passion, and it most definitely drives your desire to find a partner. You can weave an enchanting spell with the right person, and through surrendering to love can show the world just what it means to let love guide your way.

As a water sign, you feel most emotionally comfortable with others who join your element—Cancer, Scorpio, and other Pisces. You all share an ability to tune in to the nuances of feelings. However, it is with Virgo, your zodiac opposite, that you can experience the greatest challenges and most amazing chemistry. Together, you can become consummate partners and bring your dreams to life, but if you're not on the same wavelength, your castles will dissolve.

With Aries, your passion is spontaneous, but you can just as quickly feel disillusioned with one another. Taurus provides a foundation and safety net, and may enjoy your artistry while fulfilling your needs for consistency. Gemini keeps you on your toes and can leave you dizzy with laughter, although you may never fully trust one another. With Cancer, love is easy and expressing your feelings simply flows. Leo can be too demanding, especially if you feel like it's a servant-master relationship. Intrigued by Libra's elegance, you may create an artistic empire together—it's just that demands for perfection can leave you feeling too inhibited. Scorpio may seem like your soulmate, helping you open your passions while inspiring you to express your most soulful qualities. Just keeping up with Sagittarius can make your feet hurt, since what seemed real yesterday can be miles away today. You might feel safe with Capricorn, and if you are each in control of your own lives you can develop a lasting love. Whispering your dreams to Aquarius can lead to artful romance, but you may decide that friendship feels best. With another Pisces, your dreams can be encouraged and understood, but if your spirits are not in harmony you can get lost in confusion.

Making Your Place in the World

The right vehicle for expressing your imagination through your life's work can lead to contentment and true prosperity. The problem lies in determining the path that seems most fulfilling, since your wide-ranging interests can make it difficult to find one choice. Start with the idea that you may change careers over the course of your life, but seek something that inspires your faith in life itself. A career that brings more beauty into the world—like interior design, fashion, the floral industry, or landscaping—can be a good choice. Or, you might prefer a challenge to your imagination, and develop your talents in fields like music, dance, film, photography, or costume design.

Work that soothes the soul and spirit—social work, medicine, counseling, the ministry, or charitable efforts—can be fulfilling. Creating a diversion or haven for others through a restaurant, club, or amusement center can be perfect. In addition, your love for animals might prompt you to become a veterinarian or wildlife expert.

Power Plays
You know the power of faith. You've seen it in action more than once, and understand that your strength comes from a source that many cannot access. Whether your spirituality is founded on religious principles or a more eclectic path, it is through developing your compassion that you gain the greatest sense of power. For you, power for its own sake is wasted, and those who would overwhelm others with their demands or actions seem to be the most powerless in your eyes.

It's seeing yourself that can be the problem, particularly if you feel disconnected from your source. Through self-acceptance and tolerance of your own limitations, you move into unity with the universe. As you step outside of situations where you are the victim, you reclaim your power. It is a quiet force that radiates pure light, love, and timeless wisdom.

Famous Pisces
William Baldwin, Michael Bolton, W. E. B. DuBois, Fabio, George Frederick Handel, Jackie Joyner-Kersee, Joseph Lieberman, Shaquille O'Neal, Sally Jesse Raphael, Renoir, French Stewart, Sharon Stone, Laurence Tisch, James Van Der Beek, Gloria Vanderbilt

The Year Ahead for Pisces

As your life path continues to transform, you're experiencing an awakening of fresh creative impulses. Your tests during 2002 draw attention to the need for a solid foundation from which you can grow and prosper. In the process, you discover new friends, inspiring dreams, and a core of personal power that aids your ability to eliminate unnecessary elements from your life.

Under the expansive influence of Jupiter, your artistic talents blossom this year. Your thrust comes from the love in your heart that grows fuller the more you express your feelings. Whether the impulse comes from a new relationship, the significance of building a family, or a deep desire to fine-tune your artistry, this is your year to trust the voice of your ingenious muse. From January to the end of July, Jupiter travels through the heart-centered sector of your chart. Then, beginning in August, this optimistic energy moves onto the work front, when increased productivity can enhance your career. However, it's also tempting to overdo it when it comes to pushing your body beyond its capacities. If you yield to temptation and sample the dessert menu too frequently, you might not like what you discover when you step on the scale!

The limiting energy of Saturn tests your sense of security this year. Even if you need to make changes in your personal environment, you can run up against tests that shine the light on the difference between what you need and what you want. Perhaps solid-gold bathroom fixtures are not in your plans, but one thing's certain: if you overspend or commit to something you cannot handle under this influence, payback can be long and frustrating! This can be especially true when it comes to dealing with family obligations. Honoring your obligations is one thing, but you can collapse under the weight of responsibilities that are not yours to carry.

The planets Uranus, Neptune, and Pluto all move very slowly, and their strongest impact in your life will depend on the times when these influences make a critical connection (an aspect) to your Sun, Moon, or planets in your natal astrological chart. The area of your life influenced by Uranus and Neptune deals with your goals and hopes, and during the last few years you've probably had a wake-up call about the importance of targeting reasonable goals. Pluto's influence stimulates your need to explore your true calling. However, this cycle will be most noteworthy when Pluto makes a close connection to your Sun. Check the sections that follow to determine if this is the year Pluto contacts your Sun, based on your date of birth.

The solar and lunar eclipses during 2002 emphasize the need to strike a balance between home or family needs, and the demands of your lifework or career path. Establishing open and clear communication about your expectations and the expectations of others can be extremely helpful. You may also feel that it's time to break or loosen certain family ties, or to step away from traditions that have little meaning in your life. This may be part of the evolutionary process of change which occurs as you establish traditions of your own with a family of your creation. However, the changing roles in your family will also have an impact on your priorities this year.

If you were born from February 19 to 25, the universe provides a breather for your ego. None of the slower-moving planets is making a strong connection to your Sun, which means that your sense of self is intact. The tests and trials you experienced last year while Saturn was inhibiting your Sun energy are over, and some of your obligations are probably satisfied. There is one cycle you will definitely appreciate, which happens from late October through mid-December: Venus will be traveling in a harmonious connection (a trine aspect) to your Sun during this period. It's an excellent time to showcase your artistic talents. Just as important, these months can bring a special sense of satisfaction with your relationships.

If you were born from February 26 to March 3, you're feeling more sensitive while Neptune travels in semisextile to your Sun. This sensitivity can be a good thing, since the influence of this cycle helps you drop your barriers to your inner self. Delving into your psyche is easier, and opening to your spiritual essence can be exceptionally satisfying this year. The major feat involves your ability to keep your senses on alert, because it's easy to be distracted by illusion. This will be especially notable from January through the end of March, when Saturn is completing its cycle in a frustrating square aspect to your Sun. If you try to solidify plans during this time, you can be stymied by the fact that they seem to dissolve as quickly as they form. There's an unusual balancing act required if you are to make it through these cycles without feeling that you've lost track of your priorities. Begin by using the first three months of 2002 to complete projects already underway, or to tie up loose ends. Then you'll be able to step into the flow of your creativity more easily for the remainder of the year. On a personal level, the opportunity presented by this cycle of Neptune is that your intuitive and psychic insights can add a beneficial dimension to your awareness. Exercise your compassion more often, too—since your need to make a difference in the quality of life is tugging at you now.

If you were born from March 4 to 10, you are undergoing a series of transformational changes while Pluto transits in a high-friction square aspect to your Sun. This can be a very trying time, since some of the things you had counted on for your stability or security can change. Think of this as the time when your mask falls away, when you can see yourself with greater clarity. You might not like what you see, but you might also find something you treasure. This period of transformation exposes your vulnerability, while at the same time you uncover different dimensions of your true self. It's one of those times when you may find yourself asking: "If not now, when?" Hiding from yourself and from your deeper needs is simply not possible. However, you might feel powerless to do anything about fulfilling those drives. Or is that an excuse from your past? Power struggles are part of this cycle, too. The biggest issues are hiding out inside yourself, so if you wonder why you're being victimized, search more deeply to determine the part you might be playing in that picture. Extra care is also required from March through the end of June, when Saturn is also squeezing the energy of your Sun. The Saturn square to your Sun marks a period of testing, and these four months can seem like an eternity if you're not prepared for them! However, the issues that arise are not likely to come as a surprise. It's just that dealing with the realities can be exhausting. The key to both these cycles is to eliminate things, people, attitudes, and circumstances that are destructive. The very process of addressing these needs is empowering.

If you were born from March 11 to 21, you're feeling friction while Saturn transits in square aspect to your Sun this year. Some of that friction comes from the outside—from all the people and circumstances who seem to stand in the way of your progress. Before you give up and walk away in defeat, take a moment to reflect. Why are those obstacles in your life? One thing is certain: the blocks in your path demand recognition. You might be on the wrong path entirely, and the block can serve as a detour sign. Or, your path can be correct, but you might be trying to move too quickly. Saturn's influence slows your progress. It's a big-time reality check—whether you like it or not. If you are unhappy with a personal relationship, this is the year to explore what you need and how you can go about satisfying those needs. By the same token, you may find it necessary to identify what others need from you, since your responsibilities can drag you down unless you understand them. Physical ailments that appear this year can seem to take forever before you have control of them, although this can be the best time to alter your routine, diet, or lifestyle in order to get your health on track. The endings you experience during 2002 can be milestones, although you will not be able to escape dealing with your obligations or the need to take steps that can put you on a more satisfying life path. Educational pursuits and long-term projects can be part of this process, and this can also be a great time to teach or train others.

If you were born from March 13 to 18, you may wonder if somebody has turned on a cosmic fog machine! Neptune's transit in semisquare to your Sun can seem confusing, particularly if your priorities are not clearly established. The effects of this cycle are subtle, and you may not be aware of them until you realize that you've lost your way. Fortunately, Saturn's influence (described above) can actually help you stay on track. However, the temptation to stray or become distracted can create setbacks.

If you were born from March 14 to 20, the unsettling influence of Uranus can interrupt the flow of your life this year. While Uranus travels in semisextile aspect to your Sun, you can be thrown off balance by changes which are beyond your control. However, the excitement can open your creativity. You know what they say:

288 • Llewellyn's 2002 Sun Sign Book

"Necessity is the mother of invention!" This influence can also prompt you to drop unnecessary inhibitions and let your talents shine. However, it is not the best time to burn all your bridges. You may not yet be on the other side.

Tools for Change

The tension you feel now needs somewhere to go. You can absorb tension like a sponge under these cycles unless you make a concerted effort to release it and reclaim your flexibility. This requires a holistic approach if you're going to have the ultimate desired effect. That means working on body, mind, and spirit—the multipronged weapon against stress.

Body tools that can be especially effective start with regular exercise that incorporates a blend of strength training and flexibility. There are a few special tools you can include that can be especially beneficial, like the traditional Chinese healing method called gua sha, which helps to clear the lymphatic system and stimulates the immune system. In addition, bioresonaters (tuning forks), can have an amazing effect on your energy. Work with a Reiki practitioner to balance body, mind, and spirit.

To enhance your mental function, incorporate nutritional support in the form of increased omega-3 fatty acids (found in fish oils, flax seed oil, and some nuts such as walnuts). Or add an extra mental boost with ginkgo biloba supplements. Exercise your mind with word games, or stimulating computer games. Better yet, enroll in a class that is fascinating and mentally challenging!

The ultimate spiritual tool is mindfulness, which helps you stay in the moment and focus your concentration on what is before you. Meditation can also be an exceptional ally right now, and regular practice can lead to release of the unnecessary burdens of worry. Your dreams may present scattered images of confusing symbols, and work with a dream diary might be a lovely tool to incorporate into your daily or weekly routine.

Affirmation for the Year

My path is illuminated by the light of truth.
I can see my destiny unfolding.

Pisces/January

In the Spotlight

Despite power struggles, your drive to accomplish your goals takes you into record-breaking territory. The challenge is to determine priorities that will strengthen your foundation, but still give you plenty of room for progress. Friends help make your dreams a reality.

Wellness and Keeping Fit

The extra boost you gain through January 18 from Mars in your sign encourages you to focus on fitness. Strength training can be especially successful. High-risk situations should be avoided, though.

Love and Life Connections

Love grows in the fertile space of the dreams you share with your partner, and working together to accomplish your aims can strengthen your commitment to one another. You may face opposition from family, although it might be time to break away from unreasonable restraints. To reach an understanding, look for creative ways to illustrate your goals, since your family may not understand your motivations.

Finance and Success

Advancement and recognition can be your most treasured rewards for career efforts from January 1 to 20, although a raise never hurts! Before you grab the brass ring, be sure it's swinging in a direction you want to pursue. You might also be caught up in a battle that is not yours to fight, so think twice before you enter the arena. Once Mercury turns retrograde on January 18, you can take a project back to the drawing board to work out problems.

Cosmic Insider Tip

Before you reach out to rescue someone else during the Full Moon on January 28, evaluate your limitations. Otherwise, you could both sink in stormy waters.

Rewarding Days 7, 8, 12, 13, 16, 17, 18, 22, 26, 27

Challenging Days 3, 4, 9, 10, 24, 25, 28, 30, 31

Affirmation for the Month I am growing stronger every day.

Pisces/February

In the Spotlight

An unusual idea or scheme can be very intriguing, but before you sell the farm and move to the big city, take a trial run. You may be on to something big, but you could just need a vacation.

Wellness and Keeping Fit

Setting limits can be difficult if you're under a deadline, but a balance of work, exercise, and rest helps you sustain your energy and get more out of your days. Burning the candle at both ends will exhaust your vitality too quickly.

Love and Life Connections

An attraction can capture your imagination, haunting your dreams with possibility and building emotional intensity through February 14. In an existing relationship, explore your fantasies during the New Moon on February 12 as a way to build intimacy. Then, by the time the Full Moon occurs on February 27, you'll be ready to make memories as you share romantic moments expressing your love.

Finance and Success

While Mercury retrogrades until February 8 you'll benefit from brainstorming with others whose expertise helps you fine-tune a project. In the process, you may resurrect an old association which proves to be more valuable than it was in the past. Finances improve dramatically after February 11, when Venus enters Pisces. There's a slowdown from February 17 to 22, when you may need to reconsider a proposal before it is finalized.

Cosmic Insider Tip

Your situation is looking up, but your competitors are also paying attention. Use their interest to your advantage, but do not give away any secrets in your haste to prove yourself!

Rewarding Days 3, 4, 8, 13, 14, 18, 22, 23, 24

Challenging Days 5, 6, 20, 21, 26, 27

Affirmation for the Month I am grateful for the abundance in my life and share my good fortune with others.

Pisces/March

In the Spotlight

Now that you've passed some of the bumps in the road to progress, it's time to reach out to build a support team to keep the momentum going on your top projects.

Wellness and Keeping Fit

You may crave motion right now. In fact, sitting still can seem like punishment! Whether you commit to a regular walk, a daily swim, more time on the treadmill, or cycling through the woods, you'll feel an immediate surge of energy by staying active.

Love and Life Connections

The love in your heart spills over into everything you do from March 1 to 8, and can open the way for tremendous joy in your relationships. Initiate healthy changes that will clarify your needs and feelings during the Pisces New Moon on March 14. To bring your relationship into a more enjoyable focus, take time away from your regular routine and retreat to your favorite getaway with your sweetheart after March 12. But even if you can't go anywhere, keep that communication flowing.

Finance and Success

Your talents are at a premium, and others are receptive to your suggestions. At the same time, you can bring different factions together so that more can be accomplished. Misleading actions or communications can throw a monkey wrench in the works from March 13 to 23, when ignoring trouble can undermine your confidence and stain your reputation.

Cosmic Insider Tip

Flawed reasoning can motivate you to spend beyond your means during the Full Moon on March 28. Reconsider your options and postpone expenditures, unless necessity dictates otherwise.

Rewarding Days 2, 3, 4, 12, 13, 22, 23, 30, 31

Challenging Days 5, 6, 19, 20, 21, 26, 27

Affirmation for the Month I listen to others with an open mind.

Pisces/April

In the Spotlight
Your words may carry more impact than you realize—your ability to articulate your ideas is amplified. Not only can this positively influence career activities, but if there is something you need to communicate in your personal relationships, your voice can definitely sing true!

Wellness and Keeping Fit
Concentrate on nourishing your mind. Physically, review your diet to assure you're getting sufficient B-vitamins. Emotionally, clear your mind and let go of worries each day. Then, to improve your mental acuity, exercise your thinking with challenging mind games.

Love and Life Connections
Travel with your partner can be sweet, and may give you the extra time you need to reach an understanding about the things that make your relationship special. A day trip can make a difference, but if you can squeeze in a real vacation, extended travel from April 21 through the Full Moon on April 27 can be a special treat. On the family front, reach out to a sibling to touch base (or make amends).

Finance and Success
Meetings and presentations give you an excellent forum to move your plans forward. However, there can be a breakdown in communication from April 6 to 13, when unexpected events can lead to a series of misunderstandings. By April 14, progress is back on track, but caution will serve you well. In fact, a conservative attitude works to your advantage and invites the support of the old guard.

Cosmic Insider Tip
Imaginative plans and ideas are welcome, and if you want to get an idea into the public eye this is the perfect time. Watch for the emergence of a nostalgic trend early in the month.

Rewarding Days 3, 4, 8, 9, 10, 18, 19, 26, 27

Challenging Days 1, 2, 16, 17, 22, 23, 24, 28, 29

Affirmation for the Month My actions come from a loving heart.

Pisces/May

In the Spotlight
Friction at home can be unsettling, especially if others fail to understand what you're trying to communicate. An old issue can still be a thorn in your side. Before you decide the world's against you, retreat to a safe place to evaluate the contest.

Wellness and Keeping Fit
Staying flexible is more trouble that it used to be. The core of the problem can rest in your attitude about how you take care of yourself. Emotional stress can drain your vitality, too.

Love and Life Connections
Obligations at home can seem entirely too heavy if you've taken on burdens beyond your capacity. This can be a test of your ability to distribute the load of responsibility before you buckle under the weight of someone else's burden. Talk over relevant issues, reminding yourself that your needs do count for something. Fortunately, your creative approach can inspire others to help. There's also light in your heart glowing from an experience of pure love after May 21.

Finance and Success
Repetition seems to be the name of the game. The combined influences of Mercury' retrograde after May 14 and friction from Mars and Saturn can leave you treading water instead of making progress. A surge of vision and originality yields excellent results after May 21, although you might want to see where the leadership is headed after the lunar eclipse on May 26 before you expose your most valuable ideas and projects.

Cosmic Insider Tip
The old guard seems to have reinforcements, although there's room for innovation from May 6 to 18. It may just have to be presented in the guise of familiarity.

Rewarding Days 5, 6, 7, 15, 16, 24, 25, 28

Challenging Days 13, 14, 20, 21, 22, 26, 27

Affirmation for the Month I identify and honor my strengths.

Pisces/June

In the Spotlight

There's plenty of love filling your life, adding zest to your artistry and confidence in your abilities. Identifying your priorities is easier, but you're also in the flow.

Wellness and Keeping Fit

Recreation and activities that seem more like play than work give your vitality a lift. If you've been too inactive lately, this is the perfect time to enroll in a fitness or dance class, start walking, or take up a sport you enjoy. The more you move, the greater your energy becomes now.

Love and Life Connections

Venus, Mars, and Jupiter light up your love life, stirring your passions and strengthening your ability to attract what you need and want. However, the tension from the solar eclipse on June 10 draws your attention to family matters, and the best way to soften difficulties at home. The tide turns during the lunar eclipse on June 24, when others can see the purity of your intentions.

Finance and Success

Investments grow. Even if you're tempted to make major alterations in your portfolio, wait until after June 10 to act. By then, Mercury will be out of retrograde and you'll have the benefit of growth following the New Moon phase. Showcase your talents and ideas from June 11 to 14, and again after June 22. Invite others you admire to join you in efforts that can make a dent in a community concern. Together, you can all make a big difference.

Cosmic Insider Tip

Idealistic efforts go further than you first realize, which means it's important to be clear about your motivation during the lunar eclipse on June 24.

Rewarding Days 2, 3, 7, 8, 12, 13, 20, 21, 24, 29, 30

Challenging Days 9, 10, 16, 17, 22, 23

Affirmation for the Month My actions pay tribute to my ideals.

Pisces/July

In the Spotlight
Momentum continues, driven by your special talents and fueled by your passions. You can put all your efforts behind something you believe in, and feel a surge of energy that assures progress. But you can be deceived by others. Keep your eyes open!

Wellness and Keeping Fit
Feeling supercharged, you may be ready to take your fitness routine to a new level. Ignoring your limitations can lead to trouble, but working toward larger goals under the guidance of an expert can lead to amazing results.

Love and Life Connections
Renewal of an existing relationship can bring sweet rewards if you are truly committed to it. However, if you're single and looking for love, open your heart, since you can attract a delightful situation during the New Moon on July 10. What you are not interested in is repeating the same old mistakes. Consider the kind of partner you want to be, and listen to the concerns of the one you love. This is the time to shape your relationships into something rewarding.

Finance and Success
Hammer out agreements, then sign contracts from July 7 to 21 to assure success. Business meetings, presentations, and deal-making communications lift your career to a promising level, although you might be tempted to overstep your bounds after July 14. Concentrate on situations that enhance your productivity without compromising your aims.

Cosmic Insider Tip
Social activities can be the best place to meet your ultimate business connections after July 10. This is your time to see and be seen.

Rewarding Days 5, 9, 10, 17, 18, 22, 26, 27, 28

Challenging Days 6, 7, 8, 13, 14, 19, 20, 21

Affirmation for the Month I am loving, gentle, and kind—even in the face of adversity.

Pisces/August

In the Spotlight
Satisfying your demanding schedule can take plenty of energy and dedication. Carefully evaluate your promises, since you may commit to more than you can accomplish. It's time to call in reinforcements from friends and colleagues who are both talented and responsible.

Wellness and Keeping Fit
Adjustments to your daily routine can interfere with your fitness activities, and might even be a good excuse—except for the fact that you need to stay active! Care is necessary to escape accidents after August 11, when high-risk situations should also be avoided.

Love and Life Connections
Defining your role in your relationships is necessary if you're going to avoid misunderstandings. With changes in priorities and family structure, you may have taken on certain responsibilities that now should be delegated to somebody else. Open lines of communication can bring you closer to one another. The biggest issue involves a balance of power, and ample time for everyone concerned to enjoy individual activities without feeling threatened by time apart.

Finance and Success
Improvements at work results from technological advances, but a lack of training or understanding can be the fly in the ointment from August 10 to 20. Work closely with others who have expertise in areas where you feel lacking, and volunteer to help those who could benefit from your guidance. In finances, explore your joint investments. After August 7, review long-term financial plans.

Cosmic Insider Tip
If disruptions during the Full Moon on August 22 scatter your energy or destroy your ability to focus, consider taking a time out from the action to regroup.

Rewarding Days 1, 5, 6, 14, 15, 23, 24, 28

Challenging Days 3, 4, 9, 10, 11, 16, 17, 22, 30, 31

Affirmation for the Month I know what others expect from me.

Pisces/September

In the Spotlight

Your competitive edge is showing on the fringes of your usually calm exterior. However, your ability to rise above the smaller issues is enhanced. Your ideals and philosophical values are your best guideposts during the periods of greatest tension.

Wellness and Keeping Fit

Mars stirs up your energy since it's opposing your sign all month. Sports and contests can be excellent targets for your need to meet a challenge. The way you handle anger is also significant now, since attempting to repress angry feelings can lead to physical problems.

Love and Life Connections

Clear the air with your partner, but watch for power struggles if you're experiencing trouble with your family. It's time to determine where your loyalties lie and how these feelings affect your priorities. Ducking the issues will not work, but seeking answers under the guidance of a trusted advisor or mentor could be helpful. Revitalize your relationship by exploring your spiritual connections after September 8, when travel or time away from your regular schedule can provide a chance to grow closer.

Finance and Success

Legal matters and contractual negotiations fare best through September 12. However, continuing discussions once Mercury turns retrograde on September 14 can lead to significant progress. Presentations, advertising, teaching, and writing help advance your reputation this month, and business travel can be advantageous despite Mercury's retrograde.

Cosmic Insider Tip

The Pisces Full Moon (September 21) is your time to reflect on what you need most. A retreat can be beneficial, if only for a day.

Rewarding Days 2, 10, 11, 14, 15, 19, 20, 24, 29, 30

Challenging Days 6, 7, 8, 12, 13, 26, 27

Affirmation for the Month I trust my insights to provide clarity.

Pisces/October

In the Spotlight

Despite a few confrontations (or perhaps because of them), you're making progress toward your aims. Exploration of your spiritual objectives opens your mind and heart to creative possibilities.

Wellness and Keeping Fit

Inactivity is your enemy, but disciplined effort brings excellent rewards from October 1 to 14. You'll appreciate a routine that incorporates philosophical ideology and encourages a holistic approach to your health.

Love and Life Connections

To get back on track with your partner, embrace the soulful qualities that drew you together. Intimacy—emotional, spiritual, and physical—is your goal. Even if you're single, you can explore your approach to intimacy, since uncovering your fears allows you to make room for love to flow more freely in your life. Once Venus turns retrograde on October 10 you may feel you have more questions than answers when it comes to love.

Finance and Success

Review agreements and legal documents while Mercury retrogrades through October 6. Then, work toward more comfortable arrangements where joint finances are concerned. Set up a budget that allows you to get a handle on your finances. Extra care with large expenditures can help you avoid escalating costs or paying more than necessary. That "deal of a lifetime" may be a ruse designed to bilk you out of your hard-earned money, so think twice.

Cosmic Insider Tip

Power struggles with your partner might stem from differences in the way you handle your finances. Just in case, grab your goggles and dive behind the smoke screen. Is trust the issue?

Rewarding Days 7, 8, 12, 16, 17, 18, 22, 23, 26, 27

Challenging Days 3, 4, 5, 9, 10, 24, 25, 31

Affirmation for the Month Truth lights my way.

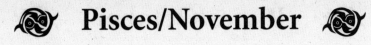

Pisces/November

In the Spotlight
It's not every day you get a second chance at something important. This month, you can recapture lost dreams, revitalize love, and reach more deeply into your soul. Or, you can drift with the current and admire the beauty of it all. Action is a valuable ally.

Wellness and Keeping Fit
Healing is a multifaceted experience. Cutting to the core of physical problems allows you to deal with rejuvenation that can make a difference. This is the time to concentrate on purification.

Love and Life Connections
To awaken love, travel outside your predictable routine—or travel, period. A romantic getaway can work wonders in your relationship from the New Moon on November 4 through the lunar eclipse on November 19. If you cannot travel, change the atmosphere at home, or make time to retreat to your favorite local haunts with your sweetie. If your passion is your creativity, that, too, can be a source of inspiration.

Finance and Success
The value of your talents is more easily recognized, and that means your finances are likely to improve. Showcase what you have to offer from November 1 to 22, launching new projects on November 4 and 5. Strengthen your association with others whose talents complement your own, and incorporate a multidimensional approach to create a more powerful effect. Your public persona is definitely out there during the Moon's eclipse on November 19.

Cosmic Insider Tip
While Venus continues her retrograde through November 21 you can eliminate elements in your relationship that stand in the way of real intimacy. It's a cosmic rummage sale!

Rewarding Days 4, 5, 8, 9, 12, 13, 14, 18, 19, 23, 24

Challenging Days 1, 6, 7, 20, 21, 27, 28

Affirmation for the Month I can let go of what I no longer need.

Pisces/December

In the Spotlight

Your desire to do the right thing can put you head and shoulders above those who prefer seizing power by less honorable means. Career efforts may be center stage, but life work and purposeful endeavors are your driving force.

Wellness and Keeping Fit

With your energy surging, you're revitalized and feeling unstoppable while Venus and Mars travel in complement to your Sun. The only problem can be establishing limits, so close your eyes when the dessert tray passes your way.

Love and Life Connections

Expressing the truth of your love turns the tide, and even resistant forces are likely to subside if your heart is pure. Expressing your affections flows beautifully, and your ability to let the light of love shine through heals old wounds and opens the way for lasting commitment. Family matters are important, too. Even a potential family crisis during the solar eclipse on December 4 can be a source of strength, when your love for one another awakens fresh potential in your relationships.

Finance and Success

Legal matters and court proceedings are favored this month, so if you have a case pending, work for progress now. Promotional efforts, teaching, publishing, and travel all lend a positive influence to your professional reputation. However, you might become distracted from December 8 to 20 and can lose momentum if you retreat before a situation ripens. It's important to stay the course.

Cosmic Insider Tip

With Venus and Mars traveling in tandem all month, you can ease the pace a bit and still get a lot accomplished. Consider it a gift.

Rewarding Days 1, 2, 5, 6, 10, 11, 16, 20, 21, 29, 30

Challenging Days 3, 4, 17, 18, 19, 24, 25, 31

Affirmation for the Month I am grateful for my life's abundance.

Pisces Action Table

These dates reflect the best—but not the only—times for success and ease in these activities, according to your Sun sign.

	JAN	FEB	MAR	APR	MAY	JUN	JUL	AUG	SEPT	OCT	NOV	DEC
Move				30	1-14	9-30	1-6					
Start a class				13-29	10, 11						4, 5	
Join a club	12, 13											
Ask for a raise			13, 14									
Look for work							22-31	1-5			19-30	1-7
Get pro advice	3, 4 30, 31	26, 27	26, 27	22, 23	20, 21	16, 17	13, 14	9, 10	6, 7	3, 4, 31	1, 27, 28	24, 25
Get a loan	5, 6	1, 2, 28	1, 2, 28, 29	24, 25	22, 23	18, 19	15, 16	11-13	8, 9	5, 6	2, 3, 29, 30	26, 27
See a doctor	4-17	13-28	1-8				22-31	1-5				
Start a diet	28, 29	24, 25	24, 25	20, 21	17-19	14, 15	11, 12	7, 8	4, 5	1, 2, 28-30	25, 26	22, 23
End relationship		27, 28										
Buy clothes							7-20					
Get a makeover		12-28	1-7, 14									
New romance					20-31	1-13	9, 10					
Vacation	7, 8	3, 4	2-4, 30, 31	26, 27	24, 25	20, 21	17, 18	14, 15	10, 11	7, 8	4, 5	28-30

The Twelve Houses of the Zodiac

You may run across mention of the houses of the zodiac while reading certain articles in the *Sun Sign Book*. These houses are the twelve divisions of the horoscope wheel. Each house has a specific meaning assigned to it. Below are the descriptions attributed to each house.

First House: Self-interest, physical appearance, basic character.

Second House: Personal values, monies earned and spent, moveable possessions, self-worth and esteem, resources for security needs.

Third House: Neighborhood, communications, siblings, schooling, buying and selling, busy activities, short trips.

Fourth House: Home, family, real estate, parent(s), one's private sector of life, childhood years, old age.

Fifth House: Creative endeavors, hobbies, pleasures, entertainments, children, speculative ventures, loved ones.

Sixth House: Health, working environment, coworkers, small pets, service to others, food, armed forces.

Seventh House: One-on-one encounters, business and personal partners, significant others, legal matters.

Eighth House: Values of others, joint finances, other people's money, death and rebirth, surgery, psychotherapy.

Ninth House: Higher education, religion, long trips, spirituality, languages, publishing.

Tenth House: Social status, reputation, career, public honors, parents, the limelight.

Eleventh House: Friends, social and community work, causes, surprises, luck, rewards from career, circumstances beyond your control.

Twelfth House: Hidden weaknesses and strengths, behind-the-scenes activities, institutions, confinement, government.

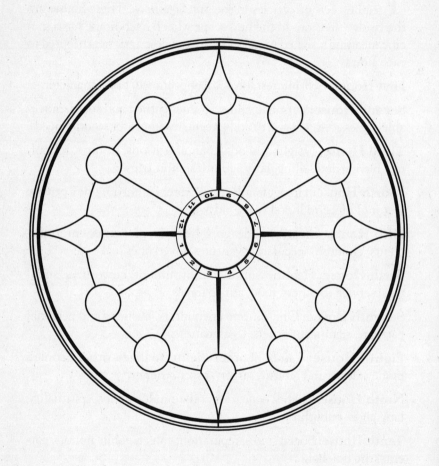

2002
Sun Sign Book
Articles

Contributors

Stephanie Clement

Alice DeVille

Marguerite Elsbeth

Phyllis Firak-Mitz

Mitchell Gibson

Kenneth Johnson

Jonathan Keyes

Dorothy Oja

Leeda Alleyn Pacotti

David Pond

The Sun and the Outer Planets

by David Pond

The Sun is the center of the solar system and the center of your self-identity, but it does not stand alone. Aspects from other planets inform and shape the Sun's expression and must be taken into account to fully understand your true nature. Aspects from the personal planets, Moon through Mars, will influence your personality. Jupiter and Saturn are the social planets and will influence your relationship to your culture and career. The outer planets are called transpersonal, dealing with forces beyond the ego-centered view of life and beyond your personal control. Aspects from the outer planets are influences from your soul, the eternal part of your being, and must be considered in that light in order to align with their energy.

In this article, we will discuss the major aspects from the Sun to each of the outer planets, but first we will explore the nature of the outer planets themselves. In the history of humanity, their discovery is relatively recent. We have known of the visible planets (Mercury, Venus, Mars, Jupiter, and Saturn) since ancient beings began watching the heavens and tracing its movements with a stick in the sand. These we can see with the naked eye, but it was not until we had access to the telescope that we became aware of the outer planets. Uranus wasn't discovered until 1781, Neptune not until 1846, and Pluto not until 1930. That they are beyond the visible realm is a clue: they exist beyond our normal realm of perception, and what works for the other planets does not necessarily work for these wanderers from afar.

The Triad of Spiritual Awakening

The three outer planets are forces that awaken us to a spiritual reality beyond our normal ego perceptions. Uranus breaks down the rigid structures that Saturn has built by confronting us with unexpected experiences and reminding us that we are not totally in control of our lives. With Uranus the unexpected happens; how we respond to this is not determined. Neptune is the imagination, which can lead us to fear or faith. With Neptune we can align with faith in our soul or indulge in the fear of the ego; the imagination can move in either direction. If fear is the response, the consciousness is driven back to the realms of thought bound by Saturn. If faith is strong, Neptune leads us to the bliss of the transcendent realms. Pluto is the planet of transformation and reveals which aspects of the ego need to be purged or transformed if we are to align with our soul's purpose in this life.

The ego, here described as your normal, everyday view of yourself, is relentless in its grip on reality. If it attempts to influence the outer planets, the ego always deflects energy from its true course, which causes the chaos that the outer planets are known for. It takes tremendous faith to surrender to the transpersonal realms of the outer planets, but the reward is well worth it. How many of us hunger to know our soul's purpose in this life? This message is encoded within the outer planets. They only create difficulty when the ego is involved—and that is the whole trick in working with them. The ego only has precedence up to Saturn; it creates trouble when it meddles in the affairs of the soul and the outer planets.

We modern astrologers talk a great deal about free will in our understanding of astrology. But free will is typically of the ego, and it essentially goes out the window in working with the outer planets. Carl Jung was once asked the question of whether or not we have free will: "Free will is the ability to do gladly that which I must," was his reply. Dare we consider destiny and fate in modern astrology? It sure helps to consider destiny when the outer planets are concerned. And isn't this where we will find the purpose that we hunger for? The soul's purpose will be revealed through the soul's realm: the outer planets.

Past Lives

Influences from the personal and social planets are straightforward and fairly obvious. As an example, if you have Mars square the Sun in your chart and you are prone to frustration and anger, it is never a mystery as to the source of your current conflict. There will be something obvious and tangible that you can identify as causing your current difficulty. This is not the case with the outer planet aspects—what you see is not necessarily what you get. Their influences are much more pervasive and insidious. To understand the aspects of the outer planets we must be willing to expand our search beyond the obvious—even into the realm of past life influences.

Although one needn't subscribe to the principle of reincarnation to benefit from astrology, considering one's birthchart as an energetic reflection of the accumulated experiences from past lives can be very revealing. This implies it was not a capricious, random event that brought you to your current birthchart. Instead, your chart reveals the work you've done, and not done, on your consciousness growth in your own past lives.

Due to the length of their orbits, the outer planets are indicative of residual issues from past lives. After all, what were you doing 84, 165, or 250 years ago? This is the length of these cycles: Uranus takes 84 years to complete its orbit, Neptune takes 165 years to complete its journey, and Pluto takes 249 years. Because of the duration of these cycles, the aspects of the outer planets tie us to cycles longer than our personal life.

Stressful aspects—the squares and oppositions—are indicative of leftover problems from when you likely misused or mishandled the energy of these planets in a previous life. The harmonious aspects—sextiles and trines—are indicative of where you are receiving benefit from using the energy wisely in a previous incarnation. The conjunction is special and is neither positive nor negative in itself.

With one of the outer planets conjunct your Sun, your self-identity is linked to that planet and you have earned the opportunity to use the energy for good or for ill.

Uranus

Uranus is electric; it quickens the energy wherever it shows up. It is the intuitive voice of your authentic self. Uranus needs to overthrow the conditioning of culture to discover its unique view of life. This is the most innovative part of yourself and connects you to the universal mind. Uranus is known for its "flashes" of insight and sudden knowing. It is the higher octave of Mercury. Where Mercury represents rational thought, Uranus represents intuitive knowing. Mercury weighs, analyzes, and generally comes to know something from the outside. Uranus enters into direct knowing, merges with what it wants to learn about, and discovers it from the inside. As a transpersonal planet, it connects you to the realms beyond self—the collective mind.

Your Sun Conjunct Uranus

You have an exciting personality. Intuitive, quick-minded, and innovative in all that you do, you can be counted on to add a unique perspective to any situation. Your independent nature requires you to be either self-employed or to work with someone who gives you complete license to do things your own way. Because of your resistance to restraints of any kind, you are much better operating independently than with a team. You are the opposite of a creature of habit, always ready to shake things up and try things a new way.

You function as an evolutionary agent in other people's lives. You have obtained the freedom of self-expression and always honor your instincts over convention. Your mental energy is boundless, and you constantly have flashes of insight that come to you unbidden. When you are interested in something, you have the capacity for instant learning and sudden knowing. You invent life as you go. You can learn to align with the quickened energy of Uranus by breathing into the energy when you feel it. This will allow you to stay in high levels of energy and use them without facing the danger of burnout.

Your Sun Sextile Uranus

You love to be in situations that require you to look at circumstances in a unique way and puzzle through the issues at hand. It is not that you have a disregard for convention, but rather that you love to stay in an attitude of discovery and are known for your ability to provide fresh insight in most situations. The higher mind and intuitive faculties are like sport for you. Your insights fit with reality. You seem to be tapped into the universal mind, and when you are solving problems or being creative it is like you are grasping ideas right out of the air.

You have an exciting personality that seizes opportunities when they present themselves. You do not need to prove your individuality; you have mastered that in previous lives, so your uniqueness and individuality add to your life and rarely stir trouble with others. Self-doubt is a stranger to you, as your experience has taught you that you are able to rise to the occasion.

Your Sun Square Uranus

The tension of the square shows that you are being tested in your ability to maintain your individuality without creating turmoil in your life. You have an independent streak a mile wide that often makes it difficult to sustain cooperative relationships. In needing to prove your independence, you constantly attract people and situations into your life that attempt to control, restrain, and restrict you. You will not tolerate this, and you rise to the occasion and prove your independence by breaking free of the situation at hand. Whether you have difficulties with commitment, or you attract people to you who have difficulty making commitments, it's an issue one way or another. Eventually you get the cosmic joke: if you need permission and approval from others to be free, you are not free in the first place.

You have likely been in intolerable situations of oppression of individual rights in a previous life and have vowed not to succumb again in this life. The tendency is to fight for your right to be free, and you need to learn how to live in a free way rather than struggle for it. It is important to stay mindful of your health, particularly the heart and nervous system. Your energy runs a little raw anyway: vitamin B can be helpful to strengthen your nervous system and protect you from burnout.

Your Sun Trine Uranus

You have an ability to express your individuality without going over the line and becoming obnoxious. You are able to assert yourself without the edge of needing to prove yourself. You have an easy way about you, in that you can trust your innovative nature to solve most any problem you come up against. Whether it be in the arts, business, or your lifestyle, your creative capacity is boundless and is demonstrated in all that you do. You have the confidence of knowing that your life is going to work out. Your brilliant ideas are often integrated with the needs of the situation at hand, and you can be counted on to offer a fresh perspective.

You are not threatened by differences in others and can even be inspired by the creativity of others without following them. You have learned in previous lives that creativity is an inexhaustible human resource, so you never hoard your insights. Instead, you willingly offer some of your best ideas to others, knowing there are plenty more where they came from.

Your Sun Opposite Uranus

The opposition aspect is just as strong as the conjunction, with one key difference: the conjunction is internal and the opposition is external. Instead of being confident about your original ideas, you tend to doubt yourself, and need a great deal of affirmation from others. Needing to constantly prove your individuality makes cooperating with others difficult. The opposition often works out through relationships, and you may find that you attract unusual, interesting, and eccentric people into your life. You are easily bored by convention and tradition, preferring to be a revolutionary in one way or another. You don't mind stirring the pot to force others to look at their lives in a liberated manner, and are most drawn to those who have broken the mold and gone their own way. You are attracted to alternative lifestyles and are quite willing to bend the rules to fit your own needs. Others have always seen you as a highly original person, and your test is to accept this about yourself without having to constantly prove it.

You have likely felt overshadowed by the genius of others in a previous life and have taken on the challenge of rising to your own greatness in this life. Try not to measure yourself against others and do watch your health. You can start running on nervous energy and forget to eat and sleep, which can lead to irritability, skin rashes, or nervous tics. As you become secure with the source of creativity, you can allow yourself appropriate rest, not fearing that somehow the creative energy will go away.

Neptune

Neptune brings the urge for transcendence—to experience the mystical and to escape the doldrums of everyday reality. Where Uranus is electric and quickens the pace of whatever it interacts with, Neptune is dreamy and pulls your attention away from your current reality through the imagination. Whether this is healthy and leads to the heights of inspiration or whether this leads to escapism and illusion is up to the individual. From the meditative bliss of spiritual union with the Divine, to getting lost in creative inspiration, to just getting lost in the illusions of fantasy, drugs, and alcohol, Neptune leads us through the highs and lows of the imaginary world.

With Neptune in aspect to the Sun, this transcendent realm holds a special allure—for good or for ill. Even if Neptune is in favorable aspect to the Sun, it still takes special training to navigate these waters. Neptune represents the notorious blind spot in your chart, until you've trained your imagination to link with true inspiration and to pull out of the world of delusions. Neptune's job is to dissolve the separate self-identity so that one can merge with the Divine. If the ego dissolves when you are meditating, this is bliss—and the point of meditation. But if the ego dissolves in the middle of an important business negotiation, this is an identity crisis! Meditating, creative activities, a mystical union with nature or music, and quiet contemplation are some of the ways to train Neptune towards its highest expression.

Your Sun Conjunct Neptune

This union brings acute sensitivity to the subtle planes of reality, and this world often seems too abrasive for the refined nature of your temperament. Many Sun/Neptune types feel like they come from another planet and wish they could go home! It is as if you have an antenna that extends a half-mile up into the heavens, and you sense the subtlest shifts in the vibrations around you. You are aware of planes of reality that others don't even know exist. If you choose to develop your spiritual nature or psychic sensitivity, you will find that you have direct access to other planes and can even develop a rapport with guides from the other side. In all ways, your sensitivity is going to be an issue, for good or for ill. Your spiritual energy affects your entire nature, so you pick up vibes, good and bad. You likely crave a life of serenity and transcendence. Your sensitivity in the body is such that you need to stay mindful of exposures to toxins, poisons and pesticides: wash your vegetables!

You have likely worked on developing your spiritual nature in previous lives by denying bodily existence, and in this life the test is to link this mystical aspect of life with the vitality of the Sun, the body, and the ego.

Your Sun Sextile Neptune

You are rarely gripped by fear, as faith is your natural orientation to life. Imagination is your friend and ally and it is not unusual for you to feel inspired. You have deep appreciation for the arts and creativity of all sorts. It is natural for you to rise above petty conflicts and to see things through a perspective that encompasses polarities. It is likely that you have been involved in spiritual paths in past lives, and all things spiritual come naturally to you because of this. You are most often able to quiet your ego without practicing self-denial. Your compassionate nature is a hallmark of your personality, and you are able to empathize with the suffering of others without getting pulled into their woes.

Your Sun Square Neptune

Your sensitivity and imagination are as much of a problem for you as they are a benefit. The needs of Neptune and the spiritual realm are at odds with the needs of your ego, so it will be a test to link them together in a harmonious way. This aspect is considered a spiritual crisis in that your soul will not allow you to find complete fulfillment in the world until you have come to spiritual reconciliation within yourself and with the Divine. It can be hard to separate fact and fantasy with this aspect. Your daydreams are often disruptive, and it is not unusual for you to believe that your life would be better if it were only different. You often lack confidence at a critical moment when you seem to need it most. This aspect is insidious and it is not easy for you to track down the source of what is currently ailing you. Your health is vulnerable to toxins and viruses, so keep your immune system strong.

In your past lives, you have likely learned to use the Divine only in times of crisis. In this life, it would be helpful for you to connect with God in times of peace. Starting the morning off with a meditation and imagining that your life is absolutely perfect just the way it is can be helpful.

Your Sun Trine Neptune

The trine between Neptune and the Sun shows a creative flow of energy between your personality and soul. You do not see God as separate from this world and are able to see the smiling face of the Divine reflected back through all creation. There is nothing of the zealot or religious fanatic in you. Instead, there is a sense of grace on your spiritual path, and it is natural for you accept other people's beliefs without feeling threatened. You have likely integrated your spirituality with your personality in past lives, and this will manifest as a powerful faith in this life, with tremendous inner guidance available when you pray or meditate. Beauty inspires you and is much akin to a spiritual experience for you. You are compassionate and able to help others without getting pulled into their sufferings.

Your Sun Opposite Neptune

Your sensitivity is as much of a problem for you as it is a benefit until you get a handle on your imagination. You are easily deceived by others because you tend to see things as you wish they were, not how they actually are. Yes, the incurable romantic in you falls in love with what you wish were true, and not always what is true. You will learn in this life that fear and faith are two sides of the same coin, and until you've learned this, you will have bouts of insecurity. Your sensitivity would be best suited for pleasant harmonious working situations. You tend to avoid conflict rather than stand up to it, so working with intimidators is simply awful for you. It is all too easy for you to sacrifice your needs for others, so be careful not to walk the path of the martyr.

In past lives you have learned to draw on the strength of the Divine in times of crisis, like an escape from terrible circumstances. In this life it is a test to align with the Divine in a more graceful way rather than just an ally in times of darkness. Psychic sensitivity and spirituality are easily developed, but here again, you must be cautious not to fall prey to false teachers.

Pluto

The Sun is the center of the solar system and Pluto is the farthest planet out, the farthest away from the center of your self-identity. Thus, the ego has little influence with the subconscious drives that this distant planet represents. Pluto reveals the deep-seated karmic patterns that have been with you for lifetimes, and points to the final transformation and purging of all that stands in the way of fulfilling your highest destiny. Pluto often leads to obsessive-compulsive behavior and, with it aspecting the Sun, it will be important for you to find healthy outlets for your need to throw yourself passionately into whatever you are doing.

In mythology, Pluto is said to wear the helmet of invisibility and thus cannot be seen directly. You become aware of Pluto in the way it shows up in your life, particularly in dealing with issues of power. The Sun, representing the ego, fears its demise in dealings with this planet of death and rebirth. The times that you fear Pluto and push it away are the times when its power over you is the greatest. It takes tremendous character strength to be willing to see the shadow side of your own character. When you are not in touch with your Pluto issues, either you attract those who misuse their power (by being controlling, domineering, manipulative, or abusive), or you misuse your own power in the same ways. The high road in dealing with Pluto issues is to be constantly vigilant for its misuse and pledge yourself to using power in such a way that benefits not only yourself but others as well.

Paradoxically, most of us would like to know what our soul's purpose is in this life, but we fear surrendering to the very voice within that knows: Pluto.

Your Sun Conjunct Pluto

You are being tested with the use of power in this life. You have charisma and magnetism that pulls people into your orb of influence, and others react to you very strongly—sometimes favorably, sometimes not. You are an extremist in most everything that you do. Destiny and fate seem to mark your life more than most. When you think back over your life, I'm sure you'll agree that destiny has played an important role. It is almost impossible for you to be in situations that you don't control, and the paradox of paradoxes is that it is not until you surrender control that your life is likely to take off in the way you really want it to. You've got to ask yourself, "Is it the power of love, or the love of power that animates my life choices?"

You may have spent lifetimes in the mystery schools and have acquired occult abilities to see into realms that others are not even aware of. This makes you aware of the darker forces in life, and you're not fooled by hidden agendas. You are a force to reckon with, and when you have pledged yourself to aligning with your highest destiny you can be a powerful force for changing the world you live in for the better.

Your Sun Sextile Pluto

Your greatest gift is your ability to be powerful without being domineering. You are able to handle the responsibility of leadership in a very admirable way: by taking charge when situations call for it, and disappearing when appropriate. Others defer to you and feel empowered in their relationship with you. You have likely worked with the spiritual disciplines of yoga and meditation for many lives, and are able to surrender your ego to a higher power because of this. You understand that surrender is not sacrifice, and this gives you a deep trust in your destiny. Your range of perception is profound and allows you to size up a situation immediately and take the appropriate action.

Your Sun Square Pluto

Your powerful will is a great gift, but also your biggest enemy. Power conflicts are not unlikely scenarios for you, and before you engage in these, please stop and ask yourself two important questions: (1) "Am I really threatened; is survival or security on the line?" and (2) "Do I really care?" If the answer is no to either of these questions, learn to step out of the way lest you become a scratching post for others to test their power on. It is likely that your most recent life ended in a sudden, abrupt way and you came into this life with the shock of that last life still lingering, so you look over your shoulder at each and every turn and wonder, "Am I safe?" You tend to respond to everything as if it were a test of survival. Try to remember that your apprehension is based on memory, not anticipation.

When survival is on the line, morals, values, and ethics fade into the background. When you feel threatened, you tend to respond with the awesome force of a hunted animal. You have an incredible will and considerable strength, and, until these are brought into alignment with your values, they create difficulty in your relationships with the world around you.

Your Sun Trine Pluto

You have learned how to draw on a higher power in previous lives, and in this life it is most natural for you to "let go and let God." Although your personal power seems considerable to others, you know that this comes from a higher source. Others are comfortable when you are in situations of leadership because you are able to draw on this higher power and fulfill the needs of the group that you serve. Instead of imposing your ideas on a situation, you simply surrender to the needs of the moment and are led to the appropriate behavior. You do not overreact to challenges, and are able to gracefully deal with most situations. Others will support your achievements in this life because you instinctively align with the greater good for humanity. You have a very strong constitution and are able to rise above petty power conflicts. Your powers of rejuvenation are both physical and emotional, and you likely have healing abilities for others as well.

Your Sun Opposite Pluto

The Sun is the center of the solar system and Pluto is the farthest planet out—and your range of perception covers this entire territory. You trigger a stronger response in others than you ever intend, sometimes bringing out the best in others and sometimes bringing out the worst. This is not dependent on your intentions or behavior; it simply comes with this aspect. Your energy provokes a subconscious reaction in others, bringing to the surface what was previously hidden, whether it be gems or garbage. You are learning about your power in this life by watching how others respond to you. There are times when you seem to get caught up in office politics and community affairs and you're not sure how you got pulled into the situation. Yes, you tend to get obsessive—so find something healthy to obsess over.

Your personal power is considerable, and when you have learned to align your power with the needs of others you can function as a powerful transformational force in their lives. Until you've connected to a higher power, the needs of your ego will interfere and you will seem like an egomaniac to others. In previous lives, you have been overshadowed by the existing powers of the time. This leads to an incredible need to prove yourself in this life. As you learn to surrender to a higher power and trust in your destiny, your light will shine brightly and you'll do good in the world.

For Further Reading

The Astrological Neptune and the Quest for Redemption by Liz Greene. Weiser, 1996.

The Gods of Change: Pain, Crisis and the Transits of Uranus, Neptune and Pluto by Howard Sasportas. Arkana, 1990.

How To Personalize the Outer Planets: The Astrology of Uranus, Neptune, and Pluto edited by Noel Tyl. Llewellyn, 1992.

Sun Signs and Your Health

by Jonathan Keyes

Five hundred years ago in Renaissance Italy, an astrologer and physician by the name of Marcilio Ficino helped translate ancient philosophical and medical astrology texts. These texts included the *Corpus Hermeticum*, a collection of writings by Hermes Trismegistos, an ancient Egyptian priest and philosopher. At the core of this text is the famous motto, "As above, so below." This phrase implies a cosmic sympathy between man, nature, the planets, and the stars.

Ficino's writings and translations became the foundation for a European rebirth in medical astrology: the study of the relationship between the stars and our health. The famous English astrologer and physician, Nicholas Culpeper, wrote compendiums describing the relationship of herbs to planets and signs. Certain herbs and foods correlated well to certain astrological configurations and were prescribed according to one's astrological chart. This practice fell into disuse in the eighteenth century when the new vanguard of scientists and doctors discarded astrology as superstition. At the end of the twentieth century, a renewed interest in medical astrology has encouraged people to look again at this ancient form of Western energetic medicine. With the growing acceptance of Chinese medicine in the form of acupuncture and Indian philosophy in the form of yoga and Ayurveda, traditional European medicine is again enjoying a rebirth of its own.

Medical astrology not only teaches us the correlations between the planets, signs, and the natural world, but teaches us a way to walk in tune with the cosmos. Medical astrology describes a universe of rhythms and vibrations, all integrating and intertwining. The natural energies and elements of the universe are found in all life and matter, and have the capability of harming or healing us depending on how we work with them. When we study our astrological chart, we begin to understand our own internal energies and the way we naturally flow in the world. Certain herbs, stones, and lifestyle choices can help augment our natural energy and bring us to our highest potential—our best resonating frequency.

Not only does medical astrology point us toward living in balance and health in our own lives, it points us toward connecting with the natural world and indeed the cosmos. Medical astrology posits that the best energy is found in the simplest of things: sunlight (fire), a gentle breeze (air), an alpine lake (water), and lush rolling hills (earth). When we choose to value these simple, precious elements, we can increase our joy and sense of awe in the wonders of everyday life. Medical astrology is not only a road towards better health but is a spiritual path towards greater harmony with the world we walk on.

Aries: The Ram

Spirit

Aries is ruled by Mars and is a vigorous fiery sign. Those with this sign have the capacity to be the pioneers, the creators, and the leaders in their community.

This sign has a lot to do with actualizing the self to its highest potential. Because it is a self-oriented sign, people influenced by Aries need to work on balancing their energies with others. It is important to honor the creative energies Aries has as its natural birthright, but not to let those energies dominate over others.

Lifestyle

Aries signs have a tendency to overdo things and burn out their fires. Though they need projects and activities to keep them happy, it is also essential to find plenty of time for rest and slowing down. Concentrating their energies in slow and direct ways can be very beneficial. This includes yoga, meditating, and cooling down periods and vacations from time to time to recharge the batteries. Aries signs would also do well to channel their energies in creative ways such as painting and making music.

Aries rules the head, and those with a lot of Aries in their chart will often have a prominent facial or cranial feature. Aries natives can also be more prone to headaches and head injuries and need to be more aware of this part of their body. Because it is a fire sign, Aries is more prone to fiery ailments like inflammations, eczema, ulcers, and circulation problems. Aries is ruled by Mars, which can signify a sometimes angry or tempestuous disposition. In Chinese medicine, anger is connected to the liver. When anger is repressed, or comes out too frequently, it can cause toxicity to the liver. It is therefore essential to nourish and tend this organ.

Exercise

Because Arians are direct and often full of bright shining energy, they need to find a healthy channel to release their power. With Mars as its ruler, Aries signs would do well to express their fieriness through physical activities. This includes aerobics, and individual sports like racquetball, tennis, and long-distance running. Aries signs could also channel their fire through dancing or martial arts. Without a channel for physical expression, Arians can sometimes feel shut down and lifeless.

Herbs

Herbs strong in iron (linked to Mars, the ruling planet of Aries) are helpful for those born under Aries. Iron helps fortify the blood and strengthen the muscles—great for the warrior sign of Aries. Iron-rich herbs include nettle, burdock, and yellow dock. If they are overdoing things, Arians would do well to take herbs that cool them down and relieve any stagnancy and tension. These herbs include dandelion, lettuce, and burdock. An Aries can take willow bark if they are afflicted with headaches. And if an Aries is having a hard time stoking his fire and feels dull and lifeless, it would be good to invigorate him or her with cayenne, hot mustards, garlic, and ginger.

Taurus: The Bull

Spirit

Taurus is the sign of the flourishing garden, the ripe fruit on the vine. Taurus signs are often strong-willed and powerfully magnetic. They are also often sensual and enjoy feeling, touching, and tasting all that life has to offer. They tend to be solid and headstrong, but they can also have a tendency to get stuck in ruts and have a hard time with change.

Taurus rules the throat, and in Indian philosophy the throat chakra is the center for self-expression and communication. People born under Taurus need to learn to develop confidence and self-esteem so they can express themselves to their fullest potential.

Lifestyle

Taurus is ruled by Venus, the planet of love, beauty, and harmony. Taurus signs would do well to increase these things and anything that helps them to be more sensual, relaxed, and in the moment. Saunas, baths, long massages, well-cooked meals, a nice glass of wine, and lovemaking are all wonderful for the spirit of a Taurus. These folks can tend to worry and obsess and deplete themselves with stagnant feelings. It is helpful to try something new from time to time, especially if they are stuck in difficult situations. Friends and family may need to lend them a hand to help them do this, as Taurus natives sometimes have a hard time doing it for themselves. They often need stability and constancy, along with strong physical and emotional connections, to feel at their best.

Exercise

Those born under Taurus do well with slow and strengthening exercise such as yoga, gardening, hiking, and weightlifting. If they are feeling bogged down and stuck, it would be best to increase the fire a bit and do more physically vigorous exercise including aerobics, dance, and bicycling.

Herbs

Taurus signs need to protect their throat from soreness and infection (often due to an inability to express themselves and move their energy). Wild cherry bark, licorice, and slippery elm are all good for this. Taurus natives sometimes need moving and stimulating herbs to remove constipation and stagnancy. These include dandelion, yellow dock, and mint.

Gemini: The Twins

Spirit

Gemini is the sign of the expressive communicator, the playful trickster, and the fun-loving friend to all. These people are known for their love of the game, the pun, the word play, trivia, and jokes. But Geminis also have a dark side. They often have a difficult time dealing with heavy emotions, and sometimes just glide along the surface, unable or unwilling to dive any deeper. In their path, it is important for Geminis to develop a conscious relationship with their darker side so that it doesn't come out in damaging ways.

Lifestyle

Geminis need outlets for their abundant interests, so it's often good to have a couple of jobs, or a job and a couple of hobbies. They also do well to have a wide social circle that can stimulate them on a number of levels. Though they tend to have a busy schedule, Geminis need to make time to slow down and relax, and find a space away from people and distractions so that they can recharge. Relaxing and breathing deeply will protect their lungs and help them focus their energies in productive ways, instead of just scattering their energies to the four winds.

Exercise

Gemini is linked to the arms and lungs and is connected to the nervous system. Geminis would do well to do slow and vigorous exercise to both cleanse their system of toxins and also strengthen their nerves and their body. Though it may be difficult for them to slow down for this pace, deep yoga, tai chi, and meditation would be wonderful for them, fully oxygenating their system and removing stress. Even paced rhythmic exercise in the form of hiking and biking would also be good for them. Anything in which they can go out into nature and breathe fresh and clean air will be healing.

Herbs

To strengthen and protect the lungs, Geminis can take mullein and coltsfoot. To help strengthen the nerves, Geminis would do well to take ginseng and lemon balm. Geminis could also use essential oils of lavender, rose, and sandalwood to help relax and protect their nervous system.

Cancer: The Crab

Spirit

Those with a lot of Cancer in their charts can be sensitive, protective, nurturing, and intuitive. They also can get moody and crabby, especially if they feel threatened or overstressed. Though some Cancers can be shy and reserved, they have a quiet power that is especially prevalent at home. Cancers need a safe home to feel strong in the world. The fundamental image for Cancer is of the Virgin Mary feeding the baby Jesus from her breast. This shows her immense capacity to love and nourish her family and loved ones.

Lifestyle

Cancer tends to be a shy and sweet presence, and these signs need to be around loving and caring people most of all. If these folks find a good environment with kind partners and friends, they will thrive. Cancers also do well to take time in and around water. This means drinking water, taking baths, and swimming as a part of regular activity. Because Cancer rules the stomach, it is essential that proper care is taken when eating and after meals. Cancers should try to eat slowly and in a nonstressed manner. It is also helpful to avoid processed foods as they are prone to disturbing the digestive tract.

Exercise

Cancers tend to be a little rounder and have a little more flesh than the other signs. They do well to do gentle, nourishing exercise that strengthens them in slow and simple ways. Aerobic exercise in the form of swimming would probably be best for this water sign. Biking, walking, and gardening would also help strengthen this sign.

Herbs

To strengthen their digestion, Cancers can take bitters before meals, including gentian and angelica. These help prepare the stomach for food and increase the gastric juices so that food is properly digested. There are a number of culinary spices that help with digestion, including peppermint, thyme, oregano, and basil. Cancers would do well to take a toning herb like nettle or licorice regularly, as these help strengthen adrenal energy and tone the whole system so they can feel calm and confident.

Leo: The Lion

Spirit

Leos are the playful lovers of the zodiac. These folks shine with the brilliance of the sun and can be gregarious, charismatic, fun-loving, and generous. They also tend towards self-centeredness, and can have a Napoleon complex if their ego is not checked. Leos enjoy being the center of attention, showing off their talents and expressing their hearts. At the core, Leos have the ability to give their creative talents to the rest of the world with an open and loving heart.

Lifestyle

Leos need to find a space to be expressive and share their talents, even if it's in a limited way. This could mean anything from joining the local theater troupe to starring in a Broadway play. They will feel nourished and strengthened when their light is shining. Acting, making music or art, directing a play, or just being the comedian at the family dinner table are ways in which Leos can express their talents. Leos need their fire sparked from time to time, whether it be through romance, a good party, a fun trip, or just a simple barbecue with the neighbors. Finally, because Leo is linked to the heart, it is helpful for Leo to meditate and visualize this center as radiant and open. Spending a few minutes at the beginning of every day doing this will profoundly and beneficially affect the path of a Leo. Leos may be attracted to stimulants like coffee and things that fire them up. These substances will eventually burn them out, however, and it is best to take them in moderation.

Exercise

Leos can help strengthen their hearts with aerobic exercise, which elevates their heart rate and helps them sweat out toxins. This can include dancing, running, team sports like volleyball or basketball, and individual sports like tennis or racquetball. Generally, it is best for Leos to do sports out in the sunlight where their energy thrives.

Herbs

Hawthorn is a good herb for strengthening the cardiac muscles. It helps the heart beat more regularly and rhythmically, which is a great preventative against heart attacks. Borage is another wonderful herb and helps with anxiety and depression associated with a weakened or stressed heart.

Virgo: The Virgin

Spirit

Virgo is the sign of purity and sanctity. It sits between the fiery exuberance of Leo and the partner-centered sign of Libra. In order to prepare for a beneficial partnership, Virgo brings us the qualities of selflessness, service, discrimination, and discernment. Virgo is concerned with separating the wheat from the chaff and removing what is self-destructive and damaging to bring in virtuous qualities that align us with what is best in life. At its worst, Virgo can sometimes be judgmental and haughty. Virgos need to watch out for being too critical of themselves and others, and focus instead on seeing the beauty and light shining from all people. Virgo teaches us to become strong, pure, and clean in preparation for merging with the lover and with the divine.

Lifestyle

Virgos can find joy in the simplest of tasks, and ultimately their goal is to find pleasure and harmony in the here and now. Washing dishes, knitting a scarf, tending a child, or even filing the taxes can be powerful and spiritual tasks if done with one's full attention and care. In Buddhist philosophy, there is a saying: "Chop wood, carry water." This implies that the most basic of tasks are what lead us to enlightenment. Virgos would also do well to focus their energies towards service in some way. Whether that be through being a healer, a church minister, a drug counselor, or even a barber, the quality of selfless service is vital for the well-being of Virgos. If there is a tendency to worry and criticize, Virgos would do well to take frequent relaxation breaks, increase aerobic exercise, and spend some time getting massages, doing bodywork, and going to spas.

Exercise

Virgos need to do exercise that tempers their tendency towards anxiety (a Mercurial function). This anxiety can affect their intestines and cause cramping, distension, lethargy, and depression. To counteract these symptoms, Virgos would do well to take walks outside in the country where the sun is shining and the air is clean. Yoga can be particularly beneficial for Virgos because it has a spiritual function of unifying the participant with the divine and focussing on strengthening the light and the holiness in our hearts and spirits. Sweating and purifying exercises, including most aerobic exercise, will help decrease tendencies towards anxiety as well.

Herbs

Dandelion and yellow dock are both purifying herbs that help remove impurities from the liver and the digestive organs. Ginger and garlic help with the process of digestion and can be taken with meals. Ginseng and nettles can be taken as nourishing tonics to strengthen the nerves.

Libra: The Scales

Spirit

We have now moved into the top half of the zodiac with the sign of Libra. Libra's opposite sign, Aries, is noted for being focused on the development of the self. Libra is noted for focusing on the cultivation of partnership. In partnership, Libra finds a mirror in order to better understand themselves. Through partnership, Libras fulfill the need to complete themselves, to find their "other half" in order to become whole. Libra is known as a social sign that is at ease with groups of people. Ultimately there is a desire for balance in all facets of life. However, this balance, as we all know, is difficult to achieve.

Lifestyle

Libras do well when they are integrated into their community and achieve a level of accomplishment and balance with their loved ones and their path. Often their struggle comes from either giving or holding back too much of themselves. Libras need to prioritize their lives to discover what is most important, and let the other tasks and activities take second place. Libras can also practice balance and serenity through the practice of breath-based meditation. Meditation restores an inner calm that allows our center and spiritual source to guide and balance us. Libra is also ruled by Venus, and Libras love nothing more than to be pampered, and to enjoy the fine and refined things in life, like dinner at a good restaurant.

Exercise

Libra is linked to the kidneys and the adrenal system. When Libras are excessively social and are caught up in pushing hard in the world, these areas can be affected and taxed. To protect the kidneys it is best to do exercise that is not overly forceful. Tai chi, aikido and chi gong are wonderful martial arts forms that stress the importance of the breath, graceful movement, and balance. Anything that involves playing against one other person, as in tennis or racquetball, can also be beneficial for Libras.

Herbs

To protect the kidney/adrenal system, it is best to take tonic herbs like licorice and nettles. Ginseng is also powerfully helpful, as it is an adaptogen. Adaptogens help our body naturally react against stress. To help strengthen the bladder and ward against urinary tract infections, Libras can take uva-ursi, parsley, and cleavers.

Scorpio: The Scorpion

Spirit

Scorpio is a powerful and intense sign. As a fixed water sign, Scorpios often act as magnets, drawing intense and powerful situations and people to them. Some of these situations may be dark and difficult. Scorpio has the ability to go down into these intense situations and draw the wisdom and medicine from an experience and come back stronger and deeper. At the core of their lesson is to transform fear into love. Scorpios can sometimes get stuck in dark and painful experiences and may have a hard time moving on. Ultimately, Scorpios teach us the lesson of letting go and loving with a vulnerable and true heart.

Lifestyle

When Scorpios have entered a dark passage in their lives, it is important not to try to rush them out of the situation, but instead to let them glean the beauty and wisdom from the experience. This can happen through seeing a counselor, writing down experiences in a journal, talking with nonjudgmental friends, and channeling their feelings through art and music. If a Scorpio is stuck in these difficult experiences, it can also be helpful to gently move them towards transformation. Moving energy through exercise, acupuncture, energy work, and prayer are all tremendously helpful for shifting and transforming.

Exercise

Scorpio is the sign of the snake and the eagle. Scorpios can do exercises that help shed the skin like a snake and spread wings to fly like an eagle. Dancing is one of the most powerful ways of shamanic transformation. Dancing can take place in the context of a drum circle, a rock concert, or even in one's home with the stereo turned up. Yoga is a wonderful way to help us shed our skin and focus any obsessive energy towards a spiritual goal. Aerobic exercise in the form of running, biking, and swimming are all great ways of shedding toxins through sweat.

Herbs
Scorpios would do well to take herbs that cleanse the body of excess toxins and poisons. These include senna, dandelion, and dock. Scorpio is also linked to the sexual organs and Scorpio women would do well to take dong quai and raspberry leaf tea. Scorpios need to avoid extreme foods like processed sugar and caffeine, as these build up in the system and can increase toxic overload.

Sagittarius: The Archer

Spirit
Sagittarius is ruled by Jupiter, which is the planet of the guru and teacher. Sagittarians often love to wander and explore, learning many different things until they decide to pass on their experiences to the greater world. They are often seen as buoyant and a consummate partyer, enjoying the fruits of life with gusto and joie de vivre. The danger for Sagittarians lies in partying too much, and in exploring so many facets of life that they can't focus strongly enough on just one particular thing. In other words, their wanderlust can be their downfall.

Lifestyle
These folks need to explore and express themselves in a number of different ways. Often not satisfied with one or two interests, Sagittarians can explore many avenues, and this is usually a good thing unless they become distracted and off-center. Because Sagittarians are a fire sign, they need a degree of play and buoyancy in their lives. Ruled by Jupiter, Sagittarians can have an excessive love for life, and need to temper themselves from time to time. Though known for a strong constitution, they can also burn themselves out

and may need to eat a diet that will help bring them back to earth (i.e. less stimulants, more root veggies). To help protect the liver, it is important not to drink to excess. In Chinese medicine, the liver is related to anger—an emotion that becomes more prevalent for Sagittarians if the liver is not nourished.

Exercise

Sagittarians can handle pretty much any kind of exercise and often enjoy a hard workout. They would do best to build and stoke their fire with regular aerobic, sweat-inducing exercise. Running, horseback riding, biking, and hiking are all wonderful for a Sagittarius.

Herbs

Sagittarius is ruled by Jupiter, which is linked to the liver. When the liver is stagnated by too many rich foods and alcohol, it is important to cleanse and detoxify this system. Lemon with hot water is a wonderful cleanser, along with oregon grape and dandelion root tea. To cool the fires when the Sagittarius is burning him- or herself out, bathe in hot water with essential oils of lavender and rose hips.

Capricorn: The Sea-Goat

Spirit

Capricorn is known for its industry and ambition. What it is less known for are its traits of sensitivity and insecurity. Capricorns usually cover this up with a sense of power and purpose. By sheer dint of will and force, Capricorns will push towards the top and try to achieve their goals. Eventually, most Capricorns come up against obstacles in their path that they cannot surmount with willpower. The ancient glyph for Capricorn is of a goat kneeling. It is this act of kneeling, or surrender, that is required for Capricorns to move further in their path. When they let go of their own need for control and authority, they become stronger and wiser beings.

Lifestyle

Capricorns can tend towards melancholy (Saturn) and anxiety and would do well to take frequent breaks, vacations, and holidays to recharge their batteries. Sun is wonderful for these folks, as it lifts their spirits. Capricorns have a tough constitution and can endure most things, but they need to allow for gentle and relaxing pursuits that do not push them so hard. If they can take up a couple of hobbies or go out to dinner and the movies once in a while, Capricorns can take life a little more easily and will enjoy it more. Massage and bodywork are wonderful for their structural alignment and peace of mind. Capricorns also have a bit of the randy Pan in them, and lovemaking helps soothe their souls.

Exercise

Known for pushing themselves too hard, Capricorns would do well to combine some vigorous exercise (which they often like and will help boost their endorphins) with a lot of gentle exercise in the form of gardening, hiking, walks in the woods, and yoga. Outdoor exercise is especially helpful for Capricorns as the fresh air and sunlight are rejuvenative.

Herbs

Horsetail and nettles are vitamin- and mineral-rich herbs that help strengthen the skeletal framework. Lemon balm, borage, and peppermint help enliven the spirit while reducing anxiety. Comfrey is related to Saturn and helps heal any wounds and strengthens bones.

Aquarius: The Water Bearer

Spirit

Aquarians are known to be a little unusual, eccentric, and progressive-thinking. These folks usually try to do things somewhat differently, and often add flavor and spice to the groups they join. Though Aquarians tend to be a little detached and rebellious from the norm, they are also often group-oriented and can be sociable. This contradiction is at the core of the Aquarian path—learning to be separate and unique within the community, while also drawing people together in a positive way.

Lifestyle

This sign is ruled by Uranus, which is linked to the nervous system. Because of this, Aquarians can often vibrate at a faster level and be more prone to anxiety and panic. It is helpful for Aquarians to take electricity breaks by shutting off the computer and the TV and take time in meditation or outdoors. Acupuncture and energy work seem to be especially useful for Aquarians. These folks also often thrive in groups, and it is helpful for them to be involved in community activities. This could be anything from being a yoga teacher to attending round-table political discussions. Anything that helps their skills as a group participant and facilitator will strengthen someone born under Aquarius.

Exercise

Again, Aquarians need to tend to their nervous system with exercise that is gentle and strengthening without overexerting the body's natural energy. Light jogging, bicycling, and hiking are a few wonderful forms of Aquarian exercise. Eastern martial arts forms are also good, as they help Aquarians become stronger and clearer channels for energy to flow through. Group sports are also strengthening, as they achieve the double function of exercise and community interaction.

Herbs

Aquarians need to tend their nervous systems. Valerian, scullcap, hops, and chamomile all help to relax the nerves. Ginseng will help stabilize the system and ward off anxiety while grounding an Aquarius. The key to a good nervous system is proper digestion and assimilation of nutrients from the diet. In this way, it is important to add culinary herbs such as thyme, oregano, and basil to meals to help process the food. Aquarians need to eat slowly and surely in a quiet and relaxed manner so that their intake strengthens them. Aquarians should avoid food that will make them uncentered, including coffee, sugar, and alcohol.

Pisces: The Fish

Spirit

Finally we come to the sign of the fish, the watery realm of Pisces. Pisceans are known for their emotional and intuitive nature. They can often pick up on the vibes from people and places and live more on a sensory level than a rational level. There is a sense of searching in these people, and they can often become lost and confused in the world, especially if they take up drugs and alcohol. To find their place in the world, Pisceans usually need to explore their spirituality and purpose on a greater level. When they can act as channels and servants for the highest good, they no longer need to see themselves as alone and foundering, but as part of a larger plan.

Lifestyle

Pisces is ruled by the planet Neptune, which is linked to the immune system. The immune system is the primary defense mechanism of the body to protect itself against the outside world. When Pisceans become weakened, they are more susceptible to disorders of the immune system and anything that compromises their boundaries. To ensure a healthy immune system and strong boundaries, Pisceans would do well to get plenty of rest, eat a nutritious diet (with regular meal times), and avoid drugs and alcohol. Drinking lots of water helps balance Pisces (a water sign) by flushing out poisons and hydrating the body. It is also important for Pisceans to be assertive and stand up for themselves when they feel as if others are taking advantage of them. Taking a few self-defense classes might be a good idea.

Exercise

Pisceans do well with flowing exercise such as swimming, ballet, and dancing. It might also be smart for them to do a stronger and more aggressive exercise from time to time to help them maintain their boundaries. These kinds of sport include martial arts, kickboxing, and fencing.

Herbs

Fundamentally, Pisceans need to protect their immune system. If a Piscean is often affected by colds and sore throats, it may be smart to stock up on echinacea and a goldenseal mouthwash. Elder and yarrow are also good herbs for flushing out toxins through sweating. Red clover and sarsaparilla help with skin-related disorders due to a poorly functioning immune system.

For Further Reading

Astrological Timing of Critical Illness: Early Warning Patterns in the Horoscope by Noel Tyl. Llewellyn, 1999.

Healing Signs: The Astrological Guide to Wholeness and Well-Being by Ronnie Gale Dreyer. Main Street Books, 2000.

Earth Signs

The Role of the Earth in Your Birthchart

by Kenneth Johnson

Do you remember when we all first saw that magnificent photograph of the Earth, taken from space? There she was, a great round ball, with pretty blue oceans surrounding her, exotic continents buckled across her body, and a soft veil of clouds half-concealing her. She looked lovely.

And she looked like a planet. We all know she's a planet, but it's sometimes difficult to perceive her that way when we're standing right here on her body and we can't see her from a distance. But that photograph made her look like just as much of a real planet as, for example, Venus or Jupiter or Saturn. And as we shall see, astrologers can make use of her in that fashion.

But if the Earth is a planet, she is also something more. She is the center of our beings. We never really get away from the fact that we live with her. And not only is she the center of ourselves, she may very well be a being unto herself. The scientist James Lovelock came up with a concept to express this idea. He called it the Gaia Hypothesis. According to the Gaia Hypothesis, the Earth is an actual living being, her own existence inextricably linked with ours in an interdependent web of life. As such, she can be reckoned a goddess. And fortunately for astrologers, the goddess already has a name and a history.

An ancient Greek poem called the "Theogony" tells us that Chaos was the first entity to come into being, but afterwards came Gaia, the earth mother herself. It was Mother Earth who gave birth to Father Sky rather than the other way around. His Greek name was Ouranos—we astrologers know him as the planet Uranus. (To the ancients, however, Ouranos was simply the sky—they were unaware of any of the planets beyond Saturn.)

Mother Earth and Father Sky mated together, and from their union all things took form. Gaia gave birth to mountains, rivers, forests, and meadows. She gave birth to a number of divine mytho-logical beings, including the Titans who lorded it over the universe before the Olympian gods arrived to replace them. When Ouranos became cruel and tyrannical, Gaia saw to it that he was slain by one of his sons, for Gaia is more concerned with the Earth (and its chil-dren) as a whole than she is with any one single individual. In much the same way, scientists who support the Gaia Hypothesis have asserted that the Earth is a "self-regulating" organism—no matter what we do to her, she always adjusts herself to new changes in her own way, and always preserves her own special sense of balance. And if we, as human beings, get out of line and try to mess with the Earth, she will almost certainly take measures to set the situation back to rights again. And when she does, we had best watch out, because she looks after her own needs first.

But how shall we, as astrologers, use the Earth in a birth chart? The answer lies in the relationship between the Earth and the Sun.

In their endless intellectual battle with the astrologers, scientists (primarily astronomers) have claimed that astrology regards the planets—including the Sun and Moon—as revolving around the Earth. This, they tell us, reflects astrology's allegiance to an ancient and discredited view of the cosmos. Thus, in their own minds, the model of the astrological birth chart—with the Earth apparently in the center—serves to discredit astrology itself.

But this simply demonstrates that the scientists are rushing to judgment without giving the astrologers a chance to explain their own point of view. For though it is true that an astrological horoscope shows all things as revolving around an apparent point on Earth, it should not be imagined that this is intended to represent astronomical reality. Instead, it simply creates an image of the way the sky seems to revolve around us, based upon our own Earth-centered point of view. In other words, it is not the Earth which is at the center of the solar system, it is you. It is your birth chart, and you are the center of your own universe. The Earth appears at the center of things because you are standing on the Earth.

And this is important as well, because the Earth is our frame of reference—and if we are not grounded and centered in the Earth, we will not be able to make much use of that which is in the sky!

In a sense, the Earth is already with us in the horoscope; not often shown, it is simply taken for granted. Many astrologers understand that if it were to appear in the horoscope it would occupy a position exactly opposite the Sun.

So you don't need a lot of exotic math to find the position of the Earth in your birth chart. It's always in the sign opposite your Sun. It's really that simple. If you are a Pisces, the Earth is in Virgo. If you are a Sagittarius, the Earth is in Gemini.

And since the Earth will always be in opposition to the Sun, then we must view them as an inseparable pair, continually magnetized to one another. In astrology, opposite signs have a reputation for being eternally in conflict with each other. But this is only half the story. The opposites actually need each other in order to reach completeness. You can't have night without day, and you can't have yin without yang. You can't have the Earth without the sky (or the Sun, which is the sky's primary "light"). Or, to put it another (and simpler) way, opposites attract. Opposites are complementary. It takes red and green together to make a Christmas.

Each sign, taken by itself, is intrinsically incomplete—merely half of a whole. If your Sun sign indicates the basic impulse of your spirit—and of the personality which houses that spirit—then your Earth sign indicates the place where the spirit comes "back to Earth," the place where it gets "grounded." It is the missing half of the total picture—the place where you achieve balance, harmony, and completeness by accessing the sign which forms the complementary opposite to your own solar nature.

Let's take each Sun sign one by one and see how the Earth might function as a point of balance or grounding.

Aries

Your Earth is in Libra. It is part of the nature of Libra to bring peace and harmony to everything it touches. Since your Aries Sun is concerned primarily with making its own passionate way in the world, it sometimes steps on the toes (or entire feet) of others. Your Libra Earth helps to ground you by teaching you to harmonize your own goals with those of others.

Taurus

Your Earth is in Scorpio. Your Taurus Sun sometimes gives you a tendency to define your world in terms of what you possess. This can isolate you from other people—like one of those mythic dragons asleep in a cave on its hoard of gold. Because Scorpio is an autumn sign which desires to merge with the world around it (whether spiritually or sexually), your Earth polarity teaches you to give a little, to sacrifice a bit of that possessive old self and start relating to the world all around you.

Gemini

Your Earth is in Sagittarius. When your "dark twin" (every Gemini has one) starts to gain the upper hand, your good-natured and good-hearted Sagittarius Earth will help you get focused and centered again back in the light. And even though practical Gemini may seem more naturally "grounded" than cosmic Sagittarius, there are times when too much practicality is nerve-wracking, and we need to remember that we are all truly "grounded" in a universe much vaster than our little selves.

Cancer

Your Earth is in Capricorn. You Moon children are, of course, deeply emotional creatures. Everything is about your feelings, right? Well, not quite everything. . . . Sometimes life simply demands that we focus on actual goals, on achievements—even if it means losing a little bit of that fireside warmth Cancer cherishes so much. Capricorn will help you get there. And don't worry about losing the warmth—it will still be there when you've finished your task.

Leo

Your Earth is in Aquarius. Ordinarily, we might think of "space-case" Aquarius as a hopelessly ungrounded sort of sign. How can you get focused on pure air? But Leo is notorious for its "me first" attitude—an attitude which, if carried too far, leaves poor Leo out of the loop. Aquarius teaches you that there are more important things in life than your own needs and wants. Put the pure air of your mind on a higher, more humanitarian level and get yourself back in the loop.

Virgo

Your Earth is in Pisces. As with the previous pair, one might find Pisces an odd place for grounding. Isn't this the sign of the endless universal ocean instead? Well, logically speaking, that's true. But Virgo often suffers from an excess of logic and practicality. Your Pisces Earth helps you realize that the whole is often more important than its parts, and that the oceanic tides of human compassion which bind us all together are far more significant than whether you cleaned the house yesterday.

Libra

Your Earth is in Aries. Therefore your Earth polarity reminds you of who you are—as opposed to who you appear to be in the eyes of others. The fiery ego-centered energy of your Aries Earth can keep you from losing too much of your individuality. When your Earth gets "activated," you may find yourself experiencing people and situations that just seem to call for a "me first" response. Listen to it!

Scorpio

Your Earth is in Taurus. As a Scorpio, you can be quite expert at understanding, using, or (at worst) manipulating others and their resources. Your Taurus Earth gets you back on the track of your own values. Sex (that famous Scorpio word) is a very good example. To Scorpio, sex is social (it has to do with meeting and connecting with people). To Taurus, it's more of a biological thing—home, family, children and so on. Taurus cools the Scorpio down.

Sagittarius

Your Earth is in Gemini. Whenever you are about to trip over your own feet because you're too busy contemplating the sky, Gemini can bring you "back to Earth" again. The busy Gemini mind can help to steer you away from solving Einstein's dilemma about the shape of the universe and help you remember to pay your electric bill—because you can't create cosmic equations if they turn your lights off.

Capricorn

Your Earth is in Cancer. Sometimes the mountain goat is so relentless in his climb to the summit of achievement that he forgets the human side of life which bustles all around him. Cancer, focused and "grounded" in the emotional realm, never forgets these matters! So your Cancer Earth is a wonderful tool for helping you to feel. It's cold at the top of the mountain. Cancer can make you warm again.

Aquarius

Your Earth is in Leo. Clever critter that you are, you've probably already caught the drift—when you're way stressed out from trying to save the world, your Leo Earth will help you to save yourself. Your Leo Earth helps you to see individuals as distinct personalities rather than as mere components in your latest philosophical vision of the universe. That's important—you make more friends that way.

Pisces

Your Earth is in Virgo. If you can't figure out how a Virgo Earth can help Pisces become more "grounded," then you're way, way deep in the ocean indeed. Pisces is the sign most likely to lose track of the details of life, Virgo the sign most likely to find them again. And the infinite compassion of Pisces may sometimes lead you into situations where you get hurt by the insensitivity of others—Virgo will teach you to protect yourself by establishing some tight boundaries.

All right. That answers the question of how it works. But what about the other all-important question: when? Astrology is concerned with nothing if not with timing, right?

Here is one method which can be used by anyone, even if you don't have a technical background in astrology. It is often said that one's birthday should be a time of meditation and reflection, a time of seeking inner empowerment for the year ahead. Our birthday is an appropriate time for such inner work because this is when the Sun returns to the exact spot it occupied at the time of birth. If, for example, you were born on May 25, you will have the Sun at three or four degrees of Gemini in your birth chart. May 25 is the day of the year when the Sun will once again return to that same degree of the zodiac—the day of the year when the specific imprint of your soul and its purpose is resonating powerfully in the sky and in the world of "time" all around us. (Of course, there is a slight variation each year, which is why astrologers cast a Solar Return chart to determine the exact moment of the Sun's return to its birth position. But for practical purposes, any old birthday will do.)

But a little bit of calculation will also reveal the day which is precisely six months distant from your own birthday—half a year away. Using our example of a person born on May 25, the half-year point will be somewhere around November 26 or 27 (depending on leap years). This is when the Sun will reach three or four degrees of Sagittarius—the "Earth point" of your birth chart. This is the day when the Sun conjoins your own personal grounding point, your point of harmony and balance. This is the day when Earth and Sun once again form a complete and total unit. If your Solar Return or birthday is a good time to assess your life's direction and purpose, the opposite point in the year is a great time to see how well that direction and purpose is actually "grounded" in the earthly realities of the world all around you. I suggest that we may use this day in much the same way as we use a Solar Return—as a day of meditation, reflection, and inner work.

In fact, if you use your birthday or Solar Return day as a time for placing yourself in the flow of your own destiny, then you can use your personal "Earth Day" to pause and ask yourself: How well have I embodied my goals and my life purpose over the last six months? Have I stayed on track? Have I done what I set out to do? And if you find yourself out of harmony or "not in the flow," then there is no better time than your "Earth Day" to get yourself back on track. This is the day when you can see precisely where you've strayed from the path, and precisely how to get yourself "grounded" to return to business.

Those who have a more technical background in astrology can, of course, take this concept even further. Any time a planet opposes your natal Sun, it is conjunct your natal Earth. Any time this situation occurs, the energy of the opposing planet has an opportunity to align itself with your basic life purpose.

This, of course, is an idea already inherent in the basic concept of the opposition. In ancient times, the opposition aspect (a planet exactly opposite any other planet) was regarded simply as a "bad" aspect. And while we may still view the opposition as a "challenging" relationship between planets, these days we also ordinarily view it as an opportunity for harmonizing the basic complementary opposites embodied in the two zodiacal signs. By paying special attention to planets which come into opposition with the Sun—and therefore into conjunction with the Earth—we emphasize the process of bringing each planet's function into harmony with our life's essential purpose (represented by the Sun).

For Further Reading

Mythic Astrology: Archetypal Powers in the Horoscope by Ariel Guttman and Kenneth Johnson. Llewellyn, 1996.

Astrology in the Workplace

by Alice DeVille

What do you like about your workplace? Does it energize you or give you the blahs? If you enjoy your work and find the environment reasonably pleasant, which facets of your workplace appeal to you the most? Is it the elevator music, the coffee service, or the state-of-the-art equipment? Does the easy commute, the convenient location, or the breathtaking view from your cozy cubicle get your vote? Are you high on the new fitness center and the convenience of the onsite post office? How about the salary level, the benefits package, or the awards program? What is your take on access to career ladders and training perks?

Each of these features sounds enticing, but they're not likely to be the main elements that draw you to your workplace. Don't worry, there are no right nor wrong answers. I just gave you an incomplete list of attractions. The organization itself may be your number one choice, along with how you relate to its mission, vision, and philosophy. And let's not forget the most important ingredient of all—the people. If you agree on giving "organization" and "people" top billing, then we're on the same page. With the help of astrology, that's what we're going to examine in this article.

The Gods of the Business World

Let's start with the role of the planets in your work environment. Planets affect the initiation of principles, vital forces, and end results of your labor. Although our primary focus is Sun sign information, let's look to the lords and ladies of the business world for a general understanding of the planets' influence. The Sun represents the dominant expression and distinct leadership style of the organization. You recognize the way the company wants to shine in the professional arena. Under the spell of the imaginative Moon, you sense worker attitudes and behavior, as well as the mood of the daily routine. Lady Luna helps you assess client needs and gain a visible niche in the marketplace. Mercury, the messenger of the gods, keeps information flowing and aids the expression of concepts and ideas. Networking in all its forms, mail management, learning tools, and communication styles are examples of Mercury at work. Cooperative ventures and diplomatic exchanges owe their success to Venus, the goddess of harmony. She keeps her thumb on the bankable assets and makes projections regarding the earning and production capacity of the firm.

Action-oriented Mars ignites competitive forces in employees by challenging initiative and keeping innovation at heightened levels. Assertive Martian qualities give the firm power over its rivals by keeping leading-edge contributions in front of consumers. Look to expansive Jupiter to capture the enterprise's underlying philosophy, politics, management climate, and compensation and rewards system. Whenever there's a merger in the wings or a move to expand in foreign markets, Jupiter's blueprint is at work. Executive authority is Saturn's domain, covering strategic planning, decision-making, and accountability for performance. Saturn's presence influences the fundamental ideals and the status of the organization in the business world.

The planetary agent of change is Uranus, known for detaching workers from fixed patterns and teaching them the fine art of independent thinking. Compromises in work practices, insurance riders, or policy amendments bear Uranus's handiwork when the futuristic planet looks at new ways to shape up tired old rules. Subtle Neptune is the power behind quiet inspiration, commitment to organizational ideals, and the fantasy side of brainstorming. She keeps track of hidden reserves and exclusive information about company changes that are in the wind but not ready for public disclosure. Pluto, the truth or consequences planet, forces the workplace to address stagnation, go through a cleansing stage, and rise to a higher plane of operation. For a glimpse into the bowels of the organization and the daily routine of the workers in the trenches, check out Pluto's retrieval system. Planets and their reigning gods not only influence the everyday business environment; they also define the critical points of the organization's framework revealed in the company's astrological chart.

The Company Chart

Every government, organization, business, company, corporation, home-base enterprise, sole proprietorship, or mom-and-pop grocer has a beginning—the company startup or opening date. Astrology views the calendar day and year as the birth date, and looks for the precise time (hour and minute) and place (city, county, state, country) your organization first opened its doors for business. This data is crucial to understanding your company's impact on the work world. A calculated birth chart of your firm contains a wealth of information about the organization's potential. You gain insight into the people who lead the enterprise, its management style, the types of employees it will attract, the client base, philosophy, and the financial outlook. The chart represents the Big Picture of the organization—the sum total of attributes the firm has to offer.

Why would you care about a company's birth date? Compatibility may make the difference in how long you work for the firm and what drives your interest. If you know your own Sun sign, you'll feel reassured when you know that you share a common outlook with your firm. An attractive starting salary may be the big draw, but is seldom enough to sustain your long-term employment. When you feel a connection to key attributes, you are likely to stick around and help build a better workplace.

The Sun sign alone may give you clues to the type of organization you are considering. How would you learn the birth date of a business? Most firms provide prospective employees with background information that includes milestone dates, the founding location, the mission, and evidence of growth and productivity.

Libraries and local government offices house historical information and records as well. In some cases, all you have to do is log on to an organization's website and explore all the links. Granted, you may have to dig deeper to obtain more precise data about the time of day the founding ceremonies took place, but the Sun sign information gets you off to a running start.

How would you use a company's birth chart, and what would you learn about it? For starters, you would find out which one of the signs of the zodiac depicts the enterprise's prominence, a quality affiliated with Sun signs. In case you don't know much about astrology, the twelve signs of the zodiac are divided by element: fire, water, earth, and air. The astrological fire signs (Aries, Leo, and Sagittarius) project vitality and put creative forces to work. Water signs (Cancer, Scorpio, and Pisces) demonstrate resiliency and appreciation for the human resources. The earth element (Taurus, Virgo, and Capricorn) prefers a strong organizational structure and thrives on strategy. Communication-oriented air signs (Gemini, Libra, and Aquarius) express thought, analysis, and flexibility.

Houses of Work

Twelve houses or "departments of life" make up the 360 degrees of the astrological wheel. Several houses provide you with talent indicators and career options. The Second House reflects possible income streams and often your personal preference for marketing your skills. The Fifth House demonstrates your entrepreneurial flair and creative outlets. When you are in a business partnership, the Eighth House shows the union's financial wellness, resources, and significant investments. The Eleventh House gives you clues about the generosity of your employer and how you'll receive benefits, raises, bonuses, and awards.

Two houses relate primarily to the work scene and your on-the-job status. The Sixth House describes the actual work you perform, your colleagues, the conditions in your work environment, and how you approach your work. This sector represents the types of challenges you face in carrying out your responsibilities and the attitudes of the people around you. Any tendencies to wimp out on the job or clash with cohorts surface in this house. Work affiliates such as clients, customers, and cooperators are primary players in your work scene. Examine this house for evidence of responsiveness, quality service, and negotiation on their behalf. If you supervise employees, the Sixth House describes their general characteristics, keys to involving and motivating them, and the types of labor and management conditions you encounter. The House takes into account the need for scheduling and monitoring of tasks and how your style aids the workplace in functioning efficiently.

Career aspirations and commitment are Tenth House matters. Your potential and how you attain recognition gets a boost. Mentors and advisors are important people who influence your career. The sign that rules your Tenth House often describes their impressive presence. Look at this house for clues about available options and evidence of your qualifications for achieving professional goals. The Tenth House depicts your attitude toward responsibility and the performance level that makes you an expert in your field. Authority figures, executives, and bosses represent the Tenth-House movers and shakers who decide how well you carry out the organization's mission and reward you for your effort. They are also the people who fire you or derail your career progress when philosophical clashes arise.

If you like the work environment and want to stay with the firm, getting along with others is essential. These houses spell out the key to survival: treat the people you work with well—one of them could be your next boss.

The Compatibility Factor

Every medium-to-large organization employs a mix of workers representative of each astrological sign. By pooling the best qualities and unique talents of your Sun signs, you and your colleagues form cohesive bonds. Respect for another's expertise evolves over time through trust and cooperation. When deadlines loom, you learn a lot about your coworkers' habits—who is a team player, and who takes a hike and leaves you holding the bag. Emerging issues affect workplace dynamics and often test alliances. Creative differences hold productivity hostage when approaches and attitudes are at significant odds. While no workplace would be healthy if workers were carbon copies of each other, a toxic work environment quickly diffuses efficiency.

With only a few employees on board, you get less astrological diversity but not necessarily reduced tension. Sometimes the workforce suffers from homogeneity and fails to understand that creative, new approaches are vital to continuous product or service improvement. Instead, individuals get on each other's nerves, because they are saying virtually the same thing in slightly different words—and nothing changes. Maybe members of these work groups share only one or two astrological signs or elements. If an isolate is thrown into the mix, this "oddball" may be ostracized merely for being different. Peers may embrace elitism and feel the misfit didn't punch the right ticket. They might appreciate their colleague much more if they knew how astrology views individuality.

If you work for yourself, think about what that's like. When you are not doing a good job of meeting client needs, who tells you that you are stuck? Probably your paycheck. The customer may say nothing, but reserves the right to go elsewhere. Naturally, you need to figure out why profits are down. I know, I know, you survey your own clients, but how unbiased is your interpretation? Even if you excel in the topnotch business skills affiliated with your Sun sign, you could use a fresh perspective. If you are a sole proprietor, consider the benefit of paying for the expertise of an outside consultant periodically. You and your business may profit immeasurably.

By now you're probably wondering about Sun sign compatibility among your peers. You know from experience that although you are cordial toward others, you don't get along with everyone at work. Yes, I know you can, yet haven't you ever wished your boss or a difficult coworker would be transferred and end your workplace misery once and for all? Maybe you thought the recurring heartburn was leftover angst from a previous incarnation (sometimes it is and you're here to balance out the old dramas). How frequently do you mentally replay a disconcerting moment involving what you thought was a personality clash long after you leave the work scene?

If you supervise the workforce, you can use astrological insight to understand the people under you and those you'll consider for future hires. It's already your job to figure out what makes employees tick and make sure the work group clicks. Astrology helps you zero in on individual strengths and build passionate, interdisciplinary teams.

Signs in the fire group (Aries, Leo, Sagittarius) and air group (Gemini, Libra, Aquarius) relate favorably to one another, as do the earth sign elements (Taurus, Virgo, Capricorn) with the water elements (Cancer, Scorpio, Pisces). The three Sun signs within each grouping or element are said to represent the optimum expression of compatibility. Because we know so much more about total chart composition when we look at the relationship of the other planets to the sun sign, this theory often contradicts itself. Yet having Sun sign information about your coworkers may help you understand the heart and soul of your team.

The sets, fire with air and earth with water, represent opposite signs to each other and therefore produce opposite energy. You would think that this dynamic would create conflict, and sometimes it does, but often the opposite sign (180 degrees away from the other) shares both similarities and differences. A magnetic draw occurs between the two polarities. The signs are both attracted and repelled by the other's traits. Each wants what the other has and feels "complete" when able to acquire the opposite characteristic, often through a relationship. When cooler heads prevail in the workplace, this tension leads to a creative exchange of ideas. The opposite effect occurs when ego bashing and hostility infect the integrity of the work just because each sign wants the last word. Neither party wants to give sufficient credit for comparable skills or admit ownership of similar flaws.

Not all members of the grouping form opposing relationships. For example, fire sign Aries opposes air sign Libra. A typical conflict these two experience at work is that Aries gets an idea and wants to run with it, but Libra needs more time to digest the new concept and wants to sleep on it. The other members of the air group, Gemini and Aquarius, form a harmonious connection to Aries. An Aries with coworkers in these signs, as well as the other fire signs, Leo and Sagittarius, would get a positive charge by collaborating with these peers. The more you know about your peers, regardless of the signs, the better you'll understand what it takes to get along.

Sun Sign Personalities at Work

If you belong to the **fire** triplicity (Aries, Leo, and Sagittarius) you exude enthusiasm and confidence in your approach to work. Career success is important to your signs. You thrive on a healthy exchange of information and a trusting work environment. The upbeat side of your nature pulls you toward mixing with people in professional endeavors as well as fun events. When the workplace offers extracurricular activities such as golf teams, company picnics, weekend getaways, and holiday parties, you participate wholeheartedly.

Your group wants to be paid well, and gravitates toward leadership positions or taking charge of projects. With a reasonable amount of independence, you stay motivated and fresh. Supervisors who keep their thumbs on your pulse drive you straight to a headhunter's office. Fire signs are generally quite outspoken and often blurt out exactly what they are thinking when put on the spot. You dislike being misquoted and can get testy if your credibility is at risk. Though quick to anger, you will get over it. Next time you're seen with your "nemesis" you're likely to be enjoying a joke or giving your colleague a pat on the back.

Nothing turns you on like competition and an opportunity to pioneer a new work concept or lead a team. Most of you like jobs that include travel, especially Aries and Sagittarius, while Leo takes the initiative on day trips, coalition building, and fundraising. You're all gung ho about sharing technology and drumming up enthusiasm for your project. Packed in your briefcase are impressive presentation kits, unique business cards, and a new laptop. Pumping money into a strategic advertising campaign is a gamble you are willing to take to win industry acclaim. No workplace would be complete without your flair for innovation and inspiration.

Members of the **water** trio (Cancer, Scorpio, and Pisces) absorb internally the vibes they pick up in the work environment. Waters work best in comfortable surroundings with an air of privacy and serenity. Many of you add personal touches to the workplace decor and often install a bubbling water garden to tune out distracting noises. When conflict and tension arise among peers, you water signs withdraw into your productive worker mode. You miss none of the dynamics that are unfolding in your midst, yet get involved only after you have time to study the angles. The workplace offers the forum for showcasing one of your dominant skills—the people-management end of problem-solving. You have a knack for putting others at ease and creating a desirable forum for addressing stressful conditions. Water signs know how to facilitate a non-threatening exchange between combatants, especially when they are not personally involved in the battle.

You know innately that power is one of your best resources and you use it persuasively to promote key projects and grab plumb assignments. Waters know how to create, plan, and execute goals, yet sometimes you hesitate at critical junctures and lose out on opportunities to shine professionally. While some of you are shy, you really fear rejection of your ideas or your skills more than failure. All you have to do is leave reticence at home and plunge into the work. You're a hot commodity and your talents are marketable.

Waters have complex mental skills, along with the patience to tackle tasks that others would find boring. Imagination and intuition kick in when you're faced with overhauling major facets of work. Cancers need the security of knowing their ideas are not merely good but highly valued. Scorpios reveal their productive efforts after doing considerable troubleshooting and testing. Pisces, sometimes a deadline dodger, delivers a high degree of ingenuity under pressure. While you water signs may lose track of time and donate unpaid hours to a worthy cause, you recognize the need to recharge your batteries. As supervisors, you are among the most considerate of the elements. You read body language with uncanny insight and know when staff members are off track. Appreciative employees like the way you encourage a balance between work obligations and family or social life. You bless the workplace with your sensitive assessment of the rules of conduct and commonsense approach in applying them.

The magic of money draws **earth** elements (Taurus, Virgo, and Capricorn) to positions of long duration and steady growth. If you are a member of this group, you know I'm razzing you a bit. Sure, you like the steady paycheck, but the benefits package is an even bigger draw. You seldom leave a job without being fully vested so you can redeem the stock options or collect earned salary on one of your favorite cash cows, unused vacation time. The truth is you're really not high on job-hopping until you have made a major contribution to the firm and gained competitive experience for following your next dream. Earth signs don't retire early unless debt load has a zero balance, and pension and financial investments guarantee a lucrative income stream.

Financial security drives you to accept responsible positions where your star rises and you earn power and prestige. You dislike chancy undertakings and organize your options toward enterprises that pay up front. Ambitious by nature, you seldom miss opportunity's knock when a new career ladder opens up. You size up mentors and look for people with integrity and authority to promote your interests. Bosses appreciate you because you are very responsive to meeting deadlines. You never hesitate to roll up your sleeves when the workload increases or pitch in when others need help. Some earth signs are conditioned workaholics, and need to lighten up by saving some of that whirlwind energy for your social life. Hang out at the opera once in awhile, or take in a dog show. You could meet a rich partner.

The banking, investing, and accounting professions draw financially astute Taurus types, while the decorating and beauty fields appeal to those of you with a creative flair. Members of this sign advocate self-development and give subordinates the advantage of on-the-job learning and classroom training opportunities. Virgos make outstanding editors, writers, medical personnel, and space management experts. Support staffs could not function efficiently without the systematic routines you Virgos implement in the workplace. Capricorn competes for administrative positions in government, politics, or the machine shop, and looks for executive roles in technology and trades industries. In whatever capacity you are employed, the solid earth element projects an aura of leadership and command of your resources. Those who put in an honest day's work easily earn your respect. The workplace functions as a clearinghouse for practical ideas, skillful negotiating, and solid achievement when earth signs lend their expertise to the business world.

The zodiac's **air** element (Gemini, Libra, and Aquarius) dominates the communications field in just about every medium connected with business. Our high-tech computer world houses the brainpower of members of your mentally adept signs. You're charged with getting the rest of us "wired up." The Internet is one of your favorite playgrounds, and you may have discovered the job you're in by surfing an employment website. You have a leading role in designing systems, engineering technological changes, and installing state-of-the-art equipment in the workplace. Many of you teach classes in software application and hold positions as network managers or web designers. While not all the computer "geeks" are air signs, you claim a solid corner of the market.

Airs have engaging personalities and relate well to colleagues. You thrive on exchanging brilliant ideas and leading intelligent discussion. Peers compliment you on your clear thinking and logical explanations. The gift of gab wins you numerous speaking engagements, presentation opportunities, and facilitation tasks. Often you're called on to fill in for your boss to explain complex proposals or long-range organizational plans. Friendly types, you know that wit and light banter belong in conversations just as much as the shoptalk. When you spot the new kid on the block, you generally break the ice and often volunteer to provide employee orientation. You make the rounds and visit every workstation or broom closet and easily chew up the better part of a workday. Let's face it, air signs: you like to talk. Among your group are incurable chatterboxes who lose track of time on the podium or on the telephone.

Many of you are masters of the written word and mothers of invention. You bring new concepts to life with your picture-perfect descriptions and eloquent writing style. When called on to give a critical opinion, you do it with class. Your quick air mind helps to bridge the communication gap when coworkers struggle with interpretation of difficult policies or work procedures. Geminis earn their living as reporters, speechwriters, and media consultants, and in various disciplines that call for manual dexterity or strong verbal skills. Travel to other sites is a routine part of your work. Your sign leans toward moonlighting, and you often draw income from more than one source. Libras excel as behavioral specialists in fields such as industrial psychology, social sciences, the diplomatic corps, or motivational speaking. Known for your interest in balancing forces, you may lean toward a career as an attorney, judge, or arbitrator. Aquarians use mental agility to fine-tune complex problems and promote product integrity. Diverse consulting fields and opportunities for inventive collaboration excite your innovative spirit. Venture capital initiatives showcase your flair for deal making, risk-taking, and diplomacy. Since air signs own the art of persuasion in the workplace, you have a leading role in selling concepts that generate enthusiasm and esprit de corps among the ranks.

Integration
This article sheds light on unique features of your workplace and the individuality of coworkers and employers. You now have greater understanding of the role that astrology plays in work dynamics, and how astrological diversity influences compatibility. Celebrate the differences. You have the tools to facilitate harmonious relationships among your peers. Use them to create a caring and participatory work climate.

For Further Reading
Charting Your Career: The Horoscope Reveals Your Life Purpose by Stephanie Jean Clement, Ph.D. Llewellyn, 1999.
Your Stars at Work : Using the Power of Astrology to Get Along and Get Ahead on the Job by Carole Golder. Harry Holt, 1998.

Women and Astrology in the Twenty-First Century

by Leeda Alleyn Pacotti

For most of the twentieth century, we women amiably stood by, allowing ourselves to be characterized as "the opposite sex," "the fairer sex," or "the weaker sex." Oh, yes, we were compliant, even jocular, no matter the name-calling. After all, we had to get along, being dependent on income-producing husbands and fathers. However, thirty-three years ago, a sexual revolution swept the industrialized world, and things changed.

The "summer of love" in 1969 openly celebrated the discovery of sexual freedom. That liberty and its expressive cohort, promiscuity, gave way eventually to individually recognized responsibility, as women and other sexually defined groups emancipated themselves, redefining awareness and roles across the social spectrum.

New freedoms led to new confidence, and women explored, then plunged en masse into the marketplace, demanding entry to occupations and professions most had previously considered out of reach. Not surprisingly, the male-dominated bastions of old guard professions rose in backlash, using a psychological warfare aimed at disrupting and destroying the inevitable onslaught of womanly infiltration. Quite a few new and unflattering descriptions were leveled at working women.

Once the gentler sex, women were now confrontational and contrary. Although women in careers, outside hospitals and schools, were a rarity as little as forty-five years ago, at the beginning of the twenty-first century all of us have trouble envisioning any pursuit that won't benefit from the perspectives and talents of the fairer sex. While we've recognized physical differences of strength, even the reserved domain of sports has fallen before the graces of women pugilists and the prowess of power babes in World Cup soccer. The weaker sex, indeed!

A Thumbnail History of Women

Because our lives span a short sweep in time, we humans tend to interpret history through the filter of present experience and reality. If we feel powerless or voiceless, we believe all generations in every culture have been without power or voice. If our circumstances are oppressed, we think oppression is a dominant historical theme. Adding to the problems of misperception and misinterpretation are historical discourses, presumed to be encompassing and factual, which were written primarily by men (after all, until the twentieth century, women in most cultures were not allowed to be educated). The viewpoint of patriarchal self-importance demonstrated the truism that "history is written by the conquerors."

While the roles and pursuits of women in our common past may have been downplayed, glossed over, or entirely omitted, literate and thoughtful women of modern times would be unforgivably remiss to ignore or forget the exploits and adventures of their illustrious or notorious predecessors. The persevering efforts and sacrifices of the unsung, who vouchsafed traditional and ancient knowledge, are frequently mischaracterized as "old wives' tales."

All of us need to remember who our generations of mothers have been. Women were instrumental in the ancient, medieval, and Renaissance worlds as queens, empresses, and high priestesses—such as Cleopatra, Theodora of Constantinople, and Isabella of Spain. Joan of Arc made an especially important contribution as a high priestess disguised as a warrior. Catherine the Great brought enlightenment to Russia. Harriet Beecher Stowe exposed the ills of slavery in the United States, while Harriet Tubman took action through the underground railroad. Eleanor Roosevelt epitomized egalitarian action by actively refusing to accept attitudes of racial segregation in her public and private lives.

Beginning in the nineteenth century, women pioneered new social vistas, taking on pressured roles. Widowed pioneer women in the Oregon Territory attained an early suffrage, becoming titled land owners and exercising the right to vote in territorial matters. Marie Curie carried forward scientific research previously done with her husband, garnering a Nobel Prize. In the early part of the twentieth century, Dr. Margaret Sanger advocated a woman's right to control the cycles and health of her body, using birth control methods to release women from the bondage of continual pregnancy and birthing, which was a debilitating social attitude left over from the Victorian Age.

Most notable are the untold stories of millions of women throughout history, from all cultures, who fought and succumbed to plague, pestilence, famine, epidemic, and catastrophe to ensure that succeeding generations of women and men could take their rightful places as productive and contributing members of society. In the modern industrial world, our gratitude goes to those women during World War II, many still living, who opened our minds to the possibilities of new careers by working wartime assembly lines, serving as test pilots, or reentering the teaching professions that women historically had to leave when they married.

The Astrological Question of "Generation"

With the proliferation of big business during the twentieth century, we have been conditioned to think of a generation as a statistical model with a duration of twenty-five years. Developed for insurance companies, this model bears no relationship to reality. Government uses it as a dictate for targeting social programs, while business employs it as a model for retirement planning. However, the twenty-five-year model has contaminated social thinking about the function of women's bodies. Its legacy is the ostracism of young mothers by promoting the idea that it is wrongful, if not outright sinful, for women to bear children in their teen years—even though this practice has always been a reality of human reproduction, occurring throughout history.

Astrology, unshackled by popular social notions, presents a more interesting perspective on what constitutes a generation. Instead of using arbitrary or fanciful age models, astrology defines a generation as a predominance of a certain type of thinking, shaped by the signs of the outer planets, Uranus, Neptune, and Pluto. Each planet endures a lengthy period or transit in each sign, which permits a reinforced stamp of consciousness on a particular population mass born during that time.

Together, the orbits of these planets bear an interesting mathematical relationship to each other, built on multiples of eighty years. Uranus and Neptune (which each have fairly round orbits with the Sun near the center) and Pluto (which has a more exaggerated elliptical orbit with the Sun placed off-center) traverse the zodiacal signs in progressively extended durations. Uranus circles the Sun in a clockwork eighty-four year period, remaining in each sign for approximately seven years. Neptune, an equally large gas giant, accomplishes its solar revolution every 164 years, residing about fourteen years in each sign. Owing to Pluto's oval orbit, which tilts away from the nearly level geometric plane followed by the other major planets, this distant planet circumnavigates the Sun in approximately 244 years.

The complexities of Pluto's orbit means that it spends unequal time in each sign. Its longest durations of about thirty years occur in Pisces, Aries, Taurus, and Gemini. Moderate transits of about twenty years come with the signs Capricorn, Aquarius, Cancer, and Leo. To balance the long transits, Pluto speeds through Virgo, Libra, Scorpio, and Sagittarius in twelve to thirteen years each. Pluto's journey through this last group of signs, beginning in 1956 and ending in 2008, underscores the exponential advancements of the late twentieth century in health and aging, social awareness of differences, biogenetic and cellular research, and communication technologies. The same journeys through these four signs were most recently observed from 1712 through 1762 (the beginning of rational thinking and new social contracts that launched the Age of Enlightenment and led to the independence of several new nations), 1466 through 1516 (the creative power-burst of published

360 • Llewellyn's 2002 Sun Sign Book

knowledge, following the Gutenberg press, that fueled the Renaissance), and 1220 through 1270 (the reorganization of civilization, known as the Gothic Period, bridging the feudal Dark Ages into the architectural and more urban Middle Ages).

Because Pluto's transit through signs is widely irregular, not obviously affecting the onset of reproduction in women, we look to other regular patterns of astrology to establish the generations. The age points of fourteen and twenty-eight, when women historically started and ended their birthing responsibilities, are neatly defined by several astrological phenomena, occurring by progression and transit. The primary significance of the combined astrological patterns is that an individual separates from birth family, particularly the mother, at about age fourteen, and gains mastery over the physical environment around age twenty-eight.

Near fourteen, everyone experiences the progressed opposition of the Moon to its natal position (detachment from the mother), the transiting opposition of Saturn to its natal position (confrontation with the father), and the transiting sextile of Uranus to its natal position (confidence within the circle of friends). Around twenty-one, each person has Uranus squaring its natal point, which jettisons the individual into self-reliance, accompanied by squares from the progressed Moon and transiting Saturn to their natal placements. Finally, at about twenty-eight, each natal chart receives a progressed return of the Moon to its natal place, as well as a transiting return of Saturn (reconciling differences with the parents), a transiting trine of Uranus to its natal position (creating an appreciation of self-accomplishment), and a transiting sextile of Neptune to its natal point (causing a desire to materialize ideals to change the world for the better).

From this simplified discussion, we expect Uranus and Neptune to play important roles in determining generational differences in thinking, with Pluto adding its own strong signature. In reviewing the movement of these planets through the signs we find that, during the twentieth century, Uranus and Neptune have conveniently changed signs at approximately the same point in time, with Uranus moving into a succeeding sign when Neptune completes one-half of its residence. Because of this coincidence, Uranus acts like a subset or secondary influence of the Neptune transit. Pluto's short residence in the signs of Virgo through Sagittarius has paced Neptune's changes, making Pluto a strong tertiary complement. (When Pluto moves quickly through signs, an important astronomical event occurs in which Pluto makes its closest approach to the Sun, traveling inside Neptune's orbit, further establishing the generational influence of Neptune.)

All this astrological and astronomical phenomena indicates that generations of the late twentieth century have a specific spiritual, emotional, and mental stamp. As a focus, we have three clearly defined generations: 1942 through 1955, 1956 through 1969, and 1970 through 1983.

The Productive Women of the Twentieth Century

As explained, the astrological generations of the twentieth century have been sped up. From astrological readings, combined with psychic perception, this century required a greater number and variety of generations because of devastating and massive population losses from two major world wars and the Asian conflicts between 1950 and 1975, as well as the pandemic influenza of 1919. The frequency of astrological generations permitted rebirth back into an originally expected life span, so that the many lives cut short could still meet the obligations of soul in the same time line.

Because reincarnation does not require a specific sexual body for the soul to meet its missions, astrological influences from Uranus (quantum thinking), Neptune (social consciousness), and Pluto (the human flaw to overcome) conspired to create time periods of acceleration toward soul accomplishments. Whether these were births of men or women, the evolution of humanity required brilliant individuals en masse, with an innate maturity, to divert and alter the recent path of self-destruction. With so many individuals needed, it is no surprise that women became as important as men, creating a groundswell to change human events. About ten months after the entry of the United States into World War II, astrological patterns indicate differences in human expression.

1942–1955: As this generational period begins, Pluto has been in Leo for about four years. Neptune shifts into Libra and finalizes the changeover in 1943. Uranus moves into Gemini in mid-1942 and takes full residence in Cancer in mid-1949.

Neptune, as the primary influence, indicates women born in this generation are deeply conscious of partnership issues, exploring the benefits of traditional and alternative lifestyles. Libra's awareness of the "other," or partner, contrives subordination to the other person's experiences, causing these women to use ingenuity to express themselves without interrupting or deterring the partner's life path. Ultimately, this generation brings equality, the lesson of Libra's scales of justice, to the fore of human consciousness.

Pluto is in Leo, imparting the human flaw of egoistic aggrandizement. Part of this flaw derives from the mothers of these women, who either worked or observed other women working important wartime jobs, as replacements for enlisted men. In the industrialized nations, as soon as World War II was over, working women were abruptly sent packing to ensure jobs for returning soldiers. Mothers of this generation lived with battered self-esteem, devalued self-worth, and a deep resentment of being considered "just another pair of hands." Those who could no longer satisfy the need for outer expression optimistically regarded husbands as the "handsome prince" who took all cares away, while at the same time despising their accomplishments. Love-hate attitudes, combined with passive-aggressive displays, were legacies to their daughters, who eventually demanded self-identity.

During the first half of this generation, Uranus is in Gemini, indicating that these women will universally enjoy a high-school education. Those who went to college used the campuses as happy hunting grounds for husbands and dropped out as they married. Gemini imparts congeniality and diversity. This generational subset used practical socialization skills as a substitute for formal learning, giving them an invaluable understanding of other women's thoughts and feelings.

Uranus in Cancer, during the second half of this generation, conflicts with Neptune in Libra. These women faced the problem of enforced domesticity—especially traditional attitudes such as keeping long hair, cooking from scratch, and the necessity of maintaining a picture-perfect home. Uranus is the planet of innovation and invention, while Cancer rules the home. These energies combined as, to gain expression, women demanded and obtained inventive appliances to care for the home and family, gaining free time.

1956–1969: At the beginning of this generation, an important astrological development occurs in which all three planets change signs. Neptune takes up residence in Scorpio, Uranus moves into Leo, and Pluto begins its shift into Virgo. With these changes, the Cold War begins, the covert land war in southeast Asia starts without a pronouncement, and body-vitalizing rock 'n' roll debuts.

With Neptune's change, the demand for expression turns inward. True to Scorpio, this generation is suspicious of other generations and keeps to itself. Neptune tends to veil the distasteful, while Scorpio revels in the mucky truth. These women are drawn to sexual excitement and sublime alteration of the mind. With an innate curiosity, deep concentration leads them to investigative research. Their role is to open the doors of science and technology, with women given open credit for their discoveries and contributions.

The stamp of Pluto in Virgo makes these women very logical and mathematical, an excellent complement to Neptune in Scorpio. This generation is preoccupied with health concerns. Pluto goes deeply into everything, and matters of the body are no exception. Influencing this generation is the idea of freedom from child-bearing, as the secrets of women's fertility are unlocked and the Pill becomes a mainstay of contraception. With bodies no longer prematurely aged from continual child-bearing, these women deal with the human flaw of self-abuse through physical neglect. Ultimately, they come to an understanding that the body is the cherished, expressive vehicle for the soul.

The first half of this generation has Uranus in Leo, putting it at odds with Neptune. On the one hand, these women want to be left to their own pursuits; on the other, they desire recognition. The demand for recognition is so strong that women venture into technological fields, which have not yet been cordoned off as a man's domain. Here, women are on an equal footing, where original thinking, coupled with Pluto's perseverance in research, really pays off. These women are the first to demonstrate unquestionably that a woman can think and achieve as well as a man.

The second half of this generation has Uranus in Virgo. Coupled with Pluto in Virgo, Uranus demands an enlightenment of health matters and the physical interrelationships within the body. No longer satisfied with being nurses, women enter even more complex biological fields, educating themselves on biogenetic research, longevity, and physical rejuvenation. This generational subset changes our concepts of aging and the body's ability to endure, precipitating valuable discoveries to repair and regenerate various physical systems.

1970–1983: As this generational period opens, Neptune quickly enters Sagittarius. Within one year, Pluto starts to shift into Libra, where it will remain until both it and Neptune change signs. In 1969, Uranus quietly entered Libra. After all the serious influence of Scorpio and Virgo in the preceding seven years, this generation seeks expression through fun and personal contentment.

Neptune is comfortable with Sagittarius, developing this sign's appreciation of personal belief systems. At the beginning of this generation, Western cultures explored eastern religions and, at times, conflicted with Asian and Middle Eastern cultures. Given the proclivity of Sagittarius to wander far and wide, social consciousness stretched to recognize the right to be different. For the first time, large populations of women became aware of each other and began to compare the differences of their social climates. The women of this generation travel the globe, looking for the common ground between themselves and women of other nations. Their task is to discover and accept humanity, despite culture, belief, or national boundary.

With Pluto in Libra, this generation explodes traditional relationships. This is a generation that made commitments at a very young age, usually without marriage. Libra includes the adversarial relationships of war, which this generation observed firsthand at home, with drive-by shootings and organized gang violence. The women did not expect to live long—a definite soul memory, as many born had immediately reincarnated from the mortally exhaustive conflicts of the recent past, only to manifest unresolved warfare on the domestic soil of former enemies. The flaw for this generation is deriving confidence from the group—leaning on the idea of safety in numbers. As they gain courage to release from group attitudes, these women mature quickly. Their lesson is to be humane, a complement to Neptune's pursuit of humanity.

As this generation begins, Uranus is in Libra, creating ingenious partnering structures. Partnering for these women is more a soul force than personal choice. Frequently, their partners have been killed or incarcerated, leaving them alone to raise children. Little has been understood about the intense familial responsibility of gangs to insure the raising of children. Women born in this time period readily accept other men in their social groups as partners and fathers and also take over mothering roles from other women. These women embody a deeply humane compassion of "all children are my children."

From 1975 through 1981, Uranus occupied Scorpio, focusing on income acquisition. At this time, interdependent financial arrangements were bolstered by exorbitant interest rates, that rose as high as 22.5%. These women expect money to be readily available and spendable. Meticulously educated and bound for professions, rather than jobs, they are not saddled with conditionally restrictive thinking, involving a "glass ceiling" or unequal pay. Because they expect, even demand, excellent salaries, they dispel forever the idea that a woman's worth is cheap labor. Their efforts give women access to monetary self-sufficiency.

Twentieth-Century Women in the Twenty-First Century

Attitudes about life span and longevity of the human body are changing cherished ideas about retirement and a satisfactory old age. Each of the three generations discussed will exert profound alterations on the social landscape.

Astrologically, the generational pattern changes. After Pluto leaves Sagittarius in 2008, it will spend seventeen years in Capricorn, twenty-two years in Aquarius, twenty-seven years in Pisces, and the remainder of the twenty-first century in Aries, becoming the imprimatur of each new generation, from 2008 through 2200. What follows are suggestions about how the twentieth century generations will influence society, swayed by Pluto's resident sign.

1942–1955: This generation got its footing while fighting for recognition of women's rights, when Pluto was in Libra. As Pluto transited Scorpio, they came on like wildcats, taking political offices as governors and congressional representatives, securing their rights through legislation. For this generation, Pluto in Sagittarius allows them to savor the recognition they've worked so hard to attain.

While Pluto is in Capricorn from 2008 to 2024, these women reach the retirement age of the old statistical model. For them, employment is a component of identity, and they will not give up good jobs or incomes that give them independence. Capricorn rouses them to demand enforcement of age discrimination laws and revision of any laws that subvert financial independence.

When Pluto is in Aquarius from 2024 through 2044, this generation enters a partial retirement. With a show of strength in numbers, these women revisit communal living. Because they did not achieve maximum earning power, they learn to join financial resources, and to underwrite experimental projects of global benefit, such as methods of harnessing renewable energy sources.

During Pluto's transit in Pisces from 2044 through 2071, these women reconcile the inner conflict between self-recognition and group effort. Philosophies derived from their experiences, preserved in social histories and commentaries, have the greatest impact on their astrological grandchildren—those with Pluto in Sagittarius.

1956–1969: Pluto in Scorpio established the scientific bent of this generation, who learned the value of shared resources during the monetary fiascos of the late 1980s. As Pluto transited Sagittarius, these health-conscious women found their demands unmet by the medical professions and plunged themselves into deeper technical issues of human biology.

While Pluto is in Capricorn these women are in their element, putting the attentive, persevering energy of their natal Pluto in Virgo to its best effort. They demand applied ethical standards from the medical professions, including the sister industries of pharmaceuticals, herbal manufacturing, and biogenetic engineering. Such ethical requirements include supervised reviews of reactions and interactions when pharmaceuticals and procedures are combined with each other.

As Pluto moves through Aquarius from 2024 to 2044, this generation withdraws from employment pursuits and turns more deeply to medical and health research. Ills, from the stress and abuse of their bodies endured in early life, become paramount, as these women research life-extending practices and remedies. Future generations will be indebted to this generation's discoveries for a lengthier, satisfying life span.

Through Pluto's transit in Pisces from 2044 through 2071, these women understand that continual work has no productive value unless it is combined with compassion for others. Now, in full retirement, they turn their energies to charitable institutions. This generation contributes an enormous awareness of the ills of society, recognizing that a healthy body demands a healthy mind. They explore and support programs in education, art, and recreation, which promote personal and social creative expression.

1970–1983: As Pluto moved through Sagittarius, this generation delayed marriage, understanding the need to choose a mate wisely. Free-wheeling Sagittarius opened a variety of occupational pursuits with excellent incomes. These professionally conscious women established themselves financially, before taking on the responsibilities of marriage and family.

During Pluto's residence in Capricorn from 2008 to 2024, this generation faces major challenges. Thoughtful about integration of commerce and society, they reject a revisiting of dehumanizing corporate practices. As Pluto spotlights problems, these women demand laws and regulations for employment security. Popular at-will work policies are scrutinized and discarded, ending anxiety over surprise terminations.

With Pluto in Aquarius from 2024 to 2044, this generation comes to full flower, championing the independence women have sought for so long. Now a reckoning force in the marketplace, these judicious women are unburdened by ideas of unequal pay or sexual discrimination. Strengthened by Pluto's transit in Sagittarius, they become more entrepreneurial and experiment with equitable business structures, developing new models of employee ownership, employment, and investment.

As Pluto transits Pisces from 2044 to 2071, these women have accumulated strong financial foundations, permitting them to expand the charitable activities of the previous astrological generation. Drawing on their innate sense of humane treatment, this generation extends its ideals of fair treatment and security beyond national boundaries, opening dialogues with women in other countries. Their philanthropy liberates the minds and bodies of repressed or subjugated women everywhere.

Taking Charge of the Future

As a final note, women of the twentieth century have been taught to succeed by emulating the styles and actions of their male predecessors. Differences between the sexes in approach and thought prove this idea unworkable. Women must set their own measurements for success, relying on time-honored strengths of patience and thoughtfulness toward others. While we may not eliminate war, conquest, or cutthroat competition, before us stretches the clean slate of the future. On it, we may write a history in which the contributions of all receive an impartial judgment.

For Further Reading

Astrology for Women by Jessica Adams. HarperCollins Australia, 1998.
Astrology: Woman to Woman by Gloria Star. Llewellyn 1999.
Women and Their Moon Signs by Jacqueline Bigar. Avon Books, 1998.

Keeping Your Sun Sign on Track

by Phyllis Firak-Mitz

O ur Sun sign is the most powerful driver of our individuality and purpose in this lifetime. No other planet quite has the strength of the Sun in determining the basic nature of our personality and the path of our destiny. Although everyone expresses their Sun sign's qualities uniquely, each of us is nevertheless guided by some of the basic principles of what our Sun signs dictate. Indeed, it can be said that even our spirit is most strongly expressed through the qualities of our Sun sign.

The more we learn to develop the essence of our Sun sign, the more we tap into our natural individuality and personal power. If we choose lifestyles, careers, and relationships that allow our Sun signs to flourish, it's likely we'll be happiest. Even if we find ourselves in circumstances different from our Sun sign's preferences, we'll be fulfilled by simply bringing the qualities of our Sun sign to whatever we're involved in.

But we have to take dominion over our Sun sign energies to bring out their best attributes and powers; otherwise, those energies might run us with their lesser urges and more limited expressions. Our Sun signs offer us a range of experiences, from the most empowering mastery to humbling self-defeat. It's up to us to develop the Sun-given qualities that serve us best and to steer clear of other solar qualities that might drag us down. Just as a mentor teaches a student about truly effective authority versus wasted effort, we need to mentor ourselves to cultivate true self-leadership and genuine expression, while learning to avoid self-sabotage. When wisely using our Sun sign's strengths, we tap into our authentic power and rely on our own wisdom to choose a positive direction for our lives.

Our Sun sign governs the type of destiny we're born to live, and supplies us with the tools and personal style we'll need to succeed. By understanding the strengths and weakness of our Sun sign we can better cultivate our gifts, as well as recognize when we're working against ourselves. If we notice that we're off course, there are things we can do to bring ourselves back into alignment. Sometimes it's the simplest shifts in our attitudes or behaviors that result in the greatest leaps in our fulfillment and effectiveness.

Here's a rundown of each Sun sign's key powers and purposes, and how to best use them to create meaningful success in our lives. I'll also discuss ways to tell whether we are misusing or weakening our Sun sign's energies, and ways to bring ourselves back on track.

Aries

If your Sun sign is Aries, your powers and destiny are rooted in leadership and initiating new pathways. You have a tremendous straightforward, enthusiastic personal presence and chemistry, and you're courageous enough to follow your instincts and vision. Your fearlessness allows you to jump headfirst into anything that attracts your attention. You are a hero/warrior at heart and enjoy gaining new ground.

You bring out the best of your dynamic Aries Sun by devoting life to the purpose of discovering who you truly are. You're happiest and most effective when you direct your competitive drive to surpassing your own personal best, and focus your conquering instincts on overcoming your own limitations. At times your destiny necessitates being solitary. But don't take that too far, or you'll feel alone in life unnecessarily.

If your Aries Sun is allowed to run rampant, your warrior nature might take over and convince you that fighting is the only way to get what you want. You'll exchange your positive outlook and purposeful activities for headstrong feelings of anger, and expend your power trying to dominate and conquer others. You'll believe that people aren't supporting you, when actually you've possibly alienated them by being overly competitive or acting in a selfish way. Because you are most exuberant when getting projects going, it's important to discipline yourself to meet the challenges of completion in order to reap the benefits of what you have sown. If you get negative feedback, evaluate whether you've allowed your willfulness to become overblown. If so, tap into the wisdom of your heart. That way you remain connected to yourself, but also make yourself available to the valuable guiding input of your spirit as well as the wisdom of others.

Patience is the one quality that can keep you from making life's biggest errors. Being a visionary, you see what is possible—but things must unfold. If you push too hard, or jump in before you are ready, you might not let things evolve the way they need to, or you might get yourself in over your head. Patience gives the beneficial universe time to assist you.

Taurus

If your Sun sign is Taurus, your powers and destiny are based on creating value and security for yourself and others. Your steadfast, calm perseverance and determination to keep going, no matter what obstacles you encounter, is a testament to your strength of character. You are loyal to the people and things you value, and your calm presence brings comfort. A cultivator at heart, you patiently sow the seeds of success and nurture along the things to which you dedicate your heart.

You'll receive the most from your abundant Taurus Sun by pursuing your purpose of recognizing and cultivating that which has true and lasting value: love of yourself and others, self-respect, and the knowledge that what you have and what you are is always enough. With that in place, you are able to wisely direct your considerable resourcefulness towards creating things of value and comfort in the world.

If your Taurus Sun pushes you around, you'll neglect tuning in to your inner source of security, and instead seek security from the temporary offerings of the world. You'll collect things or relationships as a way of defining your worth. But deep down, you'll fear lack. Others will seem to undervalue you, when actually you might not be valuing yourself and are resisting others' attempts to connect with you. If hurt, you might barricade vulnerable feelings or hold on to resentment. But that closes you off from your heart—your strongest asset. You might think stability comes from keeping things the same, and become threatened when life's inevitable changes show up. A better approach would be to accept change as life's way of offering you something of even greater value, and then set out to discover what that is. Should you get feedback that you're acting stubborn, check whether you've exchanged perseverance, which shifts and adapts as the situation dictates, with just digging in your heels, which allows no movement whatsoever, even for the better.

One of the most powerful antidotes to the fear of lack is gratitude. When you appreciate who you are and what you have, you're reminded that you've always gotten what you've truly needed. Gratitude also melts energies of resistance and opens your channels wide for both giving and receiving.

Gemini

If your Sun sign is Gemini, your powers and destiny evolve when you synthesize the multiple sides of your nature, talents, and life's choices to create an interesting and varied life. Your incredible curiosity and versatility combine to make every situation a uniquely valuable experience. You are witty, clever, and gifted at putting together ideas and/or materials in ways that are informative and innovative and spark new concepts in others. You're a communicator and teacher at heart, and no matter what avenue you use to make your point, you have much to offer.

You get the most out of your multifaceted Gemini Sun by embracing your purpose of seeking the good in all of life's experiences, including your own duality. Your life's truest excitement and magic comes from being completely involved in whatever you pursue. That way, you avoid becoming scattered, yet stay constantly intrigued with all that life offers.

If your Gemini Sun sign makes you feel scattered, it might be that you've let your multiple natures and talents run you, instead of taking dominion over them. You're interested in and good at a lot of things, but your purpose is not to do and be everything. Rather, you are designed to pick some things and invest all your talents and creativity into them, letting yourself be transformed by this experience. Boredom is sometimes a cue to move on from a situation, but usually it's a signal that you're distracting yourself from participating fully, and thus robbing yourself of a deeper satisfaction. If you get feedback that you're behaving unreliably, check to see if you fear becoming entrapped by commitment. It might be that you have yet to discover how to be fully yourself while vested in someone or something else. Challenge yourself to the vast stimulation and personal expansion that comes when you allow yourself to be completely involved.

Change is a great tonic for you, but it can also be an addiction. Before you leap from one experience to the next, make sure you've gotten as much as you can, and aren't just resisting learning something more deeply or taking on a greater challenge. The most interesting and satisfying change you can make in your life isn't of your circumstances—it's of your consciousness.

Cancer

If your Sun sign is Cancer, your power and destiny will be fulfilled by using your instincts and nurturing skills to support yourself and others. Your sensitivity and natural knowing about what is needed in any situation makes you a masterful homemaker, as well as a savvy contributor to the marketplace. You are tender and intuitive, but not a wimp: you ferociously protect all you value. You are a combination of a parent and a child at heart—at times you're the authority, at other times the innocent.

You bring out the best of your caring Cancer Sun by learning to express the life-sustaining qualities of spirit , and to receive life's ever-present sustenance through knowing you are a beloved child of the universe. As you practice skills of self-parenting, you tap into the true essence of self-fulfillment, wherein nurturing and support come from within and are bountiful. Your childlike nature keeps you imaginative and open to the wonders and magic of life.

374 • Llewellyn's 2002 Sun Sign Book

If you don't parent yourself well, your Cancer Sun's sensitivity and emotional nature can turn brooding and reactive. Instead of nurturing your strengths and well being, you'll amplify feelings of hurt and rejection over slights both real and imagined. You'll withdraw into the safety of your own controlled world while cutting yourself off from situations that could benefit you. It's important to balance the child and the parent qualities of your nature. Otherwise, you're likely to get into unequal relationships that have an unhealthy parent/child dynamic, with dependencies which ultimately limit your development. If you feel inadequate or insecure, know that it's a sign that you've neglected to tap into your inner power and skill base through which you reinvest in yourself. If you get feedback that you're overreacting, check to see if you've let the power of emotional drama replace the energy of your resourceful and knowing core.

You are learning to discern between acts of true nurturing, which empower and promote strength in you and others, with acts of indulgence, which feel good but ultimately support weakness. It's important that you take care of yourself so you can give from your overflow. If you give from your neediness (such as codependent behavior), you'll end up feeling drained and used.

Leo

If your Sun sign is Leo, your power and destiny are realized through your willingness to express and share of yourself genuinely and freely. You have a grand nature, and when you channel it into creativity and leadership you are an undeniably charismatic force. You're wired to play in life's big games and you do everything in a well-managed, stylish, and fun way. Being royalty at heart, you thrive on being magnanimous and generous to those you love.

You bring out the best of your stellar Leo Sun when you align with your purpose of cultivating and expressing through your gigantic heart. When you use love of yourself and others as your power source, you tap into the true meaning of dignity and regality: your spirit soars, your personality sparkles, and others are lifted by simply being in the light of who you are.

If you let your Leo Sun go ungoverned, you'll become controlled by your willful ego—which needs to feel superior to others, but also needs to be applauded by others for validation. You'll confuse pomposity and arrogance with true self-esteem, and feel hurt if others don't respond well to your demands. You'll consider yourself more special and important than others, which cuts you off from genuine relationships and intimacy. Or, instead of tapping into your tremendous spirit for direction, you'll try to get it from others. You'll seek worth through winning the approval of authority figures, and live your life attempting to impress others. Or, you'll seek love by knocking yourself out trying please people, hoping that their recognition will bring meaning to you. But this rarely works for long, and you'll resent your needless effort. If you get feedback that you're being controlling, check to see if you've lost faith in your ability to enjoy the magic of life. Maybe you've decided that you know better than anyone, including your maker, what's the best that could happen.

If you find you have veered from your true power source of love and joy, you can tap back into it by taking yourself more lightly. As you let yourself off the hook of your expectations, the pressure to please and the need to control fall away. You can then realign with the playful spontaneity that makes you, and life, so fantastic.

Virgo

If your Sun sign is Virgo, your power and destiny spring from your joy of service. You love organizing matters to bring out their best order and purity. Your productivity and helpfulness are inexhaustible when you know you're making a valuable contribution. God is in the details: you enjoy using your analytical skills and natural precision to attend to even the tiniest aspect of doing things right. You're a healer at heart, and find tremendous satisfaction in assisting people or situations to be as efficient and excellent as possible.

You bring out the best of your intelligent Virgo Sun by pursuing your purpose—learning to recognize the perfect order that already exists in yourself, other people, and life. In doing so, you realize you don't need to "fix" anything or anyone and thus can devote your energies to unfolding the positive potential in any situation.

If you let your Virgo Sun sign become an overbearing taskmaster, you'll become a perfectionist, deciding that nothing you have done is good enough. You'll deny yourself satisfaction over a job well done and dwell instead on the minuscule things that could have been done better. That deflates you and others. Instead of receiving joy from the details of life, you'll become overwhelmed by them, and forget the bigger picture of what's truly important. If you feel others are overworking you or underappreciating you, evaluate the way you're treating yourself. You might be guilty of expecting too much of yourself, as well as not valuing your contribution. Service to your self is Job One—if you're exhausted or resentful, you're off course. If you get feedback that you're too critical, look to see if you have channeled your analytical skills to focus only on what's wrong, and have forgotten to be part of the solution.

One simple yet effective way to shift out of the harshness of perfectionism is to set your intentions on excellence. Whereas perfectionism is intolerant and focuses on what's wrong, excellence is expansive and focuses on what's right. When aiming for excellence, your creativity peaks and your intuition guides you to do things with a brilliant grace and ease.

Libra

If your Sun sign is Libra, your powers and destiny grow from your ability to create harmony within yourself and others. Your natural understanding of relationships allows you to bring people or things together in a way that creates beauty in the world. Your charm and social skills make people feel important and at ease, which in turn allows for an atmosphere of graciousness and camaraderie. An insightful knack for recognizing multiple sides of a situation is the basis for your creativity and also makes you an excellent negotiator. You are a peacemaker at heart, and enjoy nothing more than being an instrument of balance.

You bring out the best of your elegant Libra Sun when you attend to learning to bring yourself into balance no matter what is going on outside of you. In doing so you tap into an inner peace that serves as an example and inspiration for.

If you let your Libra Sun get out of whack, you'll forget about inner balance and peace and instead demand it of the world. Idealism and demands that everything should be fair will cause you hurt and disappointment, because you'll only see how things are unfair. You'll try to make people and situations get along in the way you think is best, not considering that they have their own paths to take. You'll fear the creativity of occasional conflict and sacrifice your own needs, wants, or ideas just to keep the peace. But that's unfair to you, and creates a false peace. Or you'll attempt to avoid confrontation by becoming passively aggressive, and try to manipulate others into doing your bidding instead of risking a straight-out request. If you get feedback that you're indecisive, it might be a signal that you're trapped by a fear of not making the perfect choice. Try making a decision and investing your all into it. In doing so it becomes your best choice.

You can always bring yourself into balanced alignment by remembering that your most important relationships are with yourself and your maker. By accepting that you can't—and shouldn't—please everyone, you become free to express your genuine self.

Scorpio

If your Sun sign is Scorpio, your individuality and destiny are rooted in your ability to penetrate and transform matters. Your extreme sensitivity and uncanny insight combine to help you reveal the core nature of people and situations. That ability to uncover hidden resources, along with your talent for strategically redirecting energies, allows you to help shift what is negative into something positive, what's wasted into something useful, and what's feared into something safe. You're a detective at heart, and love nothing more than solving the mysteries of life.

You bring out the best of your powerful Scorpio Sun by directing your energies toward learning to recognize and cultivate the positive potential that's always present—even in situations that appear dark. You aren't afraid to delve into the unknown or the difficult—in fact, you're empowered by it.

If you allow your Scorpio Sun dominion over you, you can get stuck in negativity. Instead of exploring dark matters in order to transform them into something redeeming, you'll think darkness is all there is. You'll forfeit aligning with your inner power by feeling safe only when controlling others and life. You'll decide you can get what you deserve only by manipulating and seducing people and situations to giving in to you. If someone doesn't follow your plan, you'll feel betrayed and cut them off, but that isolates you. Or you'll betray your own genuine expression and develop masks or artificial roles to satisfy what you think others expect of you. Remember to use your analytical insights to expand your awareness, rather than to obsess, which contracts your awareness and causes you to miss the big picture. If you get feedback that you're overstepping your bounds, check to see if you're trying to force others to live their lives according to your rules, rather than their own.

One of the most effective ways you can shift away from negativity is to devote yourself to a higher cause, like love or service. As you rise to the challenges of something you consider worthwhile, you expand into a resourcefulness that amazes even you! And, importantly, it's the energy of love (which can be fueled by forgiveness and humor), that makes you an alchemical force of light.

Sagittarius

If your Sun sign is Sagittarius, your power and destiny are fulfilled through your enthusiastic exploration of the meaning of life. You have an inspired nature that enjoys being lifted by seeking moral, ethical, and spiritual truths. You have an innate wisdom and an intuitive grasp of the higher possibilities of life, and you teach and communicate in ways that gives others higher vision as well. You're a philosopher at heart and thrive in situations that stimulate your consciousness to expand into new territory.

You bring out the best of your gregarious Sagittarius Sun by pursuing your purpose of finding the good in life, yourself, and others. When you approach life as a schoolroom designed to teach you to recognize the divine, you become lifted by all experiences, and you find meaning everywhere.

If you let your Sagittarius Sun get off course, you'll forget that life is a learning experience, and decide you already have the answers. You'll exchange your inspired curiosity for an opinionated and righteous stance and demand that everyone around you hold the same morality and truths as you. If they don't, you'll judge them as lost or stupid and preach to them or debate with them, seeking to undermine others' personal convictions. Or you'll give up altogether and become cynical about life and contemptuous of people who have found their way. Your expansive nature needs freedom, both of thought and movement, to keep inspired and fresh. But don't confuse that with needing to keep free from commitment. You might believe that others or circumstances are confining you, when actually you're confining yourself by ignoring the valuable learning available in your situations. Should you get feedback that you're acting hypocritically, check to see if you're attempting to enforce an ideal that your humanity can't yet live up to.

If life loses meaning for you, or you lack inspiration, try returning to your student roots. This allows you to see life with new eyes, and reveals interests you might have overlooked. It's also inspiring to remember that the honor and truth you truly seek is always within yourself, even when you don't find it in the world.

Capricorn

If your Sun sign is Capricorn, your individuality and destiny are achieved by combining your strategic abilities and leadership skills to accomplish worthwhile goals. Your considerable ambition recognizes the highest potential in yourself and your circumstances, and you purposefully overcome any obstacles on your way to attaining them. Your organizational ability intuits exactly how things should be done for maximum efficiency, and your self-discipline keeps you absolutely on plan. You are a colonel at heart, and thrive on heading up difficult tasks that, when conquered, reward you with more power and prestige.

You bring out the best of your capable Capricorn Sun by directing your ambitions to achieve self-mastery. As you use the challenges of life as a forum to develop your highest character, you set your sights on accomplishing things that truly matter: inner recognition, self-direction, and accountability. With those assets you wisely manifest your destiny, and you enjoy it.

If you let your Capricorn Sun gain authority over you, your ambitions and goals will never be satisfied. You'll be driven to attain things to prove to yourself and others that you are worthy, but your need to succeed becomes more important than anyone or anything else. You'll become greedy about power and jealous of others' accomplishments, mistakenly thinking there is a limited amount of success and acknowledgment to go around. You'll suspect that others are trying to thwart your success, when it might be that you are forcing them to perform in a way that disregards their needs or rhythms. Instead of using self-discipline as a means to keep true to your purpose, you'll enforce self-denial and end up detached from the joy and sweetness life offers. If you get feedback that you're controlling, check to see if your leadership suppresses people's spirits, rather than inspiring others to bring out their best.

One way to release yourself from the pressures of driving ambition is to remember to play as you go. Take your cue from the mountain goat who eats, plays, mates, and enjoys the scenery as it climbs to the top of the mountain. In relaxing and keeping your humor, you live fully, and tap into your wisdom that knows what is really worth achieving.

Aquarius

If your Sun sign is Aquarius, your individuality and destiny come to fruition by developing your uniqueness as well as your community spirit. You are a visionary who recognizes the way humanity can evolve and grow together. Your progressive thinking attracts you to projects or technologies that support your mission of making the world a better place. As you allow yourself freedom to demonstrate your individuality, you inspire in others the freedom to be themselves. You are an inventor at heart and thrive when doing things in unconventional ways.

You bring out the best of your global Aquarius Sun as you pursue ways to translate your individuality and vision into society as a whole. When you focus on your own evolution, and lovingly participate with others, you teach by example the ways others might evolve themselves.

If you let your Aquarius Sun go off kilter, your idealism about the way people should be will keep you from appreciating who they are. You'll be impatient and opinionated about the way social progress or projects unfold, and rebellious against existing situations. Instead of joining your community in respecting the views of others, along with the evolutionary process, you'll become stubbornly dictatorial and refuse to compromise your vision to incorporate others' ideas. Or, instead of using your ability to detach and gain a better perspective, you'll just detach altogether. Disillusionment and bitterness will keep you from participating with others, and you'll distance yourself from having to deal with the foibles of humanity. But that keeps you from giving and receiving loving with others—your life's sweetest treasure. If you get feedback that you are acting aloof, check to see if you have disassociated from your feelings. You might have discarded your vulnerabilities and emotions, judging them to be distracting weaknesses, when actually they are your tools for truly connecting with others. Remember: developing your mind without incorporating the wisdom and compassion of your heart might lead you astray, or make you seem uncaring or even cruel.

You can always return to your highest ability—unconditional positive regard for yourself and others—by remembering that we are all experimenting. In doing so, you realize everyone is doing their best and learning to become what we don't yet know. When you align with an innocent curiosity about life, you free yourself from limiting expectations and open to true genius.

Pisces

If your Sun sign is Pisces, your power and destiny involve using your sensitivity and expansive awareness to align with that which brings meaning to you—such as selfless service or artistic expression. Your highly developed intuition and imagination allow you to see the greater possibilities of whatever or whomever you're involved with, and your tender compassion allows you to reach out to others in a knowing way. You have an urge to merge—you crave losing the limitations of ordinary reality to connect with the mysteries and spirituality of life. You are a dreamer at heart and thrive in situations that allow your higher visions to express themselves.

You bring out the best of your Pisces Sun when you learn to surrender your false self and limiting behaviors in order to merge with your higher self. When you practice unconditional loving and forgiveness, you touch into the sublime spiritual frequencies you seek.

If you let your Pisces Sun lead you astray, you'll surrender to activities that weaken and confuse you, instead of giving your all to activities that lift and expand you. You'll allow your will to be taken over by other people's demands or needs, or you'll give in to addictive behaviors. Your sensitivity can zoom in on suffering, and you'll believe that pain is all that exists. Considering yourself a victim of this cruel world, you'll forget that you can make choices that make you life work better. Or you'll support the weaknesses of others by believing you need to rescue them from their problems and become distracted from the responsibility of taking care of yourself. Your creativity thrives in unstructured time and free-flowing situations. But don't use that as an excuse to forget your commitments. If you get feedback that you're acting inconsistently, look to see if you're trying to escape from life, rather than learning from your experiences by lifting your perspective.

It's important that you know the difference between selfless service, which raises your self-esteem and empowers you, and martyrdom, which defeats and drains you. Your ability to recognize the oneness and connecting thread of love in all situations, no matter how fragmented they appear, is your touchstone. Living and being that compassionate oneness is the greatest gift you can give yourself and others.

Each of us is discovering how to master the energies of our Sun sign to use them for our maximum personal potential. Fortunately, we have a lifetime to do that! By reaching back to our expansive qualities and positive attributes after finding we've given in to our weaknesses, we strengthen the pathways to our true empowerment. That secures our course to realizing the highest destiny our Sun sign has to offer.

For Further Reading

Astrology: Understanding the Birth Chart by Kevin Burk. Llewellyn, 2001.

Sun Sign, Moon Sign: Discover the Key to Your Unique Personality Through the 144 Sun, Moon Combinations by Charles Harvey and Suzi Harvey. Thorsons Publishing, 1995.

The Super Natural Planets

by Marguerite Elsbeth

Uranus, Neptune, and Pluto symbolize celestial forces that constantly prompt change and growth in mass consciousness. These outer planets act as galactic messengers: they guide humanity to resonate with the greater cosmos so that we may recognize our interconnectedness with all creatures and things.

Astrologers most often view Uranus, Neptune, and Pluto as generational influences. These planets affect periods in history, entire age brackets of people, and memorable world events—yet they are thought to be difficult to understand on more immediate levels. However, because many of us now seek understanding through alternative spiritual venues, such as Wicca, Paganism, New Age philosophy, Eastern mysticism, and Western esoteric traditions, the capacity of human consciousness is expanding and deepening. Consequently, since conscious perception is the very thing that enables us to realize our external environment in the first place, the outer planets have become more personal; their effect on our everyday activities is now tangibly revealed in a variety of ways. Still, if we are to be able to recognize when and how Uranus, Neptune, and Pluto operate in our daily lives, it is first necessary to understand the relationship between the movement of the stars and planets, and life on Earth.

Cosmic Influence

There is a definite correspondence between the movement of the heavenly bodies and terrestrial existence. The signs of the zodiac, the luminaries and planets, and the division of the zodiac into houses combine to form a picture of the sky, with the Earth (and the creatures and things of Earth) in the center. Our reaction to the vibrations coming from the stars and planets is what astrology is all about. Astrology helps us to interpret the natural world, and allows us to realize our purpose on Earth in accordance with the synchronicity of nature and the cosmos.

Gravity, the cosmological power of attraction, draws every part of the cosmos towards the center. Every planet of our solar system, and every creature and thing on Earth, is subject to the pull that reaches us from the cosmos. However, we are also influenced by the gravitational forces of all the planets in our solar system, which pull us from different directions. We are most affected by the pull of the Sun, the central luminary of our solar system; the Moon, which affects our behavioral patterns, moods, and emotions; and the Earth upon which we live.

Trans-Saturnian Planets

Saturn represents a basic line of separation between these seemingly divergent cosmic and solar forces. The Moon, Mercury, Venus, Earth, Mars, and Jupiter are within Saturn's orbit, and therefore subject to the influence of the Sun's astrological ego and energy. Uranus, Neptune, and Pluto are known as the trans-Saturnian planets, because they fall outside of Saturn's orbit. They do not completely belong to our astrological solar system, and are more influenced by the energies sent out from the vastness of space. Our Sun is the intermediary between the outer planets and the Earth, and we are juxtaposed between the gravitational forces of the Sun, the Moon, and the Earth.

Saturn acts as the Sun's messenger, both by bridging the gap between the personal and outer planets, and conveying to us the ability to perceive the existence and influence of the outer planets, as well as all things that appear as externalized forms. The Sun shares these messages with the Moon, which receives and reflects the Sun's light. Both the Sun and Moon inform us of the messages collected through Saturn, in order that we may consciously act upon and/or instinctually react to the information that is passed on to us.

The Truth About Conscious Perception

Conscious perception is not based solely upon the information we receive through the five physical senses. We are cognizant precisely due to the fact that we obtain information unconsciously from the Sun, the spiritual, conscious life-center of the universe, which collects and distributes the cosmic electrical impulses that give us light and life. We are receptive to the Sun's rays due to the influence of the Moon, the subconscious soul-center of the cosmos that is responsible for the magnetic biorhythms of life.

Since the physical radiations of the Sun are actually an ocean of light that surrounds and permeates our entire planet, we quite literally live within the Sun. Therefore, our emotional bond with the solar orb is a given; we depend on it for basic survival. Moreover, because the electromagnetism of the Sun and Moon pervades all matter, we can tap into the energies transmitted by the outer planets, and indeed, everything in the cosmos, via conscious and subconscious awareness.

Sensitive people are constantly being impressed by the many different levels of consciousness, and are receptive to these supersensory impressions according to the outer planets that most affect them, as well as to the level of consciousness upon which they normally function. Impressions from the concrete or abstract mental levels induced by Uranus, for example, make their mark upon the minds of those who have attained a true measure of concentration. Scientists, mathematicians, spiritual seekers, educators, and humanitarians are all susceptible to such perceptions. Mediums, tarot readers, astrologers, and parapsychologists are exceedingly prone to receiving impressions from Neptune's etheric or astral levels, as are the vast majority of psychics. Finally, the deep-rooted emotions engendered by Pluto enable mystics, occult students, and psychotherapists to access remote regions of the unconscious mind.

Uranus: The Fifth Element

Mental telepathy, one of the supernatural abilities of the mind, is associated with Uranus, the fifth planet from the Earth and the first of the trans-Saturnian planets. This is because Uranus is a cosmic director of electromagnetic forces. It is also the higher octave of Mercury, the planet that channels these forces through our abstract and concrete mental faculties, granting us perception of size, form color, order, position, and motion. Both Uranus and Mercury are conduits of cosmic energy—nothing more. The energy we receive through them is pure and unbridled, colored only by the manner in which we consciously (or unconsciously) interpret that energy, for good or ill.

Air and ether are the spiritual elements associated with Uranus. Air, in addition to being a mixture of the invisible, odorless, tasteless gases that surround the Earth, is breath, the animating or vital principle that gives life to all physical organisms. Moreover, air, along with fire, water and earth, is contained within ether, which according to the ancients permeates all of space and is the connecting medium of the whole universe.

Uranus brings us more intuitively in touch with ether, the fifth element, than with matter, even though we tend to identify ourselves with our bodies. Yet, our bodies are not part of our essential spiritual nature, which is why we can leave them behind, during actions such as trance, meditation, astral travel, near-death experience (NDE), and actual physical demise. Our will, our mind, and our psychic life come directly from ether, and through it we are able to manipulate, move, rearrange, and employ the atoms of matter to express our thoughts and feelings, and to manifest ourselves to others. Working through Uranus, ether enables us to be aware of all the kingdoms of nature and to extend our concept of life beyond the physical plane.

Uranus in Daily Life

People with many planets in Aquarius, a heavily aspected Uranus, Uranus on the angles of the birth chart, or people who are undergoing Uranus transits generally have a strong independent streak, and a highly developed intellect with a decidedly scientific and/or occult bend of mind.

Friends, social groups, humanitarian ideals, and human fellowship are primary Uranian concerns; however, when this planet is active, it brings with it a new way of looking at things. Its approach is best met with an expanded consciousness, because Uranus sees no need for the status quo, preferring instead to break with tradition and create a new mold. Therefore, Uranus may incline you to seek out new and improved company or life-goals, in the time it takes to blink an eye.

Yet, perhaps the true cause of the divine discontent brought by Uranus has to do with apprehension regarding the course your life has taken, because your same old tried-and-true friends, methods and goals no longer satisfy your needs. Uranus induces you to ask yourself, "Do I want the rest of my life to continue along the same path, or do I want to set out in a direction more suited to my heart's desire?" If you do not realize that Uranus is asking you to take a chance by following your dreams, you may manifest this planet's energy in a variety of strange and incongruous ways instead. You may, for example, have a strong, abrupt urge to wear bright, electric colors or outrageous checks and plaids. You might seriously consider quitting your steady job to ride off into the sunset via horseback or motorcycle, or unexpectedly turn your back on mainstream religion in favor of metaphysics, astrology, or the occult. You could even drop your stable, long-term partner for someone strange, rebellious, and/or wholly unacceptable to friends and family.

Furthermore, you may be prone to sudden inflammations in the lower extremities, fractures, ruptures, lesions, spasmodic disorders, or nervous exhaustion, because your body can only handle so much energy, and Uranus gives you too much all at once.

Uranus represents a kind of cosmic shock therapy that typically leads you to seek an entirely different way of life that may seem bizarre to those who know you well and expect you to always remain the same. This is because Uranus packs a wallop in terms of electrical voltage, and odd things happen to your habitual way of thinking and being if you are not ready for it.

The cure for what ails those of you who may be sensitive to Uranus or have challenging Uranus transits is plenty of fresh air, cool water to refresh and magnetize the body, a calm and relaxed atmosphere, therapeutic massage, and biofeedback. A low-starch,

388 • Llewellyn's 2002 Sun Sign Book

low-sugar diet that includes warm, sweet, and gentle foods is also very soothing to an overelectrified nervous system.

Psychic Superconductivity

Intuition and mediumship are the mystical qualities associated with Neptune, the second trans-Saturnian planet. Neptune is also the higher octave of Venus, which channels Neptune's energy to us through the mental faculty of creative imagination.

Water is the element associated with Neptune. This liquid that descends from the clouds as rain, forming streams, lakes, and seas, is a superconductor for the magnetic creative force. It constitutes the essential matrix of all living things, and represents the principle of imaginative power in physical form.

Water is alive and responsive to our every thought and feeling through the workings of the subconscious mind, which holds the memories of all past, present, and future events through our emotions, psyche, and soul. Our bodies and the earth's surface are 70 percent water, granting all of us the innate intuitive ability to receive psychic impressions radiating from the cosmos through clairsentience, psychometrics, dowsing, and spiritual healing, in much the same way that psychics, mediums, and shamans do.

However, when functioning at optimum potential, the imagination is our greatest resource, as it is a well-known medical fact that positive mental images, visions, and dreams create wellness by increasing the number of healing cells in the body, and by helping to produce uplifting sensations of being whole, fit, and vital. Therefore, we are always in touch with Neptune through our dreams and visions, and every time we use our imaginations.

Neptune in Daily Life

People with many planets in Pisces, a heavily aspected Neptune, Neptune on the angles of the birth chart, or who are undergoing Neptune transits generally have a highly developed sense of aesthetics, a strong sympathetic nature, and finely attuned extrasensory perceptions.

Altruism, idealistic ventures, dreams, illusion, abstract thought, and the mysterious are all Neptunian concerns. Your spirituality and how you harness that energy for your personal betterment is important to this planet, as Neptune invites you to let its energy wash over you and to use a trance-like or altered state of consciousness to gain insights and heightened awareness.

However, Neptune also likes to dissolve boundaries by stretching reality to the outer limits and beyond, in a way that tends to spellbind your attention with glamour and illusion. You may, for example, speak in metaphors instead of saying what you really mean. You might become a fan of New Age music, when not too long ago you loved rock 'n' roll. You might forget your own name, yet recognize every actor in every movie, television show, and theater production. You could even give up real-time sex to have an astral love affair.

When Neptune acts upon the lower senses, you may also have feelings of depression, or doom and gloom. Usually, there seems to be no tangible rhyme or reason as to why you are feeling this way, because unless you are tapped into Neptune on a higher, more productive level, and are willing to sacrifice whatever you have going for the sake of selfless giving, this planet tends to cloud your issues.

Furthermore, Neptune-sensitive people are prone to oxygen deficiency, unexplainable glandular imbalances, energy depletion, anemia, neuroses, hypochondria, and forgetfulness. You may also feel impelled to escape from reality through drugs, alcohol, food, or other addictions.

Remedies for Neptune's more challenging energy include methods that boost, enhance, and strengthen the immune system. Spiritual beliefs that encourage the virtues of love, hope, and faith can also help. Meditation and prayer practices, positive affirmations, the active use of creative imagination, proper diet and exercise, mineral and herbal supplements, and magnetic therapy all can help to keep you vital, fit, and centered when Neptune enters your life.

Fire in the Sky

Remote viewing and clairvoyance, the abilities allowing us to see things beyond the range of the power of vision, are the supersensory gifts associated with Pluto, the third trans-Saturnian planet. Pluto is also the higher octave of Mars, which channels this energy to us through dynamic, penetrative mental and physical activity.

Fire is the element associated with Pluto, which produces the phenomenon of combustion manifested in light, flame, and heat.

This divine influence or action is also an inspiring agent that moves the intellect and emotions, and qualifies us to receive and communicate sacred revelations from the cosmos.

We all have an internal flame, a spirit that makes us 100 percent supernatural at all times. Remote viewing and clairvoyance give us the ability to see the universal truths available in the non-physical realm where all knowledge is accessible, without the limitations of space and time. However, the insights and foresights we receive through Pluto's second sight bypass the conscious mind's scrutiny and evaluation, and therefore we usually act upon these inclinations without thinking. We always have the facility of interior vision; it is more a part of our daily lives than we realize. Pluto is usually associated with death; still, dying lasts a short time, so what truly matters is transformative living. This planet activates our ability to see the truth of spiritual reality by urging us to look inward with an eye toward change.

Pluto in Daily Life

People with many planets in Scorpio, a heavily aspected Pluto, Pluto on the angles of the birth chart, or those who are undergoing Pluto transits generally are able to create, destroy, and recreate their worldview by transcending what they know.

Pluto is concerned with sex, death, power struggles, and identity crises. Its energy may be subtle, but it will hit you like a ton of bricks if you are not willing to get with the program, which is about transformation, regeneration, and rebirth. Pluto says, "Out with the old and in with the new." The question here is: what exactly do you need to change?

Usually the answer resides in the persons, places, or things that you think you want or need, yet are no longer necessary to your journey along life's path. Most often, there will be ample warnings that you must relinquish your attachments, and more often than not you resist letting go. Self-control is Pluto energy at its best, and this is the time to use it or lose it, if you don't heed the signs. You may, for example, have brushes with authority because you wave a red flag. You could play survivor on a miserable, mosquito-infested tropical island existing in a world of your own devising. You might remember long-forgotten slights and decide that it's payback time without giving fair warning to those on the receiving end of your anger. You could even become an ascetic because self-love is better than no love at all.

If we refuse to go along with Pluto's urge to eliminate outworn forms, this planet will simply have us wallow in our own misery. We may also develop ailments resulting from inflammatory and chaotic internal conditions, such as violent energy surges, headaches, sexually transmitted diseases, and sexual malfunction.

If you are experiencing Pluto problems, you will spiritually, mentally, and emotionally benefit from meditation geared toward forgiving yourself and others, and blessing and releasing old patterns. You may also want to engage in physical activity to purge your body and get rid of systemic waste. Juice fasting is another excellent way to detoxify a congested system, as is a diet that emphasizes plenty of purified drinking water, fresh, organic fruits, vegetables, whole grains and legumes, and minimal animal proteins.

Super Natural Planets

Supernatural events, such as those that occur during mental telepathy, clairvoyance, sensory awareness, psychometrics, psychokinesis, remote viewing, mediumship, and spiritual healing, are things that are deemed to be not scientifically explainable. Like the planets Uranus, Neptune, and Pluto, supernatural events relate to an order of existence that appears to lie beyond the visible, observable universe. Additionally, they seem to transcend the laws of nature and depart from what is usual or common. However, we are all beginning to recognize and acknowledge the inherent value of the application of forces that were previously considered miraculous. A variety of scientific experiments show a significant correlation between the Moon, the weather, and human emotion, for example. We consistently demonstrate a day-to-day supernatural facet of reality that coexists in perfect harmony with nature, as well as the findings of hard science and astrology.

Hence, we have a quantum-physical worldview that no longer contradicts the reality of supersensory perception, and a scientific viewpoint in which paranormal events are no longer outside the realm of possibility. The two fields are drawing slowly closer and closer together. Yesterday's miracle is today's science because serious experiments in the field of parapsychology consistently yield affirmative results indicating and affirming the presence of supernatural planetary forces.

The primary reason most people cannot demonstrate supernatural ability is because of mental chatter, or interference in the form of static electricity that may block or alter the etheric or psychic mind-stuff before it reaches conscious awareness. Intuitive tools such as pendulums, divining rods, Ouija boards, tarot cards, runes, crystal balls, black mirrors, or even a simple candle flame can help us to access the subconscious mind directly by converting faint psychic signals into forms that are able to withstand most of the mental interference we constantly experience.

Pendulums and divining rods, for instance, work through Uranus to stimulate small changes in muscle tension, micromovements of the voluntary motor muscles, and electrical impulses to and from the central nervous system. Ouija boards, tarot cards and runes operate through Neptune to produce magnetic currents, which run through the body in the form of subtle shakes, tremors, or waves. Crystal balls and black mirrors, which fall under the influence of Pluto, negate the effects of normal vision by granting us a random viewing field that enables subconscious impressions to flow in the opposite direction along the optic nerves, to the retina.

These things are always happening, but the effect is so slight that it is easily overwhelmed by the normal physical senses. All these tools function by making the most of synchronicity—the cosmic ebb and flow that connects all creatures and things. Dedicated use of any of these tools can open us up in terms of supernatural sensitivity to the outer planets, because they induce subconscious stimuli in the form of images, thoughts, ideas, feelings, and sensory impressions from the cosmic ethers. Moreover, we can read the intuitive messages we receive through these devices with the conscious mind.

We respond to Uranus, Neptune, and Pluto best when we are aware that they are constant operative factors in our lives. However, we must be able to relate these energies to some field of information, instruction, or energy distribution. Furthermore, we must be able to clearly know where these energies make the most impact—the mind, the astral body, or the physical body. The way to do this is to develop adequate sensitivity to the supernatural senses, because while all people have intuitive abilities, in most of us these abilities are far too fragile. However, the above tools can enhance the latent supernatural ability we do have, because they all rely upon tapping into the subconscious mind where our extrasensory abilities reside. Therefore, even if you believe you have little to no telepathic talent, you may be able to at least experience something of the supernatural forces inherent in and transmitted by Uranus, Neptune, and Pluto. If you focus on the feelings the electromagnetic impulses that come through these metaphysical mechanisms give you, you will begin to know, first hand, how Uranus, Neptune, and Pluto energy works for you. Later on, you can learn to heighten these sensations, and direct these energies to make specific changes in your life.

Finally, the very word "supernatural" implies that which is extraordinarily super and natural at one and the same time! Everything existing in nature is a manifestation of spirit, so how can it be said that paranormal occurrences are not in accordance with or determined by nature? Life itself is a miraculous and amazing event. Every day provides us with positive proof that there is divine intervention in human affairs. Some claim this intercession originates from the Pleiades, while others believe it approaches us through long-gone deities associated with Atlantis and Lemuria, or due to our spirit guides, animal totems, deceased relations, angels, or other highly evolved ethereal beings. There are also individuals who see paranormal phenomena as the root source of power; in fact, it seems that the more phantasmagoric the supernatural power source, the better. True, otherworldly visitors, spirits, animals, and the ancestors all may play an important role in mind-blowing incidents, but they are helpers or guides only, not the actual source of power.

The real power source is far more ancient. Electromagnetism, spiritual ether, limitless light, prana or prakriti, Great Spirit, Great Mystery, or spirit energy – all these names refer to one universal power that enters into and expands our minds to perform super, though very natural, feats through Uranus, Neptune, and Pluto, the planets that animate, ensoul, and catalyze our perceptual awareness in the here and now.

For Further Reading

How to Personalize the Outer Planets: The Astrology of Uranus, Neptune, and Pluto edited by Noel Tyl. Llewellyn, 1992.

Alive and Well with Uranus: Transits of Self-Awakening; Alive and Well with Neptune: Transits of Heart and Soul; and *Alive and Well with Pluto: Transits of Power and Renewal* by Bil Tierney. Llewellyn, 1999.

Sun Signs
and Psychic Ability

by Mitchell Gibson

The art and science of astrology in the Western world is perhaps most intimately associated with the study of the Sun sign. In a Gallup survey, more people were familiar with their Sun sign than their own blood type. The Sun sign is related to the position of the Sun in a specific constellation of stars at the time of a person's birth. These constellations were named thousands of years ago by ancient sky-gazers who were able to identify rough correlations between the shape of the stars and prominent mythological figures. The constellation Pisces resembled the shape of a fish and its name is reflective of this association. The constellation Scorpio is said to resemble a scorpion, and the constellation Virgo is said to resemble a young maiden; hence their associations with the Sun signs of Virgo and Scorpio. In this article, we will examine a scientific survey of more than 227 individuals who are gifted psychically and spiritually and determine which Sun sign occurs most commonly among the group.

To my knowledge, scientific studies of psychic ability and astrology have rarely if ever been performed in the Western world. Names of notable spiritual adepts such as Edgar Cayce, Nostradamus, Olga Worrall, Sai Baba, Cagliostro, and Padre Pio are known all over the world. If one wanted to examine which of the twelve Sun signs were most prevalent among a database of 227 such notables, one would simply complete a tally of the frequency with which the various Sun sign nativities showed up among these individuals. If the results followed straightforward statistical mathematics, each Sun sign should occur with equal frequency. In this particular case, all of the signs would show up around nineteen times. That is, 227 divided by 12 is approximately 19. When I completed this sort of random tally, with data gathered via the Hunter database, these numbers were far from the actual result. In point of fact, several Sun signs show up with such incredibly high frequencies above the expected average that I was forced to include a section on this phenomenon in my research on astrology and psychic phenomenon. In the past, I was hesitant to include such data because it was subject to considerable anecdotal bias and speculation. However in this case, it is clear that the scientific principles that define the association of particular Sun signs with spiritual abilities are sound and are removed from such bias.

One question that I like to pose at astrological conventions is, "What is the most psychic of all the Sun signs?" Invariably, in response I get a plethora of responses that reflect varying degrees of anecdotal bias and client-based information. That is not to say that these individuals are incorrect in their response, but it is clear that astrologers too often refrain from a more analytical and methodical approach to gathering their data. One's private client list of "gifted" individuals from the surrounding area does not qualify as a valid scientific sampling. In the grouping presented in this chapter, the individuals represented are taken from a time span of eight hundred years. These charts also represent nativities from people born on every continent and most of the world's countries. To date, I have not heard an astrologer give a report on a scientific statistical sampling of this nature. I hope this trend will change in the future.

When the numbers are tallied and the resulted categorized, one Sun sign emerges as the clear winner in the race for the most "psychic" of all the Sun signs. Out of the 227 charts studied in this sample, thirty-one of them represented individuals born under the sign of Pisces. If we go back to the original argument presented earlier, each sign should show up nineteen times across the sample population. This would be true if the distribution were to follow a simple random order. The fact that thirty-one of the charts were of individuals born in Pisces represents an occurrence that is 63 percent above that indicated by simple chance. How does one explain this phenomenon rationally? Before we tackle this question, let us examine three additional findings within this sampling that add further weight to the argument that certain Sun signs are indeed associated with the psychic gift.

In this sampling, twenty-five individuals were born under the sign of Capricorn. This represents an occurrence that is more than 31 percent above chance. Twenty-three individuals were born under the signs of Aquarius. Ironically, twenty-three individuals were also born under the sign of Taurus. Both of these figures represent occurrences that are more than 20 percent above chance! What does this mean? The vast majority of astrologers will eagerly guess that Pisces is logically associated with special spiritual ability because of its well-known affiliations with sensitivity and the paranormal. This is the first quantitative proof that such an association truly exists. The likelihood that Pisces would be associated with great psychics and spiritual leaders birth charts 63 percent more than random chance is highly improbable. The further scientific associations of Capricorn, Aquarius, and Taurus with the birth charts of spiritual leaders is also highly unlikely. We may never fully understand the scientific principles behind these associations, but let us examine the full data set and some of the individuals who were born under these signs.

Pisces: 31 out of 227 charts; 63 percent above chance

Pisces is well-known as a very sensitive sign. The Pisces individual often displays empathic ability and instinctively understands mystical experiences and the reality of the paranormal. Pisces is receptive by nature, and can be overwhelmed by impressions and emotions absorbed by others. Pisces is the most susceptible of all the Sun signs to outside influence. If we accept the axiom that paranormal sensitivity is by its very nature shaped by outside influences, we could scarcely create a more harmonious association between human behavior and nature as we see with Pisces. The Piscean's torrent of emotion is so deep and strong that he himself may be confused and tormented by it. The more he can impose a creative shape on it, the greater chance he has of coming to terms with it psychologically. Some of the world's greatest psychic and spiritual leaders have navigated these waters and have emerged with the wisdom and knowledge necessary to inspire the masses. Edgar Cayce, the "Sleeping Prophet," was born under the sign of Pisces. He is perhaps the most famous American trance medium of all time. His predictions and diagnostic treatments were performed while he was under the spell of a deep trance. Scientists are still studying and verifying his work years after his death. Gerard Croiset, the famous French clairvoyant, healer, and psychometrist was also born under the sign of Pisces. Other notable Pisceans gifted with heightened psychic and spiritual abilities include Meher Baba, Olney Richmond, David Bray, Jean McAuthur, Lucille Van Tassel, Kelly Quinn, Brenda Crenshaw, and Rosalyn Bruyere.

Capricorn: 25 out of 227 charts; 32 percent above chance

Capricorns come in a surprising second in our survey. Capricorns are not known to be highly spiritual or especially sensitive in the astrological sense, but our survey is replete with individuals who were born under this Sun sign. The Capricorn's mind is extremely rational and serious. His thought patterns are constructive, and he has great ability to plan ahead in detail. Capricorns are known to be cool and calculating and are not generally known to grasp new situations very quickly. However, once they understand a situation, they will never forget. Perhaps this cool and calculating demeanor helps the Capricorn to remove the external dross from situations which relate to psychic and paranormal sensitivity, and focus in on the relative essence of the matter. A number of famous Capricorns grace our survey, including Jeanne Dixon, the seeress of Washington, who became famous with her predictions regarding the assassination of John F. Kennedy. She was at one time the most famous psychic in the world. Alan Vaughan, world-renowned psychic and author, is also a Capricorn. Other famous Capricorns included in the survey were Serge Leon Alalouf, Antoinette Bourignon, Georges Gurdijeff, Raman Maharishi, Minnie B. Theobold, and Louis Claude de Saint-Martin.

Aquarius: 23 out of 227 charts; 21 percent above chance

Tied for third place in our survey is the Sun sign many people place in first position in this category in random-sample questionnaires. Aquarians are known to be original and progressive in outlook, but they can be equally stubborn and rebellious. The Aquarian mind is typically not concerned with what other people think and will often not bother to form an opinion of his own behavior. His thinking is often ahead of its time—rational, intelligent, and intuitive. His rationality and analytical nature may serve to empower the spiritual aspects of his nature. A few Aquarians included in our study are Malcolm Bessent, the Wall Street psychic who has made millions with his intuitive predictions; television psychic Kenny Kingston; author and Christian mystic Elizabeth Burrows; visionary Emmanuel Swedenborg; and physician Brugh Joy.

Taurus: 23 out of 227 charts; 21 percent above chance

The other half of the third-place tie belongs to the Sun sign Taurus. Taureans are very patient people who tend to be charming, warm, and affectionate. They are for the most part conservative people who are generous to a fault. They are psychologically content with well-established ideas and are not likely to bring up new ideas or new angles on existing concepts. The Taurus archetype would not be expected to rank highly among spiritually sensitive Sun signs. However, the most important aspect to consider when examining this ranking is the fact that science is often preempted by the reality of natural phenomenon. The steadfast nature of Taurus may well serve to balance and enhance the wellspring of natural empathy and spiritual sensitivity that is present in all signs. Rather than bragging or boasting about their proclivities, the Taurean is likely to simply accept and integrate such impressions without pretense. This in and of itself is an admirable trait in an area often filled with outsized egos and sensitivities. Famous Taurean psychics include Jiddu Krishnamurti, Jack Schwarz, Jane Roberts, Jomanda, Peter Hurkos, and Matti Vilokkinen.

Leo: 21 out of 227 charts; 10.5 percent above chance

The Leo archetype is best described as affectionate, enthusiastic, cheerful, optimistic, broad-minded, and magnanimous. Leos have a

pronounced breadth of vision, and will at once see the general
shape of a scheme or project; but will sometimes lack an eye for
detail. There is sometimes an artistic inclination that the Leo will
often use to his advantage with his pronounced constructive energies. Leo's thought processes tend to be positive, and while he may
not be a quick thinker, he will arrive steadily at firm conclusions,
and will not commit himself until he is sure where he stands. Leos
can become very flamboyant psychics who are great showmen at
heart. Some of the more famous examples of great sensitives who
are Leos are Sri Aurobindo, Rudi Schneider, Kevin Reyerson,
Debra Lynch, Ellen Yoakum, and Matthew Manning.

Gemini: 20 out of 227 charts; 5 percent above chance

Fifth place in our survey belongs to one of the most communicative
signs in the Zodiac. Adaptable, versatile, intellectual, witty, logical,
talkative, and changeable are words that would perhaps best
describe the Gemini persona. A Gemini will always be on the go,
and generally speaking will be doing more than one thing at one
time. This duality is an important part of his nature, and any
attempts to hinder this aspect of their personality would be
extremely unwise. The Gemini needs change. The Gemini mind
will have many activities at one time, and may even have several
occupations during his life. Properly motivated, he can find one or
two major themes that occupy their lives. Several Geminis have
distinguished themselves in the spiritual realms. They include Sir
Oliver Joseph Lodge, Franz Anton Mesmer, Eric Hanussen, Rex
Stanford, and Pandit Ji Gopi Krishna.

Libra: 15 out of 227 charts

Libra ties for sixth place in our survey of psychic Sun signs. However, in a concomitant survey involving the Ascendant, Libra
placed first with 31 out of 227 charts falling under this Sun sign.
According to this data, the most gifted psychics would be born with
the Sun sign Pisces and the ascendant Libra. Sri Chaitanya is the
only person in our survey who holds this distinction. Born in 1486,
this great mystic and spiritual teacher epitomizes the highest ideals
of a decidedly advanced soul. The Libran has the ability to see several sides of a problem simultaneously and as a result, he can have

difficulty deciding which side to take. He has a strong sense of justice, and will certainly do his best to see that justice is done. Libran instincts are usually right and always help him to make decisions by indicating a particular course of action. Cheerful, optimistic, and easygoing by nature, they have a natural resistance to loneliness. The intellectual kinship they will feel for one person will often be balanced by an equal and opposite antipathy for another. Thus they are able to maintain the theme so aptly expressed in this sign's glyph—a symbol of scales or balances. Paul Brunton, Ammachi, Gordon Michael Scallion, Ernesto Montgomery, Jean Forrest, Finbarry Nolan, and Deepak Chopra are Librans who have distinguished themselves in their spiritual endeavors.

Virgo: 15 out of 227 charts

The second part of the sixth-place tie in our survey belongs to the mutable earth sign Virgo. Discriminating, analytical, meticulous, tidy, detailed, and fastidious may be the words that best describe Virgo. The Virgo's flair for detail can dominate him: in his quest for perfection in minutiae he can all too easily lose sight of the overall picture. The driving motive for Virgo is to serve in one way or another. Precision and neatness are natural for him and this can build up a psychological barrier that can make Virgos seem particularly aloof. If they can work out a proper balance between the two, their charitable and giving natures can make their natural reservation seem quite charming.

The Virgo mind has the immediate instinct to break down and analyze any problem, missing no aspect or detail of the situation. The need to know, dissect, and research are paramount interests to him. A Virgo is prone to hypochondria, and if he is not careful, he will find himself the subject of his own distorted somatically-related neuroses. Several famous Virgos have distinguished themselves in the spiritual realm. They include Ralph Waldo Trine, George Bataille, Swami Sivananda, Edson Queiroz, Patricia Hough, Art Nash, and Elise Wheeler.

Sagittarius: 14 out of 227 charts

Tied for the seventh-place position in our survey is the mutable fire sign of Sagittarius. The myth of Sagittarius is associated with the centaur Chiron, who raised Jason, Achilles, and Aeneas. Chiron was famous as a prophet, doctor, and scholar, and was the son of Philyra by Cronus—who was also the father of Zeus. Sagittarians are jovial, optimistic, versatile, adaptable, scrupulous, and dependable. Their optimism can also sometimes become a handicap and they are prone to capriciousness, extremism, and a sense of restlessness. The Sagittarian mind may overlook details, but his overall sense of planning is admirable. He is at his best dealing with old problems on new lines; each difficulty will be approached from several angles, perhaps unusual ones, and there will inevitably be a great deal of refinement of ideas and conclusions. These traits should help to make the Sagittarian a fine spiritual savant, and indeed there are quite a number of individuals who have distinguished themselves over the years. They include Uri Geller, Olga Worrall, Yolanda Betegh, Aino Kassinen, Dieter Schopfwinkel, William Blake, and Sathya Sai Baba.

Cancer: 14 out of 227 charts

The second part of our seventh-place tie goes to the feminine water sign of Cancer. Cancers tend to have great imaginations and are often known for their prodigious memories. They are highly intuitive by nature and their basic instincts will usually be right. There is a tendency for the Cancer native to worry unnecessarily, and this may tend to temper his or her natural intuitive gift to some extent. Kind, sensitive, tenacious, and thrifty are traits that further describe the Cancer Sun sign. Their mood swings are the stuff of legend and a tendency toward a hot temperament is not uncommon. Some famous psychics who were born under the sign of Cancer include Greet Hofmans, Wirkus Mietek, Maxine Bell, Raymond Burgess, Arne Leine, Paul Solomon, and Murshid Inayat Khan.

Aries: 13 out of 227 charts

Rounding out the bottom of our survey is another two-way tie. Aries is a fire sign. Phrixus, son of Nepele, was falsely accused of ravishing Biadice and was condemned to death. He was then rescued by a golden ram, on whose back he escaped. When Phrixus reached safety he sacrificed the ram to Zeus. Zeus placed the likeness of the ram in the heavens and hence it became a Sun sign.

Arians are adventurous, enterprising, courageous, direct in approach, energetic, and at times impatient. Arians also have a quick wit and tend to make friends easily. The thoughts of an Aries can sometimes bound from one point to another, rather than following a logical progression, and this can lead to problems. The primitive, almost primaeval impulses of the Arian are often refreshing to others, and at times they can give their owner certain advantages in the social arena. Charles Kuntz, Ronald Lee Warmouth, William Wingfield, Ruth White, Joan Pio Prado, Serena Wright, Ram Dass, and Josephan Peladan are all examples of Arians who have become world-renowned psychics.

Scorpio: 13 out of 227 charts

The second part of the eighth-place tie in our survey goes to Scorpio. At Juno's command the Scorpion rose up from the earth to attack Orion. The Scorpion also caused the horses of the Sun to bolt when driven for a day by the boy Phaethon. Jupiter later rebuked it with a thunderbolt.

Scorpios are well-known for their strong sense of sexuality and passion. An unusual kind of intensity pervades a Scorpio's whole personality, giving him an extremely strong sense of purpose in life. The eagle was once used to represent the sign of Scorpio. This sign underlines not only a Scorpio's harsh tendencies, but also his or her power to rise above worldly difficulties. The Scorpio often finds it difficult to understand this harshness, but may use it just the same in areas of his life that require power and courage. He tends to concentrate on analyzing his reactions rather than the problem itself. These reactions have a tendency to become internalized and may erupt from the Scorpio in the form of an unwanted quarrel. The more he tries to control this repressive tendency, the better he will be able to direct his high-powered emotions in a positive fashion. When Scorpios can control their passions, they can become world-class psychics. Maha Gurr Metta, Guru Nanak, Count Karlfried von Durckheim, Joseph Issels, and Ginger Chalford are Scorpios who have mastered this trait and become notable psychics.

Psychic Implications

This list of psychic savants is by no means exhaustive. The fact that some Sun signs ranked low on our survey listing does not mean that being born under that sign is a detriment to one's spiritual development. On the contrary, one can find famous and powerful psychics under any Sun sign. The fact that Pisces is the most frequent Sun sign association in this survey, and the most well-known of all the spiritual signs, does not mean that being born under this sign will make one an immediate world-class psychic. Hard work, discipline, sensitivity, intelligence, perception, and an overall sense of wonder about the world around you are important traits for the aspiring psychic to develop. Many of the greatest spiritual leaders in the world may be found under a host of different Sun signs.

This research is part of an ongoing research effort called the Signs Project. The goal of this project is to objectify some of the claims and data found in much of the astrological literature. I also hope to add an air of credence to the too-often anecdotal and subjective efforts that permeate the field of astrology. In my new book, Signs of Psychic and Spiritual Ability, this research has been applied to over 250 psychic events, individuals, and predictions in order to elucidate an orderly and scientific method for determining the astrological markers for successful psychic and spiritual performance. Included in this work are chapters on four main subtypes of spiritual phenomena, including mysticism, psychic and spiritual healing, mediumship, and general psychic ability. My research shows that it is possible to predict the psychic and spiritual potential of any natal chart. A normative range of average, above average, superior, and outstanding has been established utilizing this research. While most people score in the average to above average range, psychically gifted individuals such as Edgar Cayce, Sai Baba, Nostradamus, Sybil Leek, and a host of other in that league score far into the outstanding range. This score is determined by using only the individual's natal information. The major Ptolemaic aspects, triangles, quads, and other multiple planet groupings are important principles that are used in the equation.

I feel that this type of data is useful for determining dates which may be used for prayer, meditation, ritual work, channeling, vision quests, and a host of other spiritually related applications that are covered in the book. I encourage all students of the art of astrology to learn more about the science of astrology and to apply some of the principles that I present in this work. Remember, astrology is one of the oldest sciences in the world and, as such, it has much to offer the inquisitive mind.

For Further Reading

Mind Trek by Joseph McMoneagle. Hampton Roads Publishing, 1993.

Psychic Exploration: A Challenge for Science by Edgar Mitchell. Putnam, 1974

Remote Viewing by Joseph McMoneagle. Hampton Roads Publishing, 2000.

Signs of Psychic and Spiritual Ability by Mitchell Gibson. Llewellyn, 2001.

Sun Signs
and Your Business

by Stephanie Clement

Almost everyone knows what his or her Sun sign is, but most of us know a lot less about how to use this knowledge to our advantage in operating our businesses or pursuing our careers. How is the rhythm of the solar year reflected in the course of daily or monthly business affairs? How does the Sun's position affect both owners and clientele?

Signs

First, consider how your Sun sign reflects your business, your attitude toward your work, and the skills you have available to accomplish the work. I have listed some keywords that indicate strong, positive business traits for each sign, as well as some less-helpful qualities to watch out for where business is concerned.

Try to be honest with yourself when you evaluate your Sun sign characteristics. When considering Scorpio (my Sun sign), I have to

Sun Sign Business Traits

Aries   Enthusiastic, purposeful, brave
             Ruthless, quarrelsome

Taurus   Humorous, practical, organized
             Stubborn, selfish, materialistic

Gemini   Adaptable, conversational
             Inconsistent, superficial, restless

Cancer   Imaginative, patient, prudent
             Frivolous, self-indulgent

Leo   Ambitious, determined, confident
             Arrogant, overbearing, stubborn

Virgo   Practical, honest, discriminating
             Indecisive, fault-finding, overly cautious

Libra   Artistic, impartial, considerate
             Extravagant, indecisive, dependent

Scorpio   Trustworthy, tenacious, aspiring
             Sarcastic, stubborn, foolhardy

Sagittarius Cheerful, honest, inspirational
             Extravagant, gullible, scattered

Capricorn Dependable, efficient, industrious
             Miserly, materialistic, unsympathetic

Aquarius   Friendly, self-sufficient, persistent
             Impetuous, rebellious

Pisces   Sympathetic, adaptable, intuitive
             Moody, indulgent, secretive

think—just what is the difference between tenacity and stubborn-ness, or even foolhardiness? Should I press so hard to make a sale that the customer may never come back to my store? Would it be good for my business to throw all available capital into one product, to the exclusion of the rest of my business? And when does this sort of foolhardy behavior erode any trustworthiness I may have earned in previous transactions? I probably don't need to say much about sarcastic behavior being detrimental to good client relationships. Having strong aspirations is an obviously good quality in a busi-nessperson, so long as they don't overrule practical decisions.

If you are honest with yourself, you can avoid the extremes of your Sun sign and cultivate a moderate style that suits your partic-ular business and will not offend your customers or clients. You don't have to give up a behavior—I can be sarcastic if I want to—but you may find you use the extreme behaviors less and less as you develop a degree of comfort in your business dealings.

Development

The second step is to think of how the Sun reflects the develop-mental cycle of the year, and how that cycle affects your particular business. The list below includes principles of the growth cycle, along with associated processes and attitudes.

Aries	Germination of seeds, infancy
Taurus	Strengthening the sprout, resources
Gemini	Flourishing of leaves, exchange of ideas
Cancer	Multiplying of buds and leaves, parental roles
Leo	Ripening of fruit, self-confidence, creativity
Virgo	Gathering, diligence, cooperation
Libra	Harvest celebration, community, partnership
Scorpio	Withering, struggle for survival, rebirth
Sagittarius	Hibernation, spiritual investigation, planning
Capricorn	Invisible life, focus on the personal
Aquarius	Waiting for spring, formation of friendships
Pisces	Seeds preparing to sprout, inner development

While you personally focus most easily on the stage in the cycle associated with your Sun sign, you also understand the rest of the cycle, and can incorporate other stages into your business plan. In fact, a complete plan may include elements of each of the steps, whether those elements are tied to the time of year or not. For example, every business has an invisible life of one kind or another. For a therapist, that might be time spent making notes concerning client sessions. For a florist it may be planning for a wedding, when you visualize the bouquets and other flowers you will need. Neither of these is reserved for the time when the Sun is in Pisces, and both are essential steps for effective action.

Elements

Third, the relationship between your Sun sign (or the Sun sign in the chart of your business) and the transiting Sun can indicate the monthly ups and downs, the best opportunities, and the most difficult challenges to your success. Each zodiac sign is associated with one of the four elements: fire, earth, air, or water. Using the following list, you can determine the element of your Sun sign and the element of the sign the Sun is in today. We will also use this list later in the article to identify the aspect (distance) between signs.

Aries	Fire
Taurus	Earth
Gemini	Air
Cancer	Water
Leo	Fire
Virgo	Earth
Libra	Air
Scorpio	Water
Sagittarius	Fire
Capricorn	Earth
Aquarius	Air
Pisces	Water

Fire/Earth

The transition from fire to earth reflects the qualities of expansion and establishment. Expansion is like dough rising and being baked to become bread. Establishment is like pottery being fired and hardened. In both cases, the materials involved are changed through the addition of heat to become useful in a new way. These kinds of changes provide a metaphor for business dealings in which one thing is changed into another.

Earth/Air

The transition from earth to air is familiar to most of us because we use this relationship every day to understand the world around us. We muck about in the practical aspects of business—the earth element. Then we pause to reflect, or rise above the details, to get a broader perspective—the air element. This close relationship between thinking and doing is taking place all the time. Without it we would have very little objectivity about our lives.

Air/Water

The transition from air to water involves the integration of, or at least awareness of the two parts of the mind—the conscious and the unconscious. The surface of a calm lake divides the water from the air. We know that there is a similar continuous connection between conscious and unconscious. In business we usually focus on conscious activities, but should remain aware that the vast majority of our customer's process is actually unconscious.

Water/Fire

The transition from water to fire is filled with emotional energy. This is an area in which we can make huge progress business-wise, if we can identify the emotional values at work in ourselves and in our clients. Getting a client or customer to decide—to change their minds—involves touching the emotional flow and subtly redirecting it. Think of the difference between a telephone salesperson saying, "This is your only opportunity to take advantage of this offer," and a salesperson telling you, "Just so you know, we are not going to be re-ordering this product, and we have limited quantities available." Both are true, but only one offers the customer a real choice.

Fire/Air

Fire and air signs never directly follow each other during the year, yet they are related through the sextile and opposition aspects. When the transiting Sun is opposite your natal Sun sign, the yearly developmental cycle is felt as the interaction of opposing forces of growth and decline. There is a strong awareness of differences. In business you can use this energy to focus on those differences as part of a continuum of energy, thereby reducing the gap between a customer's desire and the decision to purchase, or some other change in behavior. One sure way to promote this is to use your intuition to think of the client's future business relationship with you. Then ask or tell the client your thoughts. If nothing else, the client will feel you have taken them seriously enough to think about how the purchase or service will work out later.

Earth/Water

These two elements are intimately related to the growth cycle—your garden will not grow without water. Like the fire/air relationship, these signs reflect the energy of the sextile or opposition. And like the fire/air combination, they include the possibilities of awareness and opportunity. When dealing with a customer or client, you can become aware of how this other person perceives the physical and emotional results of an action. You will want to heighten emotions that are constructive and play down the less productive side. Your customer will return again and again if they feel you have considered their needs, and not just tried to make a sale.

Aspects

To figure out the aspect relationship between your sign and the present location of the Sun, begin with a list of the signs. Starting with your own sign, or the sign the Sun occupies in your business's chart, but not counting that sign, count forward or backward (whichever is closest) to the sign the Sun is in right now. For example: your Sun sign is Aries, and the Sun right now is in Sagittarius. Counting backward, you have Pisces, Aquarius, Capricorn, and Sagittarius. Sagittarius is four signs behind Aries. Now, go to the following list, which relates the distance between the signs to the corresponding aspect.

1 semisextile
2 sextile
3 square
4 trine
5 quincunx
6 opposition
0 conjunction (when the Sun today is in your birth Sun sign)

Sagittarius is four signs away from Aries, so you choose #4, the trine. Whichever number you come up with, the aspect relationship between the signs is indicative of the tone of your own thinking and your customer's thinking as well. Most of us find the trines comfortable because they involve signs of the same element. Whereas the rest of the aspects involve signs of different element, either compatible or not so compatible.

As you begin reading about the six aspects, you may notice that you are familiar with some of the energies. You probably have favorite times of the year, and they may be related to the conjunction, sextile, and trine signs. You may have months that are more difficult, and they may be related to the square and quincunx. The semisextile and opposition are sometimes helpful in that you learn how to make changes during these times. These general statements can vary, as your personal style may welcome a challenge (square) and find that very helpful, or dislike the times when things are going smoothly (trine) but little positive growth is occurring. The following information suggests the ways you can use the Sun's position to aid your business, and is based on developmental relationships between the signs.

Conjunction

When today's Sun is in your birth sign, the energies of the natural cycle align with your own cycle. Most people feel energized around their birthdays because this alignment allows you to tune into the life around you easily. If you are considering your birth sign, understanding that this is a good time for you (but possibly not so good for other people) can help you businesswise. What can you offer to other people—the best of your Sun sign—to help them? You would not want to be Aries at its most ruthless if your customer is a Capricorn or Cancer, for example, because they are feeling challenged enough already. An Aries quality that will help in most situations is enthusiasm. To spark enthusiasm in each customer is to make them feel happier at the very least, and a happy customer is more willing to buy a product than a customer you have made uncomfortable or nervous.

Another quality of the conjunction aspect is prominence. The idea here is to make some product or service more prominent by featuring those qualities that are consistent with the sign the Sun is in. All seasonal products perform this function by their very nature. Tree ornaments sell better in November than they do in May. Pumpkin decorations are a fall item. If the Sun is in your sign today, you will be more aware of product features that match the current growth cycle.

If you know your customer's birth date, you have another clue to the things that will resonate with them. Your ability to focus on features of each Sun sign will help you to sell to the "birthday shopper." Often this means selling to the birthday person's spouse or acquaintance. Since most birthday buying is done near the birth date, the Sun sign is usually the same, and the prominence of features during that part of the growth cycle will very likely strike a positive note. For example, when color choice enters the discussion, you may suggest a color that is associated with that particular Sun sign. Another less obvious focus is the place in the growth cycle. With the Sun in Leo, you might say, "This book tells how to trim off the side shoots so the main stem bears larger fruit." With the Sun in Scorpio it is too late for that tip, but focusing on the protection of rose bushes for the winter would be more timely.

Semisextile

The signs before and after your birth sign offer paradoxical opportunities. On the one hand, they are associated with the natural developmental flow from one growth stage to the next. On the other hand, they can be associated with jarring shifts of awareness from one element to the next. The elements preceding or following each sign are not particularly compatible with that sign. In both cases the key is to find the product or service features that address the developmental process in a way that makes effective use of the element and sign qualities. Each pairing of elements has a special developmental significance.

Where the developmental process is concerned, you may want to emphasize a future use that extends the life of the product in some way. "This baby crib converts into a youth bed, and you can even use the side rail as a headboard later on for a regular bed. That way the child's furniture will always match. And this furniture is made to last." Or you may want to emphasize the fact that a garment will work well from one season to the next. With electronic equipment or software, emphasizing the trade-in to upgrade feature is a good idea. All of these focus on the added value of quality, versatility, and customer service.

You can also reflect on the past with your customer. By finding out what brought the customer to you in the first place, you can make a better sale. For example, suppose you have a shoe store. In it you have all sorts of shoes—dress shoes, boots, sports shoes, and casual footwear. By listening carefully to your customer, you can determine what they need. You can ask appropriate questions to gather more information. If the customer says, "I broke my foot, and find I need extra support," you will not recommend a flimsy shoe that is destined to cause pain. You may ask, "Is there any other foot problem I should be aware of?" Then you get a more complete picture. Now you can make a more expert recommendation, and also point out features that may not be obvious. By reflecting on the past, you assure customer satisfaction in the future.

Sextile

The fire/air and earth/water relationships are involved in most sextiles. The emphasis is on opportunity. Each shopping effort affords the opportunity to spend money, obtain goods or services that are wanted or needed, and to engage in the social activities involved in commercial transactions. Each customer or client who comes to you offers an opportunity for you to help them with their purchase.

In addition, you have the opportunity to serve them without any expectation of a direct return. Because of this, I feel the sextile Sun sign moments are rich with possibility. Even if a customer cannot find what they want this time, your attitude may bring them back to your store in the future. It costs you nothing as a businessperson to endeavor to lift the spirits of every customer.

When you do focus on the transaction at hand, the sextile relationships suggest that you focus on the compatible qualities and ignore factors that are less compatible. In such cases you talk about the positives. Going back to the shoe store example, you may say, "I know you want both style and comfort. Here is a shoe that is the ultimate in support and comfort. It comes in seven colors. I sell more of this shoe than any other style in the store." You and the customer both know that the shoe is utilitarian and not the height of style, but you have indicated that lots of other people have made this choice anyway. You have appealed to the "comfort meter" the customer no doubt has. And you have addressed the fundamental need for supportive shoes, and matched it with your supportive attitude. This exemplifies the earth/water combination.

The fire/air combination is activated when the product serves a future need. For example, in a computer store you have a wide range of products for a wide range of needs. It is important to address both the current demands and the possible future uses of the system in making a recommendation. Perhaps the current demand is to keep the cost down, but the future demand is to have speed and lots of disk storage space. It is important to determine both when making suggestions. An example of this would be suggesting the purchase of a larger monitor now to avoid duplicating the expense later, and getting a system which can be upgraded less expensively to add storage and speed. These considerations are balanced by the kind of software the user will need.

The fire/air and earth/water examples share the qualities of providing the customer solid opportunities to make wise decisions. All future sales to this customer depend on getting the best "fit" among needs, desires, and pocketbook this time.

Square
The squares involve signs that are different elements, but which share a quality or mode of expression. There are three qualities:

Cardinal	Aries, Cancer, Libra, Capricorn
Fixed	Taurus, Leo, Scorpio, Aquarius
Mutable	Gemini, Virgo, Sagittarius, Pisces

The cardinal signs are assertive. They take the initiative and apply their will to whatever they do. In business, cardinal signs apply to the folks who stay in the present moment. They want to make the sale now, help the client now. Their enthusiasm is infectious, so they often do make that sale. However, they can be too intense, too forceful. Cardinal signs can be like the car salesman who doesn't want to let you leave the lot without buying a new car—whether you are ready or not. If you have a cardinal Sun sign, the transiting Sun squaring it will create pressure to accomplish things, and you need to temper your impatience.

The fixed signs are stable and methodical. Fixed signs apply to the folks who work on a plan for years, developing it slowly and carefully. Your business cannot be this slow in development, but you can benefit from consistent effort if the transiting Sun squares your fixed Sun sign. Patience in developing a sale can pay off in the long run. For example, you may work with a customer all year, helping with small sales. When the holiday season arrives, this customer may appear with an entire shopping list, asking your advice for every person on the gift list. It is your past behavior that brings the customer back.

Mutable signs are changeable. These signs apply to salespeople who are flexible enough to change gears completely when a new customer walks in the door. The are responsive to the nuances of customer behavior. When the transiting Sun squares your mutable natal Sun sign, you are able to adapt to circumstances. In fact, you are intuitively tuned to the future factors in customer and client relations. You benefit from updating your mailing list when the Sun squares your mutable Sun sign, as this is the time to be planning for that next all-important mailing.

When you are under a Sun square, look over the meanings of the two signs involved. Consider how you can blend the two energies. Can you link past and present, or present and future, in dealing with a customer, or in planning your next business move? Perhaps the fusion of fire and water sets the tone for your upcoming promotion.

Successful combination of the energies works because it aligns your actions with your sense of who and where you are at the moment.

You can tell if your customers are experiencing squares because they will be intense. They are almost driven in their actions. The cardinal signs are aggressive in demeanor, the fixed signs may be stubborn in their attachment to an idea, and the mutable signs are restless to the max. By keying in to these behavioral styles, you can focus on the present, past, or future to make the sale quickly, easily and effectively.

Trine

Most of us like trines the best. They reflect conditions where every-thing is going fairly smoothly, and all the pieces fall into place in a consistent pattern. Trines occur between signs of the same element, so there is an underlying familiarity with the energies involved.

Look at the list of characteristics for the other signs in your same Sun sign element. You probably like people who demonstrate these characteristics, and can work with them comfortably and naturally in a business relationship.

To bolster your business, examine the signs in the other ele-ments. Learn to cultivate that same comfortable style when you are faced with very different approaches. Learn to act like each ele-ment. I am not suggesting that you be false, merely that you culti-vate attitudes that work well with each of the elements. You can do this when the Sun is squaring or opposing your sign, because at that time you are intimately involved with another element and can learn about it directly. Then when the Sun forms the trine, you have actual experience of the mindset of each element to draw upon when dealing with your client or customer.

Quincunx

Like the semisextile, the quincunx relationship involves signs that are basically incompatible. They also involve pairs that are not of like quality of expression. The result is that when the transiting Sun is in this placement relative to your Sun sign, you are forced to make adjustments and concessions. If you are a car mechanic, sur-geon, or therapist, adjustment in the situation is what your work is all about, and this placement may produce some of your best work.

If you are in the legal profession, concessions are the norm. The rest of us often chafe when we have to give in to other people again and again, particularly if we have a dynamic, self-assertive style.

How should you deal with this kind of irritant, whether it be demanding customers, suppliers, or your own internal demands? First, look at the fact that adjustment is not always a bad thing. When I go to the chiropractor, after all, that is exactly what I expect. If you can put yourself in the frame of mind that adjusting your sales and service goals to suit each customer will help you, you will find that life is much easier. Give up the thought that people will adjust to you, at least in the business realm. And remember, in a few days the Sun will move into another aspect, creating either smoother sailing (trine) or more awareness (opposition).

Use this time to review your bookkeeping. Sort through the mounds of paper, clean out the file cabinets. Get a haircut. Rearrange your closets at home. Do things that utilize the intense capacity for adjustment. When you are at work, take care of all the little projects that have been sitting on your desk for months.

When all that is done, focus on the future of your business. Look at the plans you have made and see if you still feel you are moving in the right direction. Adjust your course as needed, with an eye to likely outcomes. Repaint, get the carpets cleaned, and dust off the decorations for your next seasonal promotion. Your customers will see the changes and recognize your intention to be around for the long haul.

Opposition

Awareness is the name of the game in business, and when the Sun is in the sign opposite yours you have the spotlight right on the situations you need to manage wisely. While opposing signs can mean disagreement, they are actually compatible elements and are the same quality. Thus they can work well together if given a chance. You just need to find the way to make this happen.

In business the opposition can signal understanding of a question or problem. Once the parties understand the situation, it is often much easier to come to agreement. Knowing the question—the real question—gets you more than halfway to the answer. In fact, this is true of all relationships.

One technique is to focus on any agreement in the situation. This will often depend on the quality or mode of expression. If your Sun sign is cardinal, then forthright, direct expression will work. You may need to temper aggressive urges and focus instead on bringing something original to the discussion. Express your enthusiasm for finding a solution, if nothing else. Fixed Sun signs benefit from falling back on behavior that is consistent with who they are, regardless of what the customer may be saying or doing. This involves relying on past actions to work in the present. Mutable signs may want to use logical thinking, and look to the future outcome to inform the present action. Think of how things are likely to turn out at each step of the process.

Another technique is to treat the customer's position as though it were your own. What if you had that problem or concern? What would you do? Have you ever been in a similar situation? What happened then? To the extent that it's comfortable, let the client or customer know that you are thinking about these things. It can be as simple as saying, "I know how you feel. I sometimes have to wait until the last minute to get an idea of what to get for my dad's birthday. Here's what I do. . . ." Then fill in the blank with something that suits the quality or mode of your Sun sign. This will ring particularly true when the Sun is in the opposite sign.

Groups of Customers

What about the challenge of selling a product to two or more individuals, each of whom no doubt has their own Sun sign relationship to the present moment? How can you use your knowledge of Sun signs to advantage?

1. Your conversation, regardless of Sun signs, will focus on the benefits of the products under consideration.

2. Identify who is the principal buyer. Never make the mistake that the parent in a parent/child group is the one with the money. Children often have their own disposable income, and they also often have the final say-so on the purchase. I remember a child who asked me for a particular book. She didn't remember the title, but she knew the cover was yellow. Her father indicated that knowing

this was not going to help much. I said, "Well, it isn't the usual way to find a book, but we can sure try it." We wandered around looking only at yellow books, and found it surprisingly quickly. Both child and parent benefited from my willingness to help, and we shared resourcefulness we didn't know we had. We saw these two in our store on a regular basis after that.

3. Use Sun sign knowledge to sort out whose opinion matters most. It is generally good to focus on the person who will end up with the product. While a child may not be interested in durability, you can sway the parent's opinion by pointing out the practical features of each product. Some products, like clothing, may be outgrown, or may go out of style. Quality is not a big consideration, for example, in a Halloween costume that will only be worn once.

Determine the Sun sign energy balance between the customers, and play to that energy. They may have Suns squaring each other, and their conversation will indicate little challenges. Consider the tone when one says, "What do you think?" And a remark like "Will you really use this?" can reveal historic behavior. "Does it feel roomy?" and "It's already too tight for my taste" are typical remarks from parents. "If you get the blue one, I'll get a yellow one" indicates obvious approval, which you can then support by asking what size the second customer will require.

A lot of these suggestions seem like common sense. They are listed for those occasional situations where nothing seems to be working. My own most difficult moments come when there are too many choices and no obvious way to eliminate some of them. The most helpful salesperson is the one who helps me narrow the choices by asking the right questions. Your knowledge of Sun signs can help a lot in the area. "Will you want long sleeves?" is both a seasonal and stylistic question. "This color will be good year round" is a value statement, yet relates to the season. Questions about the activities the person will be involved in may help to reduce the choices further. You may even ask, "What's your Sun sign?"

For Further Reading

Power of the Midheaven: The Astrology of Self Realization by Stephanie Jean Clement, Ph.D. Llewellyn, 2001.

The Venus Factor

By Dorothy Oja

An astrological chart is a complex map or blueprint of the patterns of your personality, including strengths and weaknesses, contradictions, and creative impulses. Each chart, although made up of the same components, is arranged in endless and uniquely different ways. The energetic connections between the planets and points of the chart create an energy flow, or a resonance, that is different from chart to individual chart. Only a competent professional astrologer can synthesize and describe the subtleties and intricacies of the combinations found in any particular birth chart. However, we can take a look at the various separate pieces of the chart in detail, to gain a greater understanding of the whole blueprint of life.

Venus in its path through the zodiac stays close to the Sun. Because of this, Venus most often occupies the same sign as your Sun, or else the sign just before or just after your Sun sign. Your Venus position is only occasionally two astrological signs in front of or behind your Sun sign. To find out where your Venus is located, you can order a basic computer printout with a basic interpretation, or consult with a professional astrologer.

Venus embodies many things in the astrological chart—attraction, affection, giving, beauty, harmony, balance, sharing, fairness, and values and valuables both tangible and intangible. However, the most prevalent understanding of Venus has to do with the function and quality of love and the relationships we forge with other human beings. We are universally interested in being loved and accepted and, in our deepest hearts, we all yearn to express love fully and completely.

It is the "Venus factor" (the sign and condition of Venus) in the chart that offers the first clue as to how a person will give and receive love, or the quality and the capability of their lovingness.

The Sun in Fire Sign Aries

If Aries is your Sun sign you will likely have Venus in Aries, Pisces, or Taurus or, more rarely, Venus in Aquarius or Gemini.

An Aries Sun combined with Venus in Aries is a zesty, fun, and highly energetic pairing. This Sun/Venus combination is preoccupied with setting and achieving goals. In matters of love, although wanting to lead, this combination is most willing to partner with others of equal drive and energy. Selfishness and vanity can get in the way of relationship harmony.

Aries combined with Venus in watery Pisces blends high energy with great sensitivity, and needs artistic expressions for well-being. This Sun/Venus combination fluctuates between extroversion and introversion, and often feels misunderstood. In matters of love, this person seeks a soul companion, one who shares deeper emotional or spiritual yearnings. Not appreciating your partner enough can cause lasting harm.

An Aries Sun combined with Venus in earthy Taurus produces an energetic seeking for security. This Sun/Venus combination will set goals to reach tangible, measurable, pleasurable results, and financial stability. In matters of love, this person desires and strives for enduring, lasting relationships and is willing to compromise—sometimes too much—in order to attain this.

An Aries Sun combined with Venus in airy Aquarius brings an unusual and accepting social interaction. This Sun/Venus combination is active in initiating relationships, and finds validation in groups and team efforts. Truthfulness and respect for individuality are essential. In matters of love, individuality and independence form an important theme, as do essential human rights.

Aries combined with Venus in airy Gemini blends energetic communication and social banter. This Sun/Venus combination is witty and entertaining, and you are likely to know where this person stands on issues. In matters of love, strong communication skills and mutual shared interests will be vital. Boredom can be an issue because this pairing needs a variety of experiences or interests.

The Sun in Earth Sign Taurus

If Taurus is your Sun sign you will likely have Venus in Taurus, Aries, or Gemini or, more rarely, Venus in Pisces or Cancer.

A Taurus Sun combined with Venus also in Taurus brings a strong sensuality and desire for financial security. This Sun/Venus combination is solid and steady and seeks to establish a secure base of operations. In matters of love, tactile pleasures and physical closeness are of primary interest. Long periods of separation will be difficult to tolerate and this combination of planets dislikes unexpected change.

A Taurus Sun combined with Venus in fiery Aries is interested in setting goals that lead to a stable position in life. This Sun/Venus combination is alert to progressing and achieving a specific level of accomplishment. In matters of love, this combination is ardent and will work tirelessly to please a partner. Avoid being too demanding.

Taurus combined with Venus in airy Gemini prefers stability but also intellectual stimulation and variety. This Sun/Venus combination may take some time to find a place, position, or even partner that suits its need for variety in expression. In matters of love, shared intellectual abilities, good communication, and interests in common will be vital. The tendency to flirtation or indecisiveness can be problematic.

Taurus combined with Venus in watery Pisces wants to provide solid service that can make a difference in other people's lives. This Sun/Venus combination is more sensitive than you may first suppose. In matters of love, this combination is likely to be charmingly romantic. Being clear about what you're feeling will prevent misunderstandings and confusion of intentions.

Taurus combined with Venus in watery Cancer enjoys nesting and homesteading, This Sun/Venus combination favors a cozy dwelling, and can have gourmet and often expensive tastes. In matters of love, the pleasures of touch, cuddling, and hugs are particularly delightful. Being supportive of family and paying attention to familial concerns are a must for peace to reign.

The Sun in Air Sign Gemini

If Gemini is your Sun sign, you will likely have Venus in Gemini, Taurus, or Cancer or, more rarely, Venus in Aries or Leo.

The Sun in Gemini combined with Venus in Gemini is an exceptionally alert and inquisitive blending. This Sun/Venus combination prides itself on knowing what's going on and connecting with others in the many environments it frequents. In matters of love, a good deal of bantering and sparkling lightheartedness is essential with like-minded friends and social companions. But too much flitting about can dissolve your bond.

A Gemini Sun combined with Venus in earthy Taurus uses information, advice, and knowledge to secure and assure a comfortable lifestyle. This Sun/Venus combination is charming and enjoys sampling the finer things of life with other witty and well-heeled companions. In matters of love, choices are made on the basis of physical compatibility, loyalty, and potential security. Acting spoiled and needing to have control all the time can get tiresome.

Gemini combined with Venus in watery Cancer gives a soft side to a sharp intellect. This Sun/Venus combination is devoted to family and can have a special relationship with a sibling. In matters of love, someone that you can be fully at ease with and talk to about deeper feelings, even insecurities, is vital for a strong bond. Whining about every little thing gets old fast.

Gemini combined with Venus in fiery Aries wants to move ahead at the speed of light. This Sun/Venus combination is quick, sharp, and sassy. In matters of love, taking the lead is common practice. This combination uses its wit to passionately pursue whatever it sets its sights on. But impulsiveness and impetuousness can land you in a hot spot before you know it.

A Gemini Sun combined with Venus in fiery Leo spreads warmth and generosity in every direction. This Sun/Venus combination values loyalty and honest self-expression most of all. In matters of love, there is a need to love deeply and passionately. Generosity, kindness, and a heap of fun come with this package. Pride can get hurt, but some genuine affection will settle the bruised ego.

The Sun in Water Sign Cancer

If Cancer is your Sun sign, you will likely have Venus in Cancer, Gemini, or Leo or, more rarely, Venus in Taurus or Virgo.

The Sun in Cancer combined with Venus in Cancer is nurturing, solicitous, and sensitive to the needs of others. This Sun/Venus combination is typically caring and understanding, and creates comforting emotional environments for family and friends. In matters of love, feeling that one belongs and is appreciated is a big issue. Insensitivity or lack of consideration can damage trust and closeness in relationships.

Cancer combined with Venus in airy Gemini is concerned and willing to communicate caring. This Sun/Venus combination values family ties and easily turns friends into a wider family circle. In matters of love, learning together and processing feelings that arise make for a strong bond. Excessive flirting can make for a great deal of insecurity in relationships.

A Cancer Sun combined with Venus in fiery Leo is a spirited, if not dramatic, energizer. This Sun/Venus combination is creative and generously shares with others. In matters of love, passion and fun go hand in hand with day-to-day activity. Childishness or acting spoiled can tarnish a really good thing.

Cancer combined with Venus in earthy Taurus is safety and security minded. This Sun/Venus combination manages to magnetize what it wants. In matters of love, this combination endures the typical trials of life with steadfastness and sweetness. Stubborn adherence to doing it your way can make for some difficult times and put obstacles in your path.

Cancer combined with Venus in earthy Virgo wants to make a difference in people's lives. This Sun/Venus combination is helpful and low-key but always gets the job done. In matters of love, being responsible, reliable, and maintaining a smooth, level energy is a big plus. However, being a workaholic will get old fast.

The Sun in Fire Sign Leo

If Leo is your Sun sign, you will likely have Venus in Leo, Cancer, or Virgo or, more rarely, Venus in Gemini or Libra.

Leo combined with Venus also in Leo is passionate and expressive. This Sun/Venus combination, when operating from the heart, spreads waves of healing energy. In matters of love, this combination is bold, dramatic, demonstrative, and loyal. Make plenty of room for fun times and laughter to keep relationships alive. Excessive pride can cause damage.

Leo combined with Venus in watery Cancer is basically caring and considerate. This Sun/Venus combination seeks self-expression and acceptance from its family and peers. In matters of love, romantic experiences turned into memories go a long way to maintaining a lasting bond. Whining or nursing hurt feelings can prevent the closeness that is desired.

A Leo Sun combined with Venus in earthy Virgo works hard to feel deserving of love. This Sun/Venus combination is chivalrous and ready to be of service. In matters of love, the little things, such as remembering the details of someone's habits, likes, or dislikes, will make the difference in a loving union. Being too fussy or picky turns off the magic.

The Sun in Leo combined with Venus in airy Gemini is friendly, warm, and gregarious. This Sun/Venus combination thrives on making friends and associations, and smiles through all the introductions. In matters of love, being on the same wavelength intellectually and having an active social life is a must. Being fickle can jeopardize a good relationship.

A Leo Sun combined with Venus in airy Libra is warm-hearted and diplomatic. This Sun/Venus combination prefers to create a dynamic partnership like no other. In matters of love, forging an equal partnership with a very special someone is a primary goal. Being grossly unfair or crude will quickly bring separation.

The Sun in Earth Sign Virgo

If Virgo is your Sun sign, you will likely have Venus in Virgo, Leo, or Libra or, more rarely, Venus in Cancer or Scorpio.

A Virgo Sun combined with Venus in Virgo strives for perfection and refinement. This Sun/Venus combination thrives when it can be of service and contribute to a system that it believes in. In matters of love, integrity is essential, as are the qualities of kindness, humility, and basic consideration. Being untrustworthy or hiding important facts will undermine your relationship.

A Virgo Sun combined with Venus in fiery Leo brings enthusiasm and a unique creativity to any task. This Sun/Venus combination works tirelessly to create warm and open environments for life to happen. In matters of love, a sustaining and generous nature wants to share the joys of life. Allowing pride to take over or being a prima donna will backfire.

Virgo combined with Venus in airy Libra works at establishing a sense of perfect balance and harmony. This Sun/Venus combination seeks to maintain beauty and appropriateness in all its dealings. In matters of love, fairness is of primary importance. Forget having privileges you are not willing to grant your partner.

The Sun in Virgo combined with Venus in watery Cancer expresses sincere concern and a nurturing helpfulness toward others. This Sun/Venus combination makes itself useful within the community that it wants to join. In matters of love, taking care of day-to-day details and basic necessities such as food become an art form. Lack of appreciation for care and comfort given to you will put your partner on strike.

A Virgo Sun combined with Venus in watery Scorpio quietly goes about its business of observing the logistics of its environment. This Sun/Venus combination quickly becomes adept at strategy in any life arena. In matters of love, physical pleasure is an integral and highly valued ingredient. Once betrayed, this person's trust is not easily regained.

The Sun in Air Sign Libra

If Libra is your Sun sign, you will likely have Venus in Libra, Virgo, or Scorpio or, more rarely, Venus in Leo or Sagittarius.

Libra combined with Venus also in Libra is a natural-born diplomat with a special gift for charming others. This Sun/Venus combination often finds itself brokering disputes and smoothing ruffled feathers. In matters of love, sweet-talking your partner to get what you want is easily accomplished. Compromising your essential needs will leave your relationship hollow.

A Libra Sun combined with Venus in earthy Virgo is a stickler for detail and has an eye for beauty as well as value. This Sun/Venus combination has talent for quality control and works well with others. In matters of love, a neat appearance and integrity of character are an irresistible combination. Nagging will easily spoil a really good thing.

A Libra Sun combined with Venus in watery Scorpio will "tell it like it is" or, anyway, as they feel it to be. This Sun/Venus combination has strong feelings and is unafraid to show them, especially in support of loved ones. In matters of love, emotional depth is sought and highly prized. Infidelity will never be forgotten and will permanently alter your bond.

Libra combined with Venus in fiery Leo is a charming winner. This Sun/Venus combination shines with graciousness and creative flair, and leads with a generous, loving heart. In matters of love, this person seeks a strong, independent, and colorful personality to participate fully in life together. Gregariousness is delightful, but egotism is a bore.

Libra combined with Venus in fiery Sagittarius is willing to take risks to initiate relationships. This Sun/Venus combination is enthusiastic, positive, and great fun to be around. In matters of love, sociability comes easily, and this person wants a partner who can be at ease in various situations. Black tie or hiking shoes—be ready for anything, but don't be a wet blanket!

The Sun in Water Sign Scorpio
If Scorpio is your Sun sign, you will likely have Venus in Scorpio, Libra, or Sagittarius or, more rarely, Venus in Virgo or Capricorn.

A Scorpio Sun combined with Venus in Scorpio is interested in powerful forces that are not obvious. This Sun/Venus combination is highly focused and can be intense, and even disconcerting. In matters of love, there's nothing lukewarm here. Passionate involvement will require that no secrets are withheld and that you keep jealousy or possessiveness in check.

Scorpio combined with Venus in airy Libra struggles with finding balance amidst strong and passionate reactions. This Sun/Venus combination wants to play with other movers and shakers. In matters of love, combining inner strength and self-possession with social agility is highly attractive. Although strong bonds are desired, don't crowd this person too much.

Scorpio combined with Venus in fiery Sagittarius is an adventurer who likes challenges and tests of endurance. This Sun/Venus combination enjoys learning new skills and seeks self-improvement! In matters of love, spontaneity, generosity and a willingness to take risks are highly valued. Just don't take independence too far—be available for relationship.

A Scorpio Sun combined with Venus in earthy Virgo has a taste for social revival and social activism. This Sun/Venus combination wants to make a difference in its chosen field of application. In matters of love, consistency and application to quality and refinement are admired. Keeping life in order is commendable, but leave some room for passionate disorder.

Scorpio combined with Venus in earthy Capricorn is a circumspect organizer with leadership abilities. This Sun/Venus combination is serious about its values and has friends in high places. In matters of love, you'll have to pass the trust test—and that may take time to develop. Be consistent, keep your word, and you're in. Break a revered rule and you're out.

The Sun in Fire Sign Sagittarius

If Sagittarius is your Sun sign, you will likely have Venus in Sagittarius, Scorpio, or Capricorn or, more rarely, Venus in Libra or Aquarius.

A Sagittarius Sun combined with Venus in Sagittarius is enthusiastic and full of life. This Sun/Venus combination is rarely bored and has many and varied interests—sometimes too many to handle. In matters of love, this combination is ready for anything and generous almost to a fault. Enthusiasm is contagious, but please don't promise more than you can deliver.

Sagittarius combined with Venus in watery Scorpio will surprise you with an exuberant exterior that contains a deeper, shadow side. This Sun/Venus combination enjoys discovering what makes others react. In matters of love, be prepared for hearty debates on current hot topics. Be completely forthcoming about relationship issues, or you'll never hear the end of it.

The Sun in Sagittarius combined with Venus in earthy Capricorn is warm and generous with a tough edge. This particular

Sun/Venus combination has big dreams and plans to achieve them step by step. In matters of love, plan to take plenty of time getting to know each other and developing trust. Don't let getting past that tough outer shell be too long an ordeal.

A Sagittarius Sun combined with Venus in airy Libra actively seeks social participation. This Sun/Venus combination brings a generous energy and a willingness to be fair in joint ventures. In matters of love, social adventures are integral to the life of the relationship. Restricting freedoms will not work, but negotiating fair-play wins every time.

Sagittarius combined with Venus in airy Aquarius brings optimistic and uniquely creative views, particularly into any human rights activities. This Sun/Venus combination is steadfast in its principles of freedom and truth. In matters of love, being honest and allowing each person the freedom to grow independently are crucial. If you really want a partner, be one.

The Sun in Earth Sign Capricorn

If Capricorn is your Sun sign, you will likely have Venus in Capricorn, Sagittarius, or Aquarius or, more rarely, Venus in Scorpio or Pisces.

Capricorn combined with Venus also in Capricorn is conscientious, well organized, and focused on achieving. This Sun/Venus combination is reliable, can handle responsibility, and likes to be the boss. In matters of love, timeliness, credibility, and commitment are important. Being a take-charge person is a plus but always running the show is not.

Capricorn combined with Venus in fiery Sagittarius is a person on an exciting mission. This Sun/Venus combination needs a stimulating cause to protect and defend, and wisdom to share. In matters of love, there's unlimited enthusiasm, generosity, and goodwill. Expressing convictions is admirable; having the courage to act on them is irresistible.

A Capricorn Sun combined with Venus in airy Aquarius is self-reliant and independent. This Sun/Venus combination believes in accountability both on the job and in basic human rights. In matters of love, being best friends first is most important. Excessive commitment phobia can cause you to lose out on some wonderful potential relationships.

Capricorn combined with Venus in watery Scorpio stores nuts for the winter. This Sun/Venus combination is interested in establishing and maintaining comfort—financially and otherwise. In matters of love, dependability and a strong committed bond, as well as a partner you can count on, are vital. Grasping what you love too tightly is the surest way to lose it.

Capricorn combined with Venus in watery Pisces is a practical idealist with a compassionate side. This Sun/Venus combination enjoys the arts, music, and the finer things of life. In matters of love, you will find an old-fashioned romantic who can incorporate love into everyday life. Be sensitive, but maintain your boundaries and those of others.

The Sun in Air Sign Aquarius

If Aquarius is your Sun sign, you will likely have Venus in Aquarius, Capricorn, or Pisces or, more rarely, Venus in Sagittarius or Aries.

The Sun in Aquarius combined with Venus also in Aquarius is independent, eclectic, freethinking, and tolerant of differences. This Sun/Venus combination is used to perceiving life differently, seeks to keep an open mind, and enjoys the group process. In matters of love, becoming best friends is the best prelude to a romantic bond. Interfering with other friendships won't fly.

Aquarius combined with Venus in earthy Capricorn enjoys maintaining long lasting friendships. This Sun/Venus combination brings a practical and commonsense attitude into its lifestyle. In matters of love, commitment is desired after certain relationship standards are met. Being immature around career responsibilities or social courtesies will create problems.

Aquarius combined with Venus in watery Pisces is socially aware and brings compassion and caring into relationships with others. This Sun/Venus combination is unusually creative and expressive. In matters of love, giving is most appreciated when it comes with truthfulness. This combination can send mixed messages or be confused by what it wants.

The Sun in Aquarius combined with Venus in fiery Sagittarius has a wanderlust that is not easily quenched—but loves to share stories. This Sun/Venus combination can tolerate being a loner or doing its own thing for a time. In matters of love, participating in a variety of adventures will bring you closer together. Excessive exaggeration or inflated ego syndrome are turn-offs.

Aquarius combined with Venus in fiery Aries is willing to be proactive for controversial causes. This Sun/Venus combination uses its natural leadership abilities to further human rights wherever it can. In matters of love, boldness and directness in pursuing a desired relationship is typical. Minimizing the "I" and maximizing the "we" in your relationship works better.

The Sun in Water Sign Pisces

If Pisces is your Sun sign, you will likely have Venus in Pisces, Aquarius, or Aries or, more rarely, Venus in Capricorn or Taurus.

Pisces combined with Venus also in Pisces is highly sensitive to environmental influences and stimuli. This Sun/Venus combination needs regular reflective time and ways to express complex feelings and emotions. In matters of love, romance and attention to the moods of the loved one are special gifts. A lack of healthy boundaries creates unnecessary complication and unhappiness.

A Pisces Sun combined with Venus in airy Aquarius easily makes many friends and acquaintances. This Sun/Venus combination is creative, alert, and generally has a good sense of humor. In matters of love, the heart rules with little fear of controversy or society's acceptance. Deliberately withholding the truth or lying will break the spell of magic and romance.

Pisces combined with Venus in fiery Aries joins a spirited energy with a sensitive idealist. This Sun/Venus combination can alternate between being shy and being direct. In matters of love, placing yourself in the path of the beloved can be a delightful choreographed coincidence. Work out indecision, because vacillating in your intentions is distressing to your partner.

Pisces combined with Venus in earthy Capricorn values refinement and consistency. This Sun/Venus combination works at self-development and can be an inspiration to those who suffer. In matters of love, supporting each other to maintain the basic concerns of life builds a strong foundation for more. Being overly dependent on others for your survival will leave you weak.

The Sun in Pisces combined with Venus in earthy Taurus is sensuous and delights in experiencing the many pleasures life offers.

This Sun/Venus combination needs the arts and music to soothe the rough edges and provide inspiration. In matters of love, consistency and closeness are highly prized. Overspending on luxuries you can't afford will create anxiety in your relationship.

For Further Reading

The Mars Venus Affair: Astrology's Sexiest Planets by Wendell Perry and Linda Perry. Llewellyn, 2000.

Venus & Mars: The Signs of Love and Passion—How They Influence Your Life and Relationships by Robert Reid. Thorsons, 1999.

It's a Trade-Off
World Predictions for 2002

by Leeda Alleyn Pacotti

After the roller coaster legal chases in late 2000 to spit out an acceptable national leader in the United States, and the ensuing catfights to divert our attention in 2001, we settle down to the regular business of living in 2002. During the last year, we champed at the bit to enjoy the fruits of our labors, only to encounter nagging quakes in the economy. We questioned why these problems continued to persist, admitting we childishly hoped they would flee with a new presidency or a new year. In 2002, all of us will be called to account for creating problems and coming up with solutions.

Topsy-Turvy Economics
In the equal-house, yearly horoscope of the world, the current ascendant is in the zero degree of Pisces, as cosmically viewed against the backdrop of the galaxy. Uranus, Neptune, and Pluto show the tendencies of population masses and are auspiciously placed in the first quadrant of the chart.

Neptune and Pluto are clearly entrenched in the First and Third Houses, respectively, while Uranus hovers at the Ascendant, preparing to enter the Twelfth House. Affected by these planets are integrated national self-images (First House) and communications, including mail and short writings, and education (Third House).

Uranus moved into Aquarius in 1996, followed by Neptune in 1998. The Aquarian influence brought the rise of the Internet as a new advertising medium. As much as this was preached, however, businessmen didn't get the hype until hazy Neptune entered Uranus's sign. A rosy glow of unreality set in, as everyone rushed to have an Internet presence. Neptune veiled the viability of website businesses as they ballooned into dot-com companies, attracting huge investments without substantiating documentation or experience. Adding to the mix, Pluto revolutionized communications globally among the population, encouraging e-mail and instant news services.

Now, as Uranus edges closer to Pisces, Internet businesses have imploded. Next year, when Neptune and Uranus are in mutual reception (residing in each other's signs), expect the Internet to shift back to an information clearinghouse, especially for publishing, databases, and nonprofit companies.

Uranus's seven-year cycles often highlight a special business group. With the coming Piscean influence, we see a push in the pharmaceuticals market, fueled in the U.S. by a presidential executive order permitting advertisement on television. No one saw the Plutonic downside, as people rushed to physicians asking for prescriptions that seemed like the balm for their ills. To counteract the growing demand for herbals, pharmaceutical companies marketed their products as "naturally derived" components from popular and exotic herbs, creating a misconception in the mass mind.

Pluto has dominion over shared resources. With its entrance into Sagittarius, the fiasco of mutual fund losses by the treasurer of Orange County, California, signaled a warning against unsecured investments. Those who believed that it couldn't happen to them will experience calamitous losses, as mutual funds scramble to find other investments that produce high returns. The expectation of retiring on interest was a pipe dream, all along.

The Return of the Mom-and-Pop Store

In 1980, John Naisbitt wrote the influential *Megatrends*. Besides identifying commercial and cultural shifts, he described an overpowering need among humans for personal and tactile interaction, dubbed "high tech, high touch." As Uranus moves toward Pisces, humans yearn for the halcyon days of strolling the neighborhood or unfolding a new letter. With giant Neptune alone in Aquarius, people are disenchanted with technological frills that don't offset sedentary work in isolated spaces, or popping, crackling, hissing phone services.

Pluto offers a solution to these problems from its residence in the world's Third House. Expect localized small businesses to flourish, catering to immediate community needs. A new pride surges from purchasing locally produced, unique products, tailored to the immediate demands of living, environment, and climate. During the previous seven-year flood of new products and services, consumers accepted a "one size fits all" purchasing convenience. Now that their incomes are curtailed, their purchasing loyalty remains in the community, especially when they can command some fulfillment of individual preferences.

Nations In Focus

When we look at national or mundane horoscopes, solar eclipses are major factors. In the world chart, we find that the Third and Ninth Houses receive the greatest influences, giving legal and religious matters, the sciences, education, and communications particularly strong emphases.

In general astrology, the cadent houses (Third, Sixth, Ninth, and Twelfth) are frequently relegated to abstract, intangible matters, making them seem insubstantial. Actually, these houses are domains of new or evolving thought, which provoke change in activities and material forms, shown by the two houses that follow them. For instance, the Ninth House, which deals with philosophical and ethical thinking, determines changes in a nation's head of state, the expression of the government, national prestige, and legislation. The Third House, which gathers general information—

especially that affecting the immediate environment—creates changes in agriculture, land use, housing, and groups that politically oppose the sanctioned government.

While we may believe that the head of state has unquestionable power, when an opposing political force becomes strong astrologically we can expect a change in leadership, a rebellion, a coup d'etat, or an honorable resignation. In 2002, several countries will experience changes in leadership, caused by altered thinking arising from the Third and Ninth Houses.

Latin America

Throughout the year, Costa Rica receives three solar eclipse influences. Beginning in December 2001, the nation is shadowed in the totality of a solar eclipse, bringing political opposition to President Rodriguez and emphasizing problems with land, housing, and agriculture. In June, the president and his government seem to gain strength, but the opposition gathers force with the ensuing solar eclipse in December 2002. During this time, it is possible the country will experience a natural catastrophe which overburdens the governmental administration but rallies local support among the clergy and legal groups connected with the government, banking, and the economic upper class. After November, the country attempts to divert attention from its woes, turning a hopeful eye to its children, sports, and other pastimes. The president uses political speeches and press releases to talk about education improvements, but professional and economic groups are not fooled. Diversions only serve to fuel the growing political opposition.

Mexico also is hit with the same three eclipses, with the June eclipse path starting at the middle of the western coast positively affecting the tourism areas of Cabo San Lucas, Puerto Vallarta, and Mazatlan. Throughout the year, Mexico focuses on its economy, foreign finance and investments, and the safety of its population. This year is a particularly good one for Mexico, as its Sun shines brightly without hindrance. Through January, legislation to improve local governments takes precedence, as more foreign investment floods in thanks to the efforts of President Fox, whose international corporate image and experience expands the treasury. After January, Mexico experiences a feeling of victory. It has attended to domestic matters and now turns its eye toward a burgeoning foreign trade. President Fox has the sanction of influential segments of society, which recognize the national and local benefits of securing treaties to strengthen Mexico's international image.

South China Sea

Like Latin America, this region experiences effects from the three solar eclipses, with the path of the June solar eclipse ending in Indonesia. From December 2001, political opposition cries out over continued economic controls exerted by the members of former President Suharto's family, and demands stringent governmental oversight, which forces President Wahid's ousting or resignation. Since the secession of East Timor in August 1999, Indonesia's stability has been rocked by another secession movement in Aceh province, which will likely remain with the nation. The opposition believes the end of the president's reign will end national breakup. Since the economic upheavals of 1997 and loss of its manufacturing base, Indonesia recognizes that any change in government must be accompanied by new thinking. A new government has the full support of the lower and middle classes, provided it expends the country's limited treasury well. Landholders, bankers, and influential members from religious groups, resenting foreign influence and any drain on their power, become the new opposition.

The Philippines experience the same eclipse influences as Indonesia; however, this nation's ills arise from domestic economics, foreign trade, and public safety. The island nation has suffered guerrilla activity from Muslims demanding an autonomous political region. Through mid-February the emphasis is on the national legislature and local governments. The press prefers strong local government to circumvent the growing tide of violence from crime and divisive political groups. Especially fearful after U.S. military base closures, landholders expect losses if a Muslim province is set up. In the first part of the year a natural catastrophe may rock the islands, unifying government on all levels. During the second half of the year, the islands may experience another catastrophe, which begs new measures to insure public safety. The administration meets the challenge, utilizing the new powers granted to local governments.

Southern Africa

During December 2002, a solar eclipse path tears through the mid-section of Angola, a country which has experienced hot and cold civil war since its independence in 1975. Opposition leader Savimbi has been so politically strong that President dos Santos created a special cabinet position for him after the last election. However, despite attempts at compromise, dos Santos has lost the sympathy of his people, who are fatigued from rebellion, scandal, and crime. With recent global warming, the country's rainfall no longer supports farming, creating a hungry nation. Conditions worsen throughout the year as hunger gives way to violence and epidemic. After mid-November dos Santos is besieged from all sides. Joining the opposition party, the press, media, clergy, educators, and wealthy landowners demand his removal. Unless the president honorably resigns he is likely to be the victim of an overthrow.

The same powerful December eclipse etches the border shared by Botswana and Zimbabwe. In the past, Botswana dealt harshly with settlers from Zimbabwe who crossed the border and made land claims. This ugliness is likely to rear up again. Closely tied economically with South Africa, Botswana ranked as Africa's fastest growing economy throughout the 1990s. With a secure manufacturing base, President Mogae prepares to tackle domestic issues affecting the population. Public health, hospitals, and the working class come to the fore. To keep the nation's high economic standard, the president knows workers must have access to the best healthcare possible. With help from the World Health Organization, the United Nations, foreign pharmaceutical manufacturers, and foreign charities, he modernizes hospitals and convalescent facilities. Through September his health programs are assailed, but do not flounder, as Angolese military deserters, criminals, and the starved flee through the Namibia panhandle and over the border into Botswana. Divisive political groups worry that these immigrants will destroy a delicate domestic balance, but President Mogae keeps his poise. After September, his efforts to protect his people garner more manufacturing and industrial agreements. Jobs for everyone is a reality.

Along the southeast coast of Africa, Mozambique chafes under the burdens of political divisiveness in its government, fueled by agricultural losses. President Chissano has been criticized for leaving constitutional reform on the table. Decreased rainfall and higher temperatures have destroyed Mozambique's agricultural base and the possibility of taking an economic lead in the south. The nation is poised for change, wanting to make a strong and deserved entrance onto the world stage. Through November, landowners concerned about property rights hamper treaty and trade negotiations, but the media follow the president around the country, where he explains his plans for a national face-lift. Chissano returns home with powerful images of parched, fallow land in the southern part of his country. After December, he lays international aspirations aside to follow Botswana's lead, and begins reforms for land, agriculture, and housing. People rally to these reforms, which are supported by several international corporate charities.

Nestled between Mozambique and Botswana, Zimbabwe encounters effects from all three influential eclipses, with the strongest occurring on December 4, 2002, tracing the nation's borders with Botswana and South Africa. Emphasized throughout the year is Zimbabwe's need to work on legislation to help its fledgling local governments. If the president works with prevailing solar energies, new domestic programs receive popular support. Until mid-April, the nation's economy and spending is the prime issue. The media, educators, and the military recognize that the treasury is in serious jeopardy. Opposing groups join the push to remedy the country's spending and production ills. For the remainder of the year, the country experiences a catastrophe in the form of massive crop failures, forging an alliance among the urban population, governmental administration, and farmers. Zimbabwe wants to feed itself instead of relying on imported assistance. Witnessing the violence and misery among emigrating Angolans, the people of Zimbabwe implore President Mugabe to modernize prisons, hospitals, and health care. Fortunately, the president listens.

Located at the southern tip of the African continent, South Africa's problems grow increasingly domestic. While the nation appears to be a power to unify the southern nations, problems of modern housing, adequate distribution of land, and farm production fuel a political opposition in its legislature at Cape Town. International sentiment that the most advanced nation in southern

Africa is ignoring domestic strife causes the president to attempt social reforms, but he is ineffectual. Until December, institutional conditions are the call to arms, as overpopulated prisons and jails are linked to outbreaks of illness, exploding into impossible conditions in outlying hospitals. The president's slow response permits a massive force to grow among the media, population, bankers, and governmental administrators, attracting even the support of criminal figures. As the year nears its end, President Mbeki uses a firm hand, reaping sanctions from foreign trade partners. The new unity has only one disruption, as property owners counter the president's suggestions to break up major land holdings to create an abundance of small farms.

Global Alliance

Australia, the United Kingdom, and the United States are still a close-knit alliance, seeking new trade alignments to cement their growing food and manufacturing needs. These three plan to sew up trade relations with reparations funds for shaky countries using the International Monetary Fund. Specifically, Australia will be linked with the countries of the South China Sea; Britain—through South Africa—with the countries of southern Africa; and the United States with Latin America. These three areas have ample populations for relocation of manufacturing and assembly plants.

Through 2002, Australians are acutely aware that revenues from international tourism have all but dried up. Making the same mistake as other Pacific countries and islands, the Australians have grown too comfortable, expecting everyone to visit and bring plenty of spending money. Government and commerce alike are embroiled in legal matters, as foreign travelers and businessmen withdraw from property investments, frightened by overplanning and tax issues. With the eclipse in December 2002, spending to induce tourism is severely curtailed. The ports at Adelaide are in the path of the eclipse, indicating a slowed entry of goods into the country. The basis of the problem lies with foreign investors, who no longer see Australia as a stable economy.

From the eclipse in December, 2001, Great Britain faces challenges to its laws and religion. The Church of England is up in arms, as it becomes increasingly clear that Prince Charles wants to marry

Camilla Parker-Bowles. The precepts of the Church of England are integrally tied to national law, making sanction of the marriage both a theological and legal boondoggle. At all costs, the government and monarchy want to avoid an unthinkable elopement and possible disinheritance of the heir to the throne. Generally, the public has grown tired of the prince's strange adventures and is very willing to see him ensconced in an obscure monarchial holding. Toward the end of the year, the queen and government attend to overspending issues to encourage greater foreign trade. During the latter half of the year, isolated but high-profile terrorist activity also creates a focus on increased public safety measures.

Still flushed from the constitutional crises of impeachment and the confused presidential election of 2000, the United States realizes the bloom is off the rose, and begins to examine what it perceives is its self-image. Through February, presidential attempts to rally the country 'round the flag, with increased federal spending on local governments, are undermined by continuing divisions among political groups in Congress. Unimpressed with presidential leadership, military leaders speak, instead of whisper, their hushed derision of the commander-in-chief, developments not lost on the president or his cabinet. In June, national attention turns to foreign relations and treaties. Expect no success from the crippled attempts of the national executive, who never enjoys popularity. This is a hard year for the United States, which hasn't really lost any international posture but bears an open internal wound of global humiliation. The woes that beset the president make it clear he will serve one term only, riding high the first two-and-a-half years on the accomplishments of the previous administration.

For Further Reading

Handbook of Horary Astrology by Karen Hamaker-Zondag. Weiser, 1993.
Horary Astrology Plain and Simple: Fast and Accurate Answers to Real World Questions by Anthony Louis. Llewellyn, 1998.
Predictions for a New Milennium by Noel Tyl. Llewellyn, 1996.

Mundane Natalogy

Angola
November 11, 1975, 00:00:00 am CET, Luanda

Australia
January 1, 1901, 00:00:00 am GST, Canberra

Botswana
September 30, 1966, 00:00:00 am EET, Gaborone

Costa Rica
November 7, 1949, 00:00:00 am CST, San Jose

Great Britain
December 25, 1066, 12:00:40 pm GMT, London

Indonesia
December 27, 1949, 00:00:00 am AWST, Jakarta

Mexico
February 5, 1917, 00:00:00 am CST, Mexico City

Mozambique
November 30, 1990, 00:00:00 am EET, Maputo

Philippines
February 11, 1987, 00:00:00 am AWST, Manila

South Africa
December 10, 1996, 00:00:00 am EET, Pretoria

United States of America
March 4, 1789, 12:13:12 am LMT, New York City

Zimbabwe
April 18, 1980, 00:00:00 am EET, Harare

The Finer Points
Houses, Aspects, and Transits
by Stephanie Clement

There's a lot more to astrology than just the signs of the zodiac. But sometimes, all the different terms and concepts can be extremely confusing. This article is intended to break down some of the finer points of reading an astrological chart, so that you can get the most from your astrological research.

The Angles and Houses

The Ascendant
The Ascendant or rising sign reflects your persona—what you choose to show to the world. Whereas the Sun sign is your individuality and does not change a great deal, you have the capacity to choose the nature and level of expression of your Ascendant. You can choose the most destructive expression, or you may choose to show a side of yourself to the world that is full of optimism, confidence, and promise.

The Ascendant is frequently useful in describing your physical characteristics and general health. Aside from geographical and ethnic realities, the rising sign shows complexion, hair and eye color, stature, and weight. A Gemini would be rather taller than average, and Taurus might be on the stocky side, within the range of genetic tendencies.

The Ascendant offers suggestions for what kind of clothing looks good, and what colors will make you seem stronger. The general shape of the head and face are linked to the Ascendant. The sign also indicates a part of the body that you can show off to good advantage. It may not be your favorite part of yourself, but it is one that will respond to careful treatment in terms of clothing, movement, etc. The Taurus may not think about the throat very much, but this is a key area to focus on to create a strong effect on others. Aquarians can benefit from careful selection of shoes, as the ankles are "the thing."

As you learn about your Ascendant, you will find a whole array of new considerations for how to present yourself to the world. Should you be flippant or stern, gregarious or darkly serious? The rising sign can provide a wealth of imaginative possibilities.

Because the Ascendant is the way others see you, physically and in every other way, it pays to understand what they are seeing. You can develop a whole range of clothing, movements, communication styles, and general attitudes based on your rising sign. You can overcome limitations in other areas by emphasizing the positives here. In this way you actively participate in creating the impression you want others to have, and you become more influential as you project a well thought-out image.

The Midheaven

The Midheaven is the part of the zodiac that is the highest (most elevated), visible point in the sky at the time you are born. If you ask the question, "How long has it been since zero degrees of Aries was at the Midheaven?" the answer tells you what degree of the zodiac is there in terms of time. If the Sun is at zero degrees of Aries, the Sun will be at the Midheaven at noon. Noon in this case is based on local time. Standard and daylight time can affect the Sun's position, placing it to one side or the other of the Midheaven point.

The Midheaven reflects what you know—or can know—about yourself. It represents ego-consciousness. Infants have little or no boundary between Self and Other. As children grow and learn, they come to understand themselves as separate beings, and they learn to depend on their own intelligence, emotions, and skills. In short, they learn about themselves as they learn about the world. The Midheaven reflects this self-awareness.

Psychologically healthy adults have a clear sense of Self, distinguished from Other. They know what their core motivations are, and they know what skills they have to achieve their physical, mental, emotional, and spiritual goals. The sign the Midheaven occupies indicates the nature of self-understanding, and provides the springboard from which you can dive into the process of gaining ego consciousness—understanding of what moves you on a deep personal level.

The Midheaven offers a way to understand yourself better, and is key to developing a flexible ego. We all know people who seem brittle and inflexible. We sense that they might "break" if they are pushed too hard in certain areas. Flexibility means developing an ego structure that can withstand the onslaught of life experiences and adapt or adjust to them. Astrology points out one path toward the development of broad-based, ego skills, and it describes both the limitations of your ego and the potential of self-awareness.

The Houses

Your chart is divided into twelve sections called houses. They are numbered from the left side counterclockwise around the chart. The chart represents the planets against a background of the signs of the zodiac, and these signs rise in clockwise motion. Thus the First House (number one) rises first, and so on. Each house includes part of one or more signs. Depending on where you were born, and the time of day, one house may include two or three signs. The farther you were born from the equator, the more likely this is to happen. There are different ways to calculate the houses, based on time or distance. Some astrologers prefer a system in which all the houses are an even thirty degrees, just like the signs of the zodiac.

Each of the houses represents an area of your life. The planets tell you what energy is involved and the signs indicate how that energy will express itself. The houses tell you where in your life the effect will be felt. The houses follow a logical order that parallels the signs to some extent. They move from the personality (First House) toward significant others (Seventh House), and from the home (Fourth House) to public life (Tenth House). All areas of experience can be found in one of the houses.

The First House

The First House begins at the Ascendant at the left side of the chart. It lies below the horizon line. The Ascendant is one of the strongest points in the chart. It is the point that was rising in the east at your birth time and place.

The First House focuses on what you show to the world. This includes the physical body and its appearance. It also includes the personality. Both of these are factors over which you have some degree of control. You can decide how to dress and how to act. You can choose to show the best of the rising sign. The First House also describes general qualities of appearance that you cannot control. Gemini rising indicates a relatively tall person, while Taurus indicates a relatively stocky build, for example.

The Sun shows your individuality. The Ascendant may sound like it does the same, but the focus is on personality. We all know people who have one kind of personality that we can see, but when we get to know them, we find something different beneath the exterior they show to us. It is that way with the Ascendant. It is the mask we show to others. There are eleven other houses that describe how we are in the world from different points of view.

The First House indicates the constitution and vitality of the physical body. Earth signs suggests a solid, grounded constitution, while air signs indicate a lighter quality that seems to float. Fire signs indicate a fiery temperament and vitality that comes in flashes, while water signs may indicate a constitution that has a rhythmic quality—an ebb and flow of energy.

When planets are in this house they have the fullest capacity for expression. The planet's energy seems to come through a wide open door into your life. This is also true of the Fourth, Seventh, and Tenth Houses. If there is a planet in the First House, its nature is prominent in the personality. If there is no planet here, then you consider the planet that "rules" the sign, and also Mars. These influences will be less forceful than planets in the house.

The Second House

The Second House indicates how you extend your personality into the world. In children this is the two-and-a-half to five-year-old stage of development, when you move outside the family nucleus and begin to make friends in a larger neighborhood. The immediate surroundings often determine the level of self-esteem. If the surroundings are secure and warm, the self prospers, while a lack of security can cause self-doubt and fear to arise.

Possessions and self-esteem are two important components of the immediate physical and emotional environment. It's interesting that these two things are found in the same house in the chart, as we don't consciously associate them with each other. When you think about it, though, it is true that what you have is often a big part of your self-esteem. Much of what we consume is chosen to make us feel better about ourselves.

Your feelings in general are part of the Second House. Beginning with your basic comfort level and reaching into deeper emotions, this house can tell you a lot about your emotional approach to life. Any planets in this house color the nature of the sign on the cusp (the sign at the beginning of the house).

The Second House also has to do with how you actually get money and material things. The sign indicates the method—the kind of effort needed to obtain income. Planets in the Second House indicate the people and activities involved. If you don't have any planets here, don't worry. The plant associated with the Second-House sign(s) will show where the money comes from, based on the house where it is found. For example, if you have Taurus on the Second House cusp and Venus in the Sixth House, then your money comes from the work environment. If Venus were in the Twelfth House, by contrast, then your income comes from private activities. If Mars is in the Second House, then some energetic activity may be involved in creating income.

How you define your personal security is a Second-House issue. The sign and any planets, by their nature, indicate what security means for you personally. You may have noticed that the things that make you happy and secure are different from other family members or your friends. Some people need a nurturing environment (Cancer in the Second House), while others are footloose and need their freedom (Aquarius on the cusp or Uranus in the house) in order to feel truly secure.

The Third House

Siblings and the immediate neighborhood are what you experienced in childhood between the ages of five and seven-and-a-half. This is the next step out into the world beyond the immediate environment of the Second House. You may have been allowed to go a certain distance from home by yourself when you were this age— across the street to a friend's house, for example.

How you tend to think is determined in early childhood, and thus is represented by the Third House. By the age of seven-and-a-half most of us have clearly defined ego structure—we understand that we are separate and different from other people, and we begin to understand how we are capable of determining the course of our lives. Many lifelong opinions are formed at this early age, based on family and neighborhood environments.

Early education is a Third-House matter. This is another powerful factor in the shaping of thought processes that last a lifetime. Learning begins before you are born, but those first years of school are critical to the development of reading, mathematical, and logical cognitive processes. The early school experience of learning to read, for example, sets the tone for a lifetime of reading.

Communication of all kinds is a Third-House activity. Planets here show the most direct means of expression. The placement of the house ruler shows another path for communication to take. The sign shows what kind of communication you are most comfortable with—air signs might indicate writing, for example, while earth signs indicate a more concrete medium of expression.

Short trips—trips through your neighborhood—are a Third-House matter. Remember that you are the one to decide what "short" means. What is in the neighborhood for one person could be across state lines, while another person's neighborhood extends only to the nearest main street. Many people feel that day trips are in the neighborhood, even if they involve train rides or short airplane flights. Some people feel their neighborhood includes entire nations or continents.

The Fourth House

Your home base can be understood by looking at the Fourth House. Home may always be the place where your mother and father live, or it may be the place where you are hanging your hat today. As with other houses, personal tastes and needs determine the meaning of home. If you grew up in one state, that may always be your home state. Most people want to have certain objects or kinds of things in the home environment that make them comfortable. Hence, all Hilton hotels have the same homey quality because they are staffed by similar people and decorated similarly. Generally speaking, the Hilton is not home.

Just as the home is where you develop the foundation of your beliefs, the Fourth House is where you look for those basic ethical and moral basics that govern your life. Fire signs on the Fourth House may indicate beliefs that are lofty, intuitive conceptions of the world, while earth signs indicate more grounded, practical considerations. Planets in the Fourth indicate the parent or other authority figure from whom you acquired your earliest ideals, most often the father.

The sign on the Fourth-House cusp (Imum Coeli or IC) indicates the deepest well of your being. The spirit that guides you is represented here, and its energy bubbles up from deep in the unconscious to emerge at the Midheaven (cusp of the Tenth House). If the Midheaven is what you know (or can learn) about yourself, the IC is the source from which that knowledge springs.

The Fifth House

The Fifth House is associated with all forms of creativity: creation, recreation, and procreation. All people have a Fifth House. Whether you have planets here or not, you are a creative being with great potential. By examining this house you can learn about how you use your talents to make a lasting impression on the world around you.

Procreation is one way to become immortal. Children carry on our ideals and enrich our lives every day. The act of conception is an expression of creative sexuality. The act of birthing is a dynamic affirmation of the desire to become a parent. The act of parenting is a lifelong process of working with your children for their highest good, thereby fulfilling your own highest creative potential.

The sign here indicates your general attitude toward children, pets, and playmates. Are you a playful Gemini, flitting from one game to the next while forming lasting friendships? Do your pets become surrogate children, demanding your love and attention, à la Virgo? Perhaps you take your creativity seriously, producing lasting monuments à la Capricorn.

You may not see yourself as particularly talented and creative. Remember, creativity can take many forms. The teacher who teaches students to read well is performing a creative act. The factory worker who takes an active interest in performing his job can be very creative in finding better ways to get the job done. The parent who protects a child from harm and guides the daily activities is actively participating in the creation of a happy, successful adult. Creativity is found in the approach toward life's activities, and the sign and planets in the Fifth House describe the approach that suits you best.

The Sixth House

Service to others and to yourself is seen in the Sixth House. This includes the work you perform and the work environment. A fire sign here does not mean you have to be a fireman, but it does indicate that your work environment should encourage intuitive and creative thought. Water signs here indicate that you would enjoy working near bodies of water. Earth signs suggest that you will be happier working at ground level. Air signs suggest some branch of the communication industry, perhaps writing or publishing. Air signs may enjoy the upper floors of buildings.

Work habits are also part of the Sixth-House picture. Earth signs may indicate a steady approach to work, while fire signs show an intuitive work-nature that goes in spurts. Water signs may need a contemplative or at least relaxed environment in which ideas and feelings can flow freely. Air signs like lots of communication among people to stimulate ideas. Each sign tells how you approach your day-to-day work activities. It would be helpful for managers and supervisors to understand the Sixth House of each employee and to make modifications in the work environment that suit each individual's needs.

Physical health in general can be defined by looking at the Sixth House. The Ascendant and First House describe the physical body and its appearance. The Sixth House indicates where physical problems may require adjustment in the form of exercise, diet, or medical treatment. The planet that rules the Sixth House is a key factor in health considerations, so its nature should be considered carefully. Other planets here can indicate strong or weak parts of the body, and potential benefits or drawbacks.

Your attitude toward your employees and other service providers can be seen in the Sixth House. While you have one approach to dealing with people, they have multiple responses. Learn about the sign on the Sixth House so that you can bring more flexibility into your dealings with employees, and you will find they respond more freely to your requests. You can be aware of individual styles without sacrificing your own priorities because each sign and planet has the capacity to respond to the others in unique ways.

The Seventh House

The Seventh House tells you about how you relate to significant others, including marriage and business partners. Because marriage is a kind of business, and you may sometimes feel married to your business partner, studying the Seventh House can give you helpful hints about how you choose both, and how you deal with them afterward. Others are significant in our lives and affect the way we feel about ourselves. You may be surprised that you actually look for the same traits in business and romantic partners!

Enemies—open enemies, that is—are seen in the Seventh House. This house is opposite the First House—you and your personality. Open enemies are out there in front of you, making themselves apparent. You may feel you have no actual enemies, but you may be able to relate to the characteristics of people who seem to irritate you for no apparent reason—people who don't seem to have your best interests at heart.

Competitors are not precisely enemies, but they meet the criteria by wanting to be better, do better, or sell more than you. Competition is one way we all grow—we see someone with greater skill and we emulate them, not just for the sake of self-improvement, but also to beat them at their own game. The Seventh House shows some of the key qualities of your competitor.

Your attitude toward partnership is seen in the Seventh House. If you have no planets here, you can still have a marriage or business partnership. It may not be the most important thing in your life, or you may find that the person you marry came to you through the activities of another house—where the ruler of the Seventh House is found. If you have the Sun in the Seventh, partners may be one of the most important things in your life. Planets here show how you tend to deal with significant others of all kinds. The sign shows qualities you look for in others.

The sign in the Seventh House often is attractive to you because you project your unconscious desires there. These individuals may have both the best and the worst traits you desire in a mate—they are able to speak to your subconscious in ways you are unaware of.

The Eighth House

The Eighth House covers sex, death, and other people's resources. Most beginning astrologers question how these areas of life are related, and the explanation offers insight into some of life's most intriguing activities. The lives of others impact our lives on a moment-to-moment basis. Every human interaction engages the mental, emotional, material, or spiritual resources of at least one other person. Sexual response and sexual expression form a fundamental area for us to cultivate the spiritual connection with others through the physical connection. Death focuses on the separation from another person who has been significant in our lives, and at the same time may put us directly in touch with that person's resources in the form of inheritance.

The sign in the Eighth indicates how you express yourself sexually, and how you respond to your partner. Consider the meaning of the sign on the Eighth in the light of intimate behavior and you may be surprised at how accurately that sign describes your sexual desires and needs. Knowing this, you can use the information to satisfy your desires more directly, asking for just the thing you want without having to guess what it is yourself.

What you receive from others in the form of inheritance is an Eighth-House matter, as are banking, insurance, and other financial issues. The sign and planets here indicate how you relate to money and financial matters in general. The aspects to planets in the Eighth show what tendencies and skills you have where money is concerned. If you have no planets here, look for the planet associated with the sign in the Eighth and check out the aspects it makes to see what other areas of your life influence money matters.

Just as the Seventh House relates others to you (First House), the Eighth House connects other people's self-esteem to yours (Second House). Often the evidence of self-worth we see in the behavior of others affects our estimation of ourselves. Your attitude toward birth, death, and self-sacrifice are all part of the way you relate to other people and their values. The Eighth House is a rich source of information about areas of life that we tend to examine only when we are forced to by circumstances and other people.

The Ninth House

The Ninth House governs areas of life that are larger than any one person's perspective. Jupiter, the largest of the planets, is associated with the Ninth House, so the subjects of philosophy, religion, law, and higher consciousness take on the scope of this giant planet.

Higher education and personal studies are Ninth-House matters. Here are found the subjects of college and postgraduate study, as well as lifetime intellectual pursuits. The Ph.D. degree is titled the doctorate of philosophy in the subject being studied because the work goes well beyond the art or science of the subject, and delves into its larger, often spiritual, meaning.

Higher consciousness is a natural outgrowth of such studies. First we learn the nuts and bolts of the language of the subject, then we learn the theoretical and practical applications of that information. Only after apprenticeship and practice of the art or craft do we reach the philosophical understanding of the material. Then we may be able to connect to a higher consciousness of the subject and gain a more global or transpersonal understanding.

Long-distance travel takes us as far from our ordinary daily living as we can go. It puts us in situations where we must engage the philosophical application of all that we have learned. We enter a different culture or subculture and we become both teacher and student in that new place. We "soak up the culture" and we share of ourselves. Travel is one way to experience different philosophies and belief systems (Ninth-House concerns).

Legal matters are revealed by the Ninth House. The law is the philosophical framework on which we base social interaction. Laws are a body of agreements for behavior. They have grown out of human experience over millennia. They may require change and adaptation from time to time, but generally they are a reflection of the underlying philosophy of a nation, state, or locality. Many current laws are found in ancient religious texts.

Religious beliefs may not always have the profound depth that study provides, but these beliefs are grounded in the higher, spiritual awareness of the Ninth House. The sign here indicates what the essential quality of religion must deliver to you, whether it be an intellectual system, emotional support structure, or practical set of rules to live by. Religious mystics are in touch with the heart of their relationship to the universe and God or Goddess.

The Tenth House

Your career is profiled in the Tenth House. The sign and planets here can be used to define one or more broad career paths, and may also provide details about how to choose the focus of career as well. Earth signs indicate careers that deal with material matters. Air signs indicate communication of all kinds. Fire signs may tend toward inspirational and artistic expression, and water signs indicate careers that focus on actual water (like sailing), or metaphorical water (such as careers devoted to change, like psychotherapy and medicine). Most careers include features of all the elements, with a strong focus on one of them, and the sign in the Tenth House is a strong indicator of the basis of your career.

What you know about yourself is indicated by the Tenth House. We have talked about the First House reflecting personality (what you show to the world). The Tenth is what you know or can learn about yourself. The sign here indicates an area where you may be rather touchy, as your ego can become involved here. This is because we use the ego to mediate with the world, and when the world applies its pressure, the ego works to prevent us from being overwhelmed. To the extent that your ego is flexible, you learn about yourself in such encounters, as well as learning about other people and the rest of the world.

Social standing and public image is a Tenth-House matter. This house is at the top of the chart, the most exposed to light. We are exposed in social situations and revealed to the world, sometimes on a ready-or-not basis. When planets move into the Tenth House by transit or progression, you may receive unexpected publicity. What you know about yourself may become public information.

Your attitude toward authority and your way of accepting responsibility are Tenth-House matters. Once you have learned something about yourself, you apply it in your life. The more you learn about the sign in the Tenth House, the better you may understand how responsibility affects you. Then you can accept the authority of your position more easily. This brings us back to career. When you understand how you work with responsibility and authority, you can be more effective in your career.

The Eleventh House

Groups and group activities are Eleventh-House matters. The sign indicates what kind of groups you will be attracted to, and planets here reflect the kinds of people in those groups. Friends are also related to the Eleventh House. Here is where you can learn about the kinds of people who appeal to your deepest being—the people with whom you most want to spend time.

Intellectual pleasure can be thought of as a sort of friend. When you are alone, what do you think and dream about? What subjects interest you? Look to the Eleventh House sign and planets for the answers to these questions.

Your attitude toward leadership can be understood by learning about the Eleventh House. Do you take a practical, earth-sign approach to leadership roles? Do you expect leaders to be practical? With a water sign here, do you expect leaders to be understanding, feeling-based individuals, able to read the emotional current of the group? Perhaps you prefer the fiery passionate leader whose charisma carries people into action, or the intellectual, orderly mind whose demands are almost always logical and clear.

Your objectives in life are reflected in the Eleventh House. Just as your personal self-esteem (Second House) follows the First House of your persona, so does your career self-esteem thrive when your goals are achieved (the Eleventh follows the Tenth House of career). This sets up an interesting situation. The signs on these houses are almost always different. Thus, your career may be practical and concrete (earth), but your goals may be more intellectual (air). The process and the goal are strikingly different.

Finally, circumstances beyond your control are reflected in the Eleventh House. We like to think we are on top of life for the most part, but each of us will have to deal with experiences where there is little or nothing that we can do to affect the outcome. How you relate to these events can be understood through the sign and planets here. If an earth sign, then circumstances place you where you cannot affect the material outcome. With a water sign, you may be unable to change the emotional impact of events. Air signs could indicate that logical decisions are made that you must accept. Fire signs could indicate actual fires, or metaphorically inspired events that take you by surprise.

The Twelfth House

Psychic and intuitive processes are the foundation of the Twelfth House. The sign here shows one of the ways in which you engage your intuitive capabilities. Planets indicate the kind of people you invite into your intuitive sphere.

Private matters are in the Twelfth House. The sign shows what you consider to be private and how you manage it. By studying this house, you can learn why other people are secretive about private matters that are of little importance to you, while you choose very differently in this area.

Institutions, such as hospitals, or prisons, are Twelfth-House places. Think of a religious retreat, a convent, or a place where you could spend time alone in contemplation. A hospital is a place where you can go for rest and regeneration, but it is away from your normal daily experience, unless your Twelfth-House interests draw you into a medical profession. Prisons offer a contained environment away from public life for individuals convicted of crimes.

Secret enemies are a Twelfth-House matter. You may not think you have enemies, but most of us know people we do not want to be around, and presumably the feeling can go both ways. The chart of a spy may be filled with the intrigue of secret negotiations, clandestine meetings, and other hidden activities. Most of us will go through life being affected very little by enemies, just as most of us spend rather a small amount of time thinking about harming the people we dislike.

The subconscious level of mind is a sort of secret enemy. We hide matters in the unconscious that we do not want to deal with in our daily lives, and sometimes these unconscious thoughts surface to irritate us, just as an enemy's barb could inflict pain. In the chart, which turns in a clockwise motion, the Twelfth House has just risen over the horizon before your birth. Thus the subconscious contains information about events from the recent or distant past that have a significant effect on your life, whether or not you remember those events. Some astrologers feel that karmic ties can be reflected in the Twelfth House for this reason.

How you "get away" from other people is shown by the sign and planets here. With earth signs you may actually move away. Air signs may cease to communicate, while water signs may freeze up. Fire signs may simply enter an altered state of consciousness where they focus on something different, and are effectively no longer present.

Aspects

The planets relate to each other when they are certain distances apart in the zodiac. These relationships, called aspects, are identified with certain kinds of action. The houses are the area of life in which your drama takes place, the signs are the setting in which action occurs. The planets are the actors, and the aspects show what kind of dialogue and action are most likely to occur.

Even if you don't know your exact birth time, you can consider the aspects (with the exception of those to the Moon), as the planets don't move far enough in one day to change the aspects very much. The Moon moves between eleven and fourteen degrees each day, so its aspects change each hour or so. An exact aspect is one where the planets are the defined number of degrees apart in the sky. Even when they are not exact (and they rarely are), the aspect is still felt. It's a little like a radio station. Even when you are not exactly tuned in, you still receive a signal.

Some astrologers believe that every planetary relationship is significant, but most have refined the list to some or all of those in the accompanying chart. I have listed the aspects in order according to what portion of the circle they involve.

Conjunction (0°): Beginnings or endings

Opposition (180°): Awareness of others

Trine (120°): Conditions of ease

Square (90°): Challenges

Quintile (72°) or **Biquintile** (144°): Talents and creativity

Sextile (60°): Opportunities

Semisquare (45°) or **Sesquisquare** (135°): Tension

Semisextile (30°): Growth (sometimes through pain)

Quincunx (150°): Adjustment

Conjunction

The conjunction aspect defines the beginning or ending of a circle. It emphasizes the point where two or more planets are, thereby giving them prominence. Therefore, what those planets represent is more prominent than would ordinarily be the case. The energy of the planets is united and magnified. The focus can result in neurotic obsession and its resultant compulsive behaviors. A more normal experience may involve intense action or emotion, but without the negative quality.

Life begins as one cell that houses all the potential for an individual human being. The progressed or transiting conjunction marks the beginning of a new cycle of activity, and the nature of the planets reflects the potential for that activity. Regardless of the nature of the planets, the conjunction itself reminds us of the principal of unity. We reconnect with the fundamental truth represented by each of the planets.

Opposition

The opposition aspect defines a polarity. All sensory awareness is based on polarities. The opposition is the only aspect where a line connecting the two planets will pass through the center of the chart, dividing the chart into equal segments. Many symbols, such as the Tao, are expressions of the polarity of light and dark, left and right. The opposition line also connects the center with the circumference of the chart, symbolizing the connection between inner and outer being.

The awareness created by this polarizing aspect can feel like a separative force. You are connected to something that has been projected by your unconscious in many cases, something you don't wish to acknowledge. The beneficial side of the aspect is that it show you an area where you can learn the value of others or the object outside yourself. The opposition defines substance by defining a polarity between two planets. This establishment of awareness can then lead to the perception of value. Thus the planets in an opposition can be understood to have significance or value as a pair, not just as two different energies.

Robert F. Kennedy had striking oppositions in his birth chart. His awareness of the power of communication and his love of power, the capacity of his emotional arguments to sway his associates, and the sheer energy he applied to his work can be found in these aspects that are all within one degree of exactness.

Trine

In childhood development, the perception of self as distinct from the rest of the world is followed by the development of the ego complex, a mediator between Self and Other. The trine aspect connects two planets that are seen to have value relative to each other, but only when they are consciously considered. A trine aspect will do nothing if you make no effort to acknowledge and activate the planetary energies.

The aspect is one of ease—the planets can act together easily and naturally. If the Sun makes a trine, or if two planets form trines in the same element as the Sun, these aspects will be the easiest to work with consciously. They will just naturally be involved in decision-making processes. The down side of trines is that they may lead to a lazy attitude. You may allow a not-so-constructive condition to exist and do nothing to change it, or you may not maximize the potential of a positive relationship. Either way, you are not taking conscious action to work with the potential. The mind must engage in order to take advantage of the available energy, and that is difficult to get started with trines.

Muhammad Ali's chart contains multiple trine aspects. He understood the grounded nature of his life and used this awareness in his boxing career. He could "float like a butterfly and sting like a bee" because he understood the source of his physical strength and power. The Sun, Uranus, and Neptune form a Grand Trine, or triangle, allowing the energies of these three planets to work very easily together. Since these planets were in earth signs, they gave him patience—he would wait for the right moment in a fight and then suddenly devastate his opponent.

Square

The square aspect connects you directly to the material world according to the nature of the planets involved. They present challenges to your course of action and demand decisions.

Squares in cardinal signs (Aries, Cancer, Libra, and Capricorn) deal with outgoing energy. They relate to activities that take us out of ourselves and into the world at large. Squares in the fixed signs (Taurus, Leo, Scorpio, and Aquarius) deal with the energy of looking inward, and relate to challenges that we find in our interior processes. The outer appearance of such a square is sustained activity. Squares in mutable signs (Gemini, Virgo, Sagittarius, and Pisces) show where the energy of the inner world is linked to the outward-moving expression directly, resulting in a wisdom and harmony that does not exist in the cardinal and fixed squares. This square is a moving, adaptable, flexible energy. It is not as clear as the other squares because it is always changing. This square is one that often results in a resolution of the energies involved. All squares connect us to the material world.

Abraham Lincoln has strong square aspects in his birth chart. Challenges he met throughout his life are reflected in these aspects, yet show that challenges need not prevent a successful career. Lincoln was a deep thinker (shown by Mercury squaring Saturn), and was also intuitive (Mercury square Neptune). The fact that Saturn was square to the Midheaven may account in part for Lincoln's melancholic manner.

On January 25, 1999, an earthquake in Colombia occurred at a time when powerful squares and oppositions dominated the chart. The outer devastation of the material world is quite evident in many areas of the chart. The inner turmoil of the people involved was extreme. For individuals with many squares and oppositions, there can be a struggle to integrate the numerous challenges into a working set of strategies and tactics that partake of the potent energy without leading to explosive outbursts.

Quintile and Biquintile

The quintile and biquintile aspects are indicative of a creative function that goes beyond the material or scientific worlds. They often indicate an organizational capacity, or the capacity to work within a group. The aspect connects two planets whose energies are well understood on the material level, and the energies can mix to provide creative solutions to problems.

Quintiles and biquintiles reflect latent talent and creative potential. Creativity at this level demands that you invest your spirit in projects, rather than your ego. Personal considerations are no longer the most important part of the decision-making process. There is often less attachment to form and less concern about limitations. The quintile family of aspects takes the energy of the planets involved, adds experience to the formula, and unifies intellect, emotion, and experience into one creative process.

Marilyn Monroe's chart has four quintiles and two biquintiles. Her acting career was reflected in these indicators of talent. She could use the energies of six different planets to achieve the expression of a role. In some areas she achieved striking success; in others she was surely unable to manifest her full range of talent.

Sextile

The sextile aspect relates planets that occupy compatible elements: fire to air, or earth to water. The aspect animates the two planets and indicates opportunities to use their energies together. You are able to create something of value, using those energies.

Sextiles contain all that is needed to produce. What you need to do is notice the opportunity, make a solid decision to move forward, and take action. You will find that the less ego you bring to this process, the easier it becomes. Your decision will be more precisely tuned to your higher needs. You don't need to push very hard with sextiles, you only need to say "yes."

If you have a lot of sextiles in your birth chart, you will occasionally find that there are many opportunities at the same time. In such a situation the decision-making process becomes even more important. You will probably not be able to test every opportunity, and, therefore, must select on the information available. Communication is a necessary ingredient. You can share your thoughts with others and get feedback. The idea is to engage your mind, gather information, and then move forward.

Bill Clinton was surely plagued by his sextiles nearly as much as he benefited from them. Mercury sextiles Mars, Venus, Neptune, and the Ascendant. The Sun sextiles Jupiter on one side and Uranus on the other. While he took advantage of his opportunities, and rose to become the president of the United States, he also fell into the trap of saying "yes" to other opportunities that led to financial and personal scandals. This is a good example of the fact that good judgment must be exercised in acting upon your opportunities.

Semisquare and Sesquisquare

The semisquare and sesquisquare aspects are "internal" in the sense that you feel their energy, but the effect may not be evident to other people. The feelings range from irritation and insecurity to agitation, all of which are somewhat counterproductive. The creative potential lies in your ability to use the tension or stress as a barometer to measure the reality of a situation.

These aspects provide one way to stimulate your psychic or intuitive awareness. When the tension become noticeable to you, take the time to sit calmly and reflect on the feeling. Allow your mind to get "inside" the feeling—let it speak to you. Whatever thoughts arise as you sit, consider them in relation to your social life, your work, and your family. You may be surprised how clear the answers become when you listen to your own internal tension.

Semisextile and Quincunx

These two aspects are indicators of growth and adjustment. Both of these conditions can be somewhat painful. They are not easy to control, and they tend to compel us to change whether we want to or not. The change is often accompanied by a realization about the self that you are unwilling to accept, at least at first. Both aspects may demand a lot of energy in dealing with those areas of your life.

The semisextile seems to bring growth through pain. We learn through this aspect to appreciate some aspect of our lives, but the flower of appreciation sometimes has thorns. The quincunx brings expansion that requires adjustment. You learn a lot about yourself and how to handle problems through this aspect. The quincunx is sometimes active at the time of an illness. This is because the body is fighting to expand its healing potential to ward off the illness or to repair physical damage.

For both the semisextile and the quincunx, you can think of one planet as the question and the other as the answer. One presents the area where growth or expansion is needed, and the other presents the method through which the adjustment can occur.

The Mayan calendar has predicted the end of the current cycle in December of 2012. The chart for this date contains a pattern of exact semisextiles and quincunxes, and suggests a global demand for growth and adjustment. Power and responsibility go hand in hand with justice and sound judgment. Growth will involve social systems and personal ideas and ideals. Change is a definite outcome of the configuration.

Adding it Together

As you begin to consider aspects in your chart, you will look at them one at a time and try to understand their energy. It is very important to remember that no single aspect stands by itself. You will find that some aspects ring true—you understand exactly what the energies are doing. Other aspects will seem foreign, or simply meaningless. As you study each aspect, make a list or catalog of the possible meanings. You will begin to see a pattern of possibilities. When several aspects express similar energies, you have found an area of concentration that you can match to your experience. The occasional aspect that does not fit into such a pattern may add some zip to your life on occasion, but does not reflect a major part of your character.

It is also true that if you have many of one aspect, you will tend to think and act according to that aspect's style. The style of the sextile is to choose opportunities; the style of the square is to respond to the material world; the style of the opposition is to gain awareness; and the style of the conjunction is to experience beginnings and endings.

Aspects that are close to exact tend to have more impact than ones that are less precise. This is like tuning your radio: you get the strongest signal when you are tuned to the exact frequency. If you have several sextiles, for example, the one closest to exactly sixty degrees may express more often and more powerfully than the others may.

Finally, each aspect has an effect in the external environment as well as an internal, psychological effect. Often we tend to focus our attention on things outside ourselves because we are trying to make something happen in the environment. You will want to consider the impact on yourself of actions and events. The opportunity indicated by a sextile may at first seem to exist in the external world, but acting on that opportunity will have an internal effect as well. When you consider the mental, emotional, or spiritual impact of your actions, you will find you maintain your balance much better.

Transits and Progressions

Just as your birth chart shows where the planets were when you were born, at any moment another chart can be created. The planets in a chart for a particular moment are called transits. As the planets move through the zodiac, they interact with each other and relate to the birth chart using the aspects that were described earlier.

Another popular kind of chart is called progressions. The planets in this chart are moved forward one day for each year of life. They reflect a different time scale—they move very slowly compared to the actual motion of the planets. Progressions show how you will respond to a larger cycle of activity, and progressed aspects are in effect for much longer time periods than transits.

The three charts are combined to forecast trends of activity and to pinpoint likely times when certain events may occur. Both progressions and transits are used to indicate action points in time, based on the potential in your birth chart. They show the ways the players in life's drama will interact with each other over time, based on individual potential as indicated in the birth chart. The house where a transiting planet is found indicates how its energy can be most easily expressed, just as the house in the birth chart shows the area of life where particular influences will be found.

It is important to remember that your birth potential determines the likelihood of events in your life. Each day there are easy or difficult transits, but they only affect you if they connect with your birth chart in some way. Today the planets may look good for an accident, but you will not have one if your birth chart doesn't show it. The same is true for winning the lottery—luck must be indicated in your birth chart as well as in today's planets.

Each planet indicates that a particular kind of energy is available in specific areas of your life, and the aspects formed to birth planets show times when that energy will be more active. The following descriptions of the planets relate to how they act in the day-to-day drama of life. You can get an idea of each transit by looking at the meaning of the planet and the sign it now occupies. Read the sections about the planet and the sign, and notice how they combine in a different way from your birth chart.

Sun Transits

The Sun brings light to the area of the chart it occupies. It focuses life energy there. You may be born with the Sun in Capricorn, a grounded, ambitious earth sign. As the Sun progresses into Aquarius, Pisces, and Aries during your life, you will find that the focus of your life changes, absorbing the qualities of those signs, and carrying that experience forward.

The daily positions of the planets are similar. As a Capricorn you may resonate to the energy of winter, but when the Sun is in Leo, you feel its light and warmth in a different way. When the Sun aspects a birth planet, that planet is in the spotlight. The "feel" of the spotlight depends on the particular aspect between the Sun and the birth planet.

Because the Sun moves rapidly through the signs, the progressions are more striking indicators of psychological and environmental forces. Progressions may indicate the entrance of a male into the picture. You may feel more determined and courageous, or possibly more "alive" in some way. Your sense of personal significance undergoes inspection when the progressed Sun forms aspects. Sun aspects affect your sense of self-esteem or conscientiousness, and often you can take pride in what you have accomplished after the aspect is past.

The Sun governs the heart and the spine. Progressed aspects can bring physical or emotional stress to these parts of the body. You may feel heartsick, or feel that you are carrying a heavy burden. Conversely, the Sun's aspects often bring the feeling of strength and vitality, uplifting the spirit and the body.

Moon Transits

The Moon's position indicates the emotional tone of the moment. The Full Moon, for example, causes changes in the physical function of the body and in our emotional response to those changes. The Moon's sign indicates that specific unconscious information may be more readily available to us, filtered through the sign so that it has a specific tone. The Moon moves even faster than the Sun through the zodiac. Thus the phases of the Moon may have more significance than the daily positions. However, some people are very sensitive to the movement of the Moon—they feel the sifting of the tides within themselves each day. The Moon moves through an entire sign in a little over two days, so its effects are short-lived. However, the Moon sometimes acts as a trigger for the transit of a slower-moving planet. In a detailed analysis of a time period, the aspects the Moon makes can tell an intriguing story of the unfolding of events.

Progressions of the Moon may indicate the entrance of a female into your life, or the influence of a female on your activities. They can indicate times when your emotions are disrupted. You may find that thoughts concerning women, your home, and children fill your time. You find that activities involve many people and ordinary activities or commodities.

Health issues revolve around the stomach, mental complaints, the eyes, and the ears. Your stomach may become the barometer of your feelings under progressed Moon aspects. You may notice changes in perception, such as changes in the ability to discern colors or sounds. Musical tastes may change during lunar progressions.

Mercury Transits

Just as the god Mercury was the messenger of the other gods, so the planet Mercury is an indicator of communication. Mercury moves faster than any other planet, so here again the influence is transitory. In addition, the planet Mercury tends to take on the character of the planet it is aspecting, so you can usually say that there is some communication concerning the other planet's nature. A third factor is that Mercury (and the rest of the planets) appears to go backward in the sky. Mercury does this three times a year. During those periods you often have a chance to review your actions and revise your plans.

Mercury often indicates what you were thinking about. Again, the nature of the other planet describes the nature of the thoughts. For example, Mars relates to energy. A Mercury/Mars aspect might indicate thoughts about physical activity, or a telephone call about some plans. The communication can occur quickly, or there may be an argumentative quality to it. Some kind of exchange is always part of the equation.

Progressed Mercury can bring you into prolonged contact with the written word, telephone or telegraph, and all forms of communication. You may find your capacity for study changes dramatically.

Health issues include a tendency to nervousness, hay fever or asthma (if you are susceptible), intense mental activity, and bowel complaints. All of these are related to your stress level is some way, and Mercury's aspects point to the kind of person or situation that is causing the stress. Clearer communication in that area helps to relieve all sorts of mental and physical symptoms.

Venus Transits

Venus brings thoughts of love and harmony into the equation. It may indicate a physical or sexual attraction—Venus can act almost like a magnet drawing you together with another person or an object, or into a social situation. The other person may be an artist or entertainer, or perhaps a younger female.

Venus in a transiting aspect can indicate a deepening of feeling, or even the beginning of love. Venus moves fairly quickly, so it indicates a momentary feeling, one that will pass within a day or so. However, when a slower-transiting planet forms an aspect with your birth Venus, this can indicate the appearance or reunion with an individual who is described by the transiting planet—a person who can become a strong love interest: if Mars, perhaps the transit indicates a strong, energetic person; if Jupiter, someone tall or large; if Saturn, someone much older or younger; if Uranus, a person who could easily become the love of your life; if Neptune, a mystical type; or, if Pluto, a person who has an overpowering effect on you, or a fanatical sort of person.

Progressed Venus can attract like a magnet. You may see more flowers and candy from your significant other! You may also have greater interest in clothing and jewelry, and your tastes in food may shift. Social events and meetings take on greater significance when Venus is active.

Venus governs the kidneys, skin, veins, thyroid, and female reproductive organs. Progressed Venus can indicate the onset of problems in these areas. Venus also is involved in sexually transmitted diseases. Not every Venus aspect brings trouble in these areas, but when you have an aspect, it is wise to moderate your diet and activities, or to take steps to protect yourself from disease.

Mars Transits

The transit of Mars indicates a part of your life where energy is being directed. It can feel like you have more physical energy to work and play. It can also feel like there is much more mental, emotional, or spiritual energy available. You will perhaps feel greater determination to accomplish what you need to do. It is important not to become stubborn in your desire to make progress, but rather to use the excitement and enthusiasm wisely. This is sometimes easy to say and more difficult to accomplish.

You may find that you are surrounded with people who express the energy of Mars clearly. They may include athletes or people interested in sports, people in the military or who have a military bearing, surgeons, doctors, and other people who may treat injuries, or possibly people who enjoy a vigorous conversation or argument.

As you use your energy, you may feel alternating periods of weakness or lack of energy. It is important to allow time for rest when Mars is present. If you become exhausted, you may be careless and cause accidents or injury to yourself or others.

Remember, Mars energy is the kind you use to do ordinary things; it fuels the body as well as your car. When Mars is active, expect to see and feel more energy in every area of your life, but particularly where the aspected planet is active. If Mars aspects the Sun, you will feel personally energized; if in aspect with the Moon, you may have very active dreams and imagination; with Mercury, your communications will be fast and vigorous; with Venus, there may be powerful sexual energy around you; with Mars, you get a chance to evaluate your life's course regarding how you use energy in general; with Jupiter, you may feel like a balloon expanding near the bursting point; with Saturn, inhibited energy, endurance, or resistance; with Uranus, sudden, surprising action; with Neptune, weakness or dissatisfaction; or, with Pluto, compulsive actions or a feeling of great power and confidence.

Jupiter Transits

When Jupiter transits or progresses to form aspects, there will be expansion. Jupiter brings hopefulness, sociability, and harmony to the other planet. There is activity along philosophical or philanthropic lines. Generally, Jupiter reflects a sense of benevolence in the area of the other planet.

Sometimes, if Jupiter indicates a too-rapid expansion, there can be loss after the expansion, or poor judgment, or other problems indicates by the aspect and the nature of the other planet. Still, the overall feeling of Jupiter is of hope, good will, and generosity.

In the environment, Jupiter is connected to merchandise, bankers, and professional people. Thus it is often involved at times when big business or career changes occur. Jupiter greases the wheels of commerce by providing the optimism to encourage taking a risk. The church or clergy may be involved when Jupiter transits your chart.

Health indications of Jupiter transits include overabundance in general. This can involve weight gain through over indulgence in food. In more extreme cases it can indicate changes in the function of liver, pancreas, and other glands, often associated with excessive consumption of alcohol, sugars, and fats, leading to problems associated with these organs. While tumors are related to Saturn, their abnormal growth is related to Jupiter.

Saturn Transits

When Saturn is strongly involved in progressions and transits, there is a tendency to concentrate and draw into yourself. You may find that you are only able to focus on one thing at a time, when you usually can keep many things balanced. There is a sense of heavy responsibility reflected in Saturn transits. You may feel that you have the weight of Saturn on your shoulders or back. There is likely to be more work, or work of a more intense, concentrated nature.

Financially such a contraction or limitation may be felt as a financial loss. Even if you don't lose property, you may feel deprived or insecure. Thus your thoughts make turn to safety issues, secrets, or worry. You may want to acquire everything you need immediately, instead of pacing your spending. In this way the very feeling of lack depletes your financial reserves.

Saturn relates to structure. It governs bones, skin, teeth, and hair. Saturnian health issues relate to deficiencies of various kinds. If there is not enough water, your digestive tract becomes sluggish, for example. Without enough vitamins and other nutrients, the bones become weak, or the hair lacks luster and strength. Saturn also indicates the chronic progress or development of disease. On the psychological level, you may feel the aspects of Saturn to its birth location very strongly. The Saturn returns at around ages twenty-eight and fifty-six may bring prominent conclusions to entire phases of life.

On the environmental level, Saturn governs utilities, minerals, grain, building materials, mines, real estate, and more. The organizational structure and policies of corporations are reflected by Saturn, while the day-to-day process of transacting business is related to Jupiter, and communications themselves relate to Mercury.

It is helpful to remember that the structuring or restructuring indicated by a Saturn transit does not in itself bring limitation or restriction. We need structure to function comfortably. If you feel isolated, you can reach out to someone else, removing the perceived barrier Saturn created.

Uranus Transits

Uranus moves very slowly by progression and by transit. Yet its aspects indicate sudden, even revolutionary change. There will be a strong desire for independence and enthusiasm for all things new and different in your life.

You may find that your intuitive abilities are stronger, or that they emerge and develop more fully during Uranus transits. This planet reflects the capacity to relate today's events to the future, and to guide your life skillfully based on your inner sense of direction. This is liberating for the soul but can cause upsets in your daily life if you allow your impulses to carry you too far too fast.

Uranus often indicates that other people are directly involved in events that affect you deeply. You may not be able to forecast who these people will be—they may remain unknown to you, too. Uranus governs inventions, from the automobile to electricity, from computers to all types of mechanical devices. It also governs antiques. This seems strange at first, but old objects are often imbued with the psychic vibrations that stimulate intuition. Professions such as astrology and psychology use the intuitive sense to help clients.

Health indications include paralysis, nervous disorders, and arthritis. The very planet that can indicate sudden movement or change also governs severe limitation of movement. Diseases with a sudden onset, like appendicitis, are related to this planet.

The overall quality is equilibrium. Uranus' energy serves to bring us back into balance. The more out of balance we are, the more striking the effect of a Uranus transit. When we are on track intuitively we feel less drama when Uranus aspects hit. Uranus is a good timer of events—many times the event happens exactly when Uranus forms the exact aspect to a planet. Don't look for events before that time!

Neptune Transits

Neptune transits bring glamour into your life. This can mean dressed-up, fantasy-related activities, or the deception of the stage magician. There is often a sense of protection that accompanies the feeling of unreality. Thus danger is sometimes a factor. You, may find yourself involved with unusual people and weird events. Yet you may also find that your psychic senses are tuned precisely.

Any progression or transit increases the imagination and sensitivity to people around you. Behavior is influenced by wishful thinking or fantasy. Scheming may develop into a pattern of action and can be detrimental to your work, as your focus on a promotion or other goal can detract from your daily accomplishments.

In your environment, you may encounter the promoter, the confidence man, and the individual who plots and schemes. You come into contact with movie stars, mystics, and psychic energy. A profit sharing venture may be presented to you.

Health issues relating the Neptune include negative attitudes, bacterial infection, and oversensitivity in the psychic area. There is a possibility of poisoning or allergic response. Thus when you have Neptune aspects you need to take care to flush the system with enough water each day, and to maintain a clean environment. At the same time your psychic senses can provide what you need to protect your health in the form of messages or dreams.

In general, the receptivity of Neptune provides the path to sympathy and understanding of other people. When you are very open to it, the energy can become confused, the psychic messages vague, and you may feel you are less capable of effective planning. It may help to logically consider what you are focused on and then use the Neptunian path of devotion to stick to the goals you have set. When your devotion is focused, it is less likely that others can derail your efforts.

Pluto Transits

Strong Pluto aspects by transit or progression indicate the influence of groups or the possibility of coercion. You may feel that any willingness to cooperate on your part opens you to being pushed—the old "give an inch, take a mile" response. Of course it is possible that you will try to take the mile yourself! The forces at work are subtle but powerful. You can benefit from careful analysis of situations. Withhold your decision until you have had time to think it through logically. Most decisions can be put off for one day without harm. Statistical analysis of a problem may be helpful. Gathering data helps to quantify the problem and point to appropriate choices.

The people in your environment who want to influence your decisions may range from highly developed spiritual beings to people on the wrong side of the law. Radio and television may play an active role in your life when Pluto is active. You may be close to drastic events that bring sweeping change, often for the better.

Health issues include allergies and hay fever. Bees and bee pollen may figure in your treatments of allergies. There may be an invasion of other organisms, such as a virus, or there may be an injury such as a puncture wound. When Pluto and, indeed, any of the outer planets, are active, you will want to be careful to focus on what you are doing and try not to let your mind wander from the task.

In general, Pluto transits bring you into contact with power. You may feel alternately powerful in yourself and pushed or oppressed because of the power others exert. You have the capacity to reach deep into the collective mind for strength, and your ability to regenerate after an injury or illness is very strong. Maintaining balance can be a challenge, but keeping your own center or regaining it will become easier as you go through the transit. Pluto brings change with no going back. When you have Pluto strong in your chart, you can be the trendsetter and an effective instrument of positive change. Pluto cleanses and revitalizes. ESP also can be an active source of data. Don't expect peace and quiet.

For Further Reading

Astrology: Understanding the Birth Chart by Kevin Burk. Llewellyn, 2001.

Astrology for the Millions by Grant Lewi. Llewellyn, 1996.

Heaven Knows What by Grant Lewi. Llewellyn, 1996.

Activities Ruled by the Planets

To check aspects for the activity you have in mind, find the planet that rules it.

Sun: Advertising, buying, selling, speculating, short trips, meeting people, anything involving groups or showmanship, putting up exhibits, running fairs and raffles, growing crops, health matters.

Moon: Any small change in routine, asking favors, borrowing or lending money, household activities such as baking, canning, cooking, washing, ironing, cleaning, and taking care of small children.

Mercury: Bargaining, bookkeeping, dealing with literary agents, publishing, filing, hiring employees, learning languages, literary work, placing ads, preparing accounts, studying, telephoning, visiting friends.

Venus: Amusement, beauty care, courtship, dating, decorating homes, designing, getting together with friends, household improvements, planning parties, shopping.

Mars: Good for all business matters, mechanical affairs, buying or selling animals, dealing with contractors, hunting, studying.

Jupiter: Activities involving charity, education, or science, correspondence courses, self-improvement, reading, researching, studying.

Saturn: Anything involving family ties or legal matters such as wills and estates, taking care of debts, dealing with lawyers, financing, joint money matters, real estate, relations with older people.

Uranus: Air travel, all partnerships, changes and adjustment, civil rights, new contacts, new ideas, new rules, patenting inventions, progress, social action, starting journeys.

Neptune: Advertising, dealing with psychological upsets, health foods and resorts, large social affairs, nightclubs, psychic healing, travel by water, restaurants, visits, welfare, working with institutions.

Pluto: Anything dealing with energy and enthusiasm, skill and alertness, personal relationships, original thought.

Planetary Business Guide

Collections: Try to make collections on days when your Sun is well aspected. Avoid days when Mars or Saturn are aspected. If possible, the Moon should be in a cardinal sign: Aries, Cancer, Libra, or Capricorn. It is more difficult to collect when the Moon is in Taurus or Scorpio.

Employment, Promotion: Choose a day when your Sun is favorably aspected or the Moon is in your Tenth House. Good aspects of Venus or Jupiter to your Tenth House are also beneficial.

Loans: Moon in the first and second quarters favors the lender; Moon in the third and fourth quarters favors the borrower. Good aspects of Jupiter or Venus to the Moon are favorable to both, as is Moon in Leo, Sagittarius, Aquarius, or Pisces.

New Ventures: Things usually get off to a better start during the increase of the Moon. If there is impatience, anxiety, or deadlock, it can often be broken at the Full Moon. Agreements can soon be reached then.

Partnerships: Agreements and partnerships should be made on a day that is favorable to both parties. Mars, Neptune, Pluto, and Saturn should not be square or opposite the Moon. It is best to make an agreement or partnership when the Moon is in a mutable sign, especially Gemini or Virgo. The other signs are not favorable, with the possible exception of Leo or Capricorn. Begin partnerships when the Moon is increasing in light, as this is a favorable time for starting new ventures.

Public Relations: The Moon rules the public, so this must be well aspected, particularly by the Sun, Mercury, Uranus, or Neptune.

Selling: In general, selling is favored by good aspects of Venus, Jupiter, or Mercury to the Moon. Afflictions of Saturn retard. If you know the planetary ruler of your product, try to get this well aspected by Venus, Jupiter, or the Moon. Your product will be more highly valued then.

Signing Important Papers: Sign contracts or agreements when the Moon is increasing in a fruitful sign. Avoid days when Mars, Saturn, Neptune, or Pluto are afflicting the Moon. Don't sign anything if your Sun is badly afflicted.

Planetary Associations

Sun: Authority figures, favors, advancement, health, success, display, drama, promotion, fun, matters related to Leo and the Fifth House.

Moon: Short trips, women, children, the public, domestic concerns, emotions, fluids, matters related to Cancer and the Fourth House.

Mercury: Communications, correspondence, phone calls, computers, messages, education, students, travel, merchants, editing, writing, advertising, signing contracts, siblings, neighbors, kin, matters related to Gemini, Virgo, and the Third and Sixth Houses.

Venus: Affection, relationships, partnerships, alliances, grace, beauty, harmony, luxury, love, art, music, social activity, marriage, decorating, cosmetics, gifts, income, matters related to Taurus, Libra, and the Second and Seventh Houses.

Mars: Strife, aggression, sex, physical energy, muscular activity, guns, tools, metals, cutting, surgery, police, soldiers, combat, confrontation, matters related to Aries, Scorpio, and the First and Eighth Houses.

Jupiter: Publishing, college education, long-distance travel, foreign interests, religion, philosophy, forecasting, broadcasting, publicity, expansion, luck, growth, sports, horses, the law, matters related to Sagittarius, Pisces, and the Ninth and Twelfth Houses.

Saturn: Structure, reality, the laws of society, limits, obstacles, tests, hard work, endurance, real estate, dentists, bones, teeth, matters related to Capricorn, Aquarius, and the Tenth and Eleventh Houses.

Uranus: Astrology, the New Age, technology, computers, modern gadgets, lecturing, advising, counseling, inventions, reforms, electricity, new methods, originality, sudden events, matters related to Aquarius and the Eleventh House.

Neptune: Mysticism, music, creative imagination, dance, illusion, sacrifice, service oil, chemicals, paint, drugs, anesthesia, sleep, religious experience, matters related to Pisces and the Twelfth House.

Pluto: Probing, penetration, goods of the dead, investigation, insurance, taxes, other people's money, loans, the masses, the underworld, transformation, death, matters related to Scorpio and the Eighth House.

About the Authors

Stephanie Clement is an accomplished astrologer with twenty-five years of professional experience. She has written numerous magazine articles and several books, most recently, *Power of the Midheaven*.

Alice DeVille has been a consulting astrologer, metaphysician, and writer for more than twenty-five years. Alice develops and conducts workshops, seminars, and lectures on a variety of subjects.

Marguerite Elsbeth is a professional tarot and astrology reader, and a practitioner of Nativism (American Indian healing) as well as European healing methods. Marguerite is the author of *Crystal Medicine*, and coauthor of *The Silver Wheel: Women's Myths and Mysteries in the Celtic Tradition*, with Kenneth Johnson.

Phyllis Firak-Mitz has been a professional astrologer in private practice for twenty years. She has a Master's degree in Applied Psychology and is an ordained minister. Phyllis specializes in combining psychology and spirituality with astrology to evolve and expand consciousness and promote personal effectiveness.

Mitchell Gibson is a well-known and highly respected medical doctor in Arizona. He is also ranked as one of the best astrologers in the world, and is a contributing author to several astrology publications and a popular lecturer. He is the author of three books; *Signs of Mental Illness*, *Signs of Psychic and Spiritual Ability*, and his newest work, *Medicine for the Soul*.

Kenneth Johnson holds a degree in Comparative Religions with an emphasis in the study of mythology. He has been a practitioner of astrology since 1974, and is the coauthor of *Mythic Astrology: Archetypal Powers in the Horoscope*, as well as the author of five other books on myth, legend, and magical lore.

Jonathan Keyes writes a regular "lunar health" column for stariq.com and has written for the *Mountain Astrologer*. He also writes a bimonthly health horoscope that can be found at astrologicalhealth.com, an astrological herbal supplement site. Jonathan is a health astrologer who works with herbs, diet, stones, and animal totems to help harmonize planetary influences for health and well-being.

Dorothy Oja is a career astrologer with twenty-eight years of experience, offering full-spectrum astrological counseling through her practice MINDWORKS. Her specialties include electional work and composite/Davison relationship analysis.

Leeda Alleyn Pacotti embarked on metaphysical self-studies at the age of fourteen. Her career encompassed antitrust law, international treaties, and governmental management. She now plies a gentle practice as a naturopathic physician, master herbalist, and certified nutritional counselor.

David Pond is a well-known national speaker and has been a full-time professional astrologer since 1976. He is the author of *Chakras for Beginners* and *The Art of Relationships*.

Notes

Notes